ROPES
OF SAND

ROPES OF SAND

America's Failure in the Middle East

WILBUR CRANE EVELAND

SERIES EDITED BY
MARK CRISPIN MILLER

INTEGRATED MEDIA

NEW YORK

Cover design by Mauricio Díaz

978-1-5040-5007-4

This edition published in 2018 by Open Road Integrated Media, Inc.
180 Maiden Lane
New York, NY 10038
www.openroadmedia.com

To
Crane and Lis
and for
Monique and Mike

CONTENTS

SERIES INTRODUCTION

I

We the people seem to have the freest book trade in the world. Certainly we have the biggest. Cruise the mighty Amazon, and you will see so many books for sale in the United States today as would require more than four hundred miles of shelving to display them—a bookshelf that would stretch from Boston's Old North Church to Fort McHenry in South Baltimore.

Surely that huge catalog is proof of our extraordinary freedom of expression: The US government does not ban books, because the First Amendment won't allow it. While books are widely banned in states like China and Iran, *no* book may be forbidden by the US government *at any level* (although the CIA censors books by former officers). Where books *are* banned in the United States, the censors tend to be private organizations—church groups, school boards, and other local (busy)bodies roused to purify the public schools or libraries nearby.

Despite such local prohibitions, we can surely find any book we want. After all, it's easy to locate those hot works that once *were* banned by the government as too "obscene" to sell, or mail, until the courts ruled otherwise on First Amendment grounds—*Fanny*

Hill, Howl, Naked Lunch. We also have no trouble finding books banned here and there as "antifamily," "Satanic," "racist," and/or "filthy," from *Huckleberry Finn* to *Heather Has Two Mommies* to the Harry Potter series, just to name a few.

II

And yet, the fact that those bold books are all in print, and widely read, does *not* mean that we have the freest book trade in the world. On the contrary: For over half a century, America's vast literary culture has been disparately policed, and imperceptibly contained, by state and corporate entities well placed and perfectly equipped to wipe out wayward writings. Their ad hoc suppressions through the years have been far more effectual than those quixotic bans imposed on classics like *The Catcher in the Rye* and *Fahrenheit 451.* For every one of those bestsellers scandalously purged from some provincial school curriculum, there are many others (we can't know how many) that have been so thoroughly erased that few of us, if any, can remember them, or have ever heard of them.

How have all those books (to quote George Orwell) "dropped into the memory hole" in these United States? As America does *not* ban books, other means—less evident, and so less controversial—have been deployed to vaporize them. Some almost never made it into print, as publishers were privately warned off them from on high, either on the grounds of "national security" or with blunt threats of endless corporate litigation. Other books were signed enthusiastically—then "dumped," as their own publishers mysteriously failed to market them, or even properly distribute them. But it has mainly been the press that stamps out inconvenient books, either by ignoring them, or—most often— laughing them off as "conspiracy theory," despite their soundness (or because of it).

Once out of print, those books are gone. Even if some few of us have not forgotten them, and one might find used copies here and there, these books have disappeared. Missing from the shelves and never mentioned in the press (and seldom mentioned even in our schools), each book thus neutralized might just as well have been destroyed en masse—or never written in the first place, for all their contribution to the public good.

III

The purpose of this series is to bring such vanished books to life— first life for those that never saw the light of day, or barely did, and second life for those that got some notice, or even made a splash, then slipped too quickly out of print, and out of mind.

These books, by and large, were made to disappear, or were hastily forgotten, not because they were too lewd, heretical, or unpatriotic for some touchy group of citizens. *These* books sank without a trace, or faded fast, because they tell the sort of truths that Madison and Jefferson believed our Constitution should pro- tect—truths that the people have the right to know, and needs to know, about our government and other powers that keep us in the dark.

Thus the works on our Forbidden Bookshelf shed new light— for most of us, it's *still* new light—on the most troubling trends and episodes in US history, especially since World War II: America's broad use of former Nazis and ex-Fascists in the Cold War; the Kennedy assassinations, and the murders of Martin Luther King Jr., Orlando Letelier, George Polk, and Paul Wellstone; Ronald Rea- gan's Mafia connections, Richard Nixon's close relationship with Jimmy Hoffa, and the mob's grip on the NFL; America's terroris- tic Phoenix Program in Vietnam, US support for South America's most brutal tyrannies, and CIA involvement in the Middle East; the secret histories of DuPont, ITT, and other giant US corpora- tions; and the long war waged by Wall Street and its allies in real estate on New York City's poor and middle class.

The many vanished books on these forbidden subjects (among others) altogether constitute a shadow history of America—a his- tory that We the People need to know at last, our country having now become a land with billionaires in charge, and millions not allowed to vote, and everybody under full surveillance. Through this series, we intend to pull that necessary history from the shadows at long last—to shed some light on how America got here, and how we might now take it somewhere else.

Mark Crispin Miller

AUTHOR'S NOTE

It is impossible to understand America's continuing failure in the Middle East without taking into account the misapplication of the CIA's responsibilities and functions in that area: the extent to which presidents have ignored its intelligence estimates; the degree to which its clandestine political action capabilities have been employed as substitutes for sound foreign policy and conventional diplomacy. What I write about the CIA's activities and failures, therefore, is not intended to be sensational, but rather to stand as a part of the truth about our presence in the Middle East.

Since May 1976 I have employed the Freedom of Information and Privacy Acts in an unrelenting effort to obtain from the CIA copies of my personnel records, including specifically any evidence that I was bound by a secrecy agreement with the agency. The CIA failed to produce even abridged copies of any document purporting to be a secrecy commitment. My May 17, 1977, appeal of the CIA's denial of documents should have been adjudicated within twenty days if the CIA had complied with the applicable statutes; nearly three years passed without any compliance by the agency.

On February 29, 1980, I informed CIA director Stansfield Turner that galley proofs of this book had been publicized in trade publications, in the press, on the radio, and circulated commercially prior to its scheduled release on May 19, 1980. No communication from the agency reached me during the ten days allowed the CIA by law to inform me if it believed that I had any obligation to submit a copy of what I have written for prepublication review. Then, in a letter delivered to me on March 20, 1980, the CIA claimed a right to review everything I'd written but advised that my commitment to allow this was too secret to send to me. Over a two-week period I discussed the CIA's demands with one of its lawyers: he insisted that I must submit anything that I had written "on the subject of intelligence" to the CIA, despite the fact that I'd become a counterespionage agent more than six years before the CIA was formed; in return, the CIA said it would declassify and send to me any secrecy agreements and contracts I'd signed with the agency. To expedite publication and any review that the CIA proved itself entitled to, I instructed W.W. Norton to send the CIA a copy of Chapters 24 through 30 of this book; they cover a period from September 1957 onward, at which point I'd changed my CIA status from "covert associate" to "contract employee." I reserved, however, my right to reject censorship unless counsel advised me that the documents the CIA had promised conveyed a legal obligation for me to submit to prepublication review.

The CIA dropped its bomb in a letter I received from it on April 4, 1980: after I'd suspended printing of this book for forty-six days, the agency wrote that it "declines to review the manuscript." The efforts I'd made since May 1977 to learn of any obligations I might have were, in the CIA's letter, called "my belated attempt to submit the manuscript [which] cannot cure any breach of duty or contract already committed." Presumably the CIA is entitled to lie before Congress, violate the rights of American citizens, employ newspapers, magazines, book publishers, press services, radio and T.V. stations for propagandizing Americans and foreigners, as well as to intervene without accountability in the affairs of sovereign nations. Nonetheless, I still believe that the First Amendment protects a citizen's right to criticize our government; I've accordingly accepted the CIA's refusal to review this book and instructed my publisher to proceed with printing and distribution.

PREFACE

I resolved to record the story of my life in the Middle East in April 1975, in Beirut, Lebanon. The port I watched burning below me had been a peaceful harbor when I'd first entered it twenty-five years before. In the past I'd been a participant in America's covert intervention in internal Lebanese affairs. The destruction of Lebanon, which now seemed inevitable, was at least in part a result of our meddling.

The contract for this book was signed in December 1977, when Anwar Sadat's mission to Jerusalem seemed to indicate that thirty years of fighting between the Arabs and the Israelis would finally end. Too often disappointed, I embarked on writing about the problems involved in past efforts to achieve peace.

I was midway through my first draft of this book when the Camp David summit meetings produced a state of euphoria. Conflict, however, soon resumed because of the intractable question of the right to a homeland of the Palestinians who'd been displaced by the creation of Israel. The presence of these refugees in Lebanon still threatened that country's survival, and I hoped that this book might help explain how the United States has evaded responsibility for its part in this human tragedy.

The initial draft of this book was nearing completion in March 1979, when President Carter witnessed the signing of an

Egyptian-Israeli treaty and predicted that peace in the Middle East would follow. But, in the meantime, new threats to the area's stability had emerged. People and political alliances with which I'd been associated now diverted our attention from peacemaking, just as they had in the past. Building barriers to communism was our objective in the 1950s, but the Baghdad Pact, like the leaders of the countries who'd formed it, had disappeared and no longer protected the interests of the West. Just like some of America's promises to the people of the Middle East, the allies we'd built up to oppose Russian influence there had turned out to be as fragile as ropes of sand.

Too often the United States has formulated its foreign and domestic policies on the short-term basis of not offending any group that might swing an election, and it is not surprising that the White House now refers to "the situation in Southwest Asia" when issuing statements relative to the crises in Iran and Afghanistan, as if these losses to the West could be segregated from the issues of human rights that America has neglected in the Middle East for the past thirty years. Now in an election year, the administration is attempting to distinguish between the Camp David Accords leading to the Egyptian-Israeli treaty and the adverse developments on Russia's border: the former heralded as a harbinger of the end of Arab-Israeli hostilities, and the latter decried as the greatest threat to peace since 1945. Both essentially relate to the single question of access to the oil resources of the Middle East; fortunately, most Americans have finally become aware of the West's dependence on the goodwill of the people who inhabit that critical area.

Our failure in the Middle East now affects the daily life of every American, and people search for contemporary explanations for the developments threatening the security and economy of the United States. Placing the blame on communism, Islam, the Arabs, OPEC and the oil companies is understandable. The American government does just that instead of facing squarely the issues of basic justice that have plagued the Middle East through the period covered by this book.

Because I played some part in shaping what America aspired to, and had to live with what we lost, I hope that this story of my own life may contribute to dispelling some of the confusion that has obscured the Middle East's problems and led to the misery and suffering that continue even now.

Wilbur Crane Eveland
Cupertino, California
January 1980

ROPES
OF SAND

I leave to my said children a great chest full of
broken promises and cracked oaths; likewise a vast
cargo of ropes made of sand.

"John Bull's Last Will and Testament,"
A Collection of Scarce and Valuable Tracts,
edited by Walter Scott,
vol. 13, p. 144 (London: 1815).

CHAPTER ONE

THE GENESIS

On January 8, 1918, President Woodrow Wilson announced America's Fourteen Point plan for a "peace without victors" that led to the armistices ending the First World War.

Just as the defeated European countries took solace from Wilson's assurances that no nation would profit from the war, so the peoples of the Ottoman Turkish Empire looked to the United States to allow them self-determination and autonomy. Although America's allies hoped to divide and annex parts of Arab Asia and Turkey as spoils of war, they were dependent upon American support in rebuilding Europe. Britain, France, and Italy therefore accepted Wilson's proposal for a system of League of Nations mandates to oversee the transition of the Ottoman Empire to independence, the shape of the future states to be based on surveys of the wishes of the indigenous peoples.

Having already divided among themselves spheres of influence in the area and made commitments to various factions in order to secure political advantage and wartime support, America's allies were hardly pleased by the prospect of plebiscites. In the Sykes-Picot Agreement of 1916, Great Britain and France had defined their claims, looking forward eventually to an Arab state or confederation within the Anglo-French spheres. Great Britain was given Mesopotamia (modern Iraq), while France took Syria (including present-day Lebanon), although Britain was granted access to the Syrian ports of Acre and Haifa. Palestine (then southern Syria) was to be placed under some form of international control to ensure universal access to the Christian, Moslem, and Jewish holy places, especially Jerusalem.

As the price of Arab participation in the war against Turkey, however, Britain had guaranteed independence and territory to the two opposing dynasties on the Arabian Peninsula: the Wahhabis, under Emir Abul Aziz ibn Saud; and the Hashemites, under Emir Hussein. Not only were Great Britain's promises to these dynasties in some ways conflicting, but its commitment that Hussein's son Feisal would rule an Arab state from Damascus clashed with the Sykes-Picot provision that Syria be within the French sphere.

Then, in 1917, further undermining its promises to the Arabs, the British government promulgated the Balfour Declaration. This viewed with favor the establishment in Palestine of "*a national home for the Jewish people*" on the condition that nothing should be done that would "*prejudice the civil and religious rights and political status of existing non-Jewish communities or the rights and political status enjoyed by Jews in any other country*."

Almost simultaneously, the new Bolshevik government of Russia made public the various secret agreements of America's allies, exposing the British and French plan to apportion the Near East between them and rule without popular consent. To counter Arab outrage over these revelations and the Balfour Declaration, Britain renewed its pledges to grant the Arabs independence and "full opportunity of once again forming a nation of the world."

On July 4, 1918, President Wilson responded to these British and French machinations in a speech denouncing all secret agreements and giving America's assurances that the Arabs under Turkish control could look forward to "*an undoubted security of life and an absolutely unmolested opportunity for autonomous development*." Thus, these Arabs had good reason to believe that the United States would be a guarantor of the independence they sought after four hundred years of Turkish subjugation.

CHAPTER TWO

JOURNEY INTO HISTORY 1918–1948

Those of us born in 1918 were promised a future in a world made safe for democracy. There would be no more wars, no secret diplomacy, no treaties dividing the world into colonial empires, President Wilson had pledged. But the U.S. Senate rejected American membership in the League of Nations, their position reflecting public opposition to involvement in the affairs of other nations.[1] As for the destinies of the people assured independence from the Ottoman Turkish Empire, few Americans understood the promises made by the Allied Powers to the Arabs. The possibility that the aspirations of these people might someday affect America's security seemed as remote as the Near East itself, then a rail-and-sea voyage of six weeks from my native state of Washington.

At the time of my birth, Spokane was still close to its frontier past. Squaws bearing papooses were a common sight; they lived in tepees on nearby reservations. Miners and loggers from Idaho came to Spokane for its brothels and speakeasies. Fort George Wright, the garrison from which the area had been settled, was still active, and the sounds of its bugle calls reached my home. While growing up, I visited the fort often, fascinated by the uniforms, drills, and

---

1   See Arthur Walworth, *America's Moment, 1918* (New York: W. W. Norton & Co., 1977), a very valuable reference book for that period.

retreat parades. I was enchanted also by my grandfather's stories of coming west to Washington Territory to homestead a farm near the place then called Spokane Falls. I made him repeat his tales of leading posses when he was a county sheriff, and I wanted to be a police chief, as he had also been, when I grew up. My urge to travel grew as I accompanied my grandfather to the distant sites of the pioneering highways he built when he became a contractor.

The depression years of my youth were lean, giving me special incentive to earn money. In high school I worked nights for Western Union, and the delivery of telegrams to passengers on transcontinental trains was part of my job. Roaming through the Pullman cars, I often dreamed that I'd be carried off with them to distant places.

Determined to see the wider world, I joined a Marine Corps Reserve battalion (lying about my age) and spent my seventeenth summer at Puget Sound Navy Yard. The next year, my last in high school, I took the West Point examinations; unprepared, I failed the written tests, and I put aside my hopes for an army commission and foreign travel for a time.

I worked in Spokane for a while, but growing restless, I set off for San Francisco, where a part-time job enabled me to take courses on the Berkeley campus until the next summer's marines encampment at San Diego called me away. Returning home, I heard of England's declaration of war on Germany and began to think of enlisting in the service. Not then fancying the life or status of a private, I decided to see what else life offered.

Christmas 1939 was difficult for me. My father was hard hit by the depression, and we quarreled about my wanderlust. During the middle of the night I started to hitchhike east. I had no definite plan; I knew only that I was determined not to return until I became successful. My timing was terrible: as I moved across the snowbound northern states, I was often left off by farmers in freezing weather, with only haystacks or culverts for shelter. Short of money, I deferred my quest for independence long enough to stay with relatives of my father in his native New Jersey.

There I learned about my paternal heritage. When I visited the home-site of a grandfather three generations removed, Major Nathaniel Crane, and was told that George Washington and

Lafayette had been quartered there while they planned raids on British stores on Staten Island, I made up my mind to enlist and seek an army commission. Again leaving at night, in order to frustrate plans of my relatives to return me to Spokane, I hitchhiked to Boston and enlisted as a twenty-one-dollar-a-month regular army private on February 13, 1940. A strong sense of controlling my own destiny accompanied this decision: my life would have started in Boston had my parents not moved from there to Spokane three months before I was born.

I was assigned to Fort Banks in Winthrop, just outside Boston. By the end of 1940 I had passed a competitive examination for becoming a staff sergeant. To prepare for the West Point preparatory school for enlisted men, I took extension courses held on the Harvard campus.

Then, in January 1941, I was summoned to the post commander's office. After warning me that my visit was to be kept secret, the colonel left me standing at attention and stalked out of the room.

A man seated on a couch behind me laughed and then said, "Relax, Eveland, the Old Man doesn't like taking orders from corps headquarters." This, it turned out, was a lieutenant from First Corps Area G-2, a military intelligence officer. Far from comfortable before this officer in civilian garb, I racked my mind to come up with what I'd done to get in trouble. Was having lied about my age to enter the Marine Corps Reserve a crime? I finally blurted out, "What's wrong, sir?"

Grinning, the lieutenant told me that I was one of ten men selected from throughout the Corps Area for assignment to secret intelligence duties. Relieved, but not knowing what was involved, I spoke of my desire to attend West Point. "We know all about that," the lieutenant responded impatiently, "but that's all off. Our country may soon be at war. Meanwhile, we have to guard against potential enemies from within. You should be flattered that you've been chosen for the Corps of Intelligence Police."

As I accepted an invitation to be seated, a blue leather folder was put into my hand. On the outside, embossed in gold, was the seal of the War Office, United States of America. Inside, printed over the outline of a badge reading "Corps of Intelligence Police," was certification that the lieutenant in the identifying photograph was "entitled to exercise the authority and perform the duties provided by law and regulations." I was duly impressed, as the lieutenant intended, but perhaps more than he knew. I was staring at the oval-shaped silver badge he held in his hand, enameled in black on its face, bearing the letters *CIP*. I was thinking of my grandfather and his days as a sheriff.

Snapping me back to reality, the lieutenant explained that the CIP had been formed in 1917 to protect the American Expeditionary Force against espionage. The only American counterespionage organization at the time, the CIP had been maintained after the armistice, although its strength had dwindled to 40 by 1938. In 1940, however, with the exposure of spy rings in the United States and the threat of war, the authorized strength of the corps had been increased to 188. I'd been chosen to be one of this number.

My acceptance was taken for granted. I was told to hurry to my barracks and pack while it was empty. I was not to explain myself to any soldiers I might meet, the lieutenant cautioned, and I would never return to Fort Banks. My records would be collected by the post commander, who would explain my departure.

Gathering my things, I accompanied the lieutenant in a staff car to a small Boston hotel. There he explained that he'd been a reporter for the *Boston Globe* until being called to active duty as a military intelligence reserve officer just a few weeks earlier. Suddenly businesslike as we entered a room reserved in my name, he passed me $200 in an envelope, saying that it was for living expenses until I'd been "demilitarized" and could report to corps headquarters at the Boston Army Base. From that day on I would never use a military title for identification; "special agent" would be my designation, and I was to say I was a civilian employee of the War Department whenever my status was asked. I'd be contacted at the hotel the following morning, the lieutenant explained. A man with identifying credentials would take me to Filene's department store to charge a civilian wardrobe for me to a covert army account. If I needed help to finance the automobile that all special agents required for their work, the man sent to contact me the next day would see to that, too. Having told me all this within two hours of our initial meeting, the lieutenant abruptly departed, leaving me to my thoughts.

Surprise slowly giving way to pleasure, I called my parents. No longer would I have to describe the prospect of rapid promotions as the reason for my enlistment in the regular army. Now they could proudly tell my friends and former neighbors that I was assigned to secret intelligence work—secret, I realized as we spoke, to the degree that I still had no idea what I'd be doing.

A middle-aged special agent called on me the following morning. Confiding that he was actually a master sergeant, he warned of the need for secrecy as we embarked on our mission to purchase clothing and a car. Soon equipped with a wardrobe, I selected a 1939 Packard coupe, which the army credit union purchased in my name under a monthly repayment schedule. It was too expensive, I knew, but I wanted it. One of my father's depression jobs had been selling used Packards. Few people could then afford one, but we at least had long rides in the country in his demonstrator. I'd resolved then to own a Packard some day. Another adolescent goal had been achieved. Military life was looking better all the time.

Given several days to find an apartment, I settled into a one-room flat with a huge bay window overlooking Beacon Street. Reporting for duty, I was ushered into the office of Lieutenant Colonel Alexander R. Bolling, the assistant chief of staff, G-2 (intelligence), of the First Corps Area (encompassing all of the New England states). A smile and a warm handshake welcomed me; to my surprise, I was gestured to a chair.

Getting right to the point, Bolling told me that army counterintelligence was understaffed and all too inexperienced, that our country was badly prepared for war, and that the secret duties I was to perform were vitally important. Such man-to-man talk astounded me, and I felt I'd been made a part of a very special team. As we talked, the reason why our work must be secret was impressed on me: spying into the affairs and activities of others ran counter to deeply ingrained American principles that held personal privacy inviolable except by due process of law. I was easily convinced, however, that the war in Europe posed a threat to America's security and that exceptional measures were necessary in times of emergency. The prospect of joining the only U.S. counterespionage organization to survive World War I gave me the feeling of being a pioneer in protecting my country from sinister enemies dedicated to its destruction.[2]

I then met my fellow special agents, twelve sergeants from the peacetime regular army. I was issued a .38-caliber snub-nosed detective special pistol with belt and shoulder holsters. My photograph was taken (in civilian clothes) and affixed to a set of credentials. The badge I was issued, tarnished from years of storage, was number 106. Although I was now equipped to represent myself as a civilian War Department employee, my credentials contained one clear indication of my real status: my enlisted serial number. But now, with proof of my affiliation with military intelligence, I was ready to protect democracy from subversion—a word I'd never used before and spelled "submersion" until I was corrected.

During my first week, I worked with an "experienced" investigator, a man who'd preceded me into the CIP by just one week. Together we made rounds of municipal and other government agencies to verify birth dates and determine arrest records or court involvements. Credit records were also valuable sources, and these, like postal "mail covers" and all other records we sought, were produced without hesitation when we displayed our credentials. We also knocked on doors, asking neighbors and acquaintances about our subject's character, morals, and loyalty. Investigations of War Department employees or candidates for sensitive assignments also entailed interviewing the subject's references, but we gave these little consideration in our conclusions, our assumption being that the comments of designated references would generally prove favorable.

I soon joined the morning-coffee conference at a restaurant near our office where most of the agents gathered. There we shared verbally our disbelief at our good fortune. There, too, we developed a system of pooling investigations by area and category. In

---

2   In 1929, Secretary of State Stimson abolished his department's intelligence activities, holding that "gentlemen do not read each other's mail." A year and a half after I joined the CIP, President Roosevelt used an executive order to establish the Office of Strategic Services (OSS).

the end, the agent responsible for a given case would integrate information acquired by his colleagues into a report. This was efficient, of course, but hardly the same as making evaluations based on firsthand knowledge.

One day a colleague told me that he'd been assigned to prepare the "full-field investigation" confirming my loyalty, integrity, and character. He needed information, he said, verifying my attendance at college courses, and was also supposed to interview my references and people who'd worked with me at Fort Banks. Suggesting that I handle these tasks, my friend proposed that I type up the final report and its conclusions for his signature, a favor I returned when his case came up. We both appeared, on paper, to be extraordinary men.

Thus validated for access to secret information, we were flooded with investigations of scientists and other professionals considered for assignment at MIT's Radiation Laboratory and the Argonne facility in Chicago. Many candidates were denied clearances by investigators who looked askance at a divorce or drinking in college. Pressure for rapid processing generally guaranteed superficial reports, and there was, needless to say, no adequate review process. Unless alerted by people we interviewed, the subjects never even learned they were being investigated. As is still the practice, the subject himself was never questioned, nor was he allowed to refute adverse reports, based as they might well be on hearsay or malice. Protection of informants' identities seemed then (as today) more important than the rights of the person being investigated. And, although possibly not interested in the position for which they were being investigated, people could be permanently categorized as unworthy of trust. (Years later, gaining access to my own government records, I found false accusations of which I'd been totally unaware and, of course, unable to challenge.)

Soon established in a comfortable apartment, I enjoyed the independence that enabled me to set the pace and scope of my investigative activities. Routine snooping and record checking became boring before long, however. Worse, I often worried about my authority, at age twenty-two, to influence the lives of people I'd never met—even my right, should I so choose, to deprive the country of the services of a talented scientist if something about his background troubled me. Impatient to get on with the business of uncovering spies and saboteurs, I discovered a bureaucratic problem: there just weren't enough spies to go around, and the FBI always moved in as soon as suspects materialized.

In spite of J. Edgar Hoover's reluctance to share the FBI's jurisdiction, however, the law entitled us to join the FBI on investigations involving War Department personnel or property. On one of these assignments I accompanied one of Hoover's much vaunted special agents—he was less than a year out of college—to investigate a fire in an army installation in Worcester. It was exciting work for a week, questioning suspects and probing through ashes, until we discovered that the enemy had been only a sinister short circuit.

The military intelligence service had no school of its own, but by mid-1941 one was organized at the Army War College in Washington. I was one of three students from the First Corps Area sent to the initial investigators' training class. Instructors came from the FBI, the Secret Service, and the Treasury Department, and one had been sheriff of Dade County, Florida. Our curriculum was ambitious for the three months allotted. Introduced by a history of espionage and military intelligence, courses included various specialties of the trade: photography, fingerprinting, mail opening, telephone tapping and recording, surveillance, surreptitious entries, interrogation, espionage law, arrest warrants, judo, and weapons practice. Class-work was supplemented by applied learning. At night we worked with teams of other federal investigators or rode with detectives of the District of Columbia Metropolitan Police. Weekends, for practice, we were assigned to teams of "hounds" and "hares," using taxis to lose our "tails" or follow our quarry. Washington taxi drivers sometimes blanched when ordered to "follow that cab," but the prevailing feeling that war was imminent, combined with a display of our credentials, produced compliance—and not a few dented fenders.

Following graduation, our records were marked to reflect the testimony of our diplomas and show that we were now "qualified investigators." I was promoted to the rank of master sergeant on a permanent basis just before all promotions became temporary in nature until the end of the war. Thus, within one and one-half years, I'd advanced from being a private to the highest enlisted grade. There were rumors that the CIP would open its own officer-candidate school and that military intelligence commissions might soon be available. The CIP was growing, 400 strong now, with authorization for another 600, and my career was growing with it.

The morning of the Japanese attack on Pearl Harbor I was readying the Packard for a weekend outing. Hearing the news on its radio, I strapped on my gun, attached a red lens to the car's spotlight, and raced down to the Boston Army Base. The shock had barely begun to register on us: we'd received no instructions from Washington, and for all we knew the Germans might land on the East Coast at any moment. Army and National Guard units were deployed along the coastline, ready to repel invaders. To have ventured out with these trigger-happy and frightened soldiers would have been suicidal. We had no choice but to sit tight. Soon we were inundated with calls from army installations reporting suspected subversive activities: a blown fuse, a lurking stranger, or a mere truck breakdown would evoke demands for investigations; but our efforts failed to produce evidence of enemy activities.

Later I was assigned to accompany FBI agents to pick up the hundreds of suspects on the bureau's automatic-arrest lists. File cards accumulated over the years now provided sufficient evidence for detention by the FBI: a German name, combined with reported attendance at a Deutscher-American Bund meeting, represented probable cause to suspect spying for Hitler; a Japanese who took photographs and was rumored to own a shortwave radio seemed likely to be an agent for Hirohito.[3] As the hysteria abated,

---

3   An estimated one million Germans, Italians, and Japanese were classified by the FBI as "alien enemies"; these people were subjected to physical surveillance, telephone taps, and hidden microphones following the outbreak of war. Although the Bureau's agents had been trained only in the apprehension of common criminals, they improvised the new techniques that were later employed in peacetime, without proper warrants, until the Watergate investigations exposed them and produced congressional pressure for new legislation. See William C. Sullivan, with Bill Brown, *The Bureau* (New York: W. W. Norton & Co., 1979).

we settled back into our routine of character and loyalty investigations. Again bored, I longed for excitement. Suddenly, relief appeared.

Although the continental United States was apparently safe, our outposts overseas still feared a delayed attack. I received secret orders sending me to the Panama Canal Zone to join the Counter Intelligence Corps (CIC) there (the CIP's name had been changed). Breaking security, I told my parents of my new assignment. After farewell drinks in Boston, accepting the toasts due a soldier leaving to fight for his country at a (secret) destination overseas, I left for New York.

Reporting to the Brooklyn Port of Embarkation with orders certifying that I was a War Department civilian employee, I watched troops in battle gear boarding camouflaged transports to sail to the Pacific and England. Assigned to a stateroom on the civilian liner S.S. *Panama*, I had further evidence of my good fortune in falling into intelligence work. I knew also that fellow marines from my reserve battalion had been mobilized and sent to the Pacific. I'd been lucky.

My ship was full of Americans returning to their homes in the Canal Zone, most of them apparently oblivious of the flow of war; many, in any case, returning to the only home they and their parents had. As we approached the mid-Atlantic coast, however, we became part of a convoy of navy vessels heading for the canal through waters in which German submarines operated with near impunity. Frequent attack drills sent us scurrying to lifeboat stations; shrill sirens on darting destroyers and subchasers penetrated the air; and, since we had no way of knowing if an attack was imminent, the voyage was far from routine.

I'd been assigned to share a stateroom with a man about my age, Neil Gellatly, who was, he said, returning to his civilian post in Panama. As we talked during the voyage, my civilian cover apparently wore thin—I hadn't been told what my civilian job was supposed to be. As Gellatly asked me questions, casually, it seemed, it became obvious that I was at a loss each time we broached the subject of my assignment. Then, returning one day to the stateroom, I found him unpacking a shirt bearing army-staff-sergeant's stripes. At this point Gellatly ended his game: he was a CIC special agent assigned to the Panama Canal Department's G-2 office, and he had known of my mission even before we left New York. I then heard the amazing story of how the army had prepared, just a few months earlier, to discharge its responsibility for counterespionage and sabotage protection of America's most vital waterway. Ordered by Washington to activate a CIC detachment, the colonel in charge of intelligence had reached no further than the enlisted typists and clerks in his office. There a crew had been assembled; pledged to secrecy; issued badges, credentials, and guns; and given an allowance to purchase civilian clothes. During the day these men performed their office duties, and at night they were turned out to look for enemy agents. That I was struggling to suppress laughter must have seemed obvious to Gellatly. There was a new plan, he assured me: an "undercover" office had been opened in Panama City, right in the heart of the cabaret district, where B-girls were suspected of doubling as Mata Haris.

During the balance of the voyage, I learned of the vulnerability of the Panama Canal, a prize the Japanese might easily have taken by continuing on from Pearl Harbor. There was still danger of sabotage and espionage by the large Japanese and German colonies in the Republic of Panama; and, Gellatly explained, our ability to detect and apprehend these people—or hostile Panamanians for that matter—was entirely dependent upon the goodwill of the government of Panama. Anti-American and nationalistic sentiment was strong, however, and many Panamanians now demanded the full independence a 1934 act of Congress had granted the Philippine Islands (to become effective in 1946). Just before my arrival, a riot by Panamanian nationalists, protesting their exclusion from the Canal Zone and their country's involuntary involvement in America's war, had been stopped just short of U.S. Army headquarters. Troops pushed these demonstrators back, but they carried with them captured machine guns, which were now displayed outside Panama's interior ministry as evidence of a capacity to start further trouble. Even with full cooperation by the Panamanian National Guard (the country's army), protecting both banks of the forty-four miles of jungle-enclosed waterway from sabotage would require many more American troops than were then based in the Canal Zone.

Debarking at Cristobal, I entered a strange outpost of America's colonial empire, a world that conjured up the British raj in Kipling's day. According to a treaty (executed under questionable circumstances with a Frenchman claiming to act for Panama), America's prerogatives were perpetual, and even the Republic of Panama had been taken from Colombia by the United States to provide labor to run the canal. Now slated to become the CIC's first "expert" in preventing and detecting attempts to sabotage the canal, I set off by train to Ancon to rendezvous with my new boss, who'd left word at the ship that he'd contact me secretly at the YMCA.

A postmidnight caller at my room turned out to be Lieutenant Albert R. Haney, the head of all (fifteen) CIC special agents in Panama—"The Chief," as he asked to be called. To prepare me for my new role, Haney assigned me a pseudonym, by which I was to be known for security purposes. I'd be operating undercover in some yet undetermined capacity; meanwhile, I was to rent a room in Panama City and refrain from establishing contacts with military personnel, even Neil Gellatly. I was given a bag containing my .38 detective special, handcuffs, and a blackjack (to be worn at all times on a key ring suspended inside my belt). The next day I was issued Canal Zone-employee ID cards so that I could shop at the commissary for white Palm Beach suits, a Panama hat, and white shoes. Thus attired in conventional CIC uniform, I was to stand by for orders from The Chief.

My first assignment was a case of suspected sabotage at Ria Hata Air Base, upcountry in the republic along the Pacific seacoast, where a small building had been wrecked by detonation of the explosives it housed. I took many pictures, collected bags of possible evidence, and then returned to my hotel to ponder the facts.

A combination of luck and simple logic enabled me to solve the case on the following day. One of the tear-gas canisters I'd taken as evidence bore marks of penetration by a .30-caliber bullet. No small-arms ammunition, however, was listed on the inventory of the destroyed building. After interrogating the men who'd been on sentry duty the night of the explosion, I finally elicited an admission from a terrified private. Half-awake, he'd heard the rattling of tin cans attached to the barbed wire surrounding the building. Assuming that this caprice of the wind signaled the presence of an invader, the sentry had fired the shot that set off the destruction I'd been sent to investigate. With a signed confession in my pocket, I telephoned news of my success to Lieutenant Haney, who authorized me to "break security" and report the next day to be introduced to the colonel in charge of intelligence for the entire Panama Canal Department.

In addition to receiving a written commendation, I was rewarded for my accomplishments as a "trained investigator" by the G-2 colonel, who assigned me a command of my own. My new title was "special agent in charge of the Atlantic Sector of the Canal Zone," and I selected my shipmate Neil Gellatly to be my deputy. Soon I had a staff of five agents in Cristobal; within two weeks I'd been made responsible for protecting half of the U.S. Navy's lifeline to the Pacific Ocean from subversive activities by our enemies.

There I again learned how vulnerable the canal was to German or Japanese attacks: from the tower of my office building I viewed the damage to an American ship that had been torpedoed by a German submarine that had penetrated the sunken steel-net barrier at the harbor's entrance. The extent to which enemy submarines were guided from the shore was a mystery to which Washington demanded an immediate solution; so, too, was the location of sub-refueling bases on the coasts of Central America or the numerous Caribbean islands.

Naval intelligence was active and cooperative, ready to assist by supplying seaplanes and ships for transportation and reconnaissance. For months my agents and I spent almost as much time over water as we did on land. We also searched the jungles for radio transmitters reported by Signal Corps operators who had heard unidentifiable sounds on the airwaves. If any enemy radios really existed in the dense bush, our mosquito-plagued treks to locate them provided ample time for the sets to be removed or hidden. And I cruised the San Blas Islands in a schooner for weeks, searching, unsuccessfully, for submarine-refueling bases that missionaries had sworn they'd seen. The results were always the same: either we were too late or we were chasing unfounded rumors.

FBI agents operated throughout Central and South America (outside their legal jurisdiction) but reported only to Hoover. Jealousy among intelligence services (the socially elite OSS now commanded the President's attention) and the ambitions of the FBI's director to expand his empire blocked the free exchange of intelligence information we might have otherwise employed to enhance the canal's security. Fortunately, Germany and Japan had priorities other than destroying the Panama Canal. Otherwise, the war in the Pacific might have been won by Japan long before the United States could have launched its island-by-island campaign to defeat the Japanese.

Meanwhile, Lieutenant Haney, keeping busy, arrested in British Honduras the "mastermind" of submarine-refueling operations in the Caribbean. It was, unfortunately, the wrong man—a rumrunner who had operated out of Belize since the days of prohibition.

My first year in Panama passed rapidly, and I was eager to return to the United States. The CIC had arranged to send its senior agents to officer-candidate schools, and finally orders leading to my commission as second lieutenant arrived. The personnel records I carried with me from Panama were endorsed to reflect a tour of "superior service." In fact, I had caught not only the Ria Hata "saboteur," but malaria (twice) and dengue fever (three times).

Now wearing the gold bars of what the troops called a "ninety-day wonder," I returned to Spokane on leave, pleased that in four years I'd accomplished my first objective in life. By this time, Washington in its wisdom had decided that each combat division, corps, and field army should have a CIC detachment. With orders to accompany a corps headquarters to Europe, I left the wife I'd just married and proceeded with my new unit over Omaha Beach and inland through France, Belgium, and Holland into Germany.

Heading a CIC-operations section, I was relatively free of

supervision by corps headquarters and moved my unit as I wished within the three-division area for which we were responsible. The generals commanding combat units looked to their own G-2 sections for intelligence concerning enemy movements; they had little interest in the CIC's assigned role of counterespionage. Provided with automatic-arrest lists of German intelligence personnel and high-ranking Nazi-party officials, I moved my men into the larger cities as soon as advancing troops could secure them (always carrying packed in our footlockers the civilian clothing that CIC regulations required).

By the time Essen fell, the German army was on the run. There was still the hazard, however, of advancing into unknown territory and encountering pockets still held by the Germans. Once, my driver and I were captured by enemy troops, who after consultation tried to surrender to us. We rejected their offer because POW facilities were already overcrowded.

The war in Europe soon ended. Flown to the United States to take leave, I was assigned to a unit scheduled for the invasion of Japan. The Japanese surrender during this period gave me the opportunity to be discharged and assigned to the military intelligence reserve. I was again a civilian. Offered a job with an import-export firm, I moved to New York City to head its office. Housing was impossible to find. Since rent controls were still in effect, no landlord wanted to offer space at wartime rates. A break came when the owner of a store I patronized offered me a furnished apartment in the Bronx just behind and above Yankee Stadium. It was a predominantly Jewish neighborhood; we appeared to be the only gentiles in our building.

Soon we discovered a major drawback to the location. Fundraising drives to buy arms for the Zionists fighting British troops in Palestine were constant. I contributed a few times but then declined further requests. My refusals were met with insults and even accusations that we were Nazi sympathizers. I then learned that coded marks had been made on doorways to advise collectors of the status of each resident. We were roused at all hours of the night; a swastika was chalked on our door. Finally, we had to move.

I was more confused than angered by the highly emotional and malicious actions of these fund raisers, who called themselves Zionists and cited claims to a Biblical birthright in Palestine. One of my employees was Jewish, a close friend since we'd met during the war in Europe. He'd been a member of the Interrogation of Prisoners of War (IPW) team assigned to my CIC detachment. He, like most of his colleagues, was from a Jewish family that had left Germany during Hitler's rise to power. Well educated, with a keen understanding of the German people, none of the IPW interpreters I worked with ever displayed vindictiveness in dealing with German military personnel and civilians whom we questioned and processed for transfer to camps in the rear. I considered their quiet dedication remarkable, particularly in contrast to the behavior of many American GIs, who seemed to delight in forcing Nazi prisoners to endure hardships—such as standing for long periods with hands above heads and being refused toilet facilities.

As a driver-interpreter, my Jewish friend had accompanied me to see the horrors of Bergen-Belsen, the British-liberated concentration camp near Hamburg that became a symbol of Nazi inhumanity. There we'd seen thousands of unburied dead and many more sick, starving, and dying prisoners too confused to understand that they'd finally been liberated. There were Poles, Russians, and, as my friend pointed out, Jews from all over Europe who had been rounded up and forced to wear the Star of David on their striped prison clothes.

Now, in New York, I asked my friend whether these were the Jews who were seeking safety in Palestine. Many were, he confirmed, but, in his view, they would be willing to go anyplace to escape memories of German persecution and were not really Zionists. That movement's real leaders, largely Polish and Russian Jews, had emigrated to Palestine during the 1920s and 1930s to acquire land for future immigration by Jewish settlers. Obviously not a dedicated Zionist, my friend criticized the concept of the Jews' being a separate and chosen people who, to survive, should never integrate themselves into the cultures of other nations.

A maiden aunt, keen on history and a family genealogist, volunteered to enlighten me further on the problems in Palestine and the role of the Crane branch of my father's family in advising President Wilson on Middle Eastern matters. She gave me a yellowed copy of a *New York Times* article of August 20, 1922, by Ray Stannard Baker, which made public for the first time a confidential report of Wilson's King-Crane Commission to Syria, which then included Palestine. More concerned just then with business problems than with the remote religious issues I'd had to move to avoid, I put this article away to read another time.

By late 1947, the Argentine monetary situation caused the head office of the company I worked for to suspend business; I was out of a job. At the time, the army was recalling reserve officers—the Berlin crisis was upon us. Now with a son to support, wanting something certain, I decided to return to active duty. Assigned to Camp Holabird, Maryland, a huge military intelligence training complex, I found that my first commander in the CIP, now Major General Bolling, was assistant chief of staff, G-2 (intelligence), of the entire army. Going to see him in Washington, I explained that I had little desire to do peacetime intelligence work. As he knew, it would consist primarily of checking out civilians for government employment. Responding to my request for help, Bolling suggested that I become a military attaché. The idea appealed to me—it would mean an assignment abroad, but not where U.S. troops were concentrated. The general said that he'd arrange the first step, an assignment to study a language at the Presidio of Monterey, California. Having summoned an aide, Bolling determined that there were three one-year courses scheduled to start at the beginning of January 1949: Chinese, Russian, and Arabic. I was invited to select one of them and let General Bolling know my decision within a week.

The next day I drove to New Jersey to collect my family. There my aunt referred to the clipping she'd given me and presented me with a just published book of Department of State documents: *Papers Relating to the Foreign Relations of the United States. The Paris Peace Conference, 1919.* In this book, she showed me the first officially released text of the report coauthored by Charles Richard Crane, President Wilson's commissioner on mandates in Turkey (and at one time the American minister to Russia and China).

Knowing that military attachés had something to do with diplomatic missions, I was now eager to learn of the activities of this man with whom I shared common ancestors (through my grandmother). Days of reading about America's role in the history of the modern Middle East led to my decision that I'd study Arabic and travel to this part of the world in which the United States had just assumed new responsibilities.

By the time I reported for language training in California, I was well aware that the Middle East might be a very strategic arena in the cold war between the Soviet Union and the West. I also understood that the peoples of that area were again looking to America to help them achieve the desires for security of life and unmolested autonomous development that President Wilson had inspired in them thirty years earlier.

CHAPTER THREE

THIRTY YEARS OF INDIFFERENCE

Woodrow Wilson's plans for an enduring peace with justice were threatened even before the Senate rejected American membership in the League of Nations. His concession to British and French demands for massive reparations from Germany eventually brought that country to the brink of revolt and economic collapse. Britain and France also wanted colonial rule over the Arab areas liberated from Turkey; they considered barely tolerable the concept of guiding new states to independence under League of Nations mandates. The idea of heeding the findings of a plebiscite in defining the areas to be mandated and their forms of government was even more repugnant to America's allies. They had plans of their own.

France, supported by the Zionists (well aware that an overwhelming majority of the inhabitants of Palestine opposed a Jewish homeland there), delayed as long as possible the formation of the Inter-Allied Commission on Mandates in Turkey. President Wilson, committed to the principle of self-determination for the Arabs, finally sent the American section of the commission alone to the Near East in mid-1919. The commission was still in Damascus when the Treaty of Versailles was signed and the concept of government under mandates was approved.

By the time the commission had completed its survey and report, President Wilson had returned to the United States to wage his unsuccessful battle for American membership in the league and ratification of the Versailles Peace Treaty. Now disillusioned and seriously ill, Wilson consigned the King-Crane Report to oblivion in the Department of State.[4] Although sentiment in the Near East strongly favored having the United States as a mandatory power, there seemed to be no possibility that Congress would agree to such foreign involvement. It did not become fully evident until the release in 1947 of the Paris peace documents, however, just how badly America's failure to assume a responsible place in the peace negotiations and treaty drafting damaged the prospects for justice and stability in the Near East.

In the end, Wilson's pledges of "self-determination" and "unmolested autonomous development" for the peoples of Arab Asia were ignored by Britain and France. The publication of the King-Crane Report revealed that Wilson's advisors had been aware of the popular aspirations of the newly liberated people and had accurately forecast the results of the failure of the United States to keep the promises upon which they had relied.

Finding the people of Syria almost unanimous in their opposition to French rule or to the detachment of Lebanon or Palestine to form separate states, the King-Crane Commission recommended that a united Syrian state be given independence and ruled by Emir Feisal of Arabia.

The Allies had accepted the principles of Britain's Balfour Declaration, and the commission gave lengthy and sympathetic consideration to Zionist aspirations for a Jewish homeland in Palestine. In its report, however, the commission opposed this after finding that the majority of the people rejected the concept of imposing a new religious community in the midst of the non-Jewish population of Palestine—nearly nine-tenths of its whole. As for Zionist claims that they had a "right" to Palestine based on an occupation two thousand years before, the commission concluded that these "can hardly be seriously considered." The commission

---

4   Named for its co-commissioners: Dr. Henry Churchill King and Charles Richard Crane. See Harry N. Howard, *The King-Crane Commission*, (Beirut: Khayats, 1963).

did recommend a British mandate over Mesopotamia (to become Iraq), and, were Palestine to be severed from Syria, proposed Britain as a mandatory power over Palestine.

In 1920, Britain and France convened the San Remo Conference to decide on peace terms with Turkey. Not having declared war on the Ottoman Empire, the United States was not a participant, nor was it consulted when the British and French used the conference to divide among themselves all oil rights within the Arab countries that had been under Turkish rule. Because of uncertainty about America's willingness to accept a political role in the Near East, and because of squabbles between the Allies, the Anglo-French mandates were not officially defined until 1923 (in the Treaty of Lausanne). Again, the United States was neither a negotiator nor a signatory.

Meanwhile, Great Britain and France had arbitrarily divided Palestine from the rest of Syria and enlarged the areas over which they had assumed "provisional mandates." First, the American and British nominee for ruling a united Syria, Emir Feisal, was ousted by French forces, which also annexed parts of Turkey to Syria. Then, despite local opposition, France greatly enlarged the Christian section of Syria (Mount Lebanon) and created an expanded state called Lebanon.

Britain annexed oil-rich Turkish territory (Mosul and Kurdistan) to Mesopotamia and delineated Iraq as an independent state with Feisal as its king. Still beholden to the Hashemite dynasty of Arabia for leading the Arab revolt against Turkey, however, the British divided Palestine, east of the Jordan River, and created Transjordan, with Emir Abdullah on its throne.

This Anglo-French game of musical chairs, contravening American promises of indigenous approval, consisted largely of drawing artificial lines on the Near Eastern map and gravely undermined the prospects of peace in the area. Moreover, these arbitrary territorial divisions were made *before* the mandates under which they would be governed received ex post facto sanction under the Treaty of Lausanne in 1923.

Between 1918 and 1949, there were eighteen revolts in Syria, and the Syrian independence promised for 1939 was not granted

by France until 1945. The French mandate over Lebanon expired
in 1941. It was not until 1944 that France agreed to Lebanese independence, and U.S. diplomatic pressure was necessary to force
French troops to leave in 1946. In 1942, troops were sent from
India and Transjordan to overthrow a nationalistic Iraqi government, illustrating that Iraq's "independence" existed in name only.

Instead of demanding reparations and seeking new territory
at the end of the Second World War, America's European allies
relied on the Marshall Plan to finance their recovery. It was the
economic impact of the war on Great Britain that brought the
United States to the fringes of the Near Eastern arena, taking over
British commitments to support Greece and Turkey against the
communists. The assistance furnished these countries under the
Truman Doctrine was extended to include Iran, where strong U.S.
pressure induced Russia to withdraw troops stationed on Iranian
soil since the end of the war. Although American involvement in
Arab affairs between the two wars had been largely commercial
in nature, postwar developments in Palestine brought the United
States squarely into a political confrontation with the Arabs.

Motivated by both humanitarian and domestic political considerations, the Truman administration facilitated passage of
the United Nations Partition Resolution of 1947, which recommended the establishment in Palestine of independent Jewish and
Arab states, joined by an economic union, and the creation of a
U.N. trusteeship over the city of Jerusalem. Vehemently opposed
to this formula, the Arab states demanded that an independent
Palestinian state replace the British mandate.[5] Legally, the General
Assembly resolution had no standing in international law, and, as
violence escalated in the Middle East, it became questionable if
partition could be enforced without intervention by outside powers. One of the King-Crane Commission's conclusions now proved
prophetic in connection with Great Britain's position: in 1919
America's investigators had concluded that "not less than fifty
thousand soldiers would be required even to initiate the [Zionists'

---

5   At the time of the Partition Resolution, Jews formed 30 percent of the
population of Palestine, owning less than 8 percent of its land.

Jewish homeland] program" and that it could not "be carried out except by force of arms." In 1947, Britain's fifty thousand troops were hard pressed to protect themselves from terrorist attacks and to cope with illegal Jewish immigration. Unwilling to force partition on the Arabs, Great Britain announced that it would relinquish its mandate over Palestine on May 14, 1948, and asked the United Nations to decide the future of that area.

Seeking additional time, the U.S. advocated consideration of a resolution establishing U.N. trusteeship over Palestine, and political solutions were being debated at the moment when British troops abandoned the mandate. Seizing an area considerably larger than that proposed for them in the Partition Resolution, the Jews proclaimed the new state of Israel, and President Truman unexpectedly extended *de facto* recognition just a few minutes later, leaving the United Nations (including the U.S. delegation) in total confusion.

Arab armies attacked the new state immediately. Wracked by dissension and equipped with inferior weapons purchased by corrupt politicians, the Arab troops were no match for the survival-motivated Israeli forces. A series of cease-fires and truces were arranged by the U.N. Mediator Count Folke Bernadotte, and then broken, always leaving the Israelis with more territory. Four days before the U.N. General Assembly was to meet in Paris to consider Bernadotte's plan for an Arab-Israeli peace settlement, he was assassinated in Jerusalem by Zionist terrorists who wanted Israel to have all of mandated Palestine. With the final weeks of a presidential-election campaign before them, neither U.S. political party wished to risk losing the Jewish vote by adopting a strong stand on settling the Palestine problem. As 1948 neared its end, the army of Israel held nearly 80 percent of British-mandated Palestine (2,500 square miles more than the 5,600 allotted in the Partition Resolution), including the new city of Jerusalem. Clearly, Israel had established by force of arms both its existence and its ability to survive against the Arabs. Approval of the Provisional Government of Israel's application for membership in the United Nations, and *de jure* recognition by the U.S. government, remained pending, however, and American policymakers sought an alternative to the Bernadotte plan. Meanwhile, President Truman's Near Eastern advisers recommended that American support of Israel's application for U.N. membership be withheld until the 1949 session of the General Assembly.

This was the situation on December 10, 1948, the day my family and I started west to the Army Language School in California. As I drove toward my first encounter with the Arabs and their language, men who would influence my own life and the course of peace in the Middle East were engaged in critical conversations thousands of miles away.

That same night, two American diplomats called at the Hotel Bristol in Paris to meet with Lebanon's delegates to the United Nations. To John Foster Dulles, acting chairman of the United States U.N. delegation, the objectives of his visit seemed almost impossible to achieve. Dulles's assistant, Samuel K. C. Kopper, a young State Department Near Eastern expert, approached this meeting with greater optimism, however. He'd worked long and hard to develop close relationships with members of the Arab delegations to the U.N. Dr. Charles Malik, the Lebanese ambassador with whom Dulles was speaking, was one of Kopper's trusted contacts. Although most State Department officials discounted Lebanon's influence in the Arab world (considering it almost a Christian country), Dulles had accepted Kopper's estimate that Dr. Malik might be the only man in Paris able to persuade the Arabs not to employ their undoubted capability of defeating a crucial resolution to be put before the General Assembly the following day.

John Foster Dulles spoke of the pending resolution to establish a U.N. Conciliation Commission, which would preside over negotiations to conclude armistice agreements between Israel and its Arab neighbors and end the fighting along mutually agreed lines. This arrangement, Dulles acknowledged to Malik, would require that the Arabs accept the existence of the state of Israel, and would also involve some injustices to the Arab people. The new resolution would supersede the 1947 Partition Resolution, leaving unsettled the future status of the 700,000 Palestinian refugees who'd been driven from their homes or had fled in panic during the fighting.

Under the new resolution, however, these Palestinians would be entitled to return to their homes at the earliest practical date or, if they elected, be compensated by Israel for loss or damage to property they'd left behind. The resolution also provided that Jerusalem and the surrounding area would be accorded separate and special treatment from the rest of Palestine, under effective control of the United Nations.

Concluding, Dulles told Malik that the United States hoped for improved relations with the Arab states. He knew that if he'd come offering a certain number of dollars in the way of economic aid in exchange for votes, his proposal would be, and should be, indignantly rejected. Nonetheless, Dulles added, he hoped that the Arab states might, at the behest of the United States, make a sacrifice and accept a painful—to them—result, in the interests of effecting peace in the Middle East. Their proposal seemingly well received, Dulles and Kopper left hoping that the next day's U.N. session might show that the Arabs would prove willing to trust the United States to show its gratitude at a later date.

That evening in Jerusalem, the American consul discussed the proposed resolution with Israel's Colonel Moshe Dayan. Dayan rejected any United Nations role in the peace talks (other than those relating to Jerusalem's special and separate status) and contended that the Arabs and Israelis must discuss peace openly as sovereign states. As he left, Colonel Dayan described Israel as being in the fortunate position of being willing and able to engage both in war and in peace talks. These conversations revealed that America now had another chance to bring peace to the Middle East, and the key question was that of whether the Arabs and Israelis were ready to make the sacrifices necessary to achieve it.

By agreeing to meet with Israel's representatives and a U.N. conciliator, the Arabs would be conceding the right of Israel to live within negotiated armistice lines. This seemed to be a reasonable concession to make in the interest of peace and in return for the right of the Palestinians to return to their homes or be compensated if they elected to live elsewhere.

As for Israel's attitude, as expressed by Colonel Dayan, it seemed strange that this state, indebted to the U.N. Partition Resolution for its existence, should decline to meet the Arabs to discuss peace under U.N. auspices. At a time when Israel still hoped for U.N. membership (and *de jure* recognition by the U.S.), one of the best ways to achieve this might be to accept the international body's role as a conciliator. Only time would tell whether Israel was prepared to live in peace with the Palestinians they'd ejected, or if Colonel Dayan and his fellow Zionists still hoped to acquire more of Palestine for a predominantly Jewish state.

CHAPTER FOUR

STARTING THE ODYSSEY

To my knowledge, I'd never met an Arab before I reported for duty at the Presidio of Monterey on January 10, 1949, nor did I have the slightest idea what Arabic looked or sounded like. Encouraging news concerning the Near East had preceded me, however, and the newspapers were filled with predictions of peace between the Arabs and the Israelis.

Just minutes before the U.N. General Assembly had voted on the resolution calling for a Conciliation Commission and defining the rights of the refugees from Palestine, the Arab states had released their supporters, whose votes would have condemned the new peace plan to defeat. Now Israel and Egypt had agreed on a cease-fire, and their representatives would be meeting on Rhodes to negotiate an armistice agreement.

With my fifteen classmates, I settled in to the study of Arabic. Instruction ran from eight until three daily; we had no other military duties. Our instructors, all male, had been born abroad, one in Palestine, five in Iraq. We studied both written and conversational Arabic, as well as the history of the Near East and Islam. To my surprise, the men who taught us seldom lobbied for the Arab cause, although they were hardly sympathetic to what they feared were Zionist plans for a Jewish state running from the Nile to the Euphrates. They made a clear distinction between Jews and

Zionists; all of them had grown up with Jews and claimed never to have discriminated against them. Now American citizens, they also seemed to accept Israel as a fact of life, concluding that corruption, dissension, and inefficiency had led to the defeat of the Arab armies.

Generally in their thirties, our instructors were a new generation of Arabs, neither rabid nationalists nor socialists. Trying to explain what the West had perceived as pro-German activity in World War II, they pointed out that nationalist movements in Iraq, Palestine, Syria, and Egypt looked to Germany for support after the British and French refused to fully honor promises of independence given at the end of the First World War. Similarly, our instructors said, the brief alliances with the Vichy French were protests against French refusals to remove troops from Syria and Lebanon.

These men also predicted an end to the rule of the pashas who had acquired power from the colonial British and French regimes. To members of the current Arab generation, our instructors told us, the fez-wearing pashas and beys, Britain's and France's surrogates, were sealing their own fate and would be overthrown one day.

At the end of January, another political development portended a permanent peace settlement in the Near East. In concurrent announcements, President Truman extended the U.S. *de jure* recognition to Israel and to Transjordan, whose armies occupied sections of Jerusalem, which the United Nations was to govern as an international city. As part of our instruction, we laboriously translated news of these events from Arabic newspapers and read the *Palestine Post* in order to learn of the Zionists' views.

Time passed quickly; graduation was set for the end of 1949. As our assignments came in, however, it became clear that those of us from the army were to go to Korea (the war there hadn't started), nor did our air force or marine colleagues receive posts in the Near East: what a waste. I had nothing against the Far East but doubted that many Arabs lived there. Fortunately, just before graduation, General Bolling arrived to inspect the school. Breaking ranks, I approached and spoke with him. Despite a berating from an irate post commander, my orders were changed and I was assigned to the attaché system and posted to Baghdad, Iraq.

As part of my preparations for this diplomatic assignment— military attachés are accredited to the host country by the Department of State, serving under the American ambassador—I went to Washington to attend both the Defense Department's Strategic Intelligence School and the State Department's Foreign Service Institute. With our wives, we were coached in protocol and diplomatic life; the list of formal clothing and uniforms we were advised to purchase used up every cent I'd saved. Finally, all my training was completed, our belongings went ahead to the ship on which we were sailing, and our family of three was now ready to enter a strange new world. I was eager to see and to learn more about it.

My eagerness notwithstanding, getting abroad proved no easy task: our ship, the *Excalibur*, was rammed in New York harbor and we had to abandon it, leaving in a flooded hold most of what we had purchased for our life in Iraq. Trying again on the *Exochorda*, we spent the twenty-one-day passage following the progress of the U.S. troops that President Truman had ordered into war in Korea. When we tied up at Alexandria, Egypt, I caught first sight of the Arab world, staring with fascination at the host of fez-topped, long-gowned, sandaled peddlers who hawked trinkets for tourists. Competing vendors of Coca-Cola and Pepsi shoved each other to make a sale.[6] Gully-gully men swallowed baby chicks, then produced them from under their fezzes. From the tumult at the bottom of the gangplank came a plethora of shrill noises and strange, spicy smells.

First rejecting the persistent entreaties and coat tugging of the many licensed guides promising unusual sights and rare bargains, I employed my Arabic to explain to the ship's agent that we wanted

---

6   Later, Coca-Cola, whose extra-sweet base used in this area had long enabled it to dominate the market, was banned by the Arab League Boycott Committee. Zionist pressure in the U.S., threatening a Jewish boycott, had induced the Coca-Cola Company to manufacture in Israel. Ford cars, Xerox, Willys Jeeps, and other U.S. products were also banned in the Arab world, as these firms had plants in Israel.

a hotel on Alexandria's fashionable beach. To my chagrin, my classical Arabic went unheeded: I was asked, in English, what I wanted. When efforts to use the Iraqi dialect I'd learned proved even less fruitful, I resorted to English and obtained a taxi. I found that I could read the street signs and advertisements as we threaded our way through the donkey carts cluttering the pier area, but conversation in Arabic was impossible, and I feared that I'd studied a year in vain.

As the summer capital of King Farouk's government, Alexandria was a startling contrast to what I'd expected of the Near East. Although veiled women scurried about the streets, the luxury hotels were crowded with Arabs wearing fashionable European clothing, speaking French as often as they did Arabic. And, with its large Greek population, Alexandria had an atmosphere as much Mediterranean as Oriental.

An overnight voyage brought us to Beirut, the terminus of our ocean voyage. I was on deck early to watch the approach to Lebanon. Again I was surprised. Expecting dull desert and a drab city, I was startled by the sharply rising mountains, with the tile-covered roofs of the yellow stucco buildings presenting a beautiful contrast to the Mediterranean's early-morning blue.

I stayed with the army attaché and was taken to meet the American minister and his small legation staff. As I soon learned, Beirut was not considered an important post in the area. A socialites' paradise, it was useful as a supply-and-recreation point for the more isolated area missions, but not as a place from which reports about Near Eastern politics would be taken seriously. The sole lesson of diplomatic value that I carried away from four days in Lebanon was that social subordinates never, never leave a cocktail party or dinner before the chief of mission and his lady do. The hair-raising drive in chaotic traffic to Beirut's tiny airport produced another impression: "The Middle East is *mejnune* [crazy]," our driver warned. "If you aren't daft when you arrive, you will be by the time you leave!"

In the C-47 (DC-3) of the air attaché from Iraq who'd flown over to fetch us, we circled four times over Beirut's rooftops and curling coastline in order to gain the altitude necessary to pass over the two ranges of mountains between us and Damascus. Past Damascus, the oldest continually inhabited city in the world, were the seas of sand in which we would find Baghdad, our home for the coming two years.

As we spotted the Euphrates River, partially obscured by sandstorms rising to nearly 3,000 feet, we were able to see Lake Habbaniya, a salt sea fifty miles from Baghdad. Called to the cockpit, I was shown rows of RAF jets at the major British base below, there under treaty rights with Iraq. Soon I caught sight of the Tigris, wending its snakelike path to join the Euphrates. The Tigris split Baghdad—the British embassy by itself on one side, the American embassy and the main part of the city on the other—thus engendering a term that defined the source of power in Iraq.[7] *Thaka sub* (the other side) referred to Britain's embassy, residence of Sir Henry and Lady Bradshaw-Mack, from which flowed all major decisions affecting "independent" Iraq's political and economic life.

Almost reluctantly descending into the heat below, we caught sight of the nearly treeless, sprawling city, distinguished only by two large mosques and their minarets, the gold-leaf-domed Shi'ite-sect shrine at Kadhimain and the blue-tiled Sunni mosque in midtown Baghdad. The rest of the city consisted of low, dun-colored mud buildings spreading back from the crowded banks of the Tigris. As we landed, turned, and taxied back down the single runway, the airport appeared deserted. We soon understood why. Within seconds of landing we'd become drenched in perspiration. As the door opened, we were blasted by furnace-hot air. The temperature was 130 degrees. Looking back toward the plane after we scrambled out of it, I saw our footprints embossed on the tarmac. This was Baghdad.

Fortunately, ceiling fans circulated the air in our new home, kept slightly cool by the thick walls. Air conditioners were not then available. Instead, camel thorn (sagebrush) was woven across

---

7   Slightly larger than California, Iraq (from the Arabic word meaning origin) was, archaeologists agree, "a cradle of civilization." The written history of this area dates back at least as far as 3000 B.C.

key windows and constantly moistened by water dripping from a punctured pipe. The evaporation, riding what breezes there were, produced a current of cool air, except during sandstorms, when everything had to be shut tight. Summers, we slept on cots on the roof, under mosquito nets, roused at dawn by the sun's hot rays.

Surrounded by towering eucalyptus trees intended as protection against desert winds and storms, the American embassy was mud colored, only two stories high, with a façade that reminded one of a miniature White House. The embassy residence was abutted on one side by the single-story chancery, in which the political and administrative sections were located. A separate building behind held the consulate and members of the CIA station; another building was the residence of the deputy chief of mission. The service attachés maintained offices in a large converted residence several blocks away, near another house, which sheltered the small economic section. Miles away, on Rashid Street, Baghdad's only main thoroughfare, was the U.S. Information Service library.

The U.S. diplomatic mission in Iraq was similar in size and quality to other American missions in the Arab world. Despite our new and larger responsibilities there, we lacked experienced diplomats capable of guiding or influencing the recently independent states of the Near East. Senior foreign-service officers with substantial knowledge of the Arabs were scarce, and there were not enough qualified junior officers to advise ambassadors as staff experts. Those few career men who agreed to more than one tour in the area were generally embittered by Washington's disregard of their recommendations. These veterans unanimously advocated that we moderate our support of Israel. The alternative, they feared, was to leave the Arabs no choice but to turn to Russia for support, leading to communist infiltration of the area.

For me, getting to know the Americans assigned to Baghdad was easy: there just weren't many of us, and common hardships—shortages of appetizing food and the harsh environment—made for a bond. As if in spite of Baghdad, official social activity was frantic, consisting frequently of two cocktail parties a night, often followed by a black-tie dinner. We passed each other coming and going more often at night than during the day.

Edward Savage Crocker, ambassador extraordinary and plenipotentiary of the United States to the Hashemite Kingdom of Iraq, had never before served in the Middle East. He'd been minister in Warsaw before coming to Baghdad, his first ambassadorial post, in 1948.

If measured by background, experience, and attitude, Ned Crocker would seem to have had no business being assigned to Iraq. Certain that America had no influence there, he was content to let Sir Henry Bradshaw-Mack attend to Western interests. Consultations concerning the relative positions of Great Britain and America in the Near East would be handled through our embassy in London or Britain's in Washington, as had been done in the past. Beyond the status of the ambassadorial appointment, Crocker liked neither Baghdad nor many Arabs, apart from his few bridgeplaying friends.

For these many reasons, our foreign-service officers in Iraq usually confined their observations and reporting to liaison contacts with the central government in Baghdad. The monarch was fifteen-year-old King Faisal II, member of the Hashemite family that the British had brought from Saudi Arabia after World War I. He was still studying at Harrow in England, and the court was controlled by a regent, Prince Abdul Illah, the king's uncle. Political affairs were managed by Prime Minister Nuri as Said (or a musical-chairs series of loyal substitutes), a Turkish-army-trained anglophile. There were few members of the younger generation in positions of influence.

The Department of State gave almost equal credence to reports on Iraq from the oil companies: visits by Exxon's "oil diplomat," Howard Page, were frequent and elicited serious attention from both Ambassador Crocker and officials of the Iraqi government. By contrast, few senior State Department officials came our way. During my Washington briefings I'd been told that the mysterious CIA had people working in Iraq. In Baghdad's smalltown atmosphere, it didn't take long to find out who the agency's "spooks" were.

That part of the CIA station in Iraq operating under diplomatic cover was so understaffed that even its two secretaries arranged communications drops and safe-house meetings with agents. Wives of the few CIA officers under "deep cover" (educational and archaeological) typed their reports and sequestered their children while their husbands met with informants at home. The chief of station in Baghdad when I arrived was inclined to accept the British view that Iraq would always remain a bastion of the U.K. His intelligence information was largely obtained through liaison contacts with the host of British intelligence officers, overt and covert, in Iraq. He frequently studied the personality profiles of Iraqi army officers we compiled, hoping to recruit some of them. Their task would be to plant communications equipment and demolitions to be used by stay-behind agents in the event of a Russian drive into the area. Almost without exception, however, his Iraqi agents had been preempted by British intelligence. Like our ambassador, the CIA reported little about Iraq that did not have a British source.

A later CIA station chief, Dick Kerin, was younger, and more imaginative; he started his own network of informants, also recruiting Iraqi civilians to work as his agents. While Britain's intelligence services relied on information from politicians, the many British officers based in Iraq, and officials of the Iraq Petroleum Company, Kerin's sources were the younger generation of Iraqis. Frustrated at being denied meaningful positions in government, they were concerned that Prime Minister Said's blind allegiance to British policies would alienate Iraq from other Arab states and lead to uprisings by the pan-Arab nationalists, students, and lower classes. When, at a weekly staff meeting, Kerin reported that most Iraqis were unhappy with government nepotism and the British-influenced expenditures of Iraq's oil revenues, he was quickly chastened by Ambassador Crocker for holding views that bordered on heresy.

About two dozen countries were represented in Baghdad's diplomatic colony, but most had small staffs, and soon I knew virtually all of the chiefs of missions and their key subordinates. Britain's presence in Iraq, however, was of another order. The British ambassador was, by treaty, doyen of the diplomatic corps and was supported by both a staff of trained Orientalists and by intelligence officers throughout the country, disguised (usually thinly) as military or diplomatic personnel or as businessmen.

If Britain could not see what was coming in Iraq, her blindness was induced by more than economic self-interest. Baghdad's only golf course, for example, was located in the enclosure of the British-operated horseracing track. The golf club was also dominated by the English. After I was elected to membership, I frequently played early in the morning on its sagebrush-lined fairways, which led to rolled sand "greens." Hoping to improve my game, I started playing with my servant, Attiyah, who had caddied for the British and played well. Discovered one day by a club member, I was warned never again to bring an Iraqi to play the course, suspended for four months, and then issued a probationary membership.

Most British holidays were celebrated in Iraq. Invited to the annual St. Andrews Day dinner, I lit a cigarette after dinner, a terrible gaffe—I'd failed to wait until King George had been toasted. And they had thought me civilized! I was, they concluded, less cultured than the few English-educated Iraqis invited as guests, exceptions to the general policy of excluding the local people from British clubs and celebrations.

In this small world, I came to know on a first-name basis not only Iraqi cabinet ministers, but also a circle of young, socially prominent Iraqis, sons and daughters of leading officials. Educated abroad, they criticized America's role in the Near East, condemned British influence, and predicted that the Iraqi government would not last long. Despite their strong feelings, we became close friends. Although they seldom spoke of it, they, like other Arabs, were convinced that the state of Israel would not have been created without American assistance. Yet, with these Iraqis as with others, I cannot recall ever hearing disparaging remarks about Jews as a people. Having once outnumbered the Arab residents of Baghdad, even the poorest Jew lived better than the average Iraqi. The 130,000 living in Iraq considered this land as their place of origin: looking back to Abraham, Nebuchadnezzar, the destruction of the first temple, and exile in Babylon, a history of 4,000 years, they, like the Christians and other minorities in this Moslem state, considered themselves, and were considered, Iraqis.

Three months before my arrival, a bomb had exploded harmlessly outside a Passover gathering, causing nearly 10,000 Jews to queue up to take advantage of the Iraqi government's policy of not restricting legal emigration to Israel. This incident prompted a series of State Department instructions that the embassy investigate predictions by the World Zionist Congress of pogroms and claims that Iraqi Jews were being prevented from leaving their country. We found that during the period of illegal immigration into Palestine, and after Israel's creation, Iraqi police had cracked down on a Zionist-organized movement smuggling Jews to Israel via Iran. This, however, had produced regulations providing for legal emigration to Israel by those who wished to leave.

Just after I arrived in Baghdad, an Israeli citizen had been recognized in the city's largest department store: his interrogation led to the discovery of fifteen arms caches brought into Iraq by an underground Zionist movement.[8] In attempts to portray the Iraqis as anti-American and to terrorize the Jews, the Zionists planted bombs in the U.S. Information Service library and in synagogues. Soon leaflets began to appear urging Jews to flee to Israel. Embarrassed, the Iraqi government launched full-scale investigations and shared its findings with our embassy. To counter outrage expressed in the world press over the bombings, the Iraqi government offered to exchange 100,000 Jews for an equal number of Palestinian refugees, an offer the Israelis did not accept. (Although the refugees had fled to adjacent Arab countries, the Iraqi offer to take such a large number set a precedent never to be repeated by the Arabs; but few Palestinians took advantage of it—they had visions of returning to their homeland, and Iraq was too far away.)

Iraq's chief rabbi, Sassoon Khedduri, frequently came to see us at the embassy. He was urging his people to be calm and to remain, remembering that they were native Iraqis first and that Judaism was only their religion, which they could practice freely as always. In spite of our constant reports that the situation in Iraq was exaggerated and artificially inflamed from without, the State Department urged us to intervene with the government to facilitate an airlift

---

8A letter from Yigal Allon (later chief of staff of the Israel Defense Force and Israeli foreign minister) revealed that he had arranged the transfer of these weapons to Iraq.

that the Zionists were organizing to "rescue" Iraqi Jews. Now portrayed in the foreign press as panicking to leave, the Jews started to depart on flights via Cyprus to Israel, which soon numbered four daily. Loath to lose these Jews, who formed the backbone of the civil service and the merchant class and who controlled most of the banks, the Iraqi government first set a deadline on applying for emigration permits and then limited funds to be taken out, eventually confiscating property that the Jews left behind. In the end, only about 5,000 remained. Although the Iraqi police later provided our embassy with evidence to show that the synagogue and library bombings as well as the anti-Jewish and anti-American leaflet campaigns had been the work of an underground Zionist organization, most of the world believed reports that Arab terrorism had motivated the flight of the Iraqi Jews whom the Zionists had "rescued" really just in order to increase Israel's Jewish population.

My first opportunity to see southern Iraq and the neighboring states came when the air attaché flew me to Dhahran, Saudi Arabia, to purchase at the U.S. airfield there goods to replace what we'd lost in our shipwreck. Because the sun's heat soon made the aircraft's engines too hot for the crew to inspect, we left just before dawn. On the city's outskirts we passed over the ruins of the great arch at Tsesiphon, crossing the barren desert to ancient Babylon. As we flew over the ruins of the Ur of the Chaldees (birthplace of Abraham, about 1800 B.C.), we saw the junction of the Tigris and Euphrates from which extended southward a marshy swamp area, until we picked up the acres of date trees marking our approach to Basra (port of Sinbad the Sailor) on the Shatt al Arab, from which Iraq's principal exports—oil and dates—were shipped.

Later we crossed over the Neutral Zone. A diamond-shaped area on the borders of Iraq, Kuwait, and Saudi Arabia, it was claimed by none of them, in deference to the nomadic tribes for whom its wells meant life or death. Below, we could see skeletons of camels that had perished just short of the water that would have saved them.

Entering Saudi Arabia's air space, we reached Dhahran. Unlike the massive British Suez base and its satellite airfields in

Jordan and Iraq, the USAF base at Dhahran and the adjacent U.S. Navy base at Bahrain had no in-place combat capabilities, yet they were essential to America's worldwide defense organization. Used for redeployment of U.S. troops from Europe to the Far East during World War II, the Dhahran airfield was now essential to the Strategic Air Command. Long-range, combat-loaded B-29s, 36s, and 47s constantly circled Russia's flanks; they were our only means of a retaliatory attack against the U.S.S.R. in the event of war. Refueling tankers, needed by these patrols, operated out of Dhahran.

The air base and consulate general there performed another role—protecting Americans who were serving in the Middle East. A diplomatic-military planning group was charged with the evacuation of all U.S. citizens in the area in case of threats to their safety. In an Arab world still embittered by America's part in the creation of Israel, such precautions seemed necessary. (Later I was sent to Dhahran to assist in this planning, when anti-Western demonstrations accompanying Iran's nationalization of British oil interests appeared likely to endanger Americans.)

Bahrain Island, headquarters of the Commander, Middle East Forces (COMIDEASFOR), proved to be nothing more than a radio-communications facility supporting the U.S. "fleet" that patrolled the Persian Gulf and Indian Ocean—one ship, a seaplane tender. Situated near the entry of the strategic Persian Gulf, this command was also close to the oil ports from which fuel was obtained to operate most of the U.S. Navy's ships abroad. Although tiny, this command was also the navy's only operational base between Naples and the Far East, and was, furthermore, a politically acceptable nucleus for expansion in time of war.

All of this illustrated how important a remote desert kingdom and an adjoining island were to America's security. On this trip I also learned the history of the participation of American oil companies in the production of Middle Eastern petroleum resources—the "black gold" on which the Allies had floated to victory in two world wars. Without friendly access to this, the United States would be unable to defend Western Europe or fight a global war, America's military planners had warned President Truman.

Defense Secretary Forrestal had gone even further and described oil from this area as being vital to the economy of the United States.

Despite all this, I learned, the American oil companies that first participated in ownership of the Middle East's oil concessions—Exxon, Mobil, SoCal, and Texaco—had done so only at the urging of the State Department.[9] At the end of the First World War, the Allies had agreed that the natural resources of the former Ottoman Empire would be available to all nations on an "open door" basis. But at the San Remo Conference (wherein the U.S. did not participate), Britain and France had divided between themselves the petroleum reserves of the area, and their national oil companies formed the Iraq Petroleum Company (IPC), forerunner of the world's greatest oil monopoly.[10] At the insistence of the U.S. government, which was unwilling to see Britain and France proceed bilaterally, American oil companies became a part of this venture—almost reluctantly, since they had what then seemed to be other adequate sources of oil. Seven U.S. companies showed initial interest, but in the end five shared a 23.7 percent ownership in IPC (in time, only today's Exxon and Mobil remained).

Not long afterward, a geologist acting for the Sheikh of Bahrain induced the Standard Oil Company of California (SoCal) to purchase for $50,000 a concession that had yielded oil in 1930. This independent U.S. entry into a British protectorate antagonized Great Britain, but with the support of the State Department, SoCal maintained its position in Bahrain. By now, in adjacent Saudi Arabia, King Ibn Saud was prepared to grant a concession, and Britain's national oil company made the king a token offer to

---

9   Throughout this book I have referred to the American oil companies by their present names or acronyms. Thus, Standard Oil Company of New Jersey is called Exxon; Standard Oil Company of New York is referred to as Mobil; and Standard Oil Company of California is abbreviated to SoCal. The Arabian American Oil Company (owned by Exxon, Mobil, SoCal, and Texaco—the Texas Oil Company) is commonly called Aramco.

10   Through interlocking production and marketing agreements, the IPC partners, joined elsewhere in the Middle East by four other American companies, had by the mid-1950s achieved domination of world oil. See Anthony Sampson, *The Seven Sisters*, (New York: Viking Press, 1975).

ensure that no American oil interests would explore there. Put off by Britain's failure to grant independence to all the Arabs, however, King Saud turned to a close adviser, the disillusioned former British Colonial Service officer Harry St. John Philby. Philby in turn summoned Charles Crane (of the King-Crane Commission) to counsel the king, and Crane arranged that SoCal be given oil rights in Saudi Arabia's eastern province at the price of a modest loan and nominal annual rental fees.

In 1939, having discovered oil in commercial quantities, SoCal was awarded a concession for all of Saudi Arabia. This time King Saud charged more: $1.5 million on signing; an annual rental payment of $750,000 while prospecting continued; and, thereafter, a division of royalties that would increase as production rose. At this point Texaco joined SoCal to extract and market this vast reservoir of oil.

After the start of World War II, these two American partners in Saudi Arabia became concerned that the British would induce Ibn Saud to terminate their valuable oil rights. In Washington, serious consideration was given to U.S.-government ownership of the Saudi Arabian concessions, but instead SoCal and Texaco were given government subsidies to construct a 1,000-mile pipeline to supply the Allies at the Mediterranean. Access to oil was now vital to the conquest of the Axis powers; in 1943 President Roosevelt declared that "the defense of Saudi Arabia was vital to the defense of the United States" and authorized the use of lend-lease funds to support King Saud's regime.

It was not until 1948 that other American oil companies were able to generate the government support necessary to break Britain's hold over Middle Eastern oil acquired at the end of World War I. The shares Exxon and Mobil held in IPC had been granted grudgingly, but only after they agreed to stay out of Saudi Arabia and other parts of the Near East. Now the United States insisted on an "open door" policy, supporting Exxon and Mobil, whose plans for Saudi Arabia had precipitated a major international legal battle with their IPC partners (at the last minute, litigation was avoided). Exxon and Mobil joined SoCal and Texaco, paying them a half-billion dollars, and the Arabian American Oil Company (Aramco) was born. Gulf Oil Company, meanwhile, now shared a concession with the British in Kuwait. The door that had been slammed shut in 1920 at the San Remo Conference was now being pried open by the Americans.

This trip proved to be only the start of my travels in the area. My duties as an army attaché involved more than just evaluating Iraq's military forces. I was also assigned to study the terrain over which U.S. military forces might operate in the event of war. I therefore spent considerable time with the tribal groups that had settled in the land the ancient Greeks named Mesopotamia—"land between the two rivers."

My first extended contact with Bedouin tribes was arranged by the paramount sheikh of the Shamar (a member of Iraq's parliament), whose people migrated each year from the northwestern Iraqi desert through the Syrian-Iraqi border and then south to the deserts of Saudi Arabia in the winter. Sharing their tents of black camel hair, I settled in for a month's stay. Everything was strange to me, beginning with the food, since it was all cooked in ghee (boiled and strained butter from fat-tailed sheep) and had a slightly rancid taste. Rice was served in abundance, heaped on large brass trays and covered with broiled mutton, lamb, or baby camel meat. Food was eaten with the hands, shot into one's mouth after being wadded between thumb and forefinger. As the honored guest, I received upon my arrival the delicacy of a sheep's eye. I swallowed it whole, struggling to imagine it was a grape. Although I became sick soon afterward, the tribe was fortunately not offended and thereafter spared me this treat.

I'd arrived wearing breeches and boots but soon changed to the aba, kaffiyeh, and agal (robe, head scarf, and cord), which offered protection from the heat and frequent sandstorms. Clad in black, only their eyes showing through the black face masks or head scarfs drawn across their faces, the tribe's women did the camp work and never joined the men in meals. Children, particularly boys, were given special treatment. All wore full-length abas. On reaching puberty, the girls changed to black and covered their faces.

I was soon accepted, a non-Arab stranger willing to conform as best he could to tribal ways. My shotgun (taken from Alfried

Krupp during the war) was regarded with awe, and I hunted birds with the men on the desert, where black partridge and bustard abounded, the sky sometimes black with swarming flocks of grouse. I also rode after gazelles with the tribesmen, with trained falcons and Saluki dogs part of the chase.

By the end of my month with the Shamar, I was twenty pounds lighter but confident, if not fluent, in my Arabic. I later went north from Baghdad with Kurdish chief Daoud Jaf (another parliamentary deputy) to his village near Irbil in the foothills of the Zagros Mountains. From there we rode horseback over mountain trails, through the gorges of the Zab River, and across plains for seven days to Sulaimaniya, capital of the Kurdish region. As our caravan approached each new terrain feature, tribesmen dashed ahead, rifles held aloft, to make certain that no Iraqi troops were nearby. At night I was regaled with tales of the Kurds' ancient history. Twenty-four centuries ago, from the peaks I'd just skirted, their ancestors had fought off the Greek "Ten Thousand," leaving their leader, Xenophon, to complain that the Greeks "had suffered worse things" from the Kurds than all of Persia's kings had done to them. Small wonder, then, that these tribesmen considered themselves superior to the modern-day amalgam of diverse cultures making up the Kingdom of Iraq, whose government was trying to suppress and integrate the Kurds.

Iraqi Kurdish leader Mulla Mustafa al Barzani was then in Russia seeking Soviet support for an independent republic to unite his tribesmen with the Kurds in Iran and Turkey. To the Iraqi, Iranian, and Turkish governments, the possibility of Moscow's encouraging Kurdish and other tribal separatist movements represented a far greater danger than did the growth of local communist parties or the threat of an invasion of the Middle East by the Soviet Union. To the West, the area's oil was of primary importance; bolstering strong central governments to control the tribes was considered the best way to retain access to the oil fields.

Reconnaissance trips took me north to Sarsank, in the Zagros Mountain foothills on the border with Turkey; there I found that Turkish was spoken as often as Arabic. Later I drove through the strategic Rawanduz Gorge in northeastern Iraq to Tehran for my first glimpse of ancient Persia. Britain's oil concession had been nationalized by Iran's government; the Iranian people seemed overjoyed at the prospect of the eviction from their country of all British nationals. Because Washington feared that Great Britain might order its troops to occupy southern Iran, I was sent to the oil fields of Iranian Khuzistan; there I found that owing to tribal ties with Iraq, many Persians spoke Arabic instead of the Iranian language of Farsi. I continued on across the Shatt al Arab to the Iraqi ports of Basra and Fao to observe the evacuation of British subjects from Abadan and Khorramshar by the landing craft whose invasion of Iran had been deterred by American disapproval. My conversations with Iraqi officials and army officers left no doubt that they were pleased to see the British forced to leave.

Returning from Basra, I stayed with the Marsh Arabs in their reed huts, built on poles in the swamps, between which they moved in round pitch-and-cane boats called kufas. I then visited Ur of the Chaldees and explored the ruins of Nebuchadnezzar's Babylon, my interest in these and the supposed site of the Garden of Eden stirred by meeting Professor and Mrs. Mallowan (Agatha Christie), who came annually to Baghdad en route to their digs in the ruins of Nineveh. The history of both civilization and Islam was all around us: Karbala and An-Najaf were, next to Mecca, the most sacred shrines of the Shi'ite Moslems.

Although I was surrounded by reminders of the area's glorious past, I sought to understand modern "Arab nationalism," the force allegedly uniting all Arabs against Israel under the banner of the League of Arab States. But after my travels, I found it difficult to consider Iraq itself as a unified nation; it seemed to be little more than an area that had been delineated as a state by lines drawn on a map by the British at the end of the First World War. More than national spirit, the Iraqis' attachment to their land was their primary allegiance. Borders meant little to the nomadic tribes, whose lands crossed national boundaries. Furthermore, the Shamar, for instance, had little in common with their fellow Iraqis: the Marsh Arabs of the south could not even communicate with them in a common tongue. For these reasons, then, I questioned the validity of claims by Iraqi politicians that their country was part of the

"Arab nation" that extended across North Africa to the Persian Gulf.

Questioning my Iraqi friends, I tried to learn how one really defined an Arab. Adherence to Islam wasn't a universal criterion: there were many Christian and other minority sects in Iraq, Syria, Lebanon, Palestine, and Egypt. Millions of Moslems lived in lands as remote as Indonesia and the Philippines, and, closer by, neither Turkey nor Iran, Moslem countries, considered themselves Arab. The bonds of a common heritage were often cited as a unifying catalyst. But what of the Egyptians? They had long regarded themselves as Africans, descendants of the Pharaohs, and as a people quite different from and superior to the Arabs from the desert.

In the end, I concluded that the true Arab was one who had lived—or was descended, without intermarriage, from those Semites who had lived—on the Arabian Peninsula: namely, the Bedouins who had moved from place to place, some of whom had settled in what we now call the Arab states. Yet there were other Semites who had also been Bedouins: these were the Hebrews, the descendants of Abraham, Isaac, and Jacob. Now, the question whether either of these Semitic peoples had the right to claim nationhood on the basis of a commonality of religion or language had brought war to the Middle East. To me, it seemed doubtful that those who proclaimed unity against Israel could ever unite as an "Arab nation." And, as Rabbi Khedduri had cautioned his people, it was possible that the Sephardic Jews of the Middle East and Africa might have nothing more than religion in common with the Ashkenazi Jews of Europe and the rest of the Diaspora, where languages and cultures differed vastly from those of their coreligionists who'd been born in Arab Asia. Thus the viability of either an all-Jewish state or a united Arab nation was still being tested.

Israel had become a nation, however; still it seemed only proper that its acts be judged as those of a sovereign state and not justified on the grounds of religion. To brand as anti-Semitic or anti-Jewish those who opposed or criticized Israel's policies amounted to ignoring the facts that the original Arabs were also Semites and that only a small fraction of the world's Jews had elected to live in Israel.

I was left to ponder all this as I finished my assignment in Baghdad and thought about the uncertain future of the area. There had been hardships, uncomfortable living, and even the death from polio of an army colleague as constant reminders that backwardness and poverty still prevailed in Iraq. Yet I had also seen some of the other side of life. I'd ridden to the hunt with King Faisal and his regent and had spent time with King Farouk's cousin in Cairo, enjoying ruling-class luxuries such as I'd never imagined.

But the world I was leaving was changing. In Egypt, a cabal of army officers had seized power and sent Farouk off to exile in Europe. King Abdullah had been assassinated in Jordan, and a political upheaval in Lebanon had changed that country's president. A military dictator ruled in Syria and its constitution had been suspended. In Iraq, in late 1952, the British embassy had been stoned, the USIS library burned, and martial law declared. If the Iraqis in power, the British, and the United States now understood the need for real reforms, all failed to understand how fast radical change would come.

It was, finally, time for me to leave. Fascinated with the Middle East, I departed, determined to return.

CHAPTER FIVE

THE VIEW FROM WASHINGTON

Back in the United States at the end of 1952, I was assigned to duties relating to the Near East in the army's Office of the Assistant Chief of Staff, G-2 (intelligence). It was an exciting time to be in Washington. As I watched Eisenhower's inauguration, I felt that a new administration could perhaps repair America's relations with the Arab world, which had been so adversely affected by Truman's recognition of Israel.

I was charged first with analyzing the military forces of the Arab states and Israel. With no more than a ragtag collection of obsolescent equipment, starved for ammunition, led by demoralized officers humiliated by the defeat and political dissension of the 1947–1948 war, the Arab armies had no capacity to back up the rhetoric of their leaders, who vowed to destroy the new Jewish state. And, with the most efficient intelligence service in the Near East, Israel could not have considered a major assault by the Arabs to be a real possibility.

The Iraqi and Egyptian forces had to make do with what remained of the surplus World War II arms Britain had provided them before the United States-United Kingdom arms embargo during the fighting in Palestine. Largely French equipped, Syrian and Lebanese forces had never seriously engaged the Jewish Haganah in combat. In Syria, furthermore, a succession of military governments had created so many rivalries within the army that preoccupation with domestic political issues seemed to preclude the capacity to wage an external war. In Lebanon, the military forces were so carefully balanced along religious and feudalistic lines that the most the government could do was to maintain internal security. As for the Saudis, their British equipment was obsolete, and the small national guard was deliberately restricted by the monarchy lest it pose a threat.

Commanded and led by British officers, the Jordanian Arab Legion was by far the most effective Arab force in the Near East. Small but well trained, its combat capabilities were limited by political considerations. Although by treaty Great Britain was obligated to come to Jordan's defense in the event of attack, the British had avoided doing so during the 1947–1948 fighting in Palestine. I'd already met the senior Iraqi officers who had commanded troops in Palestine, and most were still embittered by the quarrels between Jordanian and Iraqi leaders, which had disrupted a planned joint operation that might have cut the Jewish forces in half.

The Israel Defense Force had a potpourri of arms, some stolen from British stores, some smuggled in during the arms blockade, some manufactured in improvised armories. But the aircraft that had enabled the Zionist army to achieve superiority over the Arabs had been purchased and smuggled into Palestine by the Zionist terrorist organizations: Menachem Begin's *Irgun Zvai Leumi* and the Stern Gang. In addition to the money and guidance Russia furnished to these organizations, airplanes were delivered to them in Czechoslovakia, where Jewish pilots were trained before and after Israel became a state.

Collecting all of this information was vital to the ability of the U.S. government to evaluate the possibility of renewed fighting in the Middle East, and to assess the capacity of Israel's forces to maintain that country's defenses against attack by the Arabs. From the day the 1949 armistice agreements were signed, the Pentagon had always credited Israel with being able to repel an invasion by any one or all of the Arab armies. (Israel's initial requests for the sale or grant of U.S. armaments were based on enabling the Israelis to resist an attack by the combined Arab armies. Starting with the Johnson administration, however, the United States agreed to provide Israel with the most modern offensive weapons; these eventually gave the Israelis the capability of attacking and defeating the Arab armies on their own territory.)

In order both to limit the military power of the opposing nations and to implement the undertaking of the Tripartite Declaration of 1950 to guarantee the 1949 armistice lines, the United States, Great Britain, and France sought to control arms shipments to the Arab states and Israel. The Near East Arms Coordinating Committee (NEACC), a mechanism of the Tripartite Declaration, reviewed all reports of proposed arms purchases by the Near Eastern states and passed judgment on the approval of requests made of the declaration's sponsors. By 1953, however, political and economic considerations were weakening British and French enthusiasm for this policy, and these governments were selling arms in spite of the objections of the U.S. member of the NEACC. The best information regarding the equipment status of the Arab and Israeli armies came from military-attaché reports (such as I had prepared in Baghdad), and my job involved compiling these for navy captain James Grant in the Office of the Secretary of Defense, the U.S. military member on the NEACC.

A naval aviator throughout his career, Grant frankly acknowledged his lack of background for the task of evaluating the ground forces that were the principal combat elements in the Near East. His assignment both revealed the extent to which the navy dominated decision making concerning the area and showed the lack of available experts within the Department of Defense.

Under Secretary of Defense Charles Wilson, an assistant secretary for International Security Affairs (ISA) directed policy relating to foreign base rights, treaty organizations, and military-assistance agreements, and also represented the Defense Department on the planning board of the National Security Council (NSC), from which foreign-policy direction emanated. ISA also provided, through Captain Grant where the Middle East was concerned, day-to-day liaison between the Pentagon and the State Department. Grant's principal duties pertained to the U.S.-Turkish aspects of the NATO alliance. What time he had left he devoted to Defense's responsibilities for all the Near East, South Asia, and Africa!

My initial contacts with the Pentagon's bureaucracy revealed that its interest in the Middle East evolved from the navy's strategic reliance on the area's petroleum resources. The air force, otherwise only slightly concerned, focused on retaining rights to its airfield at Dhahran, and the army, relying almost entirely on the ability of NATO to contain the Russians, had little or no interest in planning for defense of the Middle East.

More concerned with regional defense in the Middle East was the State Department, where I had contacts through foreign-service officers I'd known in the field and through my advisory role on the NEACC. I was, therefore, able to see some continuity in the international diplomatic developments affecting American involvement in defense schemes for the Middle East.

Since 1944, successive Egyptian governments had demanded that the British evacuate their troops at the Suez base. The British had temporized, but in 1952 the avowedly pro-Western officers of the Revolutionary Command Council (RCC) ousted King Farouk, and it became clear that if the British stayed, the RCC would be unable to control radical Egyptians, who might resort to terrorist tactics. In 1951, British willingness to withdraw from Suez had been tied to a proposal that the Arab states join Britain, the U.S., France, and Turkey in a Middle East Command (MEC). Newly sovereign, acutely sensitive to slights, the Arab countries had rejected the MEC, both because it envisioned the presence of foreign troops and because it included the word "command."

Trying again in 1952, the British recommended the formation of a Middle East Defense Organization (MEDO), to be sponsored by Britain, the U.S., Turkey, New Zealand, Australia, and South Africa. France, because of its problems with Arab demands for independence in North Africa, was not included in this plan, which was to proceed with or without indigenous participation. At a later date, both the Arabs and Israel would be invited to join.

The United States, saying that the area countries themselves should be called in at the outset, correctly assumed that this organization would be rejected by the Arab governments. Although unable to agree on many questions, the Arab states were unanimously against external plans for the defense of their region. The Collective Security Pact of the League of Arab States (organized for defense against Israel, the only enemy they perceived) was adequate to defend the area, in the view of the Egyptians, who saw MEDO as just another colonialist scheme.[11]

What little the Arabs knew about communism seemed inconsistent with the principles of Islam, and they saw few Russians; but every day they were reminded that they were hosts to more than 800,000 Palestinian refugees from a humiliating war, a defeat that virtually all Arabs attributed to British and American support of the state of Israel. To those of us who'd lived in the Middle East, it was apparent that the question of the future status of the Palestinians was one that, unless it were resolved promptly, would pose a far greater threat to U.S. and Western influence in the area than would any overt moves by the communist bloc: a basic fact never properly understood in the frantic pursuit of the cold war. And by now I was beginning to learn more about the covert activities of the CIA in intervening in the internal affairs of the Middle Eastern countries—a development that further misdirected U.S. foreign policy for that area.

Concerned about economic survival, and blinded by national pride, the British were determined to remain in the Middle East. Nationalization of Britain's oil interests in Iran and the threat of losing treaty rights to station troops in Egypt, Jordan, and Iraq

---

11   Although the young Egyptian officers of the RCC—still heady from the success of their coup—may have convinced themselves that the Collective Security Pact had value in defending against Israel (or even Russia!), there remained the great weakness that had led to the defeat of the Arabs by the Zionists in 1947. The Arab country providing the largest contingent of troops was to appoint a commander for the combined army: commanding a single regiment in combat would have severely strained the capabilities of the young Egyptian colonels and majors. As for the other Arab governments, most neither trusted the Egyptians nor would have been willing to subordinate control of their armies—other than on paper, which was as far as joint Arab planning and fighting went until Egypt and Syria coordinated their forces in attacking Israel in 1973.

were further challenges, as well as the fear that the United States might become unwilling to support them as a power in the area.

In January 1953, Assistant Secretary of State, NEA (Near East, South Asian, and African Affairs), Henry Byroade was sent by Secretary of State Dean Acheson to London to meet with Foreign Secretary Eden and discuss Britain's plans for defense of the Middle East. Practically apolitical, a West Pointer who'd been made a general at the age of thirty-three and was now only forty, Byroade was an anomaly in Washington's executive branch, having been retained by Secretary Dulles from the previous administration. His predecessor was oilman George McGhee, who had championed the oil companies' successful fight for U.S. tax deductions against all royalties paid to foreign oil-producing countries.[12] Byroade had visited our embassies in the Near East, and I'd met him in Baghdad. A handsome man with an engaging personality, he was initially resented by our career ambassadors (all considerably older) as an intruder and as someone whose interests in the Near East's problems promised to be far more diverse than McGhee's oil politics.[13]

---

12   This tax advantage (later dubbed the "Golden Gimmick") so increased the net profits of the American oil companies operating in Saudi Arabia (and later throughout the world) that they "generously" offered to split Aramco's revenues fifty-fifty with Saudi Arabia. Although this substantially increased the Saudis' income from oil, it infuriated the British and French national oil companies: they saw it as a precedent threatening to disrupt their long-established fixed-fee-per-ton compensation formula. This arrangement, however, enabled the U.S. to offset to at least one Arab country the economic aid, budgetary support payments, and tax-free gifts by private donors flowing from the U.S. to Israel.

13   During the Truman administration, the Department of State had a free hand in recommending U.S. policy toward the Arab states; much of this was influenced by the senior American "oil statesmen" (Howard Page of Exxon foremost among them). Both the State Department and the oil companies drew support for their recommendations from the Pentagon (particularly the navy) because of the military's recognition of the importance of the oil-producing states of the Middle East to America's defense capabilities. On the other hand, U.S. policy toward Israel was formulated within the White House, largely by presidential assistants Clark Clifford and David Niles; they regarded the Israeli aspect of American foreign policy as being related almost exclusively to domestic political considerations.

Byroade expressed his military background in his organization of NEA—he added to his staff, an assistant for politico-military affairs which gave him an official conduit to the policy levels of the Pentagon, a channel that would enable the Department of State to keep abreast of U.S. military planning for the defense of the Middle East.

The military presence in the State Department was increased when President Eisenhower's wartime chief of staff, General Walter Bedell Smith, became under-secretary of state. Previously director of Central Intelligence, Smith, it was rumored, would give Eisenhower a direct source of information about John Foster Dulles, about whom the President knew relatively little.

I now worked under Major General Richard C. Partridge, an old-line career army officer who had little intelligence background and knew virtually nothing about the Middle East. As one of the senior members of the Washington intelligence community, Partridge had army intelligence evaluate the almost daily border incidents involving Israel and its Arab neighbors. I not only had a map of the Middle East below the glass on my desk but had also been in most of the countries and, most important, could pronounce the place names and parties concerned. The task of briefing Partridge, therefore, fell with increasing frequency to me.

With each border incident, the question was whether it was genuinely "military" in nature. Forced by the fates of war to dwell within sight or easy traveling distance of land in Israel that they'd once owned, Arab exiles often crossed the frontier to recover property or to visit relatives. On the other hand, groups of Palestinians sometimes made forays across the border to harass Israeli troops or to destroy an Israeli installation. Invariably, the Israelis would respond with pursuit or retaliatory raids. Our interest was to determine whether these incidents might escalate into serious military confrontations. At the time I became involved in these analyses, both the limited capabilities of the area armed forces and the political situation argued against resumption of full-scale hostilities. Yet, as we knew, a continuation of this trend of retaliatory or preventive raids and the use of troops against civilian incursions might set a precedent condoning independent national actions, thus circumventing the machinery that the U.N. Security Council had established to prevent border conflicts.

Responsibility for keeping the President informed of potentially dangerous situations was vested in the CIA, which had the responsibility of collating all intelligence gathered overseas. Working under General Partridge, I soon learned that the CIA had little capacity to originate useful intelligence on Arab-Israeli matters. Under Allen Dulles, the few real CIA area experts were involved in covert political activities and were less interested than the military services were in the routine tasks of reporting on current situations. The CIA intelligence analysts were undoubtedly capable but were secondary in status within the CIA to their colleagues in its clandestine service.

Within NEA in the State Department there were qualified specialists from whom I learned much about the Middle East. They argued that the establishment of Israel without equal status for the Arab state envisioned in the U.N. Partition Resolution (on which Israel's existence rested) would cause future Arab-Israeli wars from which the United States would be unable to remain aloof. No radical or innovative solutions were needed for establishing peace, these experts said. Rather, they pointed to the repeated U.N. resolutions calling for Israel either to repatriate the displaced Palestinians or compensate them for lost property if they elected not to return to their homes. Even at the cost of massive U.S. financial assistance to Israel to pay just compensation, this scheme seemed to be a real foundation for peace and held the hope that the Palestinians would integrate themselves into other countries.

These experts, unfortunately, had trouble finding an audience for their opinions: a return to previously enunciated formulas was less attractive to a new administration than were bold new solutions. Although the United States provided truce supervisory personnel and financial support to the U.N. agencies handling complaints of armistice violations and care of the Palestinian refugees, Congress made it clear that these appropriations would not be continued without signs of constructive efforts to settle the refugees permanently.

Israel announced that some Palestinian Arab funds held by a custodian since the war might now be withdrawn upon application, but Arab leaders argued that the Palestinians should accept nothing less than total compensation. And, although the U.S. had contributed over $150 million to the Arab governments for refugee aid, there was little improvement in their situation: those who had been farmers, small merchants, and laborers lived in squalid tents or tin-shack camps in Gaza, Jordan, Syria, and Lebanon, while the well educated went abroad to South America and Africa. Finally, Arab leaders felt that for the refugees to accept compensation would constitute recognition of Israel's right to occupy and confiscate Palestinian land and property. I was not alone in predicting that failure to solve the refugee problem would produce a new and very militant generation of Palestinians. By now, younger refugees were enrolled in the area's universities; yet nightly they returned to the camps to hear, from their parents, tales of homes, farms, or orchards left behind in Palestine.

By the middle of 1953, having been in Washington six months, I felt that I had some understanding of the bureaucratic structure that shaped our policy for the Middle East, and I saw increasing signs that what America did in that area would be determined and implemented by our new secretary of state, John Foster Dulles. The grandson of John W. Foster, President Harrison's secretary of state, and nephew of Robert Lansing, who had held the same post under President Wilson, Dulles seemed never to have doubted that he'd one day play a part in shaping American foreign affairs. Having been commissioned a captain of military intelligence when the United States entered the First World War, Secretary Dulles also believed that covert intelligence operations could both guide and supplement the activities of our diplomats.

At the Paris Peace Conference of 1919, Major Dulles worked as an assistant to Bernard Baruch on the Allied Reparations Commission and the Supreme Economic Council. Although his skills soon caught President Wilson's eye, Dulles's warnings against the Allies' crippling Germany economically and acquiring territorial spoils—Wilson's original position, after all—went unheeded by the President. Furthermore, Dulles watched as Wilson disregarded Secretary Lansing's opinions on the danger of the President's personal participation in the peace negotiations. Because the pitfalls Dulles had pointed out soon eventuated both in Germany's bankruptcy (followed by the rise of the Nazis to power) and in a peace treaty negotiated by Wilson that was rejected by the U.S. Senate, the new secretary of state took office with very fixed ideas about the conduct of America's international relations.

Until after the United States entered World War II, Foster Dulles maintained his antipathy toward Britain and France and his pro-German sentiments. When the Second World War ended, Dulles advocated strengthening Germany as the best means for the West to contain the Soviet Union. As for the mandates Britain and France had demanded in the Middle East at the end of World War I, the new secretary of state believed that the faster these two economically crippled European powers abandoned their claims of "special positions" with the Arabs, the better off the states of that area would be. Reparations of any type were anathema to Dulles; the claims of the Zionists that Israel should be entitled, on behalf of all the world's Jewry, to collect reparations from Germany received a cool audience from him. Finally, the secretary of state intended to take full advantage of working under a president whose military background suggested that he would delegate responsibility, and Dulles set out to implement the foreign-policy positions he'd espoused as a principal adviser during the Dewey and Eisenhower campaigns.

Encirclement of the free world by the Soviet Union was the principal danger, as Dulles saw the post-World War II international situation. Although a preventive war to meet this threat was to be avoided, Foster Dulles believed that we should stimulate a desire for freedom among the 800 million people under Communist domination. Furthermore, aware that control of the Middle East by the communists would give them access to vital oil reserves, the secretary of state advocated a policy of impartiality with respect to Israel and the Arab states until he could visit the area personally and formulate means of bringing about a permanent peace. Meanwhile, the administration's commitment to end the Korean War had to be fulfilled, and Dulles gave priority to drafting the mutual-defense pact that he proposed to sign with South Korea. This reflected the lessons taught by the Paris Peace Conference in ending World War I. Earlier, Dulles had convinced Secretary of State Acheson to delegate one man to concentrate on concluding a peace treaty with Japan and was himself named President Truman's special representative (with the rank of ambassador) for these negotiations; as such he signed for the United States the final peace documents. He'd now done the same thing for President Eisenhower in Korea; moreover, having been given an interim appointment to the U.S. Senate by Governor Dewey, Foster Dulles felt fully prepared to see the new administration's treaties and foreign policies through congressional approval.

Moving slowly at first on Middle East questions, Secretary Dulles left area problems to Assistant Secretary Henry Byroade. During this period the United States continued to press for implementation of the U.N. resolutions to compensate or repatriate the Palestinian refugees and to move from the 1949 armistice agreements toward treaties defining permanent borders between Israel and its Arab neighbors. Dulles, however, was no stranger to the Arab-Israel problem and had played an important role in facilitating the establishment of the state of Israel. As acting head of the U.S. delegation to the 1948 Paris General Assembly session, where admission of the Provisional Government of Israel was being debated, Dulles successfully lobbied for a change in U.S. plans to postpone until the following year's session consideration of Israel's admission[14] and to support the creation of an independent Arab

---

14   Headed by Secretary of State Marshall, the U.S. delegation had agreed to vote to postpone recognition by the General Assembly of Israel's admission. Instead, Marshall and his principal aide, Dean Rusk, advocated the U.N.'s acceptance of the plan drawn up by Chief Mediator Count Folke Bernadotte (just before his assassination by Menachem Begin's *Irgun* terrorists), calling for a division of the old state of Palestine into Arab and Jewish sectors. Once Marshal] was called to Washington to deal with the Berlin-blockade crisis, Dulles assumed charge of the delegation and, with support from delegates Eleanor Roosevelt and Ben Cohen, the U.S. delegation voted for the admission of Israel into the U.N.

state in Palestine. Thus, as secretary of state, Dulles had both considerable knowledge of the area's politics and some real leverage with Israeli leaders.

In May 1953, Dulles and Foreign Aid Administrator Harold Stassen made a tour of the Middle East and South Asia. Among other plans, Dulles wanted to encourage fruitful use of American foreign aid in conjunction with Arab economic development. Landing first in Egypt, Dulles heralded the RCC's General Naguib as "the George Washington of Egypt" and presented him with a pistol, a gift from President Eisenhower, thus piquing the British, who were still negotiating for base rights in Egypt. In Israel, Dulles stressed that the Arabs feared Zionism more than they did communism and that they were concerned that the United States might become the uncritical backer of what Dulles termed "expansionist Zionism." Both Israel's 1952 Status Law and the Law of Return, Dulles said, were interpreted by Arabs as indications that Israel did not intend to remain within the borders of its newly created state.[15]

---

15 The 1952 Status Law reaffirmed a fundamental precept of Zionist nationalism: the state of Israel is not created for its own nationals alone, but, rather, for the "entire Jewish people." As successor to the Jewish Agency, the Zionist Organization was recognized as having preexisting governmental status within Israel, sharing with the state the central task of gathering in all "exiles" in the Diaspora. The "cooperation of all Jews, as individuals and as groups, in building up the state and assisting immigration to it of all the masses of the people" was expected, and the "unity of all sections of Jewry" was described as necessary for this purpose.

The ensuing covenant between the government of Israel and the Zionist executive bestowed governmental functions upon the latter. There followed the Eichmann trial judgment (1961), alleging nationality status to all the "Jewish people" and a legal link between them and the state of Israel, followed by the Joint Israel-Zionist Communiqué (1964), which stressed the "dangers of assimilation" to Jews living elsewhere, and promised, in public law, to implement Zionist nationalism wherever Jews lived. To many Jews living abroad, this caused concern about dual allegiance.

Accordingly, in 1964 an anti-Zionist organization of American Jews (the American Council for Judaism) sought and obtained from the Department of State a clarification of the status of Jews in this country. In a letter of reply it was said that ". . . it should be clear that the Department of State does not regard the 'Jewish people' concept as a concept of international law."

Throughout his travels in the area, Dulles stressed the importance of expanding the area's water resources, especially to provide the Palestinian refugees with new farmland. His other primary goal was to assist the people of the "northern tier" of Middle Eastern states to defend themselves against communism.[16] In Pakistan, Dulles saw a unit of splendidly uniformed, turban-topped Pathan lancers on parade. Each man appeared at least seven feet tall. When Prime Minister Mohammed Ali apologized for an honor guard hurriedly picked from local troops (although the Pathans had in fact been flown in expressly for the occasion), the secretary of state came away convinced that this army of giants should be given weapons. Such warriors, he was certain, could stem the Red hordes.

During his stay, Dulles came to a fuller understanding of the future oil income of the Arab petroleum-producing countries. On his return, the secretary of state instructed Henry Byroade to explore the possibilities of inducing the states with oil production to contribute to a regional fund for the economic development of their less fortunate Arab neighbors. Byroade concluded, however, that considering the ill-fated MEC and MEDO defense schemes, no Western-sponsored proposal was likely to be accepted, no matter what its merits, if indeed the "haves" would help the "have nots" at all. The best the United States could do, Byroade reported, was to offer technical advice and guidance, should the Arabs be interested in forming an indigenous development bank.[17] The assistant

---

16   Acknowledging that a Middle East defense organization was not an immediate possibility and could not be imposed from without, Dulles said that he had found awareness of the menace of Soviet communism in the "northern tier" of countries bordering the Soviet Union (Turkey, Iran, and Pakistan). To these he proposed U.S. assistance to strengthen their interrelated defenses to resist the threats to "all free peoples."

17   It is interesting to note just how difficult it was for Westerners to understand the potential impact of Arab wealth. Attached to Byroade's report were quotations from conclusions reached by World Bank President Eugene Black, who had just returned from the Middle East. "The thing they [the Arabs] don't realize . . ." Black wrote, "is the absolute impossibility of spending that kind of money . . . There is no way on the face of the earth that they could possibly spend that much [$500 million] in one year."

secretary was willing to pursue this possibility further, but Dulles was unenthusiastic, since other economic and defense plans were already in his mind.

At this point, Byroade sought to obtain the views of his regional ambassadors on the need for economic- and military-aid programs for the states of the Near East and convened a meeting in Cairo in August 1953. The Office of the Secretary of Defense was to be represented at this meeting, and, in part because of my increasingly frequent liaison activities with Captain Grant, I was chosen to go. Needless to say, I was excited by the chance to return so soon to the area.

Before leaving Baghdad for Washington, the chief of Iraq's General Staff had requested that I press for Iraq's right to purchase several hundred army personnel-carrying trucks (under the reimbursable-aid provisions of the Mutual Security Act). I learned, however, that British opposition (as Iraq's "traditional supplier") in the NEACC would block such a sale, even though the vehicles were vital to Iraq's ability to maintain security in the Kurdistan area. Now, scheduled to tour, with a Department of State senior officer, all of the Arab states prior to the Cairo meeting, I faced the unpleasant task of informing General Mahmoud that the U.S. would not approve Iraq's request.

Although Baghdad was, when I landed, as hot and as sand-flea infested as when I'd lived there, I was glad to be back. It was a great pleasure to see the many friends I'd made in the past. When we met with the Iraqi chief of staff, we found that he had a shopping list of 300 trucks and 200 radio sets. Although he soon understood that it was unlikely their request would be approved, the general wanted me to at least tell him where he could buy the equipment commercially, and asked me to tell American manufacturers to

---

That Black lacked prescience is best illustrated by the oil-financed projects now underway in Saudi Arabia alone. Over one billion dollars has already been committed for the first stages of each of the two major ports through which the *Saudis* will ship the output of the multibillion-dollar refineries and petrochemical complexes the Arabs have forced the *now nationalized* oil companies to build in joint ventures and locate in the countries from which the raw oils, chemicals, and minerals are taken.

send salesmen to see him (adding, to emphasize that he'd not asked a great favor, that his country had adequate funds for such purchases, and that Iraq had long ago received its independence from Great Britain). I complied with this request on my return to Washington.

Visiting later at the Iranian embassy, my host, the ambassador, was handed a message, and suggesting that I might want to accompany him, hurriedly left his desk. In the car as we sped to the airport, he said that he'd been ordered to meet the shah of Iran's aircraft. Shortly after we'd arrived, the shah, Empress Soroya, and a small entourage landed. Only then did we learn that the Iranian monarch, alerted in advance of a coup against him, had fled Iran.[18]

Before the completion of my attaché tour in Iraq, Ambassador Crocker had been replaced by Ambassador Burton Y. Berry, a career officer for whom I'd acquired great respect. Invited by Berry to stay at the embassy, I was called to his office for drinks and a chat before dinner. He showed me a lengthy "eyes only" communication he'd received from Secretary Dulles in response to Berry's first-year summary observations, which had contained a recommendation that America exert a more positive role in guiding Iraq's future planning. In his reply, Dulles said that the United States considered Iraq to be entirely within Britain's political sphere and that in spite of the ambassador's pleas the U.S. would deal with Iraq only in a manner consistent with British objectives. In closing, the secretary of state said that the Near Eastern political scene was so delicate that all outside parties would be advised to let things settle down before advancing new proposals that might upset tradition and disturb the present balance of power.

---

18   "The Shah and his wife hastily bundled their clothes into the imperial plane and flew across the border to Iraq. For the next forty-eight hours Dr. Mossadeq was in control. Communist and nationalist mobs raced through Teheran streets screaming 'Death to the Shah!' Statues of the monarch and his father were pelted and desecrated, then toppled from their pedestals. The Mossadeq press screamed for 'revenge' and the 'gallows.' Foreign Minister Hossein Fatemi warned Iraq that harboring the monarch might lead to 'unpleasant political events.' The Shah and the Queen flew on to Rome." From the *New York Times*, August 23, 1953.

When Berry asked what I thought of Dulles's message, I responded that I was certain that new economic-development plans were being formulated in Washington, and that by concentrating energies elsewhere to relieve area tensions, these projects might work to Iraq's benefit. But Burton Berry was not to be consoled. "No, Bill," he said, "I'm through. I don't want to sit here watching things fall apart." He then showed me a copy of his letter to Henry Byroade. In it Berry wrote that Great Britain's visions of a continuing empire, the refusal of IPC to explore and produce all of Iraqi oil reserves, and the use of Iraqi Development Board funds for huge projects largely benefiting British contractors and their country's own economy would bring on a nationalistic upheaval in Iraq, from which the West would suffer badly. The Iraqis were eager for our advice, the American oil-company partners in IPC could help change the company's British-dictated policies, and, dependent upon the World Bank and U.S. economic aid, the Development Board's priorities could be realigned by our instructing the American director on its board to insist that these funds be utilized on projects of immediate benefit to Iraq's largely impoverished population. In tendering his resignation to the State Department, Berry pointedly said that he foresaw in the Near East losses similar to those that the U.S. had suffered by "letting the dust settle in China."

Going on to the Cairo conference, I joined six area chiefs of mission, representatives of the Foreign Operations Administration and the U.S. Treasury, and an officer from the staff of the U.S. Navy commander for the Eastern Atlantic and Mediterranean (another example of the navy's interest in all U.S. policies for the Middle East). Early on, the ambassadors agreed that with the possible exception of Egypt, the states of the area should not be offered American military aid at the time. Instead, the focus was on a scheme patterned after the Tennessee Valley Authority, designed for the area by American engineers, for which the U.S. was prepared to make financing available. A presidential representative, Eric Johnston, was preparing to leave for the Near East to try to persuade Israel and the Arab states contributing source water to the Jordan River to collaborate in this project. The goal was to develop hydroelectric facilities and irrigation water to benefit all the states, and, in addition, to create fertile land capable of supporting up to 900,000 Palestinian refugees on the West Bank of the Jordan (at least 100,000 of the refugees would be employed in developing the first stages of the project). It was indeed a bold and imaginative plan, holding hope of ameliorating the refugee problem as an obstacle to peace, and, equally important, of placating the Congress, whose willingness to appropriate further funds for refugee relief was now in question.

There were, of course, obstacles to the plan, at the least the problem of finding an acceptable formula for dividing the water between Israel and the three riparian Arab states (Israel, however, was to have 38 percent of the Jordan's waters, against 62 percent to be divided among the three Arab countries).

With Israel now my destination, I flew out of Cairo and landed in the Arab section of old Jerusalem. The sheer existence of an operational international airport at the crossroads of a divided city was a tribute to the U.N.'s efforts. That night, as I looked out at the city, seeing the dark stretch identified by its stillness as "no man's land," I understood how easy it would be to throw a stone, say, from Jordanian into Israeli territory.

I had little time for sightseeing and left the Mount of Olives, the Dome of the Rock, and Gethsemane behind me as I prepared to cross into Israel. Moving toward the Mandelbaum Gate and enjoined to watch out for snipers, I saw barbed wire and burned-out armored cars, reminders of the fighting, and tried to fathom how a divided city could have functioned for five years without major conflicts.

As we reached the Israeli immigration booth, I was struck by its very presence. Failing a peace treaty and the exchange of diplomats, did this not in itself constitute Jordanian recognition of the Israeli state? Our consul had provided us with "slip sheet" visas so that we could cross into Israel without voiding our passports for travel in Arab countries by having an Israeli entry stamp. As I gave my documents to the Israeli immigration officer, however, bam! his stamp had hit not the slip sheet but my passport. My protests evoked apologies, but I entered Israel with passport proof of its sovereignty. The Israelis had made their symbolic point.

Proceeding to meet the American consul general, we learned that he was stuck in what Israel claimed, and the rest of the world denied, to be its capital. The consul general's greatest problem was refusing to discuss diplomatic matters with Israel, confining his activities, instead, to consular functions. His task was delicate because Israel had notified all diplomatic missions that Israel's foreign ministry would be moving from Tel Aviv to Jerusalem. Only the Russians had recognized Israel's right to establish its capital in Jerusalem, which had been designated an international city in repeated United Nations resolutions. Given all this, we were instructed to avoid any discussions of official business with the Israelis until we reached Tel Aviv. I knew already that Israel regarded our mission as low level in status, since all policy discussions concerning U.S. aid to Israel were held in Washington. It came as a surprise, however, when our requests to visit Israeli military installations were denied.

Traveling on to Tel Aviv, we saw rusting tanks and armored cars, reminders of the terrible battles in which the Haganah had taken the strategic road to Jerusalem and occupied the New City. As we approached Tel Aviv I could see the mere twelve miles of Israel that lay between the Jordanian armistice line and the sea, leaving the fledgling state exposed to an Arab attack that could cut it in two. It was easy, then, to understand why the Israelis probably gave more credence than was due to Arab speeches threatening them.

In Tel Aviv I met with our army attaché, Lt. Colonel Michael Kane, who was eager to unburden himself about the problems he faced in dealing with the Israeli army. Unwilling to speak about classified information in his home, where, he feared, microphones had been installed, Kane explained that the internal-security organization in Israel was one of the most efficient in the world. He then said that trying to perform his duties was as difficult as it would be in an iron curtain country. The only military information he could believe from official Israeli army sources was that relating to equipment purchased in the United States, but even this was questionable. Shipping cases labeled "agricultural equipment" or "spare parts" often contained new armaments shipped in contravention of U.S. export controls.

Furthermore, Kane said, the Israeli Defense Force was capable of fully mobilizing its large reserve units and starting a war without the knowledge of the American embassy. And the CIA, he said, had absolutely no independent capabilities in Israel, depending instead on Israel's intelligence service for its information.

I'd thought Kane almost paranoid—Israel and the United States were, after all, friendly countries—but I had a lesson to learn. I was approached at my hotel by a young Israeli woman who identified herself as a reporter. Although flattered by her interest in what I'd been doing, I was unable to keep a date we'd made for later that evening when Kane explained that she worked for Israeli intelligence.

The next day, speaking with Kane and American chargé d'affaires Francis Russell, I learned that Israel had adopted as its own and was now implementing a 1944 scheme to irrigate the Palestinian coastal plain down to the Negev Desert. This plan, however, made no provision for use of the Jordan's water outside Israel and was therefore obviously illegal and prejudicial to the Arabs. Furthermore, being unilateral, the plan contributed nothing to American hopes to support cooperative ventures in the area, upon which, it was hoped, peace negotiations might be based.

Israel's diversion of water from the Jordan at Jisr Banat Yaacov in the U.N. Demilitarized Zone south of Lake Huleh had been condemned by the United Nations, and the Israelis had been ordered to stop all work. Israel's refusal to comply with this order provoked strong reaction from the United States. Francis Russell had been instructed to tell the Israelis that all U.S. aid (on which Israel's survival depended) would be withdrawn unless Israel immediately complied with the U.N. order. Furthermore, Russell was to explain that President Eisenhower had instructed the U.S. Treasury to draw up an order removing the tax-deductible status of contributions made to United Jewish Appeal (UJA) and American Zionist organizations raising funds for Israel. The power to remove the tax-exempt status of contributions to a foreign country was a matter entirely within the power of the executive branch, so this was no small threat. Although UJA funds might be earmarked for education or for humanitarian purposes, this money liberated other Israeli revenues for the purchase of arms and for the support of military forces.

After conveying the U.S. demands to Foreign Minister Sharett, Russell was given Israel's assurances that all work would be suspended on the project at Jisr Banat Yaacov, but Kane was doubtful that Israel's compliance would last. He reminded me of the drainage work done by Israel at Lake Huleh, which was diverting the source of the Jordan's waters, and of the frequent incidents of Israeli police driving Syrian fishermen from their traditional waters. Noting that these incidents had provoked the Syrians into arming the Golan Heights to protect their nationals below, Kane predicted that Israel would now feel justified in using its army in the Syrian border area in place of the police who had driven the fishermen away. Finally, Kane said, he believed Israel's long-range objective was to seize control some day of most if not all of the Jordan's headwaters.[19] As with much of what Kane told me, the very intensity of his words made me skeptical. But I listened; I still had much to learn.

---

19 After Eric Johnston was unable to reach agreement between the Arabs and the Israelis to share access to the Jordan's waters, the war Israel launched in 1967 against Syria and Jordan gave the Israelis control of virtually all the territory involved in the Johnston negotiations. From 1949 onward, U.N. and U.S. observers have always regarded Israeli raids against Syria, and its eventual conquest of the Golan Heights of Syria, as motivated by a plan to control the headwaters of the Jordan. Israel's continuing claim that its security requires retention of the Golan Heights actually translates into "security of its water sources" instead of "security of its borders" against Syrian attacks.

CHAPTER SIX

OMINOUS PRECEDENTS

My opportunity to revisit the Near East had been exhilarating, but back in Washington life was far from routine, and I was soon briefing General Partridge on new and more serious border incidents. Just after I'd left the Cairo conference, Israel had scored a major victory in the U.N.—the Security Council had passed a resolution calling on Egypt to terminate restrictions on the transit of international commercial shipments destined for Israel through the Suez Canal. Offsetting this, in Israeli eyes, was the U.S. pressure that had forced them to suspend work at Jisr Banat Yaacov. Nonetheless, with the Johnston mission in the offing, one might have expected reduced tensions in anticipation of this major U.S.-sponsored effort. Not so: attention soon focused on the Israel-Jordan border.

In early October an Israeli mother and two of her children were killed by a grenade hurled by marauders from Jordan. The Jordanian members of the U.N. commission investigating this incident had joined their Israeli counterparts in roundly condemning the raid, even asking for Israeli cooperation in tracking down the culprits. Jordan's jails were then crowded with Palestinians arrested for illegal border crossings, the Arab Legion had been kept back from the frontier in order to avert military clashes, and our comparisons of casualty figures showed that there had been far more Arab than Israeli fatalities resulting from armistice-line violations.

Now that the problems between Israel, Egypt, and Syria had been temporarily resolved, my colleagues in Washington hoped that Israel would not retaliate against Jordan. Affected considerably by Mike Kane's predictions that Israel would divert attention from Jisr Banat Yaacov and then resume work there, I found it difficult to be optimistic.

Within a few days, an Israeli army unit launched a major crossing into Jordan. The target was Qibya, a small, unarmed village well back of the border. There, fifty-three men, women, and children were murdered in their homes and the wounded were left to die, total deaths reaching sixty-six. U.N. observers sent to the scene found conclusive evidence that despite Israel's denials, organized combat troops had been employed.

When Jordan called for a Security Council meeting to condemn Israel, United States preparations for the debate included sending area experts from Washington to supplement our U.N. delegation, and I was one of those assigned. Reporting in New York to the permanent military staff advising U.S. Ambassador to the U.N. Henry Cabot Lodge, I was put to work analyzing reports received from the U.N. observers who had investigated the Qibya raid.

Prior to the U.N. session, Commander Elmo Hutchison, head of the Jordan-Israel Mixed Armistice Commission, was flown to New York. By the time I met this U.S. naval officer, he'd become a highly publicized international figure, much maligned, and a seasoned veteran of the politics of the area, although he'd had no experience in the Near East before this assignment. Because of the many times his Mixed Armistice Commission's findings had condemned Israel, he was accused in that country of holding pro-Arab sympathies. I found him a sincere man, trying to perform an impossible task. The photographs and other evidence he brought with him, in any case, left no doubt that Israeli troops had waged an unjustifiable attack on a defenseless village.

Provided a delegate's pass to the U.N., I was fortunate to be there during the annual session of the General Assembly and could travel freely through the restricted corridors of the U.N. buildings, where the famous and powerful representatives of the world's nations gathered. In those days I sported a Borsalino homburg that, in combination with my pin-striped suit and overcoat with dark velvet collar trimming its dignified navy blue, gained me entry without my needing to show my pass at the building's entrance. Checking my coat in the lobby but carrying a copy of the *New York Times* for the sake of appearance, I proceeded past the security guards into the delegates' lounge without being challenged.

The lounge was filled with clusters of seated men and women, in various national costumes, gathered in conversation, yet there was an atmosphere of quiet and calm. Magnificent high windows lined one entire wall and offered a serene view of a landscaped terrace and the East River. When Francis Wilcox, assistant secretary of state for International Organizations, walked by, I accepted his invitation for a drink at the bar. As we spoke we were joined by a man introduced as Sam Kopper. From the conversation I gathered he had something to do with oil, yet Wilcox appeared to defer to him when the subject turned to Near Eastern foreign policy. We soon moved upstairs to the dining room, and I watched the ships, barges, and tugs on the river below us. Looking at the sprinkling of famous people in the room, I thought of the distance I'd come from Spokane.

At an adjacent table sat Lebanese Ambassador Charles Malik, whom I'd met socially in Washington. With him were Pakistani Foreign Minister Zafrulla Khan and Deputy Foreign Minister Vishinsky of Russia. As we ate, Francis Wilcox offered his thoughts on what our neighbors were discussing. The Big Three foreign ministers, Wilcox said, were then meeting in London and had just reaffirmed their determination under the Tripartite Declaration to preserve the armistice lines between the Arabs and Israelis. Yet all three, apparently, wanted to avoid a Security Council meeting directed specifically at condemning Israel. Lebanon, Pakistan, and Russia had quite different hopes, Wilcox explained, if for different reasons: hence the unusual group beside us.

As lunch proceeded, I learned more of the intricacies of top-level international diplomacy. To begin with, Secretary Dulles had recently taken the unprecedented step of announcing that the United States would withhold economic aid ($60 million) promised to Israel. This might have been justified by the Qibya raid alone, but Israel, of course, had not yet been found guilty by the Security Council, only condemned by Elmo Hutchison's Mixed Armistice Commission. As Mike Kane had predicted, however, Israel had resumed work on its water-diversion project at Jisr Banat Yaacov, and this threatened to sabotage Eric Johnston's mission, which was about to depart for the Middle East.

As for Britain, it was bound by treaty to respond with military assistance, if requested, in the case of an armed attack on Jordan. If a U.N. finding that the Israeli army had invaded Jordan could be avoided, Britain might not have to comply with a Jordanian request to station troops there or risk being called on for help in the event of a future Israeli attack. The French, meanwhile, sought to stay on good terms with both the Arabs and the Israelis, especially the latter, with whom they were negotiating a large sale of military equipment, something difficult to justify in the NEACC if the purchaser had been denounced for aggression. All this, I thought, had a certain logic for the major powers but was unfortunately consistent with Arab predictions that the Big Three would fail to honor treaty commitments to small nations.

Once lunch was finished, Kopper and I returned to the delegates' lounge. As we stood at the bar, a tall, balding man, clad in a brown suit and dark horn-rimmed glasses, rushed toward the bar. As he passed us, it was "Hi, Sam" and "Hi, Jerry." Quaffing his drink in two swallows, he strode out of the room at the same pace he'd come in at.

"Who's that?" I asked Kopper.

"The American ambassador! Why didn't you salute?" This was, he explained, the Honorable James J. Wadsworth, deputy head of the U.S. delegation, carrying the rank of ambassador. Wadsworth, Kopper went on, brought brains, consistency, patience, and logic to Cabot Lodge's staff, and, as a former congressman, had great ability to negotiate compromises with foreign delegates. He also, Kopper said, was the backbone of a delegation torn between the strong wills of John Foster Dulles and Henry Cabot Lodge.

Delighted that I had found such an agreeable tutor, I listened as Sam identified the delegates passing through the lounge. At one point, Kopper introduced me to Dr. Elmer Berger, head of the American Council for Judaism, "the rabbi devoted to saving the Jews from the Zionists," Sam said. Berger, he went on, spoke for an influential segment of the American Jewish community that believed that Israel's strength and survival depended on its making every possible effort to establish peaceful relations with its Arab neighbors.

Later, at dinner, I learned more about Samuel Keene Clagget Kopper himself. Then thirty-nine, four years my senior, he'd become a lawyer before joining the staff of the State Department's Bureau of Near Eastern Affairs, serving as its deputy director from 1947 to 1949. In those years of the U.N. debate on Palestine and the formation of the state of Israel, Kopper had been a principal member of the U.S. delegation to the U.N.

Disillusioned because the Truman administration's support of Israel was not conditional on entering into peace agreements with the Arabs, Kopper had left the foreign service to become Adlai Stevenson's advisor on Middle East matters during the 1952 presidential campaign. Several American oil companies then vied for Kopper's services, and he accepted an offer from Aramco, whose parent companies (Exxon, SoCal, Mobil, and Texaco) were by then unofficially conducting American foreign policy with the Middle East oil-producing states. Initially an assistant legal counsel, Sam was soon a chief aide to the chairman of Aramco's board and, assigned as the company's observer at the U.N., a practitioner of oil-company diplomacy.

Returning to Washington when formal Security Council debate on the Qibya massacre was postponed, I came back to the U.N. in late November when it resumed and again spent time with Kopper. Drinks in the delegates' lounge and lunch in the dining room with Sam allowed me to follow the behind-the-scenes compromises involved in drafting a resolution to condemn Israel that would receive a unanimous vote. For days before the debate the U.N. buzzed with activity, the press headlined the story, and the Israelis mobilized all available pressure either to avoid the debate or to influence its outcome. I had a real sense of being present while a matter engaging the whole world's attention was being resolved.

Tension concerning the Qibya issue continued to grow. Lobbyists for groups seeking to block a debate seemed to outnumber the delegates, and New York's Mayor-Elect Wagner had taken on the Archbishop of York in the press for advocating a debate on Qibya, joining Zionist groups in calling the prelate anti-Semitic. The CIO had been mobilized by Israel; the oil companies were out in force opposing labor's position. It was obvious that the Israelis were aware of the damage that condemnation might do. At the last moment, Israel's representative (Abba Eban) introduced a lame charge against Jordan alleging that three Israeli shepherds and 150 of their sheep had been abducted, and called for immediate talks to settle permanent borders between Israel and Jordan. This move was too late, too obviously diversionary; the debate over Qibya had been scheduled and the only question remaining was that of the margin of support for condemnation of Israel.

Following the Security Council arguments as we sat together, Sam Kopper suggested that the outcome had been settled in advance, yet even he hadn't anticipated the final vote: nine to zero for the strongest censure of Israel. Lebanon and Russia had abstained, holding out for demands that Israel comply with all previous U.N. resolutions, including those dealing with the rights of the displaced Palestinians.

Rejecting the U.N.'s censure, the Israeli cabinet and Knesset stood firm in denying any military involvement at Qibya. The overwhelming evidence I'd seen confirming the participation of Israeli troops left me to wonder what might have been behind Israel's frantic efforts to avoid any debate over Qibya, even at the risk of losing U.S. financial support. Had organized retaliation now become a national policy, or had activists within the Israeli military launched the attack and later been discovered by an embarrassed government? No matter which was involved, I was certain that the Qibya massacre would drive the Arabs even farther away from the peace table.

A more significant principle was involved in the Qibya debate, however: just over five years earlier, Israel had gained admission to the U.N. by agreeing to conform to the provisions of its charter and to abide by the rulings of the Security Council, these having the force of international law. By rejecting the Security Council's findings and by embarking on a calculated policy of selective retaliatory or preventive military operations, Israel was undermining the authority of the organization to which it owed its existence. More than that, the precedent of employing force to settle disputes could (and did) lead to Israeli decisions to launch retaliatory or preventive wars against the Arabs. Qibya was a major turning point in the question of whether the Middle East would see peace or a continuing period of hostilities.[20]

---

20 The memoirs of Moshe Sharett (foreign minister at the time of Qibya) mince no words in accusing the Israeli military establishment of "manipulating facts, withholding information, and falsifying reports" in order to justify retaliatory operations. He was deeply shocked by the cover-up of the Qibya massacre. See *Yoman Ishi* (Personal Diary) by Moshe Sharett, ed. Yaakov Sharett (Tel Aviv: Ma'ariv, 1978.)

A semiofficial Israeli publication (the *Paratroopers Book*) reveals that General Moshe Dayan ordered the formation of an elite, all-volunteer unit (Unit 101) of the Israeli army to conduct reprisal raids (its first was Qibya). Led by Ariel Sharon (minister of agriculture in the present government of Menachem Begin), this unit was later integrated into the paratroop corps of the Israel Defense Force.

In 1955, Israeli military censors passed for publication an article saying that "there had been nothing reckless or impulsive about the lethal raids across the borders. On the contrary, the policy of reprisals is the fruit of cold, unemotional, political and psychological reasoning."

CHAPTER SEVEN

IN DEFENSE OF OIL, THE SHAH, AND THE KHYBER PASS

The year-end holiday season in Washington was accompanied by a welcome lull in the crisis atmosphere of the Middle East. In Israel, however, serious problems of another type loomed prominently. These involved the question of how to discharge a crippling short-term indebtedness at a time when efforts to borrow over $100 million from the American government had come to nothing. Funds usually available from private sources in the U.S. now seemed threatened by offers by the Zionist Organization of America to arrange the mass transfer of one and one-half million Jews from Eastern Europe to Israel. Not only did this pose critical problems of available space and cultural assimilation, but the Arabs also reacted with alarm over the prospect of such a huge increase in Israel's population. The appearance of many high-level visitors from Israel at the embassy parties we attended during the holidays seemed to indicate the possibility that the enthusiasm of American Zionists might be overreaching the capabilities of Israel to absorb immigrants, remain solvent, and coexist peacefully with its neighbors.

A potentially encouraging development in Israeli political life came with the transfer of the premiership from David Ben-Gurion to Moshe Sharett. The State Department's assessment of Sharett as likely to be less "hawkish" toward the Arabs than the strong "father figure" who had guided Israel since its birth coincided with the impression I'd acquired during my conversation with the new prime minister in Jerusalem. One thing about him had disturbed me, however, and that was what we were calling *fait accompli* foreign policy. The United States had made a number of strong statements to Israel warning that we considered the transfer to Jerusalem of Israel's foreign ministry to be a preface to illegally declaring the Holy City the capital of the Jewish state. When I asked Sharett how this could contribute to peace in the area, he reacted with annoyance. Israel's historic right to constitute Jerusalem as its capital had been explained to Secretary Dulles during his visit months before, Sharett told me. Why then, now that the ministry was being moved, should the U.S. show surprise in its public protests? At the time, I thought of—but did not mention—Ben-Gurion's boast that not even the U.S. had enough money to buy changes in Israel's policies. When viewed in connection with the rights of a sovereign state, this was correct. Yet, just a few days after my conversation with Sharett, the U.S. had made clear its own right to withhold foreign aid and loans when Israel's policies conflicted with our efforts to settle the differences between the Arabs and Israel. Nineteen fifty-four promised to be another interesting year in this test of national resolve.

With the start of the new year I tried to evaluate what direction I should pursue in my army career. Now thirty-five, I'd been promoted to the rank of major and had crossed the line into field-grade status. Circumstance was my greatest ally. The Middle East was now an area of critical importance, and I both knew the area and was beginning to understand how American policy was made. I still had no fixed views of my own, but, sure that U.S. military-equipment sales and grants to the area were inevitable, I hoped that our position would be based upon legitimate requirements rather than upon the political and commercial considerations that governed the decisions made by Britain and France. That the Arab armies needed weapons to maintain internal security seemed certain. As for Israel, I had reached no conclusion. Far from questioning Israel's right to a peaceful existence, I was, nonetheless, not impressed by Israeli defiance of the U.N. on both the Qibya attack and the water-diversion program. Of one thing I was convinced: we should do all we could to move the Arabs and the Israelis into the permanent peace treaties envisioned in the armistice agreements of 1949.

An important factor in my thoughts about the future was the arrival of a new army G-2, Major General Arthur G. Trudeau, to whom I'd reported my impressions of the U.N. debate over Qibya. A veteran of combat commands in Korea, the new chief of army intelligence had both a keen interest in international affairs and an instinctive understanding that the Middle East was one of America's problem areas. I liked him immediately and began to subordinate my wish to get out of intelligence to the possibility of seeking a regular army commission and utilizing my assignment to the general staff for building a secure future. A university offering extension courses at the Pentagon had evaluated my background and experience and offered constructive college credit for all but thirty term hours required to grant me a degree. I had just made up my mind to enroll in night classes when General Trudeau arranged an assignment that whetted my wanderlust and desire to return to the Middle East.

Secretary Dulles was now eager to have the U.N. focus on peacemaking efforts in the Near East, while the U.S. concentrated on the Jordan River water project to provide means of resettling the Palestinian refugees. Yet his trip to the area espousing the concept of collective security had created an opening for Britain to grasp this proposal and promote it as a means of maintaining its waning influence there. The states of the area had begun to ask Western countries for the military and economic support they thought would flow from a regional defense pact. The United States, therefore, although not eager to sell arms to the Middle East, was repeatedly being asked to do just that. Pakistan was the first state whose request the U.S. agreed to consider during the first months of 1954.

Technicians from the military services were being gathered to visit Pakistan to assess its requirements for military equipment. No intelligence officers would participate in the mission; after all, we weren't spying, but merely examining the Pakistani armed forces to determine their capabilities and armaments needs. Intolerant of such foolishness, Trudeau arranged that I be detached to the secretary of defense's office and assigned to the team as its political adviser.

The military-survey mission was led by Brigadier General Harry F. Meyers, the first army attaché assigned to Pakistan following its independence in 1947. He knew both the country and its armed forces and had postponed his retirement in order to make this trip. Although what proportion of the Middle East military-aid appropriation would be allocated to Pakistan was a closely held secret, we were authorized to recommend up to $40 million. Our conclusions would be governed solely by our evaluation of the needs of Pakistan's armed forces and their ability to utilize sophisticated military hardware.

Just as we were preparing to leave for Karachi, a telegram arrived from our embassy in London. The British, it said, had historically been the sole supplier of military equipment to Pakistan and India. Winthrop Aldrich, our ambassador to Britain, had assured the prime minister that our team would travel to England to determine what might be purchased there to outfit the Pakistani army. Aldrich added that the team might then make a courtesy visit to Karachi in order to illustrate that the British arms being sent would be paid for by the United States.

The meeting in London was typically British: against our team of ten were arrayed a number of generals and some twenty representatives of various British ministries. If nothing else, they'd wear us down. After we were informed of what weapons they could sell us, we were asked just how much we proposed to spend. Looking across the table, I could see General Meyers straining to contain himself. Finally, making an upward gesture with his right thumb, he said, "Gentlemen, this meeting is over. Our budget is secret, and we, with the Pakistanis, will decide just what types of American equipment we'll supply." As one, we stood up behind him and marched out of a room of stunned British brass and civil servants. Despite an enraged American ambassador's admonition that we await Washington's reaction to this grave threat to U.S.-U.K. relations, we flew off to Pakistan in the morning.

At the general staff headquarters in Karachi we were given the statistics on equipment and personnel we'd need as a basis for the spot inspections we planned to make in the field. At first startled that all decisions could not be made in the capital, Field Marshall Mohammed Ayub Khan flew north with us to see Pakistan's border with China. As we approached the passes of the Hindu Kush, Ayub Khan pointed out the Gilgit passes, where troops of the two countries sometimes clashed. Then, flying south, we were shown the disputed Kashmir area, where U.N. observers kept the Pakistanis and Indians apart.

A planned road trip to the famed Khyber Pass brought an overnight stay at Peshawar, the headquarters of the Pakistan army's armored forces. Although agreeing to a sightseeing excursion to Khyber, a restless General Meyers made it clear that we'd come to inspect equipment and troops. During our absence a full brigade of glistening and immaculate tanks had been lined up on the parade ground. Following Ayub Khan, we dutifully walked among the tanks, receiving salutes from battle crews lined at their sides and drivers in the turrets. As we moved to our cars, General Meyers stopped short and asked the field marshall to order his tanks to pass in review. And then it all came out: fully two-thirds of the tanks were completely immobile, and the few that groaned haltingly forward soon ground to a halt. Indeed, General Meyers had been in Pakistan before.

Despite this fiasco, the next morning Ayub Khan called a meeting to discuss what our team planned to recommend. The tall, handsome Sandhurst graduate looked squarely at the much shorter Meyers and expressed shock at news just received from Pakistan's embassy in Washington. "Can it be," the field marshall asked, "that you have only $40 million to equip us to stave off the Chinese and join Turkey in fighting the Russians? If true, Saah, you are wasting our time!"

"I don't set the figures," Meyers shot back. "Your complaint should be addressed to our ambassador." With that the general departed, and the rest of us filed out behind him. Brushing aside a now panicky diplomat sent by the embassy to advise us, Meyers said he was taking his boys down-country to visit the Wali of Swat, an old friend. So, for a day and a night we enjoyed the hospitality of one of the last independent rulers of the old Indian Empire. By the time we returned to Peshawar, tempers had cooled, and we flew back to Karachi with the understanding that the survey team's recommendation for the first increment of aid would be, appropriately, two squadrons of American tanks with a five-year supply of spare parts.

Leaving Pakistan, we stopped in Saudi Arabia for a brief inspection. Internal security—keeping the tribal leaders loyal—was the major concern of the Saudi monarchy, and we were to recommend appropriate types of small arms and transport equipment for the Saudis to purchase with several million dollars they'd set aside for this purpose. The king had absolutely no desire to create a modern military machine. Until the royal family could consolidate its control of the country, there was always the possibility that officers trained to lead combat units would stage a coup.

As we flew home, I thought back to Pakistan and wondered just who was fooling whom in these games of collective security, regional defense, and competitions to build up local military forces. Hundreds of millions of dollars would be required to fit out the well-trained but equipment-poor Pakistanis. And then what? The Russian and Chinese reactions were predictable, but such expenditures risked also inciting India, or possibly driving the Indians to Russia for matching quantities of arms. Worse, did those State Department "experts" and ambassadors who urged military-aid programs really understand anything about equipping armies? Hadn't Foster Dulles been taken in by visions of seven-foot Pathan lancers stemming the Red hordes? These same cavalrymen, now turned tankers, were the ones we'd seen at Peshawar, and without their horses they'd been helpless, immobile. Even now, I thought, floods were inundating Dacca in East Pakistan, and it seemed that our money might do more good there than it would to field a few hundred shiny tanks on Peshawar's parade ground. Perhaps, I concluded, internal security was all we should aim for in the Middle East and South Asia. Certainly local wars would then be less likely. But my thought, of course, made nonsense of the now fashionable Western-backed alliances built to "contain" Russia—or, as the Soviets undoubtedly viewed these, to "surround" them.

I was back in Washington only briefly before leaving on another mission, this time to Iraq. After thirteen months of negotiations, the United States and Iraq had signed a grant military aid agreement. Once again our embassy in London prevailed, and conferences with the British while we were en route to Iraq were part of our schedule. This time, however, the U.S. government was eager to share with Great Britain responsibility for the first grant arms-aid program to an Arab state. Israel and the Zionist Organization of America had pulled out all stops in order to block aid to Iraq, although it would be nearly two years before any equipment would arrive. Furthermore, no more than $30 million was allocated over a three-year span. Iraq's public commitment to use the arms only in self-defense or for internal security did nothing to quiet the protests. Before our departure, President Eisenhower found it necessary to announce that the aid was to help fight communism, not to assist in any local wars.

This visit to London was easier. Lists of British equipment available to supplement what Iraq already had were passed to us, and we went on our way. In Iraq, we saw that tank transporters to carry fresh equipment to Kurdistan and the mountain passes were what the Iraqis most needed. But, unfortunately for Iraq, such militarily practical units were proscribed lest they be used in a move west toward Israel. Explaining to the Iraqis that we would therefore recommend signal and light-artillery equipment, we added our conditions: we would have a large military assistance advisory group (MAAG) posted throughout Iraq to train and, as required by U.S. law, to observe the end use of all American equipment. Thus, the U.S. could block any intended aggression against Iraq's neighbors. As these discussions proceeded, I was thankful it had not fallen to me to explain how we expected Iraq to defend the mountain passes on the Turkish and Iranian borders from Russian advances without being able to move into place even the light military equipment we would supply. Once again, I thought we were deluding ourselves—or, in this case, merely bolstering a flagging British economy and Britain's waning political position in Iraq.

■ ■ ■

By the time our report on Iraq had been submitted, I learned some very good news. Henry Byroade had pressed for the appointment of an officer responsible for dealing with the Department of State on Middle East policy matters also of interest to the Office of the Secretary of Defense (OSD). It was unusual for a reserve officer to be considered for a policy job in OSD, and particularly for an officer of my grade to be charged with an area as important as the Middle East. Nonetheless, I had the job. I was not only moving from the army general staff to OSD but had once more escaped from intelligence with the support of the army's G-2, this time to one of the top staff jobs in the Pentagon. My title was "Chief of the Middle East Branch, Plans and Policy Division, Office of Foreign Military Affairs, Office of the Assistant Secretary of Defense, International Security Affairs." In short, C/MEA, P&P, OFMA, OASD-ISA.

The Office of the Secretary of Defense was a busy place, each officer too occupied to have time for the petty empire building so often characteristic of government bureaucracy. Because of all this and of the small size of the staff, I soon found that if you did your job well your advice would be heeded at the assistant-secretary and secretary levels. Being there was a great opportunity for me. In my job I worked often with the head of the Office of Foreign Military Affairs, Vice Admiral Arthur C. Davis (he was also deputy assistant secretary of defense, ISA).

In the course of my work I had to have knowledge of two National Security Council documents. The first, NSC 5428, "U.S. Policy in the Middle East," was in fact no more than a set of pious platitudes. It encouraged moves to settle the Arab-Israeli dispute; pointed to Foster Dulles's "northern tier" as the states to be encouraged in collective defense measures and to be provided arms according to their capacity to absorb them; and advocated measures to strengthen the traditional positions of our Western allies in the Middle East.

The second document, however, NSC 5401, "Denial of Petroleum Resources," was no passive policy statement. It contained plans for the military and the CIA to ensure that Middle East oil fields would be denied an invading Soviet army. If necessary, the oil fields would be totally demolished. This was essentially a navy-instigated policy, based on the recognition that even as access to this petroleum had enabled the Allies to win World War II, so the West's naval and ground forces were now similarly dependent on Middle Eastern oil. Since Western and indigenous forces were incapable of stopping a conventionally mounted Russian strike into the area, should it be executed in concert with a land attack on NATO's forces by the Warsaw Pact nations, we'd have to deny the Soviets Middle Eastern oil until our military could recover the area.

Obviously, the British, American, and possibly the French oil companies holding concessions in the area knew of this policy, since it would be difficult to place demolitions materials and technicians trained to use them without their cooperation. What choice, really, did the oil companies have? But more important by far was the question of whether any of the oil-producing countries knew what we might do to their oil reserves. I suspected they didn't. This, then, was one of our most sensitive NSC policies. It was, in fact, the *only* unambiguous policy we had for the Near East, South Asia, and Africa.

Studying this document, I was disturbed. I feared that if a Russian attack became imminent, we would follow its recommendations and be left—given the platitudes of NSC 5428 and its lack of contingency plans—to improvise according to the day-to-day pressures on the president and the secretary of state. Of course, the Joint Chiefs of Staff had plans for eventual recovery of the Middle East. But what if the threatened Russian attack didn't materialize and the Arabs, embittered by our destruction of their vast resources, invited the Soviets in as friends and not enemies? Could we then face international opinion and justify taking back what we'd destroyed?

In my new capacity, when Iraq's new chief of the general staff, General Rafiq Arif, and Major General Abbas Ali Ghalib arrived, I introduced them for talks with the secretary of defense, and then accompanied them on a tour of the U.N. (as well as an army-financed weekend at New York nightclubs). From there they proceeded to a month-long tour of defense installations in a special mission aircraft with escorts from G-2's foreign-liaison office.

Not long afterward, Admiral Davis told me that Colonel Chaim (Vivian) Herzog, defense attaché of the Israeli embassy, was coming to see him, and asked me to be present at the meeting. When Herzog arrived he informed us that Major General Moshe Dayan, Israel's chief of staff, was on his way to the United States and wanted to see the secretary of defense in order to discuss military equipment.

"Who asked him here?" Davis inquired.

"We did—our embassy," Herzog replied.

Silent for a long moment, Davis looked down at his hands and said: "You keep Eveland advised, and he'll arrange that your general meets someone." With that, the admiral stood up and shook hands. The meeting was over.

As we walked to Colonel Herzog's car, he asked why Admiral Davis had been so cool. I was honest in answering that I didn't know. I was still new at these levels, just learning what went on. As we parted, Herzog asked me to tell Admiral Davis that General Dayan also hoped to take a tour of U.S. military installations.

I'd just returned to my desk when I was told that Admiral Davis was waiting to see me. As I entered his office I found him smiling, and his smile turned to a grin when I passed on Herzog's added request. Davis had not only expected to hear from the Israelis as soon as they knew of the Iraqi visit, but he'd expected them to ask for equal treatment point for point. "If we crank up an Arab Middle East-defense organization," Davis joked, "and representatives of all the Arab countries visit for joint planning conferences, we'll have Dayan on our hands at least twice a month."

The point, Davis explained, was that the Iraqis had come on an official visit—Iraq had just signed a military-aid agreement with us. Dayan's visit was unofficial and he'd not been invited. Were the Israelis to sign a military-aid agreement with us, no doubt he'd be invited on the same terms as the Iraqis. But Israel, Davis said, was unwilling to accept military aid with the kind of conditions for the presence of American observers that we'd imposed on the Iraqis.

For these many reasons, then, the secretary of defense would not see Dayan. As deputy assistant secretary, Davis would be his host, and I would help handle arrangements for the meeting.

On the appointed day I greeted this famous general, whose combat missions dated back to the Free French action that had cost him his eye. As we walked down the corridor toward the admiral's office, I dreaded what was coming, wondering if we weren't going to be too harsh with a man whose concern reflected the position of his Arab-surrounded army. I was certain that Admiral Davis knew just what he wanted to say, and would be backed up by the White House: few if any decisions relating to Israel were taken without assurances that they would withstand domestic Zionist and congressional pressure.

Dayan came right to the point. He'd been authorized by his government to request that Israel be granted the same quantity of arms Iraq would receive from us, he said. Prepared for this, Admiral Davis replied that he was sure Congress would act favorably on any legitimate request for arms for Israel under the Mutual Security Act and that the Pentagon would recommend whatever Israel required for self-defense. Dayan smiled; Herzog had probably prepared him for a brush-off.

When Dayan passed Davis a list of Israel's needs, however, the admiral returned it without a reading, and Dayan protested that Israel was merely asking for equipment equal in value to what Iraq was to receive. Davis replied that I'd just returned from Iraq, and would probably be able to estimate whether, as we were doing in Iraq, we'd have to send fifty or a hundred U.S. military advisers with any equipment given or sold to Israel. When Dayan started to object, Davis pushed on, saying that Congress insisted on such terms in order to ensure that U.S. equipment was used only for self-defense. Surely Dayan couldn't object to that, Davis said.

But Dayan did. Israel was a sovereign country, he protested. Its defense plans and preparations were state secrets. No foreign advisers—American, British, Russian, or any other—would ever set foot on any Israeli military installation. (And none ever has, in an end-use [MAAG] inspection capacity—an exception granted by Congress in Israel's case.)

I thought this exchange would end the conversation, but, as a good general, Dayan had an alternate plan of attack and knew about our other military-equipment programs. Offshore procurement—the device through which the United States helped save the hard currency of NATO countries by assisting them to build local armaments industries—was what he asked about next. The Israelis, he said, already had an armaments industry and were selling some small arms abroad. Now Israel wanted to become a major supplier to NATO.

Parrying Dayan's suggestion, Admiral Davis pointed out that the U.S. supported offshore procurement only for and in countries with which we shared defense alliances. Therefore, Israel did not qualify. Were Israel and the Arabs to make peace and jointly defend the Middle East, Davis continued, the United States could start arms factories in all the developed states of the area.

Not finished yet, Dayan tried another tack, saying that since he'd come so far for nothing, he wanted at least to make a tour of U.S. service schools in order to observe Israeli army personnel in training. Again Davis gave nothing away, saying that responsibility for arranging such tours rested with the individual military services, that three months' planning had been required to accommodate the Iraqis—and this after their government had signed a bilateral aid agreement with the United States. Rising to his feet, Admiral Davis extended his hand. The meeting was over. I was left to accompany a silent General Dayan to the exit.

My next task was to work with the Joint Chiefs of Staff and the three services to prepare specific recommendations for a grant military-aid program for Egypt. Back in March, the decision that Egypt was eligible for such support had marked the first instance of the United States offering grant military aid to an Arab country that had a common border with Israel. We'd done this in order to ensure a peaceful departure of the British from their Middle East Land Forces' Suez base. As one price for evacuating most of its troops, Britain had sought the right to retain a garrison whose sole purpose would be defense of the Suez Canal, but Egypt had refused. In order to break the stalemate, the United States offered to provide Egypt with the arms that would enable it to defend Britain's Suez Canal lifeline. Confronted with the U.S. offer, Britain had to abandon its garrison stipulation or acknowledge that its interests in remaining were political rather than military.

Working with representatives of several government agencies, I helped prepare a determination of eligibility for President Eisenhower's approval, two important provisions of which were that the arrangements between Egypt and the United States were vital to the defense of the Near East and that no U.S. military equipment would be used to undertake aggression against any nation. In August, President Eisenhower signed a top-secret declaration of Egypt's eligibility to receive grant military aid.

Increasing grants of military aid to Iran was quite another thing, however. Preparing for a decision on this question in the NSC, I spent weeks poring over reports from our representatives in Tehran. At that time Iran had two American military missions, one to provide for internal security, the other charged in theory with providing Iran's armed forces with the capability of holding off a Russian invasion until Western forces could arrive to defend the area. In addition, having helped the shah return to his throne, the CIA was using covert funds to support a huge building up of Iran's secret service, SAVAK, to ensure the shah's political survival and suppress communism.

Although the Department of State, apparently ignoring Iran's financial and internal problems, had recommended large increases in the shipment of tanks, artillery, aircraft, and other heavy armaments to the Iranian forces, it was my job, on behalf of Defense, to draw up a position in support of the JCS planners' findings that to the contrary, internal security should be the first priority of U.S. funding in Iran.

I was nervous as I took a seat beside Brigadier General Charles Bonesteel, the Defense member of the Planning Board, at a long table presided over by Robert B. Cutler, President Eisenhower's assistant for national security affairs. A former Boston banker, he was known as "General" in recognition of his wartime service. As I looked around the table, I saw the CIA's deputy director,

Intelligence, Robert Amory, accompanied by his assistant, William Bundy. With them was Richard Bissell, an assistant deputy director of the agency's clandestine services, apparently there to ensure that the combined intelligence community's appreciation of Iran's capabilities as presented by Amory and Bundy would not detract from the case the CIA's clandestine services made for funding the shah personally and for SAVAK. As I continued to look around, I also saw the Foreign Aid Administration's assistant director (NEA), Norman S. Paul, for whom I'd acquired great respect at the Cairo ambassadors' conference.

Still scanning the faces in the room, I tried to guess just what support or opposition I could expect. Henry Byroade would be presenting the State Department's recommendation of military equipment, but I knew that as a former general he would be skeptical of Iran's ability to use this in any significant way. Norman Paul, I thought, would support me in my belief that Iran needed economic aid far more than it did military hardware. The real question was how the CIA would vote. Its clandestine operators carried great weight with Allen Dulles; giving the shah whatever he asked for would help ensure his approval of more covert activities in Iran. Amory and Bundy were brilliant and honest analysts, however; if they had prevailed with Dulles I could count on the facts to support the Defense position. Cutler, I concluded, would be the key, and I hoped that a combination of his general's stars and his banker's fiscal logic would swing the decision my way.

Papers setting forth the position of each department and agency were circulated among us. General Cutler would read each one, invite debate on conflicting viewpoints, or, possibly, simply find a paper consistent with the President's thinking and declare it to be national policy.

I was initially dismayed to see that the recommendations I'd prepared on behalf of the secretary of defense were placed at the bottom of Cutler's pile. That might not be bad, I told myself, since the others might reflect such divergent views that ours would prevail.

The general read slowly. When he reached my paper, I watched nervously when he picked up a red pencil, shook his head, and circled something I'd written. What, I wondered, had been my mistake? Then, in a caustic tone, Cutler said to Bonesteel: "who wrote this thing?"

"Major Eveland, sir; he's sitting here with me."

Red pencil in hand, peering over his glasses, the President's Adviser for National Security Affairs now addressed me directly. "Major," he said, "what in hell do you mean by 'the Iranian army's inability to intelligently and effectively absorb and employ sophisticated military equipment'? That's wrong, doubly wrong! Don't you know that?"

It seemed clear that I'd lost, but I was determined not to be cast as a complete fool. Extracting supporting evidence from my briefcase—a report from the army mission in Iran containing the identical wording and signed by the major general in command—I started to read from it. The gist was that a large shipment of olive-drab paint in drums had arrived in Iran several months before. Iranian tank crews charged with maintaining a shipment of 100 new Sherman tanks had filled their crankcases with the green paint, thinking it was lubricating oil and rendering their engines inoperable.

Even Henry Byroade, whose paper quoted the American ambassador to Iran's affirmation of the combat readiness of Iran's armor to repel the Russians, broke out in laughter. "And, sir," I said to General Cutler, "I've many more examples here to cite."

"You miss the point, Eveland," Cutler shot back. "Your paper not only splits an infinitive; it does so twice! Clean up your grammar and send the paper back to me. I agree entirely that the Iranians are far from ready for more heavy equipment, and I'll send your corrected work to the president and the NSC for final approval as U.S. policy." Then, benevolently, General Cutler smiled at me and declared the meeting concluded.

CHAPTER EIGHT

FAREWELL TO ARMS

I was still elated with my success in the National Security Council meeting when I learned that Ambassador Eric Johnston had returned from four weeks in the Middle East to report that Israel, Syria, Lebanon, and Jordan had accepted the principle of a unified-development project to share the water of the Jordan River. It now seemed possible that Arabs and Israelis would cooperate on a project of mutual benefit, which, soon after it was commenced, would also allow for the resettlement of some Palestinians in the Jordan Valley. And, I thought, such cooperation toward a common goal might be the large first step toward a final peace treaty between the Arabs and Israelis.

On October 24, Egypt and Britain signed a pact settling their dispute over evacuation of British troops from the Suez base. This was another favorable sign. With it came my involvement in still another aspect of the negotiations of America's top-secret commitment to provide arms to Egypt. Ambassador Jefferson Caffery had met in Cairo with Egyptian foreign minister Mahmoud Fawzi, and had been told that after careful consideration, the Egyptian government had decided not to ask for U.S. military aid at that time. Instead, Fawzi had strongly urged that we increase the amount of our economic aid to Egypt to allow it to make a modest start on building up military strength from its own financial resources.

Since Egypt had apparently elected to follow Israel's pattern of preferring economic to military assistance, Caffery had concluded that "the United States was relieved of its commitment to extend arms aid to Egypt."

Caffery's report set off a flurry of CIA-instigated meetings in the Operations Coordinating Board (OCB), that arm of the NSC that had responsibility for monitoring the implementation of NSC policies and approval of major expenditures of covert funds. Without argument from the State Department, the CIA pointed out that Ambassador Caffery had no entree to Prime Minister Nasser. All U.S. diplomatic negotiations concerning arms aid, they noted, had been conducted with Nasser by Kermit Roosevelt of the CIA and members of the CIA station in Cairo. Nasser, according to Roosevelt, wanted frank discussion of alternate means of providing military assistance to Egypt. The CIA planned to offer Nasser $3 million in covert funds for the purchase of "certain morale-building items of military equipment such as uniforms and staff transportation." In addition, the CIA had arranged with the Foreign Operations Administration to conceal $5 million in "nonattributed" military-aid funds within a total economic-aid grant of $40 million to allow Egypt to purchase additional military equipment "as determined by the U.S. to be desirable." No military survey team would be required under this covert arrangement circumventing the provisions of the Mutual Security Act. Nonetheless, under the CIA plan, Pentagon negotiators in civilian clothing could be sent to discuss a formal agreement for grant military assistance of $20.1 million now allocated to Egypt and to agree on how the "nonattributed" $5 million of Defense money could be spent.

Assigned to prepare the secretary of defense's position on the CIA proposal, I recommended that we oppose it as contrary to law. My position was accepted and carried to the OCB meeting. One major objection I cited was Egypt's reported need for between $50 and $100 million in U.S. arms aid. Given this, I argued, I doubted that the $8 million proposed by the CIA as a covert "sweetener" would have much effect once Nasser learned that only $20.1 million in grant military assistance would be available. And of this

$20.1 million, the Department of State was now asking that a quarter of it be diverted to Ethiopia for political purposes. Thinking back to my survey trip to Pakistan and that country's angry response to being offered less equipment than they'd expected, I concluded that we'd do better to accept Foreign Minister Fawzi's refusal through normal diplomatic channels; this covert arrangement might backfire.

In the OCB meeting my recommendation was overruled; the CIA prevailed. Furthermore, the OCB instructed Defense to select two qualified officers to go secretly to Egypt to meet with Nasser under arrangements to be made by the CIA. Still supporting me but wise enough to know when to yield, Admiral Davis had a proposal of his own. "If we can't lick 'em," he told me, "let's join 'em and keep an eye on our money." I was to be one of the two officers to meet with Nasser and was to select the other. Davis readily accepted my suggestion of Colonel H. Alan Gerhardt, who, as a friend of Byroade's, had brought me to the secretary of defense's office from G-2. To qualify himself for general's stars, Gerhardt had left OSD to take over a command, and I arranged that he be borrowed for this mission.[21]

Given that my trip to Cairo meant involvement in an operation arranged by the CIA, I began by going to see Assistant Secretary Byroade to ask if State really endorsed having covert operators of the CIA conduct American diplomacy in Egypt. When I asked Byroade if the Dulles brothers might not between them be making and implementing some aspects of American foreign policy, I was not reassured when he only laughed.

Perhaps Byroade had simply had enough of the thankless task of trying to supervise our policy of impartiality between the Arabs and the Israelis. Although he'd survived a change in administrations, he showed signs of overwork, nor was he optimistic about the prospects for peace. Furthermore, he was soon to be replaced. Two incidents had made him too hot for the administration to handle. First, in a speech in Dayton, Ohio, he'd admonished the

---

21   Other than arranging our meetings, the CIA had no control over our activities or the recommendations we would make at the end of this mission.

Arabs to be realistic and accept the state of Israel as an accomplished fact. In the same speech he'd called on the Zionists to stop appeals for unlimited Jewish immigration to Israel, which only exacerbated Arab fears of Israeli expansion. In spite of the ensuing Zionist demands for Byroade's removal, Secretary Dulles had supported him fully. But then Byroade spoke before Rabbi Elmer Berger's American Council for Judaism in Philadelphia. Though his speech had been studiedly nonpartisan, the fact that he appeared before this forum of anti-Zionist Jews brought great pressure for his resignation. With congressional elections coming up, domestic political considerations made Byroade's removal desirable. Now, it seemed, the time had come for Foster Dulles to take personal control of American diplomacy in the Near East.

Byroade would hardly disappear, however. Allen Dulles and Kim Roosevelt brought to the secretary of state a plan that Byroade found attractive as well. Ambassador Caffery had reached retirement age, and the CIA believed that Gamal Abdul Nasser would soon emerge as the new Egyptian strongman. What better person than Byroade to deal on a personal basis with the young leader of the Revolutionary Command Council officers? Just forty-one, Byroade was a member of Nasser's generation and a military man as well. For this reason, then, Byroade had endorsed both the CIA's proposals for unattributed funding of Egyptian arms purchases and my mission to determine just which types of weapons should be provided. By the time I returned from Cairo, Byroade would be ready to take up his new post and to offer Nasser the military equipment so useful in ensuring continuing Egyptian-army support of the RCC. This all sounded good to me: perhaps the State Department would regain its role, displacing the CIA, as the president's representative in Egypt, through Ambassador Byroade.

Colonel Gerhardt had accepted my suggestion that he join me on the mission to Cairo. Under the OCB's directive, we were to determine whether Nasser would sign an agreement to qualify for the $20.1 million in grant aid and advise on how the $8 million in "funny money" might best be spent. Outranked by the man I'd nominated, however, I could do nothing as Gerhardt wrote our own "terms of reference" in a letter of instructions. This top-secret letter, addressed to Gerhardt and to me, was of no practical value (we couldn't show it to the Egyptians) but spoke of such things as "exploring the nature of U.S. military requirements in Egypt," as if Nasser might be able to invite U.S. troops into the Suez base and agree to commit his country to participation in a regional defense alliance.

As if all this had not dismayed me enough, in a farewell conversation with State's Egyptian-desk officer I received his wishes for the total failure of our mission: career foreign service officers at the Washington-desk level dreaded the CIA's discussions with Nasser about arms for Egypt. Furthermore, pleased to see Byroade replaced by a career diplomat, George V. Allen, they hoped to retrieve American diplomacy for Egypt from the CIA.

Making final preparations for going to Cairo, I kept thinking that in opposing the CIA plan I'd stuck to both common sense and the letter of the law. Neither, apparently, had been enough. Since my trip to Cairo would mark my first involvement in an operation arranged by the CIA, I gave some thought to what I knew about the agency Admiral Davis had suggested we "join" to try to "control."

Just after the end of World War II, President Truman made clear his determination that the United States would not intervene covertly in the internal affairs of other nations. He signed an executive order disbanding the wartime Office of Strategic Services (OSS) and charged the Departments of State, War, and the Navy with liquidating or absorbing the OSS' foreign-intelligence-collection network. Five months later, to ensure that there would be a single source for the type of intelligence that could have warned of Pearl Harbor, Truman instructed the heads of the three departments to which the remaining OSS personnel had been transferred to form a National Intelligence Authority (NIA). With no provisions for additional funding, the NIA was to create a Central Intelligence Group (CIG), headed by a director of central intelligence, responsible for collating all intelligence acquired abroad and furnishing it to the president.

Chiefly in Europe, OSS agents and capabilities for covert action, sabotage, and counterespionage were conserved by senior veterans of that now disbanded agency who'd stayed on with the CIG, men like Richard Helms in Germany and James Angleton in

Rome. Allen Dulles, who'd directed agents against the Axis from his base in Switzerland and had helped bring about Italy's surrender, left the OSS to join his brother Foster's law firm. Before resigning, however, Dulles had helped bring to America a vital source of information regarding Russia's postwar intentions. Nazi Major General Richard Gehlen, Germany's top intelligence expert on Soviet matters, surrendered his staff and files. Alleged Soviet plans to communize Germany and to take over Poland and the Balkan states were now in American hands. Army intelligence acquired control of Gehlen's organization and turned it loose against the communists.

By 1947, Soviet-Allied friendship had turned into hostility, and it seemed that world domination was indeed Russia's ultimate aim. To meet this threat, central control of the competing U.S. armed services was essential. Furthermore, a means of providing the President with consolidated policy guidance was needed in order to deal with the complex issues of the postwar world. The National Security Act of 1947 provided for a secretary of defense, established the National Security Council "to advise the President with respect to the integration of domestic, foreign, and military policies," and created a Central Intelligence Agency to coordinate the collection of foreign intelligence on which U.S. national policy would be based. Rear Admiral Roscoe H. Hillenkoetter, who'd briefly headed the CIG, was named the first director of central intelligence (and the CIA) by President Truman.

Although designed to coordinate the overseas activities of existing intelligence agencies and to evaluate the information they acquired, the CIA soon developed a covert operational capacity of its own. The Communist coup in Czechoslovakia in 1948 and General Gehlen's predictions that more would follow helped bring about this new CIA role. With a "war scare" now gripping the American government, President Truman looked to the CIA to determine Russian intentions and find ways short of war to block them. Soon the old OSS fraternity, including Helms and Angleton, were working for a CIA adjunct under Frank G. Wisner, a lawyer who'd been a close associate of Allen Dulles during the war. Called the Office of Special Operations (OSO), Wisner's group used CIA funding, operated independently of Hillenkoetter, and was supposed to report only to the secretaries of state and defense.

The covert-operational planning of the OSO had been developed in consultation with Allen Dulles. Eager to head it, he then remained aloof after Truman's reelection quashed Foster Dulles's hopes of becoming Dewey's secretary of state. Freewheeling almost without direction, Wisner moved the OSO into clandestine political operations and psychological-warfare ventures that were theoretically subject to review (but not advance approval) by the NSC. Operating largely in Europe, principally in the Balkans, the OSO had only one area it could not enter: the Far East, where General MacArthur relied on his own intelligence sources.

The Communist takeover in China and the outbreak in 1950 of war in Korea brought about developments ousting Hillenkoetter as DCI and bringing Wisner's OSO into line. President Truman appointed General Walter Bedell Smith to head the CIA, and one of his first acts was to appoint Wisner his deputy director for plans (covert operations), with responsibility to Smith alone. Smith then met with MacArthur and used the five-star general's intelligence failures as leverage to gain acceptance of CIA personnel in MacArthur's domain.

In the fall of 1950, General Smith asked Allen Dulles to Washington to help make the CIA work. First serving as Frank Wisner's deputy, Dulles soon became Smith's own deputy and hoped to assume charge of the CIA should the Republicans win in 1952. Meanwhile, he put Gehlen and his organization in Germany under CIA control and provided funds to send agents into the Soviet Union, while Wisner's men mounted operations to encourage the peoples of Russia's satellites to revolt.

Although trained as a foreign-service officer—he had been head of the State Department's Near Eastern affairs office from 1920 to 1923—Dulles seemed to thrive on the excitement of intelligence work, which he'd first done as a young man in charge of intelligence collection at the U.S. legation in Switzerland (in 1918). Seven years younger than Foster, Allen Welch Dulles had little in common with him except the constant affliction of gout. Fond of drink, rich food, and pretty women, Allen Dulles had in fact been the first to court Foster's faithful wife, Janet, but had rejected her as dowdy and unexciting.

When Foster Dulles became secretary of state and Allen Dulles was installed as director of Central Intelligence (DCI), both the heads of armed-services intelligence and J. Edgar Hoover feared that CIA covert political action would take precedence over the collection of intelligence. This fear was confirmed when, under Allen Dulles's direction, the CIA brought about the change in government in Iran in 1953 and, in 1954, toppled the regime in Guatemala.

In addition, CIA operations had started before Allen Dulles became director that had long-range implications from which the United States might find it difficult to disengage. Stemming from his wartime OSS liaison with Jewish resistance groups based in London, James Angleton had arranged an operational-intelligence exchange agreement with Israel's Mossad, upon which the CIA relied for much of its intelligence about the Arab states. The Gehlen organization, meanwhile, was operating with abandon in Soviet-controlled areas, almost beyond the CIA's control. And, in Iran, Allen Dulles's Middle East expert, Kim Roosevelt, was building up Iran's SAVAK to ensure that the shah would not be ousted again. Now, I knew, Roosevelt's contention that Egypt's Gamal Abdul Nasser could be used to further U.S. objectives in the Near East was regarded with caution by most of the State Department experts, but the Dulles brothers seemed content to let Kim "have his head" with Nasser for the present. Given Foster Dulles's control of foreign-policy strategy, Roosevelt's plans for Nasser appeared to have government approval.

The CIA, then, both because of the Dulles brothers and because of covert work it was doing abroad, seemed now to have an active part in creating U.S. policy. It wasn't the way things were supposed to be, but there was no denying it.

Dressed in civilian clothing for the trip, both because our mission was secret and because Nasser, just rid of 80,000 British troops, had no use for foreigners in uniform, Gerhardt and I set off from New York for Lebanon. As we waited for several days in Beirut for CIA approval to proceed to Cairo, I tried to dissuade Gerhardt from speaking with Nasser about defense alliances, emphasizing the abortive British attempts to induce Egypt to join the MEC and MEDO. Nasser, I argued, would only resent any mention of trading arms for an Egyptian alliance with the West. We should discuss defense alliances, I concluded, only if Nasser brought up the subject, in which case we could point up the political problems inherent in the Arab League and its Collective Security Pact, through which the Arabs had unsuccessfully attempted to unite in opposition to the creation of the state of Israel. Although Gerhardt didn't seem totally convinced, I hoped we'd initiate our mission by discussing how Egypt might best use the $5 million hidden in the FOA funds to purchase U.S. arms of value in supporting the RCC and of use in improving Egypt's internal-security capabilities. Then we could explore with Nasser the question of his willingness to accept a U.S. military assistance-advisory group and thereby qualify Egypt to receive the $20.1 million in grant arms aid earmarked for that country by the military services.

The next morning we learned that President Naguib had been accused of implication in a plot to assassinate Nasser, who was now expected to assume the presidency, and I speculated that we'd been delayed in Beirut because the CIA had knowledge of possible trouble in Egypt. Although thankful that the agency was apparently fulfilling its assigned intelligence gathering functions, I also wondered if the CIA had plotted with Nasser to get rid of Naguib.

Miles Copeland of the CIA station met us at the Cairo airport. Six feet tall, he had a head of thick, sandy hair and wore horn-rimmed glasses over eyes that danced with excitement. Miles brandished Nasser's name liberally in sweeping us through airport formalities and in registering us at the Semiramis, Cairo's most important hotel, just one block from the American embassy. So much for secrecy, I thought. We left for Copeland's home in the suburb of Mahdi.

Well out from the new homes and apartments of Cairo's fashionable Gizera district, Mahdi was where the senior British officials who had governed Egypt once lived. Arriving at Copeland's sprawling villa, we met his wife, Lorraine, and a number of American couples, all part of the Cairo CIA station. Many had brought their children, who, with the Copelands', ran in and out of the house. There seemed to be an equal number of dogs.

Speaking with Miles and James Eichelberger of the Cairo CIA station, I learned that Copeland operated under commercial cover instead of having the embassy status that protected Eichelberger and gave him office space. It was as representative of the management-consulting firm of Booz, Allen, Hamilton International that Copeland conducted business from his home, dealing constantly with Nasser, among other tasks, except when Kim Roosevelt was in Cairo. Copeland hinted that Roosevelt had "invented" Egypt's new president and conducted high U.S. policy discussions with him much as he did with the shah of Iran, who, Copeland reminded us, had been "saved" by Roosevelt.

When Colonel Gerhardt was swept off by Lorraine Copeland to meet the ladies, Miles took me and Jim Eichelberger into his office to speak further. Wanting to learn more about our upcoming meeting with Nasser, I asked if Kim Roosevelt would come to Cairo to accompany us. No, Copeland responded, putting me in my place, Secretary Dulles saved Kim for the big things. He'd come in when the whole grant aid package was approved for announcement to Nasser. I was startled but bit my tongue. Why would the CIA have a hand in the grant-aid package? I wondered. Wasn't this something for the American ambassador to do?

I was still chewing on this when Copeland went on. Kim, he said, as I no doubt knew, had staged King Farouk's ouster and had now moved up Nasser to run the country.[22] "I didn't know,"

_____

22   In his book *The Game of Nations* (New York: Simon and Schuster, 1969, pp. 62–64), Copeland credits Roosevelt with the "peaceful revolution" that permitted King Farouk to abdicate unharmed. Planning to replace Farouk with civilian politicians, Roosevelt, Copeland writes, agreed to a military coup after deferring to Ambassador Caffery's conclusion that only the army could cope with the deteriorating situation in Egypt.

Not only does this seem totally out of character for Caffery, but I also know that the July 1952 coup caught the CIA completely by surprise. First U.S. knowledge came through Lt. Col. Evans, an assistant air attaché, who had contacts with RCC officers, and through William Lakeland, Caffery's career foreign-service second secretary for political affairs. Caffery did insist on seeing Farouk off from Egypt and thereby gained great respect from the Revolutionary Command Council, who saw that this distinguished diplomat would deal only with the legitimate head of state. Had the CIA and Roosevelt

I said. As I soon discovered, this was a favorite Copeland tactic. By including you as one "in the know," he often gained acceptance of what he'd said from those too timid to acknowledge that they hadn't been privy to his "secret."

Trying to get Copeland back to the subject of our mission, I said, "Miles, we're only here to discuss how Egypt will spend the $5 million in the FOA package on U.S. equipment for internal-security purposes."

"Oh, that," Miles replied, shrugging. "Ahmed Hussein, the Egyptian ambassador in Washington, will deliver the list to the Pentagon."

Knocked out of my real "terms of reference," I asked Copeland about the $3 million in CIA funds. "Isn't it going to be spent," I asked, "on morale-building military equipment, uniforms, and staff transportation?"

Copeland looked at me as if he'd have to teach me the facts of life. "Bill," he said, "that's already spent. I'm just waiting for the CIA finance officer in Beirut to gather up and pouch down the money so I can hand carry it to Nasser at his home."[23]

I asked Copeland how this was possible. The OCB had not approved either covert grant of funds until two weeks before.

---

not found in Nasser "another potential 'agent' like the shah," Caffery might well have continued to deal with Naguib and later with Nasser, providing wise counsel that might have averted the disastrous days for the U.S. that followed.

In 1972 I discussed with Kim Roosevelt Copeland's allegation that the CIA had arranged Farouk's ouster. Then profiting from his company's representation of the shah and the Saudis in Washington, Kim had become modest. He claimed that he'd never have been able to gain the confidence of his customer monarchs if he'd really ousted Farouk.

23   *Ibid.*, pp. 176–178, Copeland writes of personally delivering the $3 million—short one ten-dollar bill!—to Hassan Touhami, Nasser's aide. Touhami reported back that Nasser was infuriated with what he considered an attempt to bribe him and was insulted that Roosevelt would think him susceptible. Initially, apparently, Nasser planned to send the money back to Roosevelt. Then, fearing that his fellow RCC members might learn of it, he came up with another plan. A tall, thin tower was erected on an island just in front of the new Nile Hilton Hotel. Now known as the Tower of Cairo, Copeland writes, its unofficial name is *el wa'ef rusfel*, "Roosevelt's erection."

"Yes," Copeland said, "but Kim and Allen Dulles knew it was coming. I passed on the news to Nasser to bolster his morale after the attempted coup." When I asked if Hank Byroade knew about all this, assuming that these were announcements he, as new ambassador, would want to make to Nasser, Copeland said that "Kim may tell him." Copeland then explained that Byroade had earned a good rest and that his assignment to Egypt would provide it. Intimating that Nasser might soon be the spokesman for all Arab nationalism, Copeland suggested that Byroade could still function *de facto* as the assistant secretary of state for the area, with Nasser and the CIA doing all the work for him.

Long since, I'd heard more than enough but considered it essential to learn what I could, so I asked Copeland if Nasser expected us to discuss the $20.1 million in grant military aid reportedly rejected for the time being by Foreign Minister Fawzi. Copeland said that Nasser probably regarded such a small offer as an insult, that he would hand Gerhardt and me a list of a hundred million dollars or more as an appropriate initial program. Hearing this, I wondered if Miles had encouraged Nasser to believe that we'd given our minimum figure and would be prepared to negotiate upwards. Whatever the facts, I told Copeland that $5.5 million of that $20.1 million was probably going to Ethiopia, and, furthermore, that the Pakistanis might have the balance before Gerhardt and I got back to Washington. Grinning, Miles suggested that there were other ways of getting into Defense funds. "You and Al should be prepared to talk big money when you meet Nasser tomorrow night," he said.

When Gerhardt and I finally departed for our hotel, I carefully avoided any discussion of our mission during the ride back to town. I feared that if I told Gerhardt what Copeland had said, he'd fire off a message to the Pentagon insisting that our mission to Egypt be terminated. I was confident that we could deal well with Nasser and was reluctant to jeopardize this opportunity to meet him. We'd be better off, I concluded, knowing just what the CIA had promised and how Nasser really felt about accepting a military advisory mission.

At the appointed hour the next evening, Al Gerhardt and I were collected by Copeland at the hotel entrance. Uncertain of

where we'd meet Nasser, I questioned Miles about the arrangements. "Junior's safe house," was the answer. "It's located in Mahdi
not far from my home." Junior! Who in hell was he? I wondered,
expecting he might be a batman, or enlisted servant, assigned to
Egypt's new president. "I'd better tell you about Junior," Copeland
said. "He's an army major, one of Nasser's closest confidants, a top
man in the secret police and the man who arranges my meetings
with Nasser in the CIA safe house to which we are going." Junior's
real name, we learned, was Major Hassan Touhami. "You'll like
this young fellow," Miles said as we drove past the side of a tree-
shrouded villa and parked behind the house. "Just don't take him
too seriously."[24]

As we entered the villa by its back door, we were greeted by a
smiling Major Touhami. Copeland still grinned as he introduced
us, but he displayed deference to Hassan as our host. We were
early, deliberately, expecting that Nasser might be precise in keeping the appointment. As we waited, Miles teased Touhami about
the secret police following the "two American colonels" (being still
a major, I was flattered). Touhami insisted that he was merely trying to protect the "important representatives of America's secretary of defense."

Just as I lit a cigarette to calm my nerves, I heard the rear door
open and saw Nasser and a tall, thin man come toward us. We
jumped to our feet as Nasser asked which one was Gerhardt. Identifying himself, Al found a huge hand extended in greeting. "And
you must be Colonel Eveland," said this tall, husky man, whose
face was as handsome as the one I'd seen in posters all over town.
(Copeland had obviously promoted me, yet Nasser seemed to
know that Al Gerhardt was the senior "colonel.") Nasser's shiny
white teeth showed as he grinned and shook my hand warmly,
then introducing Major General Abdul Hakim Amer, the new

---

24   Just how important "Junior" was, and continues to be, has since been
revealed. As chief aide to Nasser until his death, Touhami was appointed
"deputy prime minister at the palace" by President Sadat and later met secretly
in Rabat with Moshe Dayan to conclude the arrangements leading to Sadat's
historic trip in 1977 to Jerusalem. As a key adviser, he accompanied Sadat to
the Camp David summit meetings with President Carter.

chief of Egypt's general staff. Why not, I thought, let Nasser hear my best classical Arabic, since this was normally used in speech-making. I was sure that I'd do better than I had with Alexandria's guides four years before, *"le ash sherif ya Hadrata ar rais, wa rais arkan al jaish; ahlan wa shalan* (I am honored, O Excellency the president, and chief of the general staff; this is your house and we are your family)." I'd done the right thing: Nasser broke out into a loud laugh of appreciation. At that point Copeland lied, describing me as a scholar of Arabic. He added, undiplomatically, that I'd been an army attaché in Baghdad.

Nasser laughed again and said that I must be acquainted with his old friend that sly fox Nuri as Said. I acknowledged this, knowing that the two Arab leaders would gladly murder each other. I was worried that already we were treading too close to Nasser's suspicions that Iraq might join up with a Western defense alliance, but the president seemed unperturbed and asked if we'd like to talk about military equipment for a time before Hassan Touhami served one of his home-cooked Egyptian dinners. Hakim Amer, he said, had brought along a list.

At Nasser's suggestion we sat at the dining-room table. He then took off his jacket and tie, saying we should do the same thing so that we might talk in comfort. From his pocket Nasser took two packs of Kents and placed them on the table. Hassan rushed off to produce large ashtrays for all of us. Other than to shake hands and pass brief greetings, neither Copeland nor Touhami had uttered a word. It was obvious that Nasser's presence commanded any audience; he was accustomed to taking the lead. He sat with hands crossed on the table and a wide toothy grin—one cigarette was already in the ashtray and he'd lighted another. He was a magnificent-looking man, in good shape, with a large head and close-cut, slightly kinky black hair with traces of gray sprinkled through it. Having melted us with his smile, he said, cordially, "You men have come a long way to see us. We appreciate it and want you to know you're welcome." His English was flawless, with only the slightest trace of an accent.

We started to examine the several pages Hakim Amer passed us, but Nasser abruptly suggested that we look at them later.

Asking me about just how U.S. aid was furnished, he listened attentively as I described both the survey team and the military advisory group that would work out with the host country's armed forces a detailed program of equipment and training aid. Hearing this, Nasser said that there was no way he could survive politically if he permitted American officers and soldiers to take up posts on Egyptian soil. Egypt had just, after thirty-two years of "occupied independence," arranged for the evacuation of the 80,000 British troops at the Suez base, and the recent attempt on his life had been caused in part by reaction to his agreement that the British might return under certain conditions.

Knowing that Nasser was right, I suggested that we could send only a small mission, which could wear civilian clothing when visiting any large city. Nasser laughed, asking if I'd ever seen a general who could do without the perquisites of his rank, a soldier-driven staff car with a starred flag denoting his rank. I remained silent, and General-to-Be Gerhardt didn't argue the point.

"So that we can't do," Nasser said, "at least not right now."

We then moved on to talk about the mutual-aid agreement, which Nasser said he had looked at briefly. "Half the secretary of defense's office must be lawyers," Nasser joked, referring to the agreement's length and fine-print provisions. Although Al suggested that a relatively abbreviated agreement was possible, Nasser didn't really seem interested. He continued to chain-smoke, his eyes darting about nervously. I wondered if he was seeing us just to be courteous.

At this point, just as I'd feared, Al Gerhardt launched into a discussion of regional security and defense of the Middle East against the Soviets. To my surprise, Nasser seemed to urge him to go on, and for twenty minutes Al held forth about NATO, SEATO, and the need to defend the Middle East against our common enemy, the Russians.

Nasser finally interrupted Al to say that he was hungry, and while we ate there was little in the way of serious conversation. When our discussion resumed, Nasser said that our common enemy was not Russia but Israel. He wasn't just talking about what the Arabs believed, he said, but considered American attachment to Israel dangerous for us in the long run. Furthermore, he said, he'd seen no signs of Russian hostility except to the defense organizations we were erecting to surround the Soviet Union. Hakim Amer added that the Arabs already had their own defense organization, which was adequate to protect them from any external threat. Apparently having heard this too many times, Nasser asked if we'd like a drink.

As we sat with our whiskeys, I decided to risk talking about the Arab League's Collective Security Pact. As I expected, Nasser said that Egypt, contributing the largest military force, would be in command of the combined Arab armies, and that Hakim Amer would lead the forces. Taking a chance on being kicked out of the room, if not the country, I asked Hakim Amer, who had been promoted from major to general in one jump, just how much combat command experience he'd had and what senior-staff-college training. This, thank God, didn't faze him. He'd learn, he said, although he was young. Furthermore, he told us, the war against the Jews was the only type of combat experience he needed. Egypt, he concluded, would be fighting to defend its own land, not on distant shores as America had done in its wars, and the defense of one's own homeland instilled a brand of patriotism and desire for survival that we couldn't appreciate. He had made some good points, I had to admit to myself.

Nasser had listened patiently, but I felt that he either expected the CIA to produce a miracle or he'd agreed to see us merely out of Arab hospitality. We spoke for another few minutes, and soon it was midnight. The meeting was over.

As I put on my jacket, I pulled out a folded, legal-size copy of the Arab Collective Security Pact and, in jest, asked Nasser whether he would just sign "this" now and allow us to get arms shipments underway. When he asked what it was, I said, only half-incorrectly, that it was a mutual-security assistance pact. Smiling, he said, "Tomorrow, perhaps. I'm too tired to write just now." I was sure he'd joined in my joke, or had he? I knew Arabs put no store in written agreements: good faith of the parties was all that really mattered. Perhaps, as Fawzi had told our ambassador, Nasser just didn't feel the time was ripe. In any case, I hoped that the CIA hadn't promised that they could do things more inexpensively and without papers being signed. If so, we'd have a very angry Arab on our hands when he discovered that neither Kim Roosevelt nor Allen Dulles, nor, for that matter, Foster Dulles, could alter the laws in this case.

Back at our hotel, Al and I looked over the list of equipment Hakim Amer had prepared: bombers, tanks, heavy artillery—the showy weaponry all armies liked to produce in major parades. At least $100 million would be needed to pay for just a few of these items; the $20 million first authorized would be barely a drop in the bucket. I was glad, therefore, that we hadn't discussed equipment with Nasser. From military attaché reports I'd prepared my own list, largely motor-transport and communications gear to enable Egypt's infantry and armored divisions to function as combined tactical units—not glamorous at all, but they were essential as the first step in building a combat-worthy army.

While Nasser might have admitted to himself that these basic items were of the highest priority, I doubted that he would have said so in front of Hakim Amer. Although they had been badly beaten in the 1947–1948 war, the Egyptian armed forces generally and the RCC officers especially had fought well with little modern equipment; now they needed to see new military hardware to restore confidence in themselves. Little would be gained by discussing this further with Nasser, I felt, and I concluded that it might be better not to meet with him again on this trip. I was sure also that Washington would reject the Egyptian list out of hand: only defensive equipment would be offered, lest a threat to Israel become involved.

Although I now hoped that there would be an end to the CIA role in military-aid negotiations with Nasser and a return to conventional procedures, I had little reason to be heartened when I saw Copeland the next morning. Exuberant as always, he wanted to show us what the CIA was doing to support Nasser and his regime. In a modern apartment building on Gizera Island overlooking all of Cairo, he introduced us to Frank Kearns, a veteran of the CIC with whom Miles had served and now described as a correspondent for CBS news. According to Copeland, Kearns was actually part of the local CIA station and was operating under-cover. Certainly, since Kearns failed to ask us for details of our mission or our talk with Nasser, it seemed that he had little interest in providing CBS with a major news story.

Eichelberger was also present, and Copeland explained that he'd joined the CIA from the J. Walter Thompson advertising agency. Eichelberger now functioned as the "idea man," dream-ing up ways to popularize Nasser's government in Egypt and the Arab world. The CIA, Copeland said, had brought out a leading American authority on "black" and "gray" propaganda, to advise the Egyptians on newspaper and radio activities. They had also brought in a number of Germans to coach the Egyptians, includ-ing the famous Otto Skorzeny, who had rescued Mussolini. Gener-ally ignored and underpaid by the Egyptians, most of the Germans were disenchanted and wanted to leave.

Eager to tell us more, Copeland described the new broad-casting equipment that the CIA was setting up in Egypt, which would be the most powerful in the entire Middle East.[25] Clearly, I thought, the CIA had launched an enormous operation in Egypt, perhaps the largest of its kind since the inception of the agency. I was certain that the more conservative leaders of Iraq, Jordan, Lebanon, Saudi Arabia, and the Sudan would not be pleased.

There seemed to be no end to the surprises Copeland could reveal. What disturbed me most was the youth and apparent immaturity of the people, who seemed to have been given a free hand. Furthermore, there was no resemblance between what I was seeing here and what I'd learned while in Washington about how our government made and implemented foreign policy. It was really frightening, and I wondered how an old-line ambassador like Caffery put up with it.

When I spoke that night with Caffery's deputy chief of mission, G. Lewis Jones, a fine diplomat whom I knew from Washington, he asked me if I'd seen the Eichelberger-Copeland operation. From

---

25   This radio, the Voice of the Arabs, worked so well that we later found it necessary to finance stations in other locations to counter a gift that had been turned against our interests.

his tone I was certain that he found the CIA's high-flying maneuvers as scary as I did. Lewis said that he had instructions from Henry Byroade to arrange that we dine with the ambassador, a protocol-ridden ritual requiring an hour's briefing by Lewis's wife, to be certain that we'd observe the proper formalities. Although only the Cafferys and we would attend, black tie was the uniform, red roses for the ambassador's wife were to arrive precisely one hour before us, and there would be no talk of business until Jefferson Caffery took us to the smoking room for brandy, coffee, and an exactly one whiskey nightcap.

The next day Copeland told us that no further meetings with Nasser would be necessary. The Egyptian equipment list was being sent to Ambassador Hussein in Washington; a team of Egyptian officers would follow in a week or so to discuss specific items with technicians from the three military services. When I asked whether Nasser had changed his mind about accepting a military-assistance advisory group, Miles said we had erred in discussing this in front of Hakim Amer. "Junior," Copeland said, was the man whom Nasser would send to Washington to talk about a MAAG and how this matter might be handled unobtrusively. "So Nasser was still interested?" I asked. "Definitely," Miles replied.

Dinner with Ambassador Jefferson Caffery the next evening was an experience I'll never forget. He was a formidable man, erect, keen-eyed, and appearing much younger than of retirement age. No other American was likely to equal his thirty-five years as a chief of mission: he'd moved to Cairo after serving as our first post-World War II ambassador to France. And no one—certainly not Kim Roosevelt, as Miles had implied—could doubt that Caffery had played the decisive role in the Anglo-Egyptian negotiations on the evacuation of British troops from the Suez base.

A kind host, the ambassador asked us very little about our meeting with Nasser, and we volunteered nothing more than he sought. Had we gushed with enthusiasm and predicted great results, he would have classified us with Copeland, and his CIA colleagues, and I suspected that Caffery's imminent retirement was the only reason he'd agreed to tolerate them. I departed knowing that I'd been in the presence of one of the great American diplomats of our time and did not envy Henry Byroade the task of following him in Cairo. Brilliant as he was, Byroade didn't have Jefferson Caffery's prestige and reputation: I suspected that Foster Dulles would be giving orders to the Cairo embassy, instead of basing U.S. policies toward Egypt on Byroade's recommendations.

As for the arms Egypt required to counter the increasing tempo of Israeli attacks against Egyptian civilians, installations, and military formations in Gaza and the Sinai, I had no doubt that Israel's Mossad was fully aware of our mission to Cairo and had already organized the Zionist lobby in the United States to block a grant aid agreement. In any case, I was now certain that the CIA was even less qualified than the Department of State to determine what the military-equipment requirements of foreign armies might be.

I left Cairo with the feeling that Nasser had detected the State Department's reluctance to implement President Eisenhower's arms-aid commitment to Egypt; unless Henry Byroade could present a convincing military argument for building up Nasser's armed forces, I was afraid, our mission would become a casualty to domestic American political considerations.

CHAPTER NINE

AT THE HIGHEST LEVEL

Back in Washington, Al Gerhardt returned to his command at nearby Fort Meade, leaving to me the task of writing the report on our visit to Cairo. When I learned from Kim Roosevelt that the officers Nasser was sending to continue the arms negotiations would not arrive for several weeks, I decided to postpone our report until after their meetings with military technicians produced agreement on the types of equipment we'd be sending to Egypt.

I soon spoke with Roosevelt again, when he called to say that the shah of Iran would be arriving shortly on an unofficial visit and hoped to see the secretary of defense. Although we both knew that the Department of State was trying to discourage the shah's trip, Kim explained that the Iranian monarch would come in any case. He was still without an heir, and unless Empress Soroya, whose examination by specialists at Johns Hopkins had been arranged by the CIA, could bear a son, a royal divorce was inevitable.

When the shah arrived, he met with the President, Vice President Nixon, and Secretary of State Dulles, none of whom gave him much encouragement about the arms he sought almost as fervently as he did an heir. Late one afternoon, State's Iranian-desk officer informed me that the shah would come to the Pentagon the next morning and asked that I make appropriate arrangements to receive the visiting chief of state. Because Defense Secretary

Wilson was out of town, the shah would have to meet with Deputy Secretary Robert Anderson. Anderson's aides brushed me off as if I were daft: surely, they complained, I must realize that such a busy official's schedule was booked weeks in advance.

Admiral Davis was my last hope, but his secretary said it was the admiral's afternoon for flying and he'd gone to Anacostia Naval Air Station across the Potomac. Rushing there, I arrived at flight operations to find two brown-shoe (naval aviator) admirals checking in from the flight over the capital that had qualified them for that month's flight pay. Davis and JCS chairman Admiral Radford were preparing to head for the officers' club and a drink when I announced to Admiral Davis that we had another "General Dayan problem" on our hands. Once I explained that this one involved the shah of Iran, however, the wheels of the Pentagon began to spin with amazing speed—lubricated, as it were, by oil from the wells of Iran. Deputy Secretary Anderson had formerly been a secretary of the navy: the admirals would have him waiting at ten the next morning. My job was to have a guard of honor and the Marine Band standing by for the shah's arrival. A few telephone calls, citing the JCS chairman as my sponsor, produced everything I needed, including a relaxing drink before dinner at home.

The next morning I was on my own again, however, and, apart from the impressive ceremonial aggregation I'd assembled, I stood alone at the Mall entrance to greet the shah. As national anthems were played, I discovered that I'd rushed out without my uniform cap, and I wasn't sure how to salute bareheaded. I muddled through somehow, certain that the two admirals and others likely to be called into a meeting with our distinguished visitor had found things to do elsewhere.

After I'd introduced myself to Iran's ruler—not daring to remind him that we'd met in 1953 when he'd stopped in Baghdad on his way to a brief exile in Rome—I finally got him up to Anderson's outer office. As we were ushered into the deputy secretary's huge suite, I caught sight of Admiral Radford and the JCS brass exiting through the door at the other end. Although I couldn't read the title of the policy document in Radford's hand, there was no doubt in my mind that it was NSC 107. Now the policy of

discouraging arms for Iran that I'd helped formulate would be disclosed to the shah, and I had visions of being placed in the hot seat
and asked to defend it. Mohammed Reza Pahlavi knew precisely
what he wanted: destroyers, jet fighters, and tanks headed his list.
To my surprise, I was saved by Robert Anderson's apparent failure
to understand or heed the briefing he'd just been given: somehow
the shah left with the impression that his priorities were quite new
to us and that Anderson would look into the requests very carefully. Later, recounting details of the meeting to Admiral Davis, I
was told that Anderson's ploy had been quite deliberate.

For over two years, now, I'd followed Western maneuvering to
bring the states of the Middle East into a regional defense alliance.
Although Britain's grandiose scheme to join distant members of
the Commonwealth (Australia, New Zealand, and South Africa)
with an indigenous organization for the area's defense had been
rejected out of hand by the Arabs, subtle British influence (and the
lure of U.S. arms grants) induced Pakistan to sign a defense treaty
with Turkey in April 1954. Caught by surprise, the State Department at first said nothing, but by the year's end Foster Dulles was
describing this move by the Islamic East as a gain for the West.

The first sound basis for defense of the Near East emerged from
the provisions of the Suez-base agreement (signed in October 1954
with considerable U.S. assistance). The new Anglo-Egyptian pact
allowed British troops to reoccupy Suez in the event of an attack
on any Arab state or Turkey—a member of NATO. This, however,
had not satisfied Great Britain: there was still its unpopular treaty
with Iraq, where renewal was improbable and abrogation a constant threat. Foster Dulles's "northern tier" concept was just what
the British needed to persuade Iraq to sign a defense agreement
with Turkey. Once more, the Department of State was caught off-
balance, especially when the U.K. announced its intention to join
the Turco-Iraqi alliance and urged that the U.S. immediately do
the same.

As logical as this latest pact might have seemed as an arrangement paralleling Egypt's commitment in case of an attack on Turkey (or the Arab states), it gave no consideration to the realities of
inter-Arab political jealousies. For the Egyptians to subordinate

their sovereignty in the event of aggression against Turkey was one thing; for Iraq to enter into a bilateral pact with the Turks was, in Nasser's eyes, an affront to the Arab League and to the entire concept of Arab unity. Soon Radio Cairo's CIA-furnished propaganda apparatus was screaming out attacks against Iraq and the "Western imperialists" behind this move to split the Arabs. First threatening to withdraw from the Arab League (which was legally impossible until 1960), Nasser instead announced plans to promote a counteralliance with Syria, Saudi Arabia, and Yemen.

Unprepared, U.S. policymakers were once more in the position of reacting instead of having alternatives prepared in advance. Now an additional complication was involved: if the U.S. should join, as the British were urging, in a pact embracing Iraq, as an Arab member, it appeared essential to undertake to defend Israel from the Arabs or insist that the Israelis, too, be accepted as members.

It was finally apparent from Admiral Davis's explanation that what I'd heard in Secretary Anderson's office was part of the belated scrambling by the U.S. to develop some sort of a policy to cope with the *fait accompli* with which Britain's machinations had presented us. Iran was the gap remaining in the "northern tier" as the secretary of state had envisioned it, and we'd decided to plug this hole with American initiative, using the shah as our instrument. That we had leverage to play this card seemed certain, as the admiral described just how strong our hand was.

First, in what was to become the most publicly flaunted CIA "secret" accomplishment, Allen Dulles and Kim Roosevelt restored the shah to his throne in 1953, improvising a plan called Operation AJAX. Britain's SIS alleged (and still does) that Roosevelt really did little more than show up in Iran with CIA funds to encourage agents the British had organized and then released to American control.

That Britain alone could not have salvaged Iran's economy, bankrupt after forty months of shut-down petroleum production, was incontestable, though. This had taken the efforts of Herbert Hoover, Jr. (then a special assistant to Secretary Dulles), and Howard Page of Exxon to negotiate the agreement Iran signed with a U.S.-U.K. oil cartel to start Iranian oil flowing to Western Europe again. Unprecedented antitrust exemptions were necessary to permit American oil companies to participate in this consortium, but after the President declared Iran vital to the defense of the United States, the Department of Justice had reluctantly granted them. Now, the State Department went along with a JCS proposal that the shah and his country become a key link in the defense of the entire Middle East.

One thing remained to be done, and only the Shahanshah (king of kings) himself could do this. A still valid Soviet-Iranian friendship treaty gave Russia the right to occupy part of Iran, should that country join or serve as a base for pacts directed against the Soviet Union. Thus, should the shah be willing to stand up to almost certain adverse Russian reactions and threats of war and become America's contribution to the "northern tier" (in lieu of pact membership), we'd be willing to view favorably his requests for additional military equipment—no matter whether the olive-drab paint went into the crankcases or adorned the outsides of the tanks we shipped to Iran.[26] So ended my first lesson in the give and take—as opposed to logic—of foreign relations and defense alliances.

These developments alerted the military services to the advantages of nominating senior officers to OSD positions dealing with Middle East plans and policies, and, as a major, I was now supervising assistants who outranked me. Eager to retain me in my position, Admiral Davis offered a proposal that would allow me to continue on another basis. As a reserve officer, I had the option to request relief from active duty, and advocating that I do this, Davis said that he'd recommend my appointment to one of the civil-service supergrades exempt from the regular rolls. My reservations about giving up the military career I'd sought since my youth soon disappeared when the admiral proposed nominating

---

26   Iran's final decision to join the Baghdad Pact with Turkey, Iraq, Pakistan, and Britain was announced in October 1955. Soviet protests followed immediately. Rejecting Russia's objections, the shah asserted that Iran's membership "was essential to Iran's prosperity" and that the Soviet protest constituted "interference in Iran's internal affairs."

me as a GS-18—the equivalent of a lieutenant general on the Pentagon's "simulated rank" scale. While my conversion to civilian status was being processed, I remained on my job as a consultant to the secretary of defense.

Soon afterward, I was nominated to the permanent staff of the OCB. I especially welcomed this opportunity to move up to the executive office of the president and to learn how policy was coordinated on the White House staff. Located next to Blair House and across Pennsylvania Avenue from the executive-office buildings, the OCB's staff was charged with monitoring interagency implementation of NSC policies through working groups composed of senior representatives of the departments and agencies concerned. It also reviewed all proposals for clandestine political-action operations abroad and major expenditures of covert CIA funds.[27]

Briefed by Elmer Staats, executive secretary of the OCB and head of its permanent staff, and told by him that he hoped I'd stay on with the staff once my super-grade appointment was approved, I was assigned the desk from which I'd exercise my responsibility over NSC policies relating to the Middle East and Africa. From my office I could look across the street to the Oval Office end of the White House. Contemplating my new situation, I thought it would be impossible for me to be closer to the seat of America's policies and power without moving into 1600 Pennsylvania Avenue.

Not long afterward, I met with Sam Kopper. "I hear that you're working for the President now," he said. "How would you like to become an ambassador?" Used to Sam's jokes, I laughed, but he was, in his fashion, quite serious. I should realize, he said, that few of the foreign-policy pronouncements emanating from Washington made sense to the people or governments of the Middle East.

27 The OCB's membership consisted of the under secretary of state (as chairman), the deputy secretary of defense, the director of Foreign Operations, the director of Central Intelligence, and a representative of the President. At the time I joined the OCB permanent staff, these members were Herbert Hoover, Jr., Robert Anderson, Harold Stassen, Allen Dulles, and Nelson Rockefeller (representing the President). Brought along by Rockefeller, Henry Kissinger was then a consultant to the OCB. (Its executive secretary, Elmer Staats, is now comptroller general of the United States.)

Some of our diplomats in that area felt the same way; unfortunately, they had resigned themselves to accepting losses in America's political influence. Those U.S. envoys who attempted to defend our policies were generally too new at their jobs to be effective in dealing with the local governments; therefore, other channels had to be used if U.S. interests were to be preserved in this vital area. How, Sam asked, did I think this was being done? Remembering my experience in Cairo, I thought Kopper might say it was through the CIA, and I decided to hold my tongue.

Urging that I look realistically at America's position, Sam explained that retaining access to the petroleum resources of the Middle East and the transportation routes to ship this oil elsewhere was the only justification for the defense alliances that U.S. foreign policy now encouraged. Aramco and its parent companies understood this, but they could also foresee a day when the energy requirements and economies of the West would be dependent on Middle East oil. Few Arab political leaders were aware of this yet, and not even the U.S. Navy could envision a future in which this oil would be as vital in peacetime as in war. In Sam's opinion, our priorities in diplomacy were reversed: instead of trying to convince the people of Asia and Africa that they were threatened by communism, we should seek to understand this huge segment of the world's population and endeavor to preserve our interests within the framework of their own aspirations.

For these reasons, then, his company was stepping up its government-relations activities in the Near East and, through organizations of the U.N., Kopper was following the tendency of many newly independent nations to adopt positions of neutrality in the quarrels between the East and the West. Furthermore, the present generation of senior Aramco executives was nearing retirement age, and new people with experience in the Near East were needed to assist and eventually replace them. Asked whether I'd be interested, I told Sam that I would like to have specific details about what his company had in mind for me.

The next evening, I dined with Kopper and several Aramco executives, who made a formal proposal that I go to work for them. They told me that in Egypt, Lebanon, and Syria the company employed local representatives to maintain contact with the governments of these countries. In Dhahran, the company's dealings with the provincial governor related mostly to training and employing more Saudis, also helping the most enterprising of these to become contractors to the oil company. A senior vice-president resided in Jidda, on the Red Sea, but in the capital, Riyadh, Aramco did not have regular contacts with either the royal family or the younger, educated Saudis who would someday influence their country's policies toward the West. As I understood it, I'd set up in a large villa at the desert capital and maintain a kind of open house to receive the royal princes and senior government officials. Oriental in its furnishings and in the hospitality it would offer (a library of Islamic history and culture would be provided), this would be a place for getting to know the Saudis on a personal basis. Lobbying and pressure tactics would be proscribed, yet my mere presence would provide better opportunities for gaining the confidence of government officials than those available to the U.S. ambassador in Jidda. Envisioning a comfortable setting to perfect my Arabic and become a real expert on Islam, I expressed genuine interest and asked for some time to think about it. Now my aspirations related to emulating Charles Crane, who had once been considered one of America's foremost authorities on the Arabs and Islam.

I had another reason for my interest in this job—the frustration of working in Washington that had caused Sam to leave the State Department. I was thinking in particular of my report on the Cairo mission. Under constant prodding from Al Gerhardt, I'd completed a summary of our discussions with Nasser. From the start of our mission, I'd been dismayed by Gerhardt's "terms of reference," including his notion that we should comment on the feasibility of negotiating an arms-aid agreement with Egypt. (We'd had one since 1952!) By contrast, the OCB's instructions had asked that we report on "what grant military assistance should be furnished the Egyptian government." My conclusion in the report left it absolutely clear that Nasser was still interested and that the procedures through which grants and sales of arms were made were being followed (by the team of officers Nasser had sent to negotiate with our technicians).

After signing the report I had called Gerhardt to have him assure me that he'd come to the Pentagon and add his signature to mine. In advance, Admiral Davis signed the cover memo transmitting our report to the OCB, and I left these papers with Davis's secretary, with instructions that they be sent on once Al had added his signature.

I gave no further thought to this matter until a summary of the status of military-aid agreements crossed my desk at the OCB. I was startled to read that the military services had actually reserved $35 million for grant aid to Egypt—not $20.1 million— and that these funds had now been released instead to other countries. Why? Because, I read, of a Defense Department finding that Nasser refused to sign a military-aid agreement with the United States. Were they talking about my report? This was crazy.

Furious, I searched in vain for a copy of the report I'd prepared for Gerhardt's signature, but there was no record of its existence at State, Defense, or in the OCB—it had vanished without a trace! Yet the Egypt-desk officer at State (who'd wished me "failure" on our mission) now officially attributed Nasser's refusal to the findings of our mission to Cairo, and funds even greater than we'd known were available were now irretrievably lost.[28] The reversal of my recommendation that we not provide Iran with additional arms had been explained to me, but in this case involving Egypt, it seemed that I'd been deliberately kept in the dark.

Given all this, I had a real interest in Aramco's offer. Oil diplomacy was looking better all the time. I was still weighing my plans when Sam and I attended a reception given by Lebanese ambassador Charles Malik. Shortly after we arrived, Kopper introduced me to Senator Hubert Humphrey and then left, after describing me as an administration expert on Middle East policy. What a dirty trick! Humphrey immediately backed me into a corner and launched into a lecture about how difficult Secretary of State

---

28   In 1978, under the Freedom of Information Act, the Departments of State and Defense furnished me all documents relating to the Cairo mission. It was then that I confirmed that my report had never been registered in the Department of Defense files. It will probably never be known who used my Cairo mission to block military aid to Egypt.

Dulles was making it for the Congress to support the administration's foreign policy. Obviously no fan of Foster Dulles, Humphrey described how the secretary talked down to the Senate Foreign Relations Committee as if they were schoolboys.

Under full steam, Humphrey spoke of the just concluded conference of Afro-Asian nations held in Bandung, Indonesia, where twenty-eight neutral countries had vowed to oppose pro-Western alliances such as the Southeast Asia Treaty Organization (SEATO). Humphrey warned that a new bloc of unaligned nations would someday haunt U.S. efforts to dominate the U.N. and to manipulate tame, unrepresentative governments. Foster Dulles, Humphrey went on, was unable to perceive anything but immorality in the actions of the leaders of emerging nations and saw rejection of alignment with the West as motivated by the devil himself.

Although I knew that the OCB had formed a special working group to deal with the conference and had sent observers discreetly to monitor its proceedings, I'd never given much thought to the possibility that neutrality could be turned from isolation into a force competing with the East-West powers. Fortunately, Humphrey never sensed my ignorance: he was a monologist.

As the crowd thinned out, Charles and Eva Malik asked that Sam and I remain behind. Preparing to depart shortly for Lebanon, where he would become foreign minister, Malik said that he wanted to tell us about something he doubted Secretary of State Dulles would understand. Not merely aware of the Bandung Conference, Charles had just returned from Indonesia, where he'd represented Lebanon as a delegate. Now he was alarmed, fearing that the neutral nations might soon mobilize into a powerful force. (A Harvard Ph.D. in philosophy, a leading churchman, and fervently pro-West, Malik saw no room for neutrality in the East-West struggle.) In Sukarno, Nehru, and Tito, Malik discerned leaders who, courted by both Russia and mainland China, would unite to lead the underdeveloped nations of Asia and Africa, long ignored by the West. He was particularly worried by Nasser, describing him as completely mesmerized by the speeches of this new political grouping and the attention it had showered on him as the man who had most recently evicted the British.

That evening before we left, feeling that I'd learned a great deal, I asked Malik if he'd be willing to present his views on Bandung before the members of the OCB. He said he would, and I promised to make the necessary arrangements.

When I broached this at the OCB staff meeting the next morning, Elmer Staats agreed that having the board members hear Malik would be useful, and then asked me to come to his office for a private meeting. Allen Dulles, he told me, had requested that I be lent to the CIA for a special assignment. The task was to work with Ambassador Moose in Syria to assist in encouraging pro-Western Syrian political leaders to put aside their personal quarrels and unite behind a strong candidate to replace the interim president, who'd served since Syria's military dictator had been forced to flee his country. Staats said that the OCB favored Dulles's request. Feeling that I had little room to refuse, I agreed to meet that afternoon with representatives of the CIA.

Kim Roosevelt came to my office with Richard Bissell, who, like Kim, was an assistant deputy director of the CIA's directorate of plans (DDP—through which covert political-action activities were conducted overseas). Dick Bissell, a tall man whose appearance and speech matched his professional background, began by conveying Allen Dulles's congratulations on my mission to Nasser. Kermit Roosevelt explained what the CIA had in mind for me. "Poor Jimmy Moose in Damascus" was, he said, way over his head in trying to cope with the rapid pace of Syrian political developments and, because he was an introvert, had few contacts with the people who would determine Syria's future. Therefore, Roosevelt said, Allen and Foster (the Dulles brothers, to whom he always referred in that order) had agreed that the CIA should step in to ensure that the U.S. was on top of the situation. State and the CIA had decided, I was told, that I could use my contacts in the Arab world to expand the horizons of the Damascus embassy for a few months and then return to my desk at the OCB.

While Roosevelt apparently had authority to be speaking as he did, I'd met James Moose at the Cairo ambassadors' conference in 1953 and had concluded that he was one of our more perceptive and experienced envoys. Had he been consulted in all this? I wondered. I suspected not. He seemed very much the traditional senior career diplomat, precise and, I thought, unwilling to delegate to others the prerogatives with which the President's personal representative to a foreign country was endowed by both custom and law.

When I asked what Roosevelt thought Ambassador Moose's reaction to my presence would be, he said that if I was willing to take the assignment, the secretary of state would simply notify Moose that I was on my way. Put off by this, I said that I'd not consider the assignment unless it was completely endorsed in advance by the ambassador and clearly acceptable to Assistant Secretary of State George Allen. Both Bissell and Kim hastened to assure me that Allen had been informed already, and pointed out that the OCB's agreement to my absence showed that this wasn't purely a CIA idea.

I then mentioned the offer I'd received from Aramco and said that I would have to be sure that nothing associated with the Damascus trip would in the future prejudice my possible employment by the oil company. Because of this, I insisted that I be supported by Department of State travel orders and able to operate in the open with the full knowledge of the embassy's staff. Undaunted, Kim agreed and proposed that I meet with Deputy Assistant Secretary Jack Jernegan, who was in charge during George Allen's absence from Washington, and set up arrangements with which I'd be comfortable. If my conditions were met and I decided to accept the assignment, a CIA man in charge of Syrian affairs, Walter Snowdon, would contact me to arrange funding for my travel and other expenses. Because Allen Dulles was personally behind this, a single predeparture meeting with Snowdon at my convenience would suffice to get me off to Damascus.

When I was alone again, I pulled out my files of State telegrams from Damascus. One immediately caught my attention: the new chief of staff of Syria's army had approached Ambassador Moose, through an intermediary, asking if the U.S. would sell arms to Syria under the reimbursable-aid provisions of the Mutual Security Act. This kind of thing was right up my alley, I thought. It seemed that Syria's new civilian government was willing to reverse the previous Syrian position of refusing to sign any type of foreign-aid agreement with the United States. If so, I might be of real value to Ambassador Moose in expediting the approval in Washington of arms sales to bolster army support of the Syrian government.

Sam Kopper was still in town, and I asked him if I could postpone acceptance of Aramco's offer for a few months in order to permit my travel to Syria on a Department of State assignment. Kopper spoke of pipeline transit rights that Aramco would soon have to negotiate with the Syrian government, and encouraged me to take whatever time was necessary to familiarize myself with that country's complex politics; anything I learned would be of value to his company, he said. I then went to see Jernegan, who'd conducted the Cairo ambassadors' conference, and I asked for his frank views concerning the Department's and Ambassador Moose's attitude toward my working for the CIA in Syria. Jack was pleased that I'd consider the assignment, and he agreed to query Moose to be certain that I'd be welcome. As I left, I felt excitement at the prospect of being able to return to the Near East and to become a part of its political evolution.

CHAPTER TEN

SPOOKY CORRIDORS

I soon got a call from Jack Jernegan, who told me that my diplomatic passport was ready and read a message from Ambassador Moose welcoming me. Pleased that this crusty career diplomat had agreed to my mission, I was glad to have evidence that I'd be able to work openly in Syria and not be involved in secret meetings with CIA personnel.

Alerted by Kim Roosevelt, the CIA knew of Moose's response, and I received a phone call from a man who identified himself as Walter. Clearly this was Snowdon, but he said he'd heard I was planning a trip abroad and wondered if I might be able to look up an old friend of his. Considering this subterfuge silly but assuming that there might be some method to the CIA's madness, I agreed to meet him the next day. Then, just playing the game, I thought, I added that I'd picked up my passport and would collect my travel orders as soon as I'd chosen a departure date. Snowdon cut me off quickly and, after reconfirming the time of our appointment, said that he'd be waiting outside the main entrance of the Roger Smith Hotel. He'd be carrying a copy of the *New York Times* so that I'd be able to pick him out.

How professional all this was, I thought—as long as too many people weren't carrying the *Times* while waiting at the same door. It seemed ludicrous. Here I sat in offices Roosevelt and

Bissell had felt free to come into, but Snowdon and I were playing cloak-and-dagger.

When I reached the Roger Smith the next day, I approached a man whose face was hidden behind a copy of the *Times* and found that I'd guessed right. As we went in for a drink in the hotel's cocktail lounge, I had trouble taking the whole business seriously: Snowdon resembled Mickey Rooney in size and appearance. Passing me a large manila envelope, he whispered that what I'd need for my trip was inside it. When I said that I wouldn't be leaving until June 6, Snowdon seemed irritated. This would be my one contact with the agency, he told me, and I was not to go near a CIA building. Since I'd made trips to the CIA's headquarters compound before, I considered this precaution strange, to say the least. He then asked for my passport and seemed unhappy that I'd been accorded diplomatic status. I had no idea why.

I was asked to memorize some names, which were under no circumstances to be written down. First, I now had a new name—Perry M. Chapworth—by which I would be known while working with the agency.[29] Snowdon instructed me to get used to my pseudonym and to perfect a signature to go with it.

The second name he gave me was that of Walter Campbell, the CIA chief of station in Syria. I was not to see him on my arrival but instead make an appointment to see the ambassador. Later, Campbell would send instructions for our first meeting. Perhaps naturally obstinate, or because I knew how small our embassy was and had just learned, from Snowdon, that Campbell's office was located in a mid-floor alcove between the embassy's second and third floors, I suggested that Campbell might simply join the ambassador and me behind closed doors when I arrived. "Too insecure," Snowdon said. "Secretaries and local employees might notice." This, too, seemed insane: Campbell had State Department cover. Why would I avoid him?

---

29   Pseudonyms are devised in the following way: using an old telephone directory from the Australian outback, a young clerk in the CIA opens a page at random, closes her eyes, points a finger, and finds a name.

I was given several papers to sign—as Perry M. Chapworth—during moments when no one was watching. I signed a cash receipt for $2,000 for travel expenses, and a form on which I wrote instructions for banking my salary. Finally, there was a paper referring to the funds I'd be advanced and the monthly "fee" for my services. This required me to acknowledge that I was an independent contractor and not an employee of the CIA or the U.S. government. It seemed a standard receipt form, presumably to preserve "security," but I was glad that my assignment would involve nothing illegal, since the government could deny knowing me. That was all; my State Department orders would be waiting in Jernegan's office.

As I cleaned out my desk at the OCB the next day, I received a call from Snowdon informing me that plans had been changed. First, I was not entitled to a diplomatic passport—not even Mr. Roosevelt had one—and I was to apply for a lower-status special passport instead. I was angry, but before I could tell Snowdon what he could do with his instructions, he said that Allen Dulles had asked to see me before I left.

As if by magic, all of Snowdon's super-secret injunctions disappeared the moment I met the assistant he sent to my office to escort me. As we drove down 17th Street, he pointed out the row of temporary World War II wooden buildings lining the reflecting pool to the Lincoln Memorial, explaining that this was where the headquarters of the CIA's clandestine services housed its staff. He and his colleagues, Snowdon's assistant said, represented themselves as civilian employees of the military services and had cover telephones for receiving outside calls running from military switchboards.

After parking, we entered the rear of "K" building. They ran—three city blocks—from "L," where the top brass had offices, to "I," where we'd find the Near East and Africa (NEA) Division. After showing his ID card, Snowdon's assistant signed me in and I received a visitor's badge. Snowdon was waiting for us at the end of the building. He took me to meet Roger Goiran, chief of NEA, of the agency's Directorate of Plans (DP). Speaking with a trace of a French accent, Goiran told me of Ambassador Moose's withdrawn nature and the difficulties Walter Campbell was having in overcoming Moose's dislike of covert intelligence operations. Saying that he'd heard I knew and got on well with the Arabs, Goiran suggested that I might keep the ambassador occupied while Campbell went about the CIA's business. Describing the Damascus chief of station as an experienced and capable operator, Goiran said that the two had served together in the OSS. As for himself, the NEA chief told me he had come to headquarters from Iran, where the agency had been "remarkably successful."

Since Goiran seemed uncomfortable, as if tolerating me under instructions, I was glad when the call came announcing that he, Snowdon, and I could leave to see Allen Dulles. On the way out we bumped into Goiran's deputy, Archibald Roosevelt (Kim's cousin). About five foot eight, wearing dark horn-rimmed glasses, Roosevelt came over to welcome me, putting out his hand and pumping mine with a motion that seemed to start at his shoulders and extend out through his fingers. For me this was a long-awaited encounter: Archie had once been an army attaché in Baghdad, and I'd studied many of his excellent reports on the Marsh Arabs and the Kurds.

We had little time to talk, however—Goiran hurried us out of the building to his car, a Rénault. Why, I wondered, wasn't he in Paris or Indochina, where he'd blend in without needing cover? But then I realized that assigning him to an American embassy in one of those places would be like hanging a sign reading "CIA" around his neck.

We drove past the Lincoln Memorial, cutting across Constitution Avenue to 23rd Street, and turned into the drive leading to the cluster of sandstone buildings from which the CIA operated openly. Although I'd attended meetings in adjacent buildings, this was the first time I'd been in the headquarters of the world's largest intelligence organization.

Going by elevator up to the top floor, we were soon led into a large office where, at the far end of the room, sat the gray-haired man for whom I'd be working. Allen Dulles was on the phone, leaning back in a high-backed leather chair, a foot propped up on a wooden wastebasket. Pipe in hand, he gestured us toward a grouping of leather chairs and a sofa in front of his desk and continued his conversation. One white, one red, and another black telephone like the one he was using stood on the credenza behind his desk. I assumed that neither the White House nor the CIA's operations room now demanded his attention.

Finishing his call, Dulles extended his hand and said, "Welcome, Eveland. Glad to have you aboard and that you could find time to see me before you took off." Moving to a leather armchair by Dulles's desk, I had time to study him while he dipped his pipe into a large brown glass bowl and slowly tamped layer after layer of tobacco, carefully shaved off the excess, then replaced the bowl's cover. He was a kind-looking man with a wide oval face and thinning gray hair parted almost in the middle. He wore round, frameless glasses; a full, neatly trimmed bushy silver moustache tapered down to the edges of his lips.

Breaking the silence, he asked when I'd be leaving and how much time I could spare the CIA. I explained that June 6 was my target date and that I planned to spend a day in Beirut before driving over the mountains to Damascus. That was fine, Dulles said, and he wanted me to be sure to see his man Zogby, who had charge of the CIA station in Lebanon. I laughed to myself and turned to look at Snowdon for a moment. He must have been crushed, having given me the impression that he was revealing a national secret by identifying Walter Campbell, with whom I'd be working in Damascus.

Then, referring to Ambassador Moose, Dulles said he hoped I'd work closely with "Jimmy"—a good man, he said, who'd been in the area since the days when Dulles had directed Near Eastern affairs in the Department of State. "You know him, of course?" Dulles asked, and I said I did. Then, offhandedly, Dulles observed that the CIA's man in Syria wasn't very strong but assured me that the man soon to replace him, Vernon Cassin, had been highly recommended. "Another name," I thought, "another state secret to be memorized but not written down." I also wondered how Goiran felt about hearing his boss's opinions of Moose and Campbell.

To my surprise, Dulles then mentioned Charles Malik, saying he regretted that all the OCB members had been unable to hear him, adding that he'd heard from Elmer Staats that Malik had made a deep impression on the OCB staff. Dulles then brought up Nasser and, after praising me for the trip I'd made, spoke of continuing negotiations with the Egyptians, which he was sure would lead to some sort of arms shipments. Finally, he told me to use my own good judgment in Syria. He doubted that the conservative politicians in Syria had the "stomach" to save their own country but hoped I might prove him wrong. Embassy reports that the Syrian army wanted to buy trucks and some arms from us also interested him. He remarked that I knew more than he did about such things and that he hoped I'd let him know personally if arms sales might be the key to enabling senior officers to control younger ones who had leftist tendencies.

"Do you have any questions?" Dulles asked. If I had any, I wasn't about to pose them now and risk damaging the carte blanche mandate I'd just received. Our meeting ended with handshakes and his best wishes for my pleasant voyage.

Speaking with Goiran after we left Allen Dulles's office, I expressed my irritation about the downgrading of my passport. Goiran apologized, saying lamely that Snowdon had only been following CIA regulations. When I said that I'd decided to limit my CIA trip to three months instead of four, Goiran was not displeased. From our whole conversation I concluded that I was an outsider imposed on career people who'd be glad to see me gone.

The next day I went up to Jack Jernegan's office in the State Department to pick up my travel orders. Finding that they had not yet been typed up, I read what had been authorized by the CIA and learned that they merely authorized me to travel to Damascus "at no expense to the Department of State." This was absurd, I thought: even the Damascus-embassy administrative officer would identify me as a spook before I ever met Walter Campbell.

Jernegan was sympathetic, fortunately, and authorized me to dictate my own travel orders to his administrative officer. Thinking on my feet, I improvised this wording for official travel to Syria (and return to Washington):

"To assist the Ambassador in the establishment of a new consulate in Aleppo, Syria, and to assist Embassy officials in the administrative organization of the Embassy in Damascus."

This formula, I thought, would withstand scrutiny at any diplomatic mission abroad. It owed no thanks to the CIA, of course, and I was dismayed by their pretense of secrecy when the most basic and revealing details were overlooked. If the CIA didn't feel obliged to provide me cover, now at least I had an unclassified State Department document I could show to Syrians, the press, or American friends, while having never to deny or affirm that I'd heard of the CIA.

CHAPTER ELEVEN

WAIT AND SEE

By the time I reached Lebanon I was relaxed, no longer annoyed with the low-level CIA officers, and elated to be again in the Middle East. After visiting friends and Aramco's office, I went to see Ghosn Zogby, the CIA's Beirut chief of station, who was carried by the American embassy as a first secretary, political.

Although my name meant nothing to Zogby's secretary, the sight of my State orders was enough to induce her to usher me in. Zogby was a portly man whose collar and tie could scarcely contain his bulging neckline; the buttons running down his shirt seemed on the verge of popping. Forty years old, he had unmistakable Levantine features that would have identified his ancestry even had he not had a common Lebanese name. Showing him a copy of my orders, I joked that they were false. "My name," I said, "should appear in your files as Perry M. Chapworth, and I bring you greetings from Allen Dulles and Archie Roosevelt." To be sure I'd made my point, I mentioned that Kim Roosevelt and Dick Bissell had conjured up my mission and that I'd be off the next day to Damascus to work with Walter Campbell, who'd been notified of my assignment by Walter Snowdon and Roger Goiran.

Zogby's eyes bulged as I reeled off these names, but finally he grinned, stood up, and shook hands again, saying that his pseudonym was Kennard and that he was pleased to have a new KUBARK hand aboard. Not wanting to display my ignorance as to what a KUBARK was, I thanked him and asked him to cable Campbell that I'd arrive in Damascus the next day. Zogby then dictated a message filled with code names. I couldn't follow much of it, but the first word had been KUBARK, followed by "staffer" and my pseudonym. I concluded that KUBARK was the cryptonym for CIA.

When I described my assignment to Zogby, he made repeated offers of assistance, and I left hoping I'd find other CIA officers as cooperative as he was. Heading for Damascus, I hired a cab, and soon we were climbing into the mountains. The highway up to the top of the first range consisted of a series of narrow hairpin turns, which my driver, like others, took without fear of meeting cars coming from the opposite direction. Apparently Allah watched over us. Finally, we dropped down through more gradual curves until I caught sight of the flat, fertile Bekaa Valley.

Passing through Syrian immigration at Riyaq, we followed a route through the 8,000-foot mountains above us and then descended alongside the River Barada into the outskirts of Damascus. High above the city's generally low profile rose the minarets of the eighth-century Umayyad Mosque, fourth holiest in all Islam.

Settling into my room at the New Omayad Hotel, I looked out at Damascus's nearly deserted streets, so different from Beirut's bustle, suddenly felt the weight of the 6,000 miles I'd traveled, and slept. I woke the next morning, sunlight pouring through my room's windows, startled until I remembered where I was. It was time to get to work.

Going to the American embassy, I was soon in the office of Ambassador James Sayle Moose, Jr. I'd met him at the Cairo conference and found him a very serious man, intolerant of fools. He was now fifty-two, three years into his second tour in Damascus, and had also served in Lebanon, Saudi Arabia, Iraq, and Iran. A policy-level assignment in Washington preceded his appointment as our first ambassador to Syria, when the mission's status was upgraded to that of an embassy in 1952. All of this, coupled with his service in Paris at a time when France had ruled Syria under mandate, provided Moose with superb qualifications for his position.

Although he received me cordially, the ambassador's welcome left no doubt that the opening gambit was mine, so I passed him my State Department travel orders. Suddenly smiling, Moose said he was glad that Washington had finally recognized the importance of having a consulate in Aleppo. Caught in my own trap, I decided not to mention that I'd devised this wording myself. Referring then to the other section—that I'd assist in the administrative organization of the embassy—the ambassador said that he assumed that this part was merely CIA cover but that he'd go along with the ploy and assign me office space from which I could work.

The ice now broken, Moose said that he was discouraged by U.S. policy for the Near East but still hoped that we might belatedly recognize the danger inherent in Syria's political disintegration. A leftist-oriented or communist-dominated government here, he said, would clearly threaten U.S. interests in Turkey, outflank all of the states of the NATO alliance, in fact. Furthermore, he worried about continuing American deference to France's fancied "special position" in the Levant (Syria and Lebanon) and was especially concerned by our failure to face up to the consequences of Syria's conservative parliamentary majority giving way to the well-organized, French-educated minority of socialists and crypto-communists.

The ambassador seemed to be hoping that I'd say my presence was proof that the embassy's repeated warnings had finally found an audience at the NSC policymaking level. I couldn't encourage him. The very logic and dispassion of his telegrams from Damascus accounted in great measure for the lack of attention with which they were met. Moose was the epitome of a professional diplomat and rejected the "squeaking wheel" approach of demanding the "grease" of NIACT (night-action message) crisis attention. As for changes in national policy, I'd concluded that only threats of war or schemes to defend against it could spur the NSC to action. To the Pentagon's planners, a stable Syria meant secure lines of communication to the oilfields and Russia's borders, and the military brass were unlikely to react until these routes were denied us. The

Department of State—now absorbed in Foster Dulles's search for an overall solution to the Near East's problems—regarded Syria more as an irritant: an obstacle to the Johnston mission, a country plagued by border clashes with the Israelis. I didn't dare tell the ambassador that Allen Dulles had challenged me to prove wrong his estimate that Syria's conservative politicians didn't have the guts to save their own country.

That Moose wasn't expecting easy solutions came to light when he explained why he'd waited to call in the CIA's chief of station. First, the ambassador wanted to satisfy himself that I hadn't arrived with plans for covert political action or visions of curing Syria's ills by funding the country's political conservatives to embark on programs we'd be unable to sustain. For Moose, none of this had any point until policymakers in Washington defined U.S. objectives in Syria in terms compatible with Syria's own interests and our ability to support to the limit anything we asked the Syrians to do. It would be a mistake, he thought, to encourage Syrian political leaders to risk their futures by aligning themselves with the United States, when even he was uncertain whether we yet had a Near East policy or were merely reacting to emergencies as they occurred. So far, so good, I thought. The two of us certainly viewed America's shortcomings in the same way, and, to my surprise, Moose had defined Syria's problems without once mentioning Israel as the sole cause.

Despite all this, the ambassador said, there might be a way for the U.S. to encourage and strengthen the civilian government that had replaced the previous series of military dictatorships. It now seemed possible that Syria would alter its position of being the only state in the area to refuse any type of U.S. economic or military assistance. Informal inquiries had reached the embassy regarding our willingness to permit the Syrian army to buy arms in the United States under the reimbursable-aid provisions of U.S. mutual-security legislation. Should a formal request be received, my background could be of value. A prompt response to Syria's request to purchase equipment to maintain internal security and defend the country's borders, Moose believed, might induce relatively pro-West or politically uncommitted nationalist army officers to support a strong civilian government. Otherwise, he said, they would not oppose a leftist takeover in the army.

Delighted that what Moose proposed could be implemented openly, I saw some possibility of success through a combination of the ambassador's support and my Department of Defense connections. I'd now met on behalf of the CIA with this most conventional of diplomats, and all had gone well.

At this point, CIA station chief Walter Campbell was called in to join us. Apparently convinced that I had Allen Dulles's ear, Campbell showed no curiosity about what the ambassador and I had discussed, went through the necessary courtesies, and departed. Shrugging his shoulders, Moose led me out to meet the members of the embassy's political section.[30] This done, I went below to seek out Richard Funkhouser, a close friend of Sam Kopper's whom I'd known in Washington as the State Department's expert on petroleum affairs. Having predicted an ignominious end for shortsighted oil-company policies in the Middle East, Dick had been relegated to Damascus to head our economics section in a country where no oil production existed. A second secretary in the section, Arthur Close, was introduced to me as he darted in with a report to be signed while Funkhouser and I talked. Later, on my own, I went in search of the mid-floor CIA office to which, back in Washington, Walter Snowdon said I'd be secretly summoned. Baffled, I'd just passed the entrance for the second time when I felt a hand on my shoulder. "In here, Bill. I'll show you the way to our office." It was Art Close, a wide grin on his face, delighted that I'd not earlier known of his real job. One of Snowdon's security measures, I was certain.

The windowless and stuffy small room whose ceiling conformed to the slope of the stairway above it was the headquarters of all CIA operations in Syria. If ever a place for undisturbed plotting existed, I was in it, and I determined to make my office downstairs where large rooms with bright windows provided a feeling of reality.

---

30   Robert Strong, deputy chief of mission; William Brewer, head of the political section; and his two assistants, Edward Waggoner and Alfred L. "Roy" Atherton.

Walter Campbell and I again spoke briefly, and again he had no questions about my mission, no inquiries about how high up the CIA's totem pole I'd been allowed to venture in Washington. And, best of all, he gave no indication that I'd be under any supervision. Art Close then took me to a room on the embassy's roof and introduced me to the career CIA girl who encoded and decoded CIA messages and spent the rest of her time maintaining the station's records and handling its finances. I also met the CIA radio operator, who relayed and received through U.S. stations in Cyprus and Asmara all diplomatic and CIA communications with Washington and other missions overseas.

Now, Close said, I'd met the entire CIA station, with the exception of Keith Williams, whose cover kept him away from the embassy despite the fact that he presumably represented the (CIA-funded) American Friends of the Middle East. Because of Williams's "deep cover," Art explained, we'd have to rendezvous some dark night at one of the "safe houses" that the station maintained for clandestine contacts.

I left the CIA hutch more than a little dazed. Here, in a country where communism posed a real threat, there was a staff of five. In Egypt, however, the CIA was building an empire behind Nasser. I wondered if the agency had its priorities straight.

Speaking further, Ambassador Moose and I reviewed Washington's latest plan to relieve tensions in the Near East. Recognizing that steps to solve the Arab-Israeli problem were essential to denying the Soviets opportunities for exploiting current enmities and further dividing the Arabs, Secretary Dulles had created within his own office the Middle East Policy Planning Group to concentrate on means of achieving peace between the Arab states and Israel. Code-named "Alpha" and headed by Francis Russell (who'd been returned from Tel Aviv for the assignment), the Group had the President's permission to draw on any department or agency of the executive branch for support. This sounded good, Moose said, provided that bipartisan congressional support could be counted on to ensure that domestic political considerations in the U.S. did not interfere with the shaping of foreign policy. When I told him

I'd arranged informally to have my former colleagues keep me posted on the progress of Alpha and other planning for the area, Moose looked pleased and volunteered to share with me all sensitive communications he received from Washington.

Appraising the diplomatic corps accredited to Syria, the ambassador said that he thought highly of the envoys of Great Britain, Iraq, and Turkey (Sir John Gardner, Abdul Jalil ar Rawi, and Adnan Kural). They, too, he said, were concerned with what we termed the "leftist drift" in Syria. When I explained that I'd known Rawi since my tour in Baghdad, Moose encouraged me to seek his views on Iraqi activities in Syria and offered to inform all three envoys that I was visiting Damascus as a Department of State observer. What surprising cooperation, I thought.

Although I was apparently free to make contacts and form my own conclusions about Syria, Moose did issue one caveat. Meeting Ambassador Clerac of France would be a waste of time, he warned. Like his government in Paris, Clerac saw the extension of American, British, Iraqi, and Turkish influence in the Levant as a greater danger than communism. Having belatedly recognized that its oppressive rule and commercial exploitation during the mandates had created strong anti-French feelings, France was now trying to consolidate what influence it retained. In Syria this meant appealing to cultural ties with the French-educated intellectuals, most of whom, unfortunately, were ultranationalistic or leftist-oriented radicals. Angered by the Arab independence movements in North Africa, France was restricting her arms sales to the Arab states; instead, she was offering the latest jet aircraft to the Israeli air force, and modern French tanks bolstered Israel's armed forces.

In Moose's opinion, the ability of Syria to survive as an independent, constitutionally governed country would depend on the results of the coming presidential election, which might prove the last opportunity for Syria's two largest and most conservative political parties (the Nationalists and the Populists) to unite to elect a strong president able to control both the leftist parties and the army. But these large political blocs, composed primarily of wealthy landlords and merchants, were divided by petty jealousies. Again, France was an obstacle, taking the position that a victory by the conservatives would provoke a pro-leftist army coup d'etat. The French, therefore, were encouraging a francophile independent political leader whose ambitions for the presidency had little chance of success. Furthermore, the ambassador said, the French were reported to have moved ex-dictator Shishakly to Lebanon so that he would be ready in case of a conservative standoff creating a demand for his return.

Moose also described conservative political leader Rushdi Kikhya as one of the few men capable of winning the presidency with the support of both the Populists and the Nationalists. Characterizing Rushdi Bey as a man who shunned social functions and never called on the American embassy, Moose added that it might be useful for me to seek him out and encourage him to unite and lead the conservative politicians.[31] Already, then, it seemed that the ambassador was asking me to perform the mission Allen Dulles had assigned me. Nonetheless, I considered it strange that the embassy was not initiating discussions with Kikhya. I received my answer when Moose reiterated his reluctance to encourage Syrians to risk their futures, adding this time that there was little value in doing so unless we could promise a change in U.S. policies toward Israel. As I left, he warned that no matter who won the election, the junior army officers might take over the government and seek arms from any source, should Israel continue military actions against unarmed civilians within Syrian boundaries. I wondered, hearing this, if Syria's future did not in fact depend upon the external pressures to which it was exposed.

Nothing I'd been told during my Washington briefing by the CIA had indicated that the Damascus station had anything but an intelligence-gathering capability. Perhaps now, however, Moose had seen in my presence a "covert" role for the CIA, in the sense that I could try to induce Syrians to do things by promises unlikely to be kept. Whatever I implied or said could always be repudiated. In fact, having left the army before I had obtained approval of my

---

31   Although in Iraq the Turkish honorary titles of bey (sir) and pasha (lord) still prevailed, they were used less frequently in Syria; in Egypt, both titles and wearing the fez (tarboosh) were banned by the RCC.

civil-service status, I was expendable, both in Washington and in Damascus. Whatever I did would be a risk, then, and I'd have to be careful. I could best protect myself, I thought, by keeping Moose informed of everything I did.

Getting more of my bearings, I had dinner with Art Close, who was the workhorse of the Damascus CIA station, performing full-time cover duties as a diplomat and spending his evenings making clandestine contacts with agents. The son of pioneer mission-ary educators, Close had grown up in Syria and Lebanon before attending Princeton and moving straight to the CIA. The Near East was part of his life, and he intended to stay.

Art told me, sadly, that our local CIA station had no assets of real political stature and, like the embassy, had little more than second-hand knowledge of what went on outside the capital. He described Syria as being slightly larger than North Dakota, with the same agricultural focus in its economy, and a climate similar to that of Southern California. Aleppo, in the north, was, he said, important to the country both politically and economically. Like Moose, Close hoped we'd establish a consulate there. Otherwise, we had no real idea of what transpired in most of Syria. Worse, we had virtually no contacts with those Syrians termed by the ambas-sador "leftist" or "procommunist."

Close had arranged a late-night meeting at the home of Keith Williams, the station's deep-cover officer, and I was urged to do what I could to lift the morale of this man whose isolation from American officials was discouraging him. Because both Wil-liams and his wife needed cheering, Close explained, they were dispensing with the precaution of a safe-house meeting. Setting off on a circuitous drive through the city, we ended up, finally, nearly where we began. Noticing my confusion at our route, Art explained that the European sector of Damascus was small and that an American who lived elsewhere would immediately attract suspicion. Although Keith and Art were almost neighbors, Close made the long drive to try to discourage surveillance.

There was little of real value I could tell Williams; nevertheless, he greeted me warmly, and we talked for hours while I filled him in on the Alpha Group, the NSC and OCB, and other Washington organizations to which he'd never been exposed. I could sympathize with him: he'd probably joined the CIA expecting a life of excitement and then received an assignment barring him from open contact with U.S. officials. Despite their deep-cover status, however, Williams and others sent abroad in covert capacities by the CIA still received the same allowances, home leave, and area-rotation benefits as their colleagues operating under embassy cover. This illustrated a fundamental weakness in American foreign-intelligence operations: we were still too comfort and status oriented to "bury" people under deep cover for long periods of time. Soviet agents and those of some of our allies took such assignments knowing that they would never have official status and that they might be required to remain in place even if diplomatic relations with the country in which they resided were severed (as later became the case between the United States and Syria).[32]

By now I perceived that we had little real knowledge of who the so-called leftists and communists were, what motivated them, and whether or not their objectives were more nationalistic than anti-Western. Determined to learn more, with Ambassador Moose's approval I sought out the Iraqi and Turkish ministers.

As I'd hoped, Abdul Jalil ar Rawi remembered me from Baghdad and Washington. Extremely fond of Americans, Rawi had tried to extend his assignment in Washington, but his real discontent stemmed from the fact that he didn't actually represent the Iraqi government in Syria. Both Iraqi Crown Prince Abdul Illah and Prime Minister Nuri as Said, Rawi complained, hoped that Iraq would take over Syria, if for different reasons. Nuri as Said had always considered Syria a logical part of a greater Iraq—the Fertile Crescent, including Jordan as well—and was certain that one day the divided Syrians would either call for Iraq to solve their

---

32   Because of his isolation, Keith Williams met most of his agents in Beirut, and he was soon transferred there permanently. First using as cover a CIA-subsidized airline-service company (Transocean), he was assigned to work with Air Jordan, to which the CIA provided support (as it did to Iranian Airways). Later, he returned to Lebanon in the guise of a major American oil-company (Mobil) employee.

problems or welcome a takeover by the Iraqi army. Ever responsive to the British, Nuri seemed content to await the signal from London as to the time and manner of an Iraqi takeover.

By contrast, the crown prince, who hoped to restore Hashemite rule over Syria, was constantly plotting to encourage pro-Iraqi Syrians to call for a monarchy. Ignoring Iraq's foreign ministry, these two conducted their intrigues in person or through the military attaché, who, to Rawi's great relief, had been banned from Syria and now operated from Beirut. Considering all Iraqi aspirations to rule Syria foolish, Rawi wrote reports stressing the desire of most Syrians for complete independence from either Iraqi or Egyptian influence.

Like Moose, the Iraqi minister considered Rushdi Kikhya a desirable candidate for the presidency. In close contact with Syrian politicians, however, he considered it likely that former president Shukri Quwwatly would be elected. A weak man, in Rawi's opinion, Quwwatly had recently returned to Damascus, beholden financially to the Saudi Arabians and Egyptians who had supported him in exile. Nonetheless, Rawi considered him preferable to having another military dictatorship. I was urged to encourage Kikhya and assure him that the U.S. looked favorably on his candidacy. If in the end Quwwatly were elected, Rawi said, we should provide military equipment to support the conservative army officers who could keep him in power and enable him to resist the leftist army clique.

In Washington I'd often suffered through Rawi's complaints about how unrealistic the U.S. foreign policy in the Near East was, being more favorable to Israel than to the Arabs. Now I faced him with a dramatic change in our policy, one I was certain neither the Arabs nor the Israelis could condemn as biased. The previous day Secretary Dulles had offered large-scale U.S. financial aid for the resettlement of the Palestinian Arabs and the development of regional irrigation programs, as well as an undertaking to guarantee any frontiers on which Israel and the Arab states could agree. Proud that the Alpha Group had devised this response both to the demands of Arab politicians (as surrogates for the Palestinians) for resettlement of the refugees and also to the appeals of the Israelis for secure borders, I asked Rawi what more the U.S. could do.

Ignoring entirely what the U.S. was offering the Palestinians, Rawi shrugged off Dulles's plan as a futile gesture, saying that Israel would reject our proposal for two reasons: an increase in the Arab population of Israel would be contrary to the Zionist goal of an all-Jewish state; and secure Israeli borders would deprive Zionists of the crisis appeals for the foreign aid upon which Israel was financially dependent. I'd heard these arguments many times, but now, since they came from a man quite willing to criticize his own government but never the Arabs as a bloc, I couldn't help wondering if the Arabs might be underwriting a self-fulfilling prophecy. The bandwagon of politicians espousing the rights of the Palestinians was overcrowded with opportunists counseling the refugees to reject settlement offers. If the Palestinians could speak for themselves, and if the hardworking settlers of Israel were freed of pressures to accept more immigrants, these two ancient Semitic neighbors might be able to live together in peace. Once more, it seemed that external pressures were affecting the destinies of the people most concerned, for if Zionist plans for massive immigration to Israel materialized and the more radical Palestinians organized themselves into a political movement, the situation with which we were now dealing might become explosive.[33] I left Rawi disappointed, convinced that our conversations to come would be confined to the subject of Syrian politics.

Adnan Kural, the Turkish minister, was a descendant of the Turks who had ruled Syria for centuries, and he seemed both to understand the Syrians and to sympathize with their aspirations for independence from foreign influence. Like Rawi, he anticipated that Shukri Quwwatly would become Syria's next president.

---

33 The manner in which these two factors had emerged as obstacles to peace over the ensuing fifteen years became evident in 1970. Speaking from Kuwait (where the PLO leader Yasser Arafat had once worked as an engineer), an Al Fatah official, Hani Al-Gahassan, warned on April 14, 1970, that "any Arab leader signing a peaceful settlement with Israel will be signing his own death sentence." The May 18, 1970, issue of the National Observer carried a story ("Zionist Role in the U.S. Raises New Concern") by Lawrence Mosher quoting Gottlieb Hammar, chief Zionist fund collector in the U.S., as observing: "When the blood flows, the money flows."

Kural recalled, however, that Quwwatly had once fled Syria when internal problems with the army appeared, and observed that the former president might not have the courage that had characterized his opposition to French rule. Certainly he would find it difficult now to oppose the policies of Egypt and Saudi Arabia, where he'd been given asylum; and if subjected to pressures from Turkey, Iraq, or the U.S., Quwwatly might lead Syria into an alliance with Nasser.

We spoke during the ensuing weeks, and Kural finally told me that he differed strongly with his own country's view that the nationalists of Syria's Ba'athist party should be considered pro-communist. The West, he said, should cultivate the socialists and the Ba'athist nationalists instead of ignoring them and forcing them to seek strength through alliances with Syria's Communist party.[34] Strong both in Iraq and Syria, he went on, the Ba'ath had great appeal because it espoused a revival of Arab nationalism, appealing to former Islamic glory. This was quite different, Kural insisted, from Nasser's nationalism, which cloaked his desire to become the sole leader of the Arab world. If we only showed a willingness to understand the Ba'aths' aspirations, the Turkish minister suggested, we might be able to influence them constructively.

Again differing from officials in Baghdad and Ankara, Kural also rejected Iraqi plots or Turkish border harassment as means of justifying outside intervention in Syria. Memories of the Ottoman Turkish occupation still lingered, and Israel had friendly relations with the Turks. Iraq, so long as the monarchy ruled there,

---

34   Led by two schoolteachers, Michel Aflaq and Salah ud-Din Bitar (later to be prime minister several times), the Ba'ath Party took its name from the Arabic word *baath*, meaning "renaissance." Its objectives were defined as "Freedom, Unity, and Socialism," although its socialistic concepts embraced more national-improvement goals than economic principles. Active also in Lebanon, Iraq, and Jordan, the Ba'ath was unattached to any specific leader for its leadership within the Arab world and thus differed from Nasser's brand of Arab unity and single leadership. The leader of Syria's Communist party, Khalid Bakdash, was more a disciple of the French type of Eurocommunism than an inflexible adherent of Soviet communism.

was considered a tool of the British by the Syrians and other Arabs. In Kural's view, the United States would do best to encourage the development of a totally independent Syria, one that could some day feel strong enough to make peace with Israel and remain neutral in the West's conflicts with Russia and China. We should, he concluded, openly support a civilian Syrian government—probably headed by Quwwatly—built around army support, and both independent and unaligned.

I asked Kural if he'd ever presented his views to his government in Ankara. He said he hadn't, knowing that they would be unpopular, and urged that I not quote him in State Department messages—these were all repeated to Ankara and might lead to his transfer if they were discussed with the Turkish foreign ministry. Receiving my assurances that I could protect his privacy and still use my own channels to ensure that his views were considered by top policymakers in Washington, Kural concluded by saying that Turkey, the U.S., and Britain all erred in expecting Syria, Egypt, and other states of the Near East to take sides in the East-West struggle. The interests of the states and peoples of this area were not identical to ours, he said, and by portraying political alignment with the West as the only alternative to communist subjugation, we were only strengthening the nationalistic elements that advocated emphasis on Syria's interests alone. Ba'athist appeals for agrarian reform and arms without "strings" from any source were in themselves inducements for the new generation of Syrians to reject the traditional conservative politicians and senior army officers. The wealthy landowners thought only of profits, just as the merchants had profited by speculating in inferior arms during the Palestinian war. These factors, the Turkish minister said, had very little to do with forces outside Syria.

Particularly because Kural's views were not affected by his perspective on the merits of the Arab-Israeli problem, I resolved to report them to Allen Dulles and request that they be passed to Francis Russell's Alpha Group. Perhaps there they might be expressed in terms not offensive to Foster Dulles's rejection of neutrality as a concept of independence. As for Ambassador Moose, I was sure that he was sincere in believing that the aspirations of

Syria's nationalists were identical to those of the communists, and that therefore both factions must be opposed.

With Ambassador Moose's blessing, I arranged through Rawi to meet Rushdi Kikhya just before the presidential election. This tall, taciturn Syrian politician didn't impress me as a man with behind-the-scenes maneuvering talents, nor did he display any of the qualities of a strong leader. Straining to carry on a conversation, I asked him if there was anything the United States could do to encourage Syria's two major conservative parties to set aside their differences and unite in the interests of their country. Silent for a long period, he teased his worry beads and looked at the floor, finally saying that it was too late. I was speechless, wondering if this was the type of leader who represented Syria's conservatives, now convinced that those in this country who had the most to lose were unwilling to help themselves. Under the circumstances, it seemed, the best we could hope for was the election of Quwwatly and the support of his regime by the senior army officers. When the election came, Shukri Bey Quwwatly was elected Syria's new president, just as Rawi had predicted.

Not long afterward, my replacement in the Pentagon sent a top-secret personal letter filling me in on recent U.S. thinking about the sale of arms and regional defense in the Middle East. In late July 1955, Ambassador Byroade had cited confirmation that the Russians were offering to barter weapons for Egyptian cotton to justify Department of State approval of Egypt's urgent request to purchase $28 million of military equipment in the United States. The Egyptian government had also asked if it might pay in local currency, since it was short on dollars. In sending this request to Defense, the State Department advised that it had anticipated Egypt's terms and had already informed Byroade that we opposed extending either credit or grant assistance to Egypt. Egypt's shortage of hard currency, State felt, would be a desirable brake on the Near East's becoming involved in an arms race.

Clearly, my friend wrote, State had been searching for some way to turn down the Egyptian request. The Defense Department, nonetheless, worked out ways for Egypt to purchase some arms with local currency—with the air force selling sixteen aircraft on credit terms and the army offering twenty tanks by converting Egyptian pounds into dollars. These offers had never left Washington, however, and it appeared obvious that Secretary Dulles was still raging at Nasser's "immoral" decision to join the Third World nations that advocated neutrality. Foster Dulles was determined to punish Nasser by denying arms to Egypt, my friend concluded, but just how we could block an Egyptian-Soviet arms deal was something neither Byroade nor the Pentagon could fathom.

Now that Syria's new president had been elected and a reasonably conservative cabinet appointed, I saw no other means of assisting the embassy overtly in the absence of a formal Syrian request to purchase U.S. military equipment. I decided to share what I'd learned from my Pentagon friend with Ambassador Moose, in order to illustrate that even should the new government approach us for arms, the secretary of state's attitude concerning arms sales in the area rendered very dim the prospects of approval of a Syrian request. Moose reminded me that in April 1955, the U.S. had denied Syria's formal application to buy, through commercial channels, sixty American tanks of World War II vintage. As a result, Syria had purchased Russian tanks from the Czechs. Still unwilling to see the Syrians become dependent upon the Soviets for military equipment, Moose hoped that I'd stay on long enough to work with him in trying to change Washington's apparent embargo on arms sales without regard for the merit of the request.

Moose had been informed that President Quwwatly and the Syrian chief of staff, General Shawkat Shuqayr, had now agreed to shun a military pact with Egypt and would approach the U.S. first in seeking new equipment for their army. Shuqayr, the ambassador had learned, had further assured Quwwatly that the army would stay out of politics. The ambassador had already met with the new president and had been told that General Shuqayr was preparing a list of equipment to be purchased. I was asked to see the army attaché, Colonel Robert Molloy, and arrange that the two of us meet with the chief of staff.

Bob Molloy loved secrecy, and an aura of conspiracy surrounded all that he did. When I crossed the street and entered his office he closed and double-locked the door, and looked furtively about as if fearful of hidden microphones. He agreed that I should accompany him to see Shuqayr but urged that the meeting be conducted in absolute secrecy, since knowledge that we were considering arms sales would, he feared, encourage the leftist junior officers to seek an offer from Russia. Molloy knew a Syrian newsman who was close to the chief of staff, he said, and this man could arrange a secret meeting. What foolishness, I thought: even when I wanted to do something openly, our embassy made it cloak-and-dagger.

Having decided that he would accompany us, Ambassador Moose told Molloy to set up the clandestine meeting with General Shuqayr. Although I'd never met the chief of staff, I had studied his background. Born in Lebanon, Shuqayr came from the Druse tribes that were scattered through Lebanon, Syria, and Israel as a result of the World War I mandates. That he now commanded the Syrian army seemed to indicate that the Syrians preferred an outsider rather than one of their own. The Druse, whose secret religious rites made them anomalies in the Middle East, were also a minority sect in Syria, and this again raised the question of how one really defined an "Arab," or even a "Syrian."[35]

We met General Shuqayr at the home of the journalist who'd arranged the meeting. Although the official cars parked outside revealed the participants' identities, Bob Molloy busied himself closing all window shades and searching out monitoring devices. No eavesdroppers having been discovered, we finally got down to business. In answer to Moose's opening question, Shuqayr acknowledged that tentative Soviet offers of barter arrangements for weapons had been made, but these were, so far, only inquiries of interest. The general said, that Syria wanted to purchase 1,700 heavy-duty trucks and 850 cargo trailers from the United States. It was a modest list, I thought, certainly justified by Syria's widely separated population centers. But I suspected that the list would engender opposition in Washington: the trucks could also be used, of course, to move soldiers in the direction of Israel.

---

35   Lt. General Hafez al Assad, president of Syria since 1970, is a member of the minority Alawite sect from Northern Syria.

Although the United States considered France to be the traditional supplier of arms to Syria, Shuqayr observed, now that the French were selling arms to Israel he anticipated that Syrian requests to the French would be turned down. The United States would, he hoped, agree to help him stave off requests by his officers to buy Soviet arms. We could expect a formal request from the Syrian foreign ministry the next day, the general told us as we parted.

The next morning I joined the ambassador to read a long telegram he had drafted to urge an immediate and favorable response from Washington to Syria's request to buy arms from the U.S. government. As if in anticipation of this position, a telegram arrived from the Department of State saying that the United States was not inclined to favor reimbursable military-aid agreements with Syria (or Egypt) at this time. Moose was now crestfallen: the first opportunity for the United States to support Syria's new conservative government now seemed lost.

Seeing both French and Israeli pressure behind Washington's message, Moose said that he intended to proceed with his recommendation and to warn that unless our position was reversed we'd have to reconcile ourselves to there being great quantities of Soviet arms in Syria. He then wondered aloud just how Secretary Dulles expected his "moral considerations" to prevent the Russians from providing the Arabs with arms, which, he said, could of course be moved directly to Israel's frontiers. Coming from James Moose, this was a ringing statement of frustration. He knew well that neither U.S. intelligence operations nor propaganda campaigns would be able to reverse what might result from the establishment of an openly pro-Soviet Syrian government.

Remembering my predeparture conversation with Allen Dulles, I secured Moose's endorsement of my plan to cable to the CIA director a summary of all this. In what I learned was the first "eyes-only Ascham" (Dulles's pseudonym) message to be sent from Damascus, and also the longest of any kind, I spared few words in predicting that Soviet arming of the Arabs was now at hand. A cable from Washington next day said that Dulles would receive my message in London, the first leg of a trip he was making to CIA stations around the world (except for those located in the Near East). This gave me another idea, and I went to see the ambassador. Telling him that I believed the best chance of changing Foster Dulles's mind was to have Allen Dulles warn him that Syria was "on the brink" (a favorite expression of the secretary of state) of concluding a Soviet-arms deal, I announced that I was leaving for London to meet personally with the DCI. Moose laughed but wished me well. Walter Campbell was busy packing for his move, so I didn't trouble him with my plans.

Stopping in Beirut, I was soon aboard a DC-6, which, in those days, took all day with three stops in Europe to transit the distance from Lebanon to London. During the flight, I concluded that I'd done all I could do in Syria. Unless Dulles offered encouragement that the U.S. position on arms to Syria would be reversed, I'd consider my CIA mission at an end—and I'd packed with this in mind.

Once more I found Allen Dulles in a cordial mood. With a copy of my long cable before him, he asked me to repeat General Shuqayr's assurances that Syria had not concluded a barter agreement to obtain Russian arms. As I did this and gave him a copy of the list of the transportation equipment Syria wanted to buy from us, a telegram arrived from Ambassador Moose confirming that the government of Syria had made a formal request to purchase the U.S. equipment.

Although Dulles was pleased that the Syrians had turned to us, he stated that Britain now opposed any arms sales to the Near East (except to Iraq as a Baghdad Pact member). His brother, he said, was considering following Britain's lead. This news distressed me, especially when the DCI confirmed what I'd heard about large secret-arms sales by France to the Israelis. These deals, Dulles told me, were being winked at by the British and Americans. France would not be joining the Baghdad Pact and was contending that sales to Israel would indirectly strengthen Western defense capabilities in the Near East. He ignored my question about how Israel, surrounded by a sea of hostile Arabs and constantly complaining that insecure borders threatened its survival, could possibly participate in the defense of the area against Soviet attacks.

Referring instead to Egypt, Dulles explained that the CIA was now certain that Nasser had in hand a firm Russian offer of heavy military equipment in exchange for Egypt's cotton crop. The Egyptian president now apparently took the position that he'd been patiently negotiating for U.S. arms for a year but had experienced nothing but obfuscation and delays on our side.

Obviously sympathetic to Nasser's position, Dulles further explained that Israel's policies toward Egypt seemed to be directed at blocking any U.S.-Egyptian agreement on arms. First, he said, speaking in the strictest of confidence, attempts to sabotage U.S. offices in Egypt and attribute this to Egyptian terrorists had been traced to Israel's Mossad.[36] Furthermore, Dulles said, Israeli reprisals against attacks by the Egyptian-armed fe-dayeen, now operating from the Gaza Strip and Sinai, had escalated beyond possible justification. An Israeli army raid on an Egyptian military installation in Gaza, leaving fifty-four Egyptians dead and another fifty wounded, had brought unanimous condemnation of Israel by the Security Council, a temporary withholding of U.S. economic aid previously promised to the Israelis, and further calls by the U.N. for a cease-fire after the Israelis once more sent their forces into Gaza. At this point, President Nasser informed the U.S. that he would be unable to resist public pressure for retaliation, or even remain in office, unless America agreed to sell Egypt the arms it had long since requested.

When Dulles asked how I thought Syria would react to a Soviet-Egyptian arms deal, I responded that both Ambassador Moose and I were certain that the Syrians would also turn to the Russians. What, I asked Dulles, was the present status of Egypt's request for U.S. arms? Again, speaking for my private information only, he answered that the CIA had arranged for an approach to the highest levels of our government by Nasser's personal representative, Major Hassan Touhami. Even as we spoke, Kim

---

36 Mossad's role in the Cairo bombings became public knowledge in 1960–61 during an investigation of what was called the "Lavon Affair." This brought about the resignation of Defense Minister Pinchas Lavon and ended the political career of Prime Minister Moshe Sharett.

Roosevelt was escorting Touhami around Washington to meet with officials in the Departments of State and Defense. In summary, Allen Dulles said that he hoped Roosevelt's efforts, and the CIA's estimates of the implications of an Egyptian-Russian arms deal, would prevail.

Obviously in no position to express my real feelings on the subject, it nonetheless occurred to me that the Dulles brothers were now negatively influencing American policy. If another man headed the CIA and had the fortitude to risk his career and reputation, he would exercise his legislatively defined responsibility to warn the President that the secretary of state's policies were inviting the Russians to become a determining political presence in the future of the Middle East. Clearly, Allen Dulles's loyalty to Foster Dulles stood in the way of his carrying out this higher duty. As these thoughts about the two brothers crossed my mind, Allen Dulles urged me to return to Syria and prepare with Ambassador Moose a comprehensive written justification for the sale of U.S. arms to Syria. If I'd cable him a copy of this, Dulles added, he'd see that his brother gave it full consideration.

Flattered, I agreed to stay on until the Syrian-arms matter was resolved one way or the other. Hearing this, Dulles invited me to consider remaining until the end of 1955 in order to assist him in other area matters, as well as in the transition of chiefs of station in Damascus. When I said that I'd first have to check on Aramco's reaction, Dulles said that he'd be happy to intervene with the oil companies if I thought it would help. Not wanting to be linked with the CIA, however, I rejected this offer.

Leaving Allen Dulles, I contemplated my present position with the agency. My unilateral decision to fly to London had gone unchallenged, and the precedent of my dealing directly with Dulles had been established. I had also communicated with him by cable on a personal basis, and Dulles's messages to the CIA's Washington headquarters and the Damascus station saying that I was returning to the Near East on a special assignment for him made it clear that I was operating under his personal direction. This all affected my thoughts about staying on: if I were acting as Allen Dulles's field representative on Near Eastern matters, I might find working for the CIA more attractive.

My need of some type of official identification prompted my next move. London was crowded in September, and my problem in arriving without hotel reservations had been solved by a chance meeting with Lewis Jones, who was passing through en route to his new assignment as minister-counselor at our embassy in Teheran. Thanks to Lewis's personal introduction to the manager, I'd been put up at one of London's most exclusive hotels (the Connaught), but when asked for my card, I'd been embarrassed to have to say that I had none with me. Now I headed for Harrods for a remedy. After selecting the finest parchment stock, I wrote out the wording for two different calling cards. On one, there appeared below my name "Operations Coordinating Board, Executive Office of the President, Washington, D.C."; on the other, "Department of State, Washington." I walked away aware that I'd taken one more step toward extending my original three-month mission. And should I change my mind, I thought, I'd have some souvenirs at the CIA's expense.

Lewis Jones and I sat together on the following day's flight to Beirut, and I questioned him about conditions in our embassy in Cairo as he'd left them. Ambassador Byroade's position, as Lewis described it, was nearly hopeless. His appointment to Egypt, although it had been dreamed up by the CIA, had been welcomed by Foster Dulles because Byroade was showing too much initiative in the execution of U.S. policy for the Near East. But now, Jones said, Byroade was irritating the secretary by overreaching what Dulles considered the scope of an ambassador's responsibilities—Byroade was urging changes in the secretary's policies, drawing to his attention the possibility of Nasser's doing things that Dulles considered immoral. Worse, Ambassador Byroade was beginning to wonder whether he or the CIA represented the U.S. in Egypt and in dealings with Nasser. Miles Copeland had in the past been seeing the Egyptian president at will, promising all kinds of things beyond his control, and the large CIA contingent now was dealing with the Egyptian government at almost every level, as well as with the influential Egyptian press. Not only an admirer of

Ambassador Byroade, Jones was also a career diplomat and made a strong case that we should have left the arms discussions with Nasser to Ambassador Caffery, and later to Byroade, in order to avoid giving the impression that the CIA could find shortcuts to circumventing arms-aid regulations.

When Jones and I then spoke about the future of the Egyptian and Syrian arms requests, I was not reassured by his expressed opinion that the U.S. would turn down both governments. He had no answer—because there just wasn't one—to my question of how the United States and Great Britain expected to prevent Soviet-supplied armies from renewing hostilities with Israel as soon as they learned how to use new Russian equipment. Laughing, and averring that I was being too practical, Lewis said that he was sure Foster Dulles, in all his wisdom, would handle that problem when and if it occurred.

CHAPTER TWELVE

APPLE-PIE DIPLOMACY

Having stopped in Beirut on my way to Damascus, I was still there when Sam Kopper flew in, as exuberant as ever. Sitting on Sam's balcony at the Hotel Saint Georges, we were working on a fifth of White Label, watching the sun sink into the sea, its pink rays reflected by the remaining snow on the mountains, when Kopper winked at me and placed a call to the president of Lebanon. Within an instant, it seemed, I learned that we were invited to dinner at the presidential palace. I made a note to myself never to underestimate the abilities of Samuel Keene Claggett Kopper.

On our way to the palace, Sam told me of President Chamoun's background. Then fifty-five, he'd been trained as a lawyer and had been a member of parliament and a cabinet minister for ten years before his appointment, in 1944, to represent Lebanon as minister to the Allied governments in London. Kopper had first known him as Lebanon's delegate to the newly formed United Nations; according to Sam, Chamoun had provided moderate and constructive Arab approaches to the controversial debates on Palestine. Long a fighter for Lebanese independence, Camille Chamoun had also been an early spokesman for Arab nationalism and against colonialism. Now in the middle of his six-year term as president, he was struggling to keep Lebanon from involvement in inter-Arab feuds and the radical anti-Israeli nationalism that he believed had nothing constructive to offer.

When we arrived we were met by a tall, elegant, attractive woman, Zelpha Chamoun, who embraced Sam as if welcoming a brother back home. Chamoun himself then entered the room. Strikingly handsome with steel gray hair, he was muscular and immaculately groomed. Respectfully addressing Chamoun by his title, Sam then moved forward and was embraced by the president, who stood more than a foot taller than him. When joined by their two grown sons, Danny and Dory, the Lebanese president (a Maronite Catholic) and his wife (a Protestant, half-English, half-Lebanese) completed a family grouping such as one might expect to see living in Paris, London, or New York. I felt comfortable immediately.

By the time we'd finished dinner, coffee, and several drinks, the Chamouns and Kopper had spoken at length about old friends, their times at the U.N., and world personalities of whom I'd only heard. When it was nearly midnight, President Chamoun asked if I'd be staying long in the area and what my duties were. Before I could answer, Sam made a joking reference to my involvement in U.S. arms sales and in making usually ignored recommendations concerning U.S. policy in the Near East. Continuing from this, Chamoun said that Lebanon was less interested in buying from the U.S. military than in selling Lebanese products to it. Summoning a servant, he ordered that a large crate of Delicious apples be sent to our car. There were already too many private arms loose in his country, Chamoun complained. Lebanese apples, however, were a major source of his country's foreign-exchange income. If I could arrange for the U.S. Sixth Fleet and our armed forces in Europe to purchase them, my contribution to Lebanon would be far greater than if I arranged the sale of tanks to its army. The majority of Lebanon's population depended on agriculture for their living, the president explained, and our help in this manner would be felt directly by the people upon whom his country's stability depended. It seemed an overwhelmingly sane request for American assistance to the area, and I promised to do what I could. With warm farewells, we left soon afterward.

The apples Chamoun had given us had a strange yield. When Sam asked what we should do with them, I, coming from the apple-growing state of Washington, said: "Make apple pies of them, you fool. What else are nice red apples for?" Beaming, Sam had the apples sent to the hotel's chef with instructions to incorporate the entire box into four great apple pies. It was a disconcerted *chef de cuisine* who, under Sam's direction, put the concoction he'd created into four large silver salvers, each nearly two feet in diameter, which would be protected in transit by the domed covers of soup tureens.

Now, Sam said, he was going to explain diplomacy to me. The basic requirement of negotiation and conciliation, he continued, was to establish a common interest upon which all parties could agree. Once this had been discovered, even those holding seemingly irreconcilable positions would have to concede that mutual interests really existed. Working from this foundation, an approach to the main issue could be made with some prospect of success. To treat the disputed areas first, however, was to invite certain failure.

Moving to specifics, Kopper described a problem about which he'd learned from Chamoun. Two Arab ambassadors accredited to Lebanon were now funding a campaign of subversion to bring down the local government. Yet just eight years before, at the U.N., the same men had worked hard in the overall interests of the Arabs with two Lebanese delegates, now Lebanon's president and foreign minister. Tempers were strained, Sam said, and Chamoun was preparing to order Foreign Minister Charles Malik to demand the recall of these ambassadors who had once been their friends. During his days at the United Nations, Sam had done much for the U.S. in persuading these four Arabs to be reasonable when the partition of Palestine was at issue. Now, to remind these men of the past, Kopper was going to send each a gift of their favorite American dessert, deep-dish—and these dishes were deep—apple pie. If the gifts were followed by calls on the offending ambassadors, Sam said, he was certain that he could induce them to agree that dividing the Arab world by subversion could serve only one cause in the area—Israel's.

Next Sam reminded me of what Chamoun had said about how we might best assist Lebanon and its people. America's diplomatic efforts, Kopper feared, had unfortunately placed too much emphasis on dispensing aid to encourage the building of defense alliances, the acquisition of Western base rights, and the modernization of indigenous armies—all directed against the only enemy we seemed able to perceive, Russia. But what of the welfare of the people and the economies of the countries upon which we must ultimately depend in the Middle East? No matter how much of this military activity we subsidized, it still detracted from constructive approaches to ensuring long-range stability. If, in frustration, the people someday rose up against the politicians who used our aid to consolidate their positions, we might, Sam predicted, find ourselves on the outside looking in toward an area now ripe for communist subversion.

Concluding his discourse, Kopper pointed out that there was no more common denominator in America than good old apple pie. It had appeal at all levels of our population, just as our foreign policies should to the people abroad. All this, Sam decided, meant that we should consider what he'd now decided to call "apple-pie diplomacy," before it became too late.

I was preparing to leave for Damascus when Kopper arranged that I fly there with him on the private plane of John J. McCloy, who was on his way to Saudi Arabia. Secretary of war under Roosevelt, McCloy was now head of the Rockefellers' Chase bank, which was financing oil companies developing new fields in the Middle East and around the world. He was, Sam told me, probably as influential as any American in U.S. oil diplomacy in the Middle East.[37]

Speaking with McCloy during the flight, I learned that Chase was receiving constant requests from the new King Saud for loans against future oil-royalty earnings and that this perturbed the

---

37   Involved with U.S. Middle Eastern oil policies since the time of President Roosevelt's consideration of American-government ownership of the Saudi Arabian concessions, McCloy and his law firm figured prominently in the tax exemptions and antitrust waivers through which major U.S. oil companies prospered, nearly tax-free, abroad. In addition to heading the Chase bank, McCloy also represented the Rockefeller brothers' legal interests, including those relating to their holdings in companies making up Aramco.

British government. The king was squandering money, as were the many princes, and Saud had become a major backer of anti-Western political activity in the Near East. Intensely jealous of the Iraqi and Jordanian monarchies, his activities were designed more to bring them down than to harm the United States. Not a man of strong character, King Saud was easy prey to those seeking funds to undermine the Hashemite dynasties. He was flattered, too, by those proposing Saudi alliances with Egypt and Syria, apparently not understanding that their objective was the extinction of all monarchs, Saud included.

The British, McCloy explained, were constantly imploring the U.S. government to force Chase to cut down or control Saudi Arabia's oil revenues. Our talk of Saudi sovereignty and reluctance to interfere with private industry was rejected by the British as either naive or as camouflage for American plans to replace Britain in the Near East. Now, using the Trucial Sheikhdoms (on the Persian Gulf), where they had absolute control, the British were creating border incidents on Saudi Arabia's eastern flanks, which showed promise of leading to major tribal wars. McCloy, therefore, was going to see King Saud to explain the extent to which his foolish policies were making it difficult for Chase to continue the very loans upon which Saud was almost dependent. I now understood why Aramco's management had sent Sam Kopper to follow McCloy's activities closely. (Wearing another hat on this trip, Kopper was also helping Adlai Stevenson prepare Middle East policy positions for use in the next year's presidential campaign.)

When we landed in Damascus I immediately drafted and sent a cable to Washington describing what McCloy had explained to me about his mission. When I then told Sam what I'd done, he laughed. "Colonel, you've still got so much to learn." Taken aback, I asked him what he meant. McCloy, Sam said, would undoubtedly be addressing King Saud in the name of President Eisenhower and Foster Dulles. Before leaving the United States, he explained, McCloy had probably told the American government just what he intended to say on its behalf. "Don't ever underestimate John McCloy's power," Sam warned, and added that the fact that I'd been able to learn of McCloy's plans couldn't hurt: it would show that I was doing my job.

Within a few days, Vernon Cassin, the new CIA chief of station for Syria, arrived. I was prepared for the worst. While in Beirut, I'd had dinner with Zogby and his wife. They had described Cassin as a complete professional who went by the book, and warned that he would resent my presence in Syria and my relationship with Allen Dulles and other top-level personnel. In time, Zogby suspected, Cassin would find allies in the senior level of career CIA men and make things difficult for me. When I showed my dismay, Zogby suggested that I work out of his office and commute to Syria when necessary. In fact, Zogby said, he had already made this recommendation in a letter to the Roosevelts.

In the flesh, Vern Cassin seemed to conform to Zogby's appraisal. Tall, with crew-cut hair, in his early thirties, the new COS (chief of station) seemed uncomfortable in my presence. He'd followed the Walter Snowdon pattern in arranging our first encounter: a cryptic note, discreetly dropped on my desk by Art Close, summoned me to a meeting in the CIA warren an hour after the embassy's closing time. Cassin's piercing eyes surveyed me, darted about the room, then blinked as he made his first comment on my operational techniques: couldn't I write shorter cables, to save money? Knowing that the cable Allen Dulles expected me to draft jointly with Ambassador Moose would be a long one, I dealt with Cassin's suggestion—and ended the meeting—by saying that I'd communicate in the future from Beirut, where Zogby had offered me access to his station's automated coding and transmission facilities. In effect, I'd just transferred myself to Lebanon.

Talking with Ambassador Moose, I learned that he was no longer so pessimistic about the U.S. role in Syria and now welcomed Allen Dulles's help in Washington to obtain approval of the arms sale. This, he thought, might permit President Quwwatly to maintain a constitutional government with support from General Shuqayr and the army.

Moose was heartened, he said, because in spite of Saudi, Egyptian, and French pressure influencing internal and foreign affairs in Syria, the country now had an anticommunist president presumably willing to keep the country uncommitted and dedicated to strengthening it internally. Thus, Moose now felt, if the United States could make policy decisions about Syria on the basis of what benefited Syria and the United States alone, we stood a good chance of reversing the leftist trend that had caused our previous concern. Coming from James S. Moose, Jr., I thought, this amounted to almost unheard-of optimism.

Now, since Allen Dulles had agreed to give serious consideration to our opinions, Moose charged me with drafting a joint cable integrating his views with what I knew of Defense and JSC policy considerations. All this, Moose hoped, would enable Dulles to endorse Syria's request for arms before the OCB as being consistent with America's long-range interests in the Middle East.

While I worked on the cable, I referred to the implications in Syria of a Soviet arms deal with Egypt, but my final argument pointed up how seldom the U.S. had found favorable opportunities for enhancing its position in Syria. Could we, I wrote, pass up this chance while we awaited the elusive Arab-Israeli peace agreement?

Moose approved my cable and added some news to it. President Quwwalty had ordered released from prison conservative officers arrested by the army's proleftist G-2, Colonel Abdul Hamid Sarraj, and had also pledged that all procommunist officers would be purged from the armed forces "within one week." Quwwatly and General Shuqayr were sending to Washington the journalist who'd arranged our meeting with the chief of staff, empowering him to press for approval of Syria's request to buy U.S. arms. Because of this, rather than build up hopes to the extent that an anti-U.S. reaction would follow refusal, Moose felt obliged to inform Shuqayr of the possibility that the U.S. might suspend all arms sales to the Near East.

Taking a taxi to Beirut, I sent my long cable to Allen Dulles, then went for lunch to the Hotel Saint Georges, whose bar was a haven for the foreign press corps. There I joined Sam Pope Brewer, Middle East Bureau Chief of the *New York Times*, to whom Sam Kopper had introduced me. I'd found Brewer a trained listener and also a man with enough facts accumulated during two previous assignments to the area to draw his own conclusions. Kopper had said that Brewer was one of the few newsmen who'd never betrayed a confidence and, as a valuable source of what went on behind the news, someone I should get to know better. Having just received my new calling cards, I passed Brewer an OCB card to support Sam Kopper's description of my duties as involving area-policy coordination. After drinks, Brewer and I agreed to meet for dinner.

When he joined me that evening, Sam was carrying the just released translation of Nasser's September 27 announcement of an agreement with Czechoslovakia to exchange arms for Egyptian cotton. Shaken, I told Brewer that I feared that Soviet influence had now entered the Near East to stay. As he opened the cables the *Times* had sent him to give background for the story they'd ordered on local reactions, Sam read and passed to me the text of U.S. statements about the Egyptian deal. At the U.N. our officials had acknowledged that the United States had rejected an Egyptian request, in June, for heavy military equipment, because we feared that it "would alter the balance of forces in the Middle East." Furthermore, in 1954, according to these sources, Egypt had rejected a mutual-security agreement with the U.S. under which American arms "could not be used for aggression." Reading this, I couldn't suppress a four-letter statement of disgust. When Brewer asked what was bothering me, I explained that Egypt had signed an arms agreement with the United States in December 1952, containing precisely these restrictions on the use of our arms, and added that I'd personally conducted the 1954 negotiations with Nasser.

There was also a joint statement, from Secretary Dulles and British foreign secretary Macmillan, saying that the United States and Britain "have for some time been in close consultation with each other" regarding "arms-supply policies in the Middle East," and that the United States and Britain were in "complete harmony" on the subject, basing their policies "on the desire, on one hand, to enable the various countries to provide for internal security and for their defense, and, on the other, to avoid an arms race that would inevitably increase tensions within the area."

I shook my head. It was obvious that such obfuscation would badly set back our position in the area and certainly damage for years the prospects for peace. Everything I knew made me conclude that Foster Dulles had simply been induced to go along with the British in order to crush Nasser. All the rest was no more than double-talk.

Later that night, while Sam typed away on his story, another cable came in. Assistant Secretary of State George Allen was being sent by Secretary Dulles to Cairo for talks with Nasser. As if to convey the impression that the Egyptian-Czech arms deal didn't concern us, the trip was billed as a routine area visit by Allen to several countries to "discuss current problems." I'd had enough of that baloney for one night and left Sam to his work.

Driving into Damascus to meet Ambassador Moose the next day, I had the feeling that it was all over now, that we'd soon be seeing Soviet tanks and trucks on these streets. Determined to try, I asked Moose if he'd support me if I flew immediately to Cairo to plead with George Allen for favorable consideration of the Syrian arms request. He gave his approval but said that he was afraid my mission would be fruitless.

I was met at Cairo airport by Charles Cremeans, with whom I'd worked when he was the CIA's principal analyst for the Middle East on the National Board of Estimates. Filling me in, Cremeans said that Foster Dulles's abrupt decision to send George Allen had angered Nasser, who anticipated an ultimatum, and the CIA was now desperately trying to mollify him. Kim Roosevelt and Miles Copeland (now based in Washington) had flown in before Nasser's announcement and were optimistic that Roosevelt still might induce Nasser to cancel the Czech-arms deal. When Cremeans told me that he now dealt with the Egyptian minister of interior and frequently saw Nasser himself, I asked him, jokingly, if he might be teaching them how to dominate the Arab world. More seriously than I'd expected, Chuck said that this had been the original CIA plan but that now the agency was attempting to direct Egypt into fields compatible with U.S. objectives. Here, I thought, was one of the CIA's most scholarly analysts, a former university professor in Cairo, now engaged in covert political action instead of gathering intelligence about what Nasser's intentions might actually be.

On my way to see George Allen the next day, I encountered Ambassador Byroade in his outer office, dictating telegrams. "Have at him while he's free," Byroade said, and I wondered if he thought that I, too, might have come as another CIA "expert" hoping to get into the Egyptian-arms act. "If I can make a strong-enough case for Syria on behalf of Moose and myself," I told him, "perhaps Allen will remember that the world doesn't revolve around Cairo alone." Byroade smiled, and I felt somewhat better.

George Venable Allen was no run-of-the-mill assistant secretary of state, having spent twenty-five years in the diplomatic and consular corps and been ambassador to Iran, Yugoslavia, and India. Obviously uneasy with his current assignment, he seemed relieved when I said that my only interest in the Egyptian-arms deal was its possible effect on future Syrian actions. He sat silent as I described the situation in Syria as Moose and I perceived it. When he asked if negotiating an arms agreement with Syria would be decisive, I replied that it would not unless it was followed promptly with sales of equipment. Allen doubted, he said, that "in his present mood" the secretary would consider it, but invited me to state my case in writing.

Getting to work, I quoted Ambassador Moose's opinion that Syria now had in hand a Soviet proposal to barter cotton for arms and pointed out that a month had passed since Syria's formal request to purchase a small number of military vehicles. This request had been left unanswered, I wrote, apparently because of Washington's unwillingness to take a stand either way. Unlike Egypt, I argued, in Syria both the Communist party and leftist groups were well organized and operating openly, putting strong pressure on the new government to accept the Soviet-arms offer. Trying to be sure to fill Allen in on Pentagon planning, I emphasized that the entire "northern tier" defense concept depended upon unrestricted access to lines of communication from the Mediterranean, through Syria, and on to Iran. In conclusion, I stressed that although responding favorably to Syria's request might be construed as entering into a Middle East arms race with the Soviets, the alternative was to be forced at some future point to dislodge Russia from this vital area. If for the second time in one year, we turned down Syrian attempts to obtain arms, we'd have little reason to condemn a decision by Syria to resort to other sources. To this memorandum I attached a copy of my joint message with Ambassador Moose to Allen Dulles, then sent a cable to Moose summarizing what I'd written.

Although I'd expected to encounter frantic conferences in progress, I returned with my report to learn that Roosevelt was off playing tennis, that Ambassador Eric Johnston, who'd flown in for the emergency, was napping, and that Henry Byroade was at my hotel for a steam bath. Free to see me, George Allen praised what I'd written but then said that he could be of no help to me, that nothing he might do would make any difference. When I asked if Allen Dulles's support of Syria's application in the OCB and NSC wouldn't influence policy, Allen deliberated and then replied almost with reluctance. "You should know," he finally said, "that contrary to anything you've learned about Washington, the entire foreign policy of the United States is—and has been for months—in the hands of a not easily influenced man: Secretary of State John Foster Dulles."

Prior to the July 1955 Geneva summit conference, Allen explained, the President had accepted Secretary Dulles's "Open Skies" proposal to the Russians and believed that this presaged the end of East-West conflicts throughout the world. Since August the President had first been on vacation and then hospitalized by his heart attack. Now, while the President's condition remained in doubt, it would be foolish to expect the Secretary of State to accuse Russia of violating the "Spirit of Geneva."[38] Had Nasser just been patient and aware of the dangers to Egypt that came from communism, Allen said, Secretary Dulles would have had time to persuade the Russians to withdraw the Czech-arms offer and

---

38   Although Russia eventually rejected the U.S. proposal ("Open Skies") of reciprocal inspection of air bases and defense installations, Bulganin's acceptance of Eisenhower's promise that the U.S. would never take part in an aggressive war produced what was known as the "Spirit of Geneva." East-West cooperation to end the cold war seemed possible now, and at Geneva, Khrushchev had assured Foster Dulles that there would be no Soviet arms sales to Egypt.

there would have been no reason for the present crisis in Cairo. It seemed to me that it might have been easier if we'd sold arms to Egypt on credit and been able to control their use, so I pressed on with my questions.

What, I asked, about reports that Allen had arrived to deliver an "ultimatum" to Nasser? Did anybody really think that a threat to withhold $50 million in economic aid from Egypt would induce Nasser to forego Soviet arms when Israel's forces were killing Egyptian soldiers 200 miles away in Gaza? There would be no threats, Allen responded. Together with Britain, we were refusing Israel's arms requests in order to avoid future clashes. Risking Allen's irritation, I continued and said that this overlooked the fact that France was shipping its most advanced Mystère jets to the Israelis. Should it, I asked, now come as a surprise if Syria and Egypt bought Russian MIGs to defend against Israel's air force? While not challenging my point, George Allen was clearly losing his patience. Indicating that our conversation was over, he suggested that I await the outcome of his meeting with Nasser. Then, he said, we'd know what the Egyptian-arms deal was all about and could assess what its impact in Syria might be.

Leaving Allen, I went over to the office of Jim Eichelberger of the Cairo CIA station. He was talking to Miles Copeland about Ambassador Byroade and his relations with Nasser, which, according to Miles, had deteriorated to the point where "even Kim Roosevelt might not be able to save Byroade's skin." According to Copeland, some young Nasser supporters had cornered the embassy's labor attaché and accused him of being a spy. Then, while Egyptian police stood by watching, the attaché had been savagely beaten. "Is he one of your people?" I asked Eichelberger. "Hell no," he replied. "If he had been, Byroade probably wouldn't have been angry at all."

Impatient, Copeland said there was more to it than that. I listened incredulously as he insinuated that, had Byroade not protested to Nasser about the beating, Roosevelt and Copeland might have quashed the Czech-arms deal, or, at the very least, induced Nasser to associate it with enabling a strong Egypt to enter into peace negotiations with Israel. I'd already had evidence that Copeland tended to exaggerate, and the wagging of my head must have been obvious. Undaunted, Miles then said that Byroade had cracked under the strain, that he was now spending his time chasing women, and that George Allen's mandate included telling Ambassador Byroade to pack up and leave.

Tired of this gossip, I asked Copeland what had transpired during Major Hassan Touhami's visit to Washington to buy arms for Egypt. Miles complained that the Pentagon was the obstacle, that no one in the military believed that "Junior" was making Nasser's last-opportunity plea for help in averting a deal with the Russians. Now certain, from what George Allen (and my Pentagon friend) had told me, that the negative U.S. position had its roots in the State Department, I asked Copeland if he and Roosevelt might not have encouraged Nasser to believe that the Pentagon would overrule the secretary of state. My suggestion that the CIA had made promises it couldn't keep had no more effect on Miles than water on a duck's feathers, but I continued to press for the answer I sought. What, I asked him, had gone wrong during my meeting with Nasser the previous year? "You offered him peanuts, tied up in all sorts of strings," Copeland said. "This isn't just a two-bit nation; our meager offer to Egypt made Nasser believe that we considered his country just that."

"Then how much did he expect?" I asked.

"Multiply it by ten; say two hundred million," Miles estimated.

"It couldn't be that you led him to expect that much, could it?" I countered.

"We didn't originate that kind of thinking," Copeland shot back. "It was John Foster Dulles who first put those figures in General Naguib's head when they met in Cairo in 1952."

Because Secretary Dulles didn't share with the Pentagon news of all the commitments he made, I couldn't be certain whether Miles was bluffing, so I changed the subject and asked what had brought Eric Johnston to Cairo. That should be obvious, Miles said. The CIA had put him together with Nasser to sell the Jordan Valley Development Plan. My mind was boggled. What kind of logic dictated counting on a man who sat 400 miles from the Jordan's headwaters—which Nasser had never laid eyes on—to persuade the heads of three Arab governments that Nasser's agents and propaganda were trying to unseat to agree on this complex project? "Unless Nasser supports Johnston's Plan, it will fail," was Miles's answer to the question I was preparing to ask. I'd had enough of this crazy talk and left the room.

The next morning I received a cable from Ambassador Moose confirming his agreement with the cables to Allen Dulles I'd attached to my memorandum for George Allen. Asking that I inform Allen of this, Moose expressed his belief that the simple authority to negotiate an arms-aid agreement with Syria would be of doubtful value unless we were prepared promptly to sell at reasonable prices the equipment General Shuqayr had requested. Handing this message to Allen, I found him gloomily preoccupied with Nasser's delay in receiving him, quite happy to accept Moose's proposal that the Syrian question be discussed in Beirut, where the assistant secretary planned next to meet with our ambassadors to the Arab states. While I expected that nothing new would emerge at this conference—convened as an elaborate justification to show that Allen's dash to Cairo was part of a larger trip—I took the first plane to Lebanon, in order to sit with the senior envoys assembled in the hope that George Allen might announce a new U.S. policy to counter Russia's entry into the Near East arms-sales contest.

When he arrived the next day—apparently uncertain of his own future after failing to budge Nasser an inch—Allen was less frank with his own people than he had been in describing to me Secretary Dulles's personal direction of all U.S. policy for the Middle East. The gathering did, however, illustrate the mixed backgrounds of the advisers on whom the Department of State would have to rely for guidance at this critical juncture in the future of the Near Eaat. Our ambassadors to Iraq and Jordan were just embarking on their first Near Eastern assignments (Waldemar Gallman, like his predecessor Edward Crocker, brought experience in Poland to Baghdad; Lester Mallory had dispensed economic aid in Latin America before becoming ambassador in Amman). Tours as chief of mission in Indochina had qualified Donald Heath for home leave before taking over in Lebanon; and a brilliant "Old China hand," John Emmerson, had been sent over from Karachi, meanwhile, to hold the fort in Beirut.[39] Back from "exile" in Czechoslovakia was George Wadsworth, now en route to take over in Saudi Arabia. Although he was a seasoned Near Eastern veteran, either prudence or diplomacy stilled his inclination to remind us how prescient had been his 1947 warning that U.S. endorsement of Zionist plans for Palestine would bring Russia into the area as a political power within twenty years.

Ambassador Henry Byroade, meanwhile, was conspicuously absent. With Eric Johnston, Roosevelt, and Copeland still freewheeling in Cairo, he obviously considered refuting Roosevelt's allegations that he was unhinged to be more urgent than hearing George Allen improvise again. That left James Moose as the only chief of mission who'd lived with American policy for the area during the previous three years. Soon aware that Allen had no guidance to convey from Washington, Moose, Wadsworth, and I headed over the mountains to Syria.

Back in Damascus, Ambassador Moose and I found the Department of State's position on Syria's arms request contained in a personal cable addressed to me by Allen Dulles. It said that the entire U.S. arms policy for the Near East was being reevaluated and that no sales could be made at this time. Meanwhile, Dulles advised, the views of our embassies in London and Baghdad were being solicited regarding the possible effect of selling arms to Syria as a counter to the anti-Israeli pact Nasser was proposing for Egypt, Syria, and Saudi Arabia. Moose, Wadsworth, and I sighed in unison at the prospect of a decision about our policy toward Syria being predicated on factors other than what was best for Syria and America's position there. Worse, expecting Ambassador Gallman to provide qualified advice was illusory: although undoubtedly experienced in diplomatic negotiations, his only previous dealings

---

39   Like Moose's deputy, Robert Strong, John K. Emmerson was a victim of the McCarthy-era vindictiveness that precluded Senate confirmation of well-qualified senior diplomats who'd served in China for any ambassadorial post. Emmerson never overcame this barrier and retired in 1967 as a "diplomat in residence" at Stanford. Robert Strong was finally assigned as ambassador to Iraq, just before the 1967 break in Iraqi-American diplomatic relations that still continues.

with the Near East had been years earlier while he was serving at our London embassy; and his principal contact then had been Sir Michael Wright, now Britain's ambassador in Baghdad. Since Gallman had no background in current Arab politics, his advice could be expected to reflect Britain's desire to keep Syria weak, in order to permit its eventual takeover by Iraq. I'd already experienced the deference Ambassador Winthrop Aldrich in London accorded British wishes, and it seemed to me certain that as in the case of Egypt, America's policy on arms for Syria would really be Great Britain's.

With the Egyptian-Czech arms deal now a reality, it was possible that not even our sale of transportation equipment to Syria would preclude that country from later accepting a Soviet barter-arms offer should Israel again attack. Still, in anticipation that the Israelis would now demand arms to offset those Egypt was to acquire, Moose believed that we should not turn down the Syrians.

As the ambassador had anticipated, the United States soon decided to sell Israel "significant" quantities of arms. Because new sales of French aircraft to the Israelis had been disclosed, I concluded that a major arms race was about to begin. With the end of the year approaching, Washington had still not made a decision on approving Syria's request, and Ambassador Moose suggested that I might do more to force the issue by returning to the United States.

While I was preparing to leave, news came of a large Israeli attack on Syria that had left fifty-six Syrians dead, and an additional thirty taken prisoner.[40] In discussing this incident with Moose, I expressed my belief that the leftist politicians and army officers finally had all they needed to justify a Soviet-arms agreement, since the government of Syria now vowed never again to be caught unprepared against border attacks. The ambassador went even further, arguing that the Israelis had acted in full knowledge that Syria would turn to Russia for help. Israel, then, he said, could

---

40   The Israeli attack was debated in the Security Council after an intensive U.N. investigation. On January 19, 1956, a unanimous resolution was passed condemning Israel for a "flagrant violation" of the cease-fire and armistice agreements.

justify its requests for Western arms as anticommunist rather than anti-Arab.

The Department of State promptly announced suspension of consideration of all arms sales to the Arabs and the Israelis. And there was bad news elsewhere as I left Beirut to fly to Washington. Lebanon was filled with American and British civilians who'd been evacuated from Jordan, where anti-Western riots had been precipitated by a British mission to press for Jordanian membership in the Baghdad Pact.

The long flight home gave me time to reflect on the losses we had sustained in the Near East during 1955. Above all, it seemed that we'd let slip by what might be our last opportunity to prevent war in the area. What I'd seen in Cairo and Damascus provided ample proof that U.S. policy decisions gave little account to the advice and warnings of the two capable ambassadors representing the United States in these capitals. For nearly half the year, our foreign policy had been improvised by a strong-willed secretary of state making decisions for an absentee president. That we'd acted in concert with Britain with respect to Nasser and to arms sales to the area could hardly be seen as encouraging, since neither common motivations nor joint long-range plans were involved. To Prime Minister Eden and his government, the Egyptian president represented an implacable enemy to be crushed at any cost. Annoyed that Nasser had gone beyond passive neutrality and now recognized Communist China, Foster Dulles wanted to slap his wrist smartly, yet the secretary of state still countenanced the CIA's concept of using Egypt to constructively influence the other Arab states.

As for France, our ally in NATO had nonetheless embarked unilaterally on its own course in the Near East. Finally, the Israelis' aggressive posture seemed devised to exacerbate the area's instability, and I kept wondering why. Perhaps, I thought, Israel now considered time its enemy, concluding that only dramatic illustrations that the armistice lines drawn six years earlier were still insecure would induce the Western powers to pressure the still economically dependent Arab states to agree to make peace. No matter what the logic of this strategy, it had worked against the West's interests, and the Soviet Union now had a significant politico-military position in the Near East, having leapfrogged the entire "northern tier" and NATO. The Zionists had brought Soviet arms into the Near East in 1947 in order to win statehood for Israel; now Egypt and Syria were turning to the same source for arms to repel attacks by Israel's armed forces. The American reaction to the recognition of Communist China illustrated Foster Dulles's "selective" application of standards of international morality: Great Britain and Israel both recognized the mainland Chinese; yet when Egypt and Syria took similar measures, Dulles elected to treat these "immoral actions" as slaps against him personally.

CHAPTER THIRTEEN

PEACE OR PLOTS?

The mail from Damascus that awaited me in Washington included a Christmas card from Roy Atherton. He also enclosed a translation of an article from An Nasr, a Damascus daily that received support from Soviet and local Communist-party funds. "A prominent American personality," it read, "left Damascus after spending a few months, during which he contacted a number of political and nonpolitical personalities. It was said that this personality was entrusted with a very serious mission by the brother of Mr. Dulles, U. S. Secretary of State, who is chief of the Central Intelligence Agency."

Although, of course, the article could have been sheer speculation on the part of An Nasr, it was equally possible that Syrian intelligence had recruited or planted an agent among the local employees of our embassy. In either case, the article could be used for black propaganda purposes: an intelligence service would take an article from a paper it controlled and then distribute the item throughout the area as an authentic press report. I had to wonder, therefore, what this would do to my future in the Middle East.

The next day I saw Sam Kopper and told him about the An Nasr article. Kopper still didn't know that I was working for Allen Dulles. Shrugging off the item as unimportant, Sam suggested that I use it as a pretext to see Dulles and seek his help in another matter. The Syrians, he said, were planning to construct their first oil refinery at Homs, astride the pipeline that carried oil from Iraq's Mosul and Kirkuk fields to the Mediterranean. Although its Trans-Arabian Pipeline Company's route crossed southern Syria, Aramco as a company had no interest in the Iraq Petroleum Company's pipeline through Homs. Yet two of Aramco's parent companies (Exxon and Mobil) owned part of IPC, and all questions of pipeline rights and royalties were of concern to the interlocking major American oil companies producing in the Middle East. Under its pipeline agreements, Syria had rights to take a portion or all of its transit payments in crude oil for domestic refining. Syria, Kopper explained, had invited Russia and Czechoslovakia to bid for the Homs refinery, and this posed the threat of a communist country's being able to divert or block a portion of the Iraqi oil production flowing to Western Europe.

Sam proposed, accordingly, that I try to encourage both the Department of State and the CIA to make sure that an American company had an opportunity to tender for the engineering and construction of the Syrian refinery. He had, he said, already discussed this matter with Howard Page of Exxon. Since Page was one of the executives to whom I'd report as Aramco's representative in Riyadh, I'd greatly enhance my standing by working with him to keep a Soviet-bloc refinery out of Syria.

Oil-company interests and my personal goals aside, Sam's proposal seemed to me to be the first practical approach I'd heard to a sound U.S. program for assisting Syria. U.S. arms sales risked heightening the area tensions we were trying to assuage and would also deplete the country's dwindling foreign-exchange reserves. In addition to saving on the cost of imported fuel, an efficient refinery would benefit the economy of northern Syria, where many conservative Syrian politicians had their strength. If the CIA could give hidden money for arms aid to Nasser and get nothing in return, why couldn't such funds be used to subsidize a Syrian refinery and avoid the ponderous formal agreements that I doubted any Syrian government would be able to sign with the United States and survive?

Sam and I spoke further about how to proceed, but already I was seeing some benefit in the *An Nasr* article. If I returned to Syria to openly discuss the refinery project with officials of the government—as I had done with the arms sale—my actions would belie any accusations of involvement in clandestine political action. And if Syrian conservatives really wanted to counter the leftists, *An Nasr's* allegations of my high-level Washington connections would lend substance to my ability to ensure that a U.S. refinery could be provided on a basis competitive with any offered by the Soviet bloc.

When I saw Allen Dulles the next day, he had a proposal to make. As I knew, he said, the Egyptian-Czech arms deal had produced diverse reactions among the U.S., British, and French governments, whose Tripartite Declaration commitments to prevent a Near East arms race were now subjected to their first real test. Big Three meetings were scheduled for February 1956, Dulles explained, but the United States and the United Kingdom hoped to resolve their differences in advance. At the end of January Prime Minister Eden would confer with President Eisenhower, with preliminaries to this meeting set for the coming week. British Undersecretary for State Evelyn Shuckburgh and his staff would meet with the Department of State, George Allen acting as host. Dulles wanted me to attend these meetings. Usually; he said, Kim Roosevelt would participate on behalf of the CIA, but the British now associated Kim with the buildup of Nasser and believed that he'd dispensed huge sums of CIA money to instigate troubles for Britain in Saudi Arabia and the Persian Gulf states. Not wishing to expose Roosevelt to British questioning, Dulles said, the CIA would not be represented openly at all. But if I ostensibly attended on behalf of the OCB, my presence would be warranted; and this, both Dulles brothers had agreed, was what I should do.

Pleased that the cover I'd devised for employment by the CIA overseas would now be ratified in Washington, I accepted this proposal at once. Meanwhile, I'd meet with Francis Russell and his Alpha Group to familiarize myself with current U.S. planning for the Near East.

I then brought up the Syrian-refinery idea and found Allen Dulles enthusiastic. He proposed that we discuss it with Under-Secretary of State Hoover and offered to arrange a meeting soon.

Furthermore, Dulles said, he hoped that I'd take on the task of returning to Syria to determine the chances of the project's being accepted.

When I mentioned the *An Nasr* article, Dulles suggested that I make my headquarters in Beirut for a few months and visit Damascus only as the need arose. To facilitate this, my assignment would be broadened to include regional responsibilities with State Department backup orders to authorize my traveling throughout the entire Middle East. The prospect of having such credentials pleased me, and there was the further benefit of eliminating possible oil-company reservations about my activities by showing new orders for area travel. There was still the problem, however, of whether our ambassadors in the area would accept my visits on the basis of travel orders that might bear an indication of their CIA origin. Dulles's solution was simple: I was to draft a State Department telegram advising that I'd be working in the area on plans of the Alpha Group. He would then have his brother sign and send it.

While spending an afternoon with Francis Russell, I was brought up to date on how the Alpha planners saw the Near East situation. To begin with, there had been substantial progress toward resolving the crucial issues that divided the Arabs and the Israelis. In response to American urging Foreign Minister Moshe Sharett had submitted significant Israeli concessions as part of a comprehensive plan for permanent peace treaties with the Arabs. Along the lines of Eric Johnston's Jordan River Valley Plan, the Israelis were willing to join in unified development of the Jordan and Yarmuk valleys. Furthermore, Israel had now agreed to compensate the Palestinian refugees for all property they had left behind. Although the option of repatriation, contained in the U.N.'s resolutions, had not been volunteered by Israel, this was considered tolerable, since in fact only a small fraction of the refugees could be expected to elect to return.

Also included in Sharett's seven-point peace plan were provisions for the normalization of relations between the opposing parties. Natural lines of land communication between Egypt and Lebanon were offered; Jordan would have free port facilities at

Haifa and a road across the Negev to Egypt; Arab planes would be free to overfly Israel; and, to permit natural frontiers, Israel agreed to accept minor border adjustments.

This was indeed a heartening breakthrough in our search for peace, and from this initial position there seemed to be room for negotiation. That the United States would have to foot a large part of the bill for compensating the Palestinian refugees and for a major part of the water-development scheme appeared to be a reasonable price to pay compared to that of financing Israel's strained economy and its part in an arms race. Since this might be our last chance to promote a settlement while we still had the economic and political leverage to bring both sides into line, I wondered what forces outside the Near East might become involved. Could Britain and France put aside their political and commercial aspirations, for example, and might Russian adventurism play a role?

First, Russell and I discussed Russia's role. Traditionally, we'd assumed that Soviet objectives included gaining control of the oil fields of the Middle East and acquiring access to the warm-water ports of the Mediterranean. Yet the Alpha Group had no evidence of Russian success in lining up the Arabs against Israel or the West, and there were many reasons to conclude that the Soviet Union wished to avoid involvement in the Middle East, at least until it could quiet unrest developing within the satellite countries of the Soviet bloc. There had been, of course, the Egyptian-Czech arms deal and there might be another arms agreement with Syria; but we had left the Russians an opening to capitalize on our own mistakes and procrastination, and we'd failed to restrain the Israelis in their retaliatory raids against the Arabs. Even so, it would take at least a year for the Egyptians to learn to use effectively such arms as they received. Until then, we had both time and means to induce Nasser to subscribe to a plan for area peace.

One such inducement was the Aswan Dam, which we, the World Bank, and Britain were considering financing. Our ability to participate in this scheme was, however, not certain, Russell cautioned. There would be domestic opposition in Congress from both the southern cotton bloc (eager to keep Egypt's cotton off the market) and from Israel's supporters, and also from

Treasury Secretary Humphrey, who felt that British manufacturers and contractors would benefit tremendously even though the United Kingdom's cash contribution would be nominal. The Egyptians would also have to take steps to ameliorate relations with the Sudan, through which the headwaters of the Nile flowed.

Then, perhaps assuming that Allen Dulles had told me of another reason for Kim Roosevelt's absence from the U.S.-U.K. meetings, Russell spoke of the plans the Dulles brothers had made to bring Nasser and Ben-Gurion into personal peace negotiations. Former Deputy Secretary of Defense Robert Anderson was discussing this prospect with Nasser in Cairo; Kim Roosevelt had made the arrangements with the Egyptian president, and James Angleton (head of the CIA's counterintelligence division) was dealing with Ben-Gurion. So far the prospects of this plan were encouraging, in spite of the fact that neither Nasser nor Ben-Gurion trusted the other. Foreign Minister Sharett's comprehensive peace proposal had been advanced as a prelude to Egyptian-Israeli agreement to enter into negotiations. The problems, as Russell saw them, were twofold: there was the question of whether Nasser could persuade any other Arab state to agree to make peace with Israel; and Ben-Gurion's truculent attitude left the impression that he'd rather have arms for dealing with Nasser than negotiate the peace proposals Sharett had persuaded Israel's Mapai party to approve.

Apropos of the discussions in which I'd be participating the following week, there were other difficulties involving the British, who were trying to isolate Nasser and to establish Iraq as the major power in the Near East. Britain's influence over Jordan was clearly ending, and only a U.S. offer to take over the United Kingdom's subsidies would enable King Hussein to refuse Saudi offers of funding in return for an inflexible stance in opposition to peace with Israel. British instigation of Iraqi designs on Syria was suspected by the French, and both Egypt and Saudi Arabia were sure to consider a Syro-Iraqi merger as a move directed against them by the West.

Overall, the Alpha Group had concluded, it was impossible to predict what French policy for the Near East would be. Beset by domestic political problems stemming from North African Arab independence movements, the French seemed intent on striking out against Nasser by offering to arm Israel. In fact, it appeared that only France's commercial and cultural interests in the Levant barred an open French-Israeli alliance. Yet France was also dependent on Arab sources of oil and was a shareholder in Iraq's petroleum production. Furthermore, the French would suffer financial losses under the Sharett peace plan. Through commercial control of the Port of Beirut, France benefited from tolls on freight and would not gladly see this traffic diverted to Haifa, an equally logical entrepot for goods destined for the inland Arab states.

For these many reasons, then, the United States would have to take strong positions with both Britain and France during the Tripartite meetings, if an Arab-Israeli peace settlement were to stand any chance of success. This illustrated a problem inherent in employing the CIA to conduct diplomacy through its liaison channels: unless the United States informed its European allies of the peace initiative then underway, both Britain and France could be expected to proceed with their efforts to isolate or bring down Nasser—obviously our key to engendering Arab support for peace treaties with Israel was the Egyptian president.

When Russell finished his summary, my elation over Israel's proposals was considerably tempered. Yet, for the first time since the end of the 1948 Palestine fighting, there seemed to be international recognition that continuing hostilities in the Near East might lead to a global war. It had taken the Egyptian-Czech arms agreement to make this point, but if the United States, Great Britain, and France could agree on a plan based on Israel's offers, peace in the area seemed a real possibility. In fact, Russia hardly seemed to be the real villain: setting a common policy with our allies was essential. Otherwise we'd be handing the Soviet Union opportunities far more attractive than any of their planners could possibly devise. I was now eager to find out how much of America's secret planning would be revealed to Great Britain's representatives. We would cover all matters to be discussed between Eisenhower and Eden; should the prospects of peace between Egypt and Israel not dominate the discussions, this could indicate that the Dulles brothers were intent on pulling off a "coup" of their own.

■ ■ ■

When our meetings with British Undersecretary Evelyn Shuck-burgh and his team opened, any hope I had that Britain might respond with us to Israel's peace overtures disappeared as soon as I looked at the agenda. The Arab-Israeli dispute appeared only as a subheading under a discussion of U.S.-U.K objectives in the Middle East, for which only one half-day had been reserved. Yet, over the course of the six-day conference, two full days would be given to "Policy with Respect to Conflicts between Saudi Arabia and the [British] Sheikhdoms of Eastern and Southern Arabia." I felt only more depressed when Shuckburgh led off with a lengthy discourse on Britain's traditional interests and spheres of influence, thus taking up all of the first day's meeting.

In the summaries I prepared nightly for Allen Dulles, I began by calling attention to what Shuckburgh said was Britain's "paramount interest" in the Middle East—"oil, nothing else." As for the Baghdad Pact, under George Allen's questioning Shuckburgh conceded that it had little if any military value. Rather, its benefits were entirely political: although Great Britain's bilateral treaties with Iraq and Jordan might not be renewed, the pact offered a means of maintaining British bases and troops in both countries.

Another point Shuckburgh made at length was that Saudi Arabia was Britain's *bête noire*, and he wanted to discuss "what can be done to bring about a fundamental change in the government of Saudi Arabia." To me, as I wrote in my summary, that sounded as if the British wanted a coup to eliminate the Saudi monarchy and planned to try this with or without the help of the CIA.

I noted also that the U.S. agenda item dealing with anti-Western dissension growing in Kuwait, still under British protection, was viewed by the British with equanimity. A few rag-tailed communists were involved, Shuckburgh said, claiming that the real danger was in Jordan, where, with Saudi financing and Egyptian goading, the communists had instigated the riots against the Baghdad Pact. This didn't tally with what Francis Russell had told me about disaffected Palestinians being behind our troubles in

Jordan, and friends in Beirut had warned me that the Palestinian refugees were organizing in Kuwait. I wondered if both we and the British weren't underestimating the Palestinian movement in Jordan and Kuwait, terming it "communist" simply because we didn't know what it really was.

Through the days of talks that followed and while position papers were written on joint U.S.-U.K. matters of agreement, my mind kept going back to Shuckburgh's opening statement about Britain's need for oil. I wondered if the British really regarded peace among independent states of the Middle East as the best means of ensuring continuing access to the area's oil fields, or whether they hoped, instead, to retain control through what the British diplomat had jokingly referred to as their "tame Arabs." The "leftist drift" that America feared in Syria was hardly mentioned, and then only by Shuckburgh in the context of a close affinity between the Iraqis and the Syrians. And when George Allen had described Britain as vulnerable to attacks against colonialism, Shuckburgh had rejected this point with considerable heat. Yet if one examined Nasser's anti-Western outbursts, one saw that he struck out more often at foreign troops and bases than he did at our role in creating Israel as a Jewish state.

Finally, in a British-prepared summary of the meetings, I noticed a cryptic reference to "encouraging and finding scope for a more positive Egyptian leadership" should Nasser continue his present policies: a coup, I took that to mean. As for an Arab-Israeli peace settlement, there were only two areas of agreement: no arms sales in the Near East, and support of the Johnston Plan for the Jordan River. While reading this paper I looked around the conference table to the place occupied by Ambassador Byroade, who'd been brought back from Cairo to attend the meetings. Was it possible, I wondered, that the CIA was using Robert Anderson to discuss with Nasser a plan for peace with Israel without informing our own ambassador? This did seem consistent with Kermit Roosevelt's allegations that Byroade has lost all rapport with Nasser, and, if Foster Dulles no longer trusted his own chief of mission in Egypt, it was quite possible that the Dulles brothers had also decided to exclude the British and French from knowledge of their peace planning. I wondered how much they had told President Eisenhower to prepare him for the Big Three meeting—there was no question that he regarded preserving the Atlantic Alliance as being America's highest priority.

After the Shuckburgh meetings, I went with Allen Dulles to meet Under Secretary of State Herbert Hoover, Jr. I described Syria's plan to build its first refinery and noted that it would be in our interests to see that an American firm underbid the Russians and Czechs. I thought I'd stated my case succinctly and was just congratulating myself when Hoover said, "Who in hell put you up to this?" Startled, I said, "No one specifically, sir. The embassy would favor it and I know the oil companies would, too."

To my relief, Hoover replied that he thought the idea might have originated with the British—they were adept, he said, at devising expensive projects for the United States to finance. Knowing from Russell that Hoover disliked both the Aswan Dam plan and the Baghdad Pact because of the advantages the British had found in them, I responded that I believed that the Syrian refinery was favored by Howard Page of Exxon. This remark changed the whole atmosphere, and the under secretary asked what the U.S. government could do. Dulles then explained that I was being sent back to Damascus to determine whether the Syrian government would accept a low American bid or whether the Russians already had a decisive edge. Agreeing that this made sense, Hoover said that he'd discuss the proposal with the American oil companies involved in IPC and asked that I notify him before I left for the Near East.

As Dulles and I prepared to depart, he mentioned the U.S.-U.K. meetings and added that I'd been in attendance. "Damn it," Hoover exploded, "we didn't want any CIA people there!" When I described my OCB "cover," the under secretary seemed to be relieved. At that point Allen Dulles decided to remain on to speak privately with Hoover—another sign, I suspected, that we weren't telling the British what the CIA was doing in Egypt and Israel.

Once my business in Washington was finished, I learned from Hoover that he'd arranged for Howard Page to see me in Exxon's New York offices on my way back to Syria. When I asked how my role in this matter had been described to Page, the under secretary said he couldn't remember just what he'd said. The odds were, I thought, that at least one senior executive of an Aramco parent company now knew that I worked with the CIA.

In order to set the date for my departure, I met again with Allen Dulles and explained my plans. My review of the U.S.-U.K. conference papers had convinced me of a need for more understanding about whether the British might undertake unilateral covert action in Egypt or Saudi Arabia. I proposed, therefore, that I book passage on the same BOAC flight on which Evelyn Shuckburgh would return to England and try, in passing conversation, to learn more. Dulles perceived no objection and wished me good luck.

Weather delayed my flight's landing in New York, and I barely had time to see Howard Page and hear that he'd arranged that I meet in London with an American refinery-engineering company, Procon, that had its international offices in England. At least I'd been spared a long conversation during which Page might have asked me point-blank if I worked for the Central Intelligence Agency.

The flight with Shuckburgh was not very productive, perhaps not surprisingly, since the Eden-Eisenhower meeting was pending and the Washington meetings had impressed me as being more a British effort to explore America's intentions than to arrive at an agreed agenda for the Eden-Eisenhower conference as a prelude to the Tripartite summit. We did, however, talk about Iraq, and when I expressed my fears that Iraq's government might try to take over Syria by a coup or by force, Shuckburgh reacted with anger: "Perhaps you'd prefer to have the CIA's Nasser in control of Syria instead." In reply, I said that it might be preferable to allow the Syrians to determine their own fate, but Shuckburgh rejected this as impossible. Nasser, he argued, wanted to take over Syria and was acting for the Russians as their tool in the Middle East.

The cocktails we were drinking may have loosened Shuckburgh's tongue: he went on to say that U.S. money paid to King Saud was financing Nasser's Syrian quest, adding that I should have realized that stopping this was what the Washington meetings had been all about. Then, before we parted, Shuckburgh opined that someday America might wake up and realize that Iraq represented the salvation of the West in the Middle East.

As I sat thinking, adding Shuckburgh's remarks to what I'd heard in the U.S.-U.K. meetings, it seemed plain that for the British an Arab-Israel peace agreement was far from being what they sought; nor, it was obvious, had agreement been reached on a common U.S.-U.K. policy for the Middle East. Getting rid of Nasser and Saud had priority with Britain; setting up the Iraqis would be the next step; and, sometime later, the issue of peace between Israel and its neighbors could be approached. Now all the glow that I'd felt when Francis Russell described Moshe Sharett's plans for a comprehensive peace seemed to be fading away.[41]

---

41 See Sharett, *op. cit*, vol 5, pp. 1316 and 1328. During these days (January 1956) Foreign Minster Sharett continued to argue within his party for a continuation of the CIA peace probes, and against a preemptive war against Egypt by Israel. In expressing his doubt that Nasser would attack Israel, Sharett cautioned against provoking the Arabs militarily and stressed the need for Israel to expand its international ties, while continuing to seek arms from the United States. On June 17, 1956, Premier Ben-Gurion appointed Golda Myerson [later Meir] to replace Sharett as foreign minister, reportedly because Sharett was too cautious in his policies toward the Arab states and because he had failed to obtain U.S. arms for Israel.

No comparable opportunity to bring peace to the Middle East has since occurred, and one must wonder what might have happened had the United States conducted its peace negotiations through normal diplomatic channels, and in concert with Britain and France, who, with Israel, soon adopted their own secret plans for dealing with Nasser.

CHAPTER FOURTEEN

GAME PLANS

While in London, I met with Procon's executives, who, alerted by Exxon, agreed to send an engineer to Syria to obtain the refinery data and start work on their tender. When I arrived back in Damascus, I described to Ambassador Moose and Dick Funkhouser (of the embassy's economic section) the project as it existed so far, agreeing that I'd work in the background to arrange a fair hearing for the U.S. bid by the conservative politicians. Moose and I then discussed American arms sales to Syria and the U.S.-U.K. talks I'd just left. The Department of State had, I learned, sent out the Pentagon's pricing of the trucks and trailers Syria sought, but as I looked at the list I feared the deal would never go through. Just one cargo truck with trailer would cost twice as much as the reconditioned Czech tank they would haul. Furthermore, the price list was qualified as being for information only and was accompanied by a statement that no U.S. agreement to sell the equipment had been reached.

As he read over my notes of the Washington conference, Moose smiled when he saw that so little time had been devoted to the Palestine problem and to Syria. Venturing one of the few jokes I ever heard him make, the ambassador asked me if the summaries hadn't been written "by the foreign office in London."

When I left the embassy I went to the New Omayad to meet Michail Bey Ilyan, leader of the conservative Populist Party, who was staying at the hotel and with whom I'd talked at length many times since my assignment to Syria. A Christian and a wealthy landowner from Aleppo, Ilyan had once served as Syria's foreign minister. In the past he'd invariably greeted my return to Damascus with great eagerness, hoping that I might convey news that America had devised some miracle to put Syria and the Near East back on their feet. I felt embarrassed this time, aware of how Ilyan, like most politicians of the area, examined microscopically each U.S. press statement and official comment. For these men, America was endowed with power and wisdom. Each word and phrase, they believed, had been carefully thought out, with long-range objectives subtly hidden inside. If they'd only known how many off-the-cuff statements came out of Washington, how many of our officials had to consult maps before discussing the area, their confidence in the West would have been badly shaken.

Nonetheless, I had not sought out Ilyan just to acknowledge that nothing constructive concerning Syria had come out of the highly publicized U.S.-U.K. talks in Washington. Instead, I hoped to build up the idea of a U.S.-subsidized refinery as proof that America was more interested in Syria's economic ills and the welfare of its people than in emulating the Soviets' offers of expensive armaments.

Telling Ilyan that since the U.S. had induced Israel to offer concessions that the Arabs had long demanded, we planned to accord first priority to pressing for negotiations leading to Arab peace treaties with the Israelis. I'd been sent back to Syria, therefore, to ask Ilyan and his friends to give us time, to do everything possible to block a Soviet arms deal with Syria. In return, we'd bolster their efforts by arranging that Procon's refinery bid be lower than what the Russians or Czechs would charge for building one. In addition, I pointed out that American companies had pioneered refinery technology and that the Soviet bloc could at best offer nothing but inferior imitations. Although this proposal was obviously not what Ilyan had expected, he finally agreed to go along. At least, I thought, I'd made a start at gaining some time.

■ ■ ■

It was now time for me to move to Beirut. After settling in to a studio room at the Hotel Excelsior, I went to visit Ghosn Zogby at the CIA station. He was pleased to see me, and I looked forward to working with a man without ambitions for building an empire, who, rather, said that he was grateful for any additional intelligence coverage I might provide. To avoid misunderstandings and jurisdictional problems, we went to explain my assignment to Ambassador Donald Heath. Already alerted by a telegram from Foster Dulles, Heath offered me access to all embassy communications and seemed to take it for granted that having me based in Beirut would pose no problems. As I left, he handed me a large manila envelope that had been sent by pouch from the OCB. Showing its secret contents to Zogby, I broke out laughing, amused at just how effective my Washington cover had been. Assuming that I'd be involved in support of the Eden-Eisenhower meetings, the State Department's secretariat had sent to my former Washington office a complete set of talking-brief papers for use by the President during the two days he and Eden had conferred.

That meeting, in fact, had produced a communiqué, issued by the two heads of government, containing bold promises to strengthen the 1950 Tripartite Declaration (to limit arms shipments and use force if needed to prevent a Middle East war). Beyond deploring disruptive Soviet tactics, this was about all the two leaders said. As I read the stack of position papers I'd received, I saw one that revealed how we were being outmaneuvered again. It dealt with arms shipments, and while only the U.S. and U.K. had been involved in the Washington talks, it anticipated with distressing accuracy what the French position would be in the Tripartite talks that followed. Although the 1950 Declaration applied only to the Arab-Israeli conflict, Britain and France now wanted to expand it to cover their colonialistic problems. France sought to use this vehicle to curb arms in North Africa, while Britain wanted to exclude them from Saudi Arabia. Square in the middle, we had commitments to sell arms to the Saudis as a condition of renewing our 1951 Dhahran Airfield Agreement, and access to our North

African USAF bases depended upon the goodwill of the Arabs there. Also, we opposed arms sales to Israel, although we and the British acknowledged that the French would probably go ahead with them in spite of our wishes.

Although this presidential paper was headed "Arms Shipments to the Near East," it contained not a single reference to the Egyptian-Czech agreement or to U.S. objectives of using arms sales as leverage to bring about an Arab-Israeli peace. It seemed clear, then, that both Britain and France intended to do as they wished while the U.S. remained committed to using force, even outside the U.N., if large-scale fighting again broke out in the Middle East. I felt for Francis Russell and his Alpha planners: it seemed all the more certain that to the British and French, peace in the area was at best of secondary priority.

Still mulling over the papers I'd received, I was taken around by Zogby to meet the key operational members of his station: Raymond Close, Eugene Trone, and James Barracks. Ray Close (brother of Art, who was with the CIA in Damascus) handled a few Lebanese politicians from the Bekaa Valley. In addition, he dealt with the old-time American residents of Lebanon, who had for years been friends of the Close brothers' parents. Gene Trone was the principal contact with the Syrian Socialist Nationalist Party (known as the SSNP in Syria and in Lebanon as the PPS—*Parti Populaire Syrien*). Dedicated to Syrian-Lebanese unity, which had existed prior to French separation of the two countries at the end of World War I, this party had been outlawed in Syria. Now, with the tolerance of the Lebanese government, it was based in Lebanon's mountains.

Jim Barracks, a noncareer employee still weighing whether he wished to become part of the CIA, had been sent specially to Lebanon to handle contacts made by the Roosevelt cousins. One of his informants was Mohamed Khalil Abu Rish—generally known as Abu Said—whom I'd known since 1950 as *Time* magazine's capable local stringer.[42] During the Palestine fighting, Abu

---

42   By custom, many Arab men proclaim the achievement of producing a son by adopting the son's name and prefacing it with Abu—literally, "father."

Said had worked for Sam Brewer; and he was a fixture at the Hotel Saint Georges bar, where most foreign correspondents congregated. When Zogby told me that Abu Said had been "recruited" by Archie Roosevelt (the first chief of the Beirut station) and was one of the CIA's most capable "agents," I was shocked to recognize that such description of casual informants was part of the way in which overseas stations impressed Washington with the number of "intelligence assets" they controlled. It was clear to me that Abu Said had never been anybody's agent—he happened to believe that Americans were friends of the Arabs. If he could help, without straining his conscience, by passing on some of the information he acquired in abundance, he'd give it to Jim Barracks or Sam Brewer for the *New York Times*, although *Time* always had his first allegiance.

Remaining behind to chat with Ray Close and Barracks, I learned of their frustration over the manner in which Zogby evaluated and reported information he received from the station's informants. Speaking of Abu Said (a Palestinian now carrying a Jordanian passport), Jim complained that Abu Said constantly came up with significant information about the refugees that neither Zogby nor the CIA in Washington seemed to care about. Perhaps, I thought, this was only a reflection of Lebanon's attitude then that the Palestinians in their tin-hut camps were no more than a nuisance, although, as victims of the war with Israel, they also provided the Arabs with some political clout.

By contrast, I learned, Zogby had his own principal informant, Samir Souki, upon whom he depended almost exclusively for reports, which he accepted without question and immediately sent off to Washington. An Egyptian who'd somehow acquired a Lebanese passport, Souki had been a U.P. stringer in Palestine, and then worked for *Newsweek* until an American correspondent, Larry Collins, took over in Beirut.[43] Now Sam Souki was associated with Harry Kern (a close friend of Allen Dulles and Kim Roosevelt) in

---

43 After leaving Beirut in 1958 to take over the *Newsweek* bureau in Paris, Collins earned fame writing books. His *O Jerusalem* became a bestselling account of the Palestine war.

a service called *Foreign Reports*, which was sold to oil companies interested in the Middle East.[44] From Sam Brewer, who'd known Souki for years, I learned that taking money for information didn't bother Samir Souki in the least.

Zogby liked and trusted Souki, who frequently visited the chief of station in the embassy's CIA offices, where he wandered about as if he were part of the staff. Extremely close to the Egyptian ambassador and still owning property in Egypt, Sam Souki was a man whom neither Barracks nor Close trusted, nor did they like being exposed in the CIA's offices when Sam came around. Since my position was even more delicate, I soon refused to call on Zogby if the CIA secretaries said that his favorite informant was there. That Zog was the CIA's chief of station was certainly no secret: Sam Brewer and most American reporters called on him from time to time. Deciding to counter potential suspicion of my association with Zogby with apparent candor, I told Brewer and his colleagues that the CIA's director was a member of the OCB, so I naturally knew about some of the things the agency did and in fact on occasion used their communications channels for sending sensitive messages.

In this period there were many sensational headline stories in the European press about high-level meetings of the Western powers for dealing with the Middle East. Constantly used was the phrase "the threat of war," and from press briefings and leaks it appeared that the Big Three might be preparing to intervene militarily. An international tempest seemed to be brewing, according to the headlines, yet no matter what the view from Washington, London, or Paris, there was little to be seen on the spot in the Near East. The "crisis" in fact did not exist. The talk itself was what was dangerous, but our British and French allies seemed to want it that way.

---

44   Often serving as the CIA channel to the Japanese government, Kern, like Kim Roosevelt, had no compunctions about parlaying his CIA-associated access to high foreign officials into personal gain. In February 1979 the *New York Times* described Harry Kern as having represented the Grumman Aircraft Company (Roosevelt represented Northrop in Iran and the Middle East) in arranging the Japanese-jet-fighter sale that had shrouded the Japanese government with scandals. He reportedly was paid a commission on each sale.

This point was first impressed on me by Charles Malik, Lebanon's minister of foreign affairs. He said that he'd concluded, after a careful analysis of the European press, that the stories being circulated were strengthening Israel's hand. While not suggesting that Israel wanted war, Malik pointed out that the Israelis would be foolish not to take advantage of the "crisis" in order to justify large shipments of arms. Russian reaction to the possibility of Western intervention, he pointed out, had been strong, leaving Israel an opening to predict the bombing of Tel Aviv by Russian-supplied Egyptian jets. Malik proposed, therefore, that we shut down the high-level conferences. Matters might then cool down before we backed Nasser and the Arabs into a corner. If not, they'd have no face-saving alternative except to revive their threat to eventually wipe Israel off the face of the map.

Considering Malik's warning sound and to be worthy of Washington's attention, I dictated a cable to report it and passed the draft to Zogby for review. Delighted, Zog urged me to send the message but said that first he'd have to give me a Beirut-station pseudonym to use in place of the foreign minister's true name—a routine security measure, I was told. The next day Jim Barracks caught me at the hotel and broke out laughing as he explained that Zogby was boasting of Malik as the station's highest-level agent: I'd recruited the foreign minister as an agent, it seemed, simply by using his new code name in my report to CIA headquarters.

A note left at my hotel summoned me to a meeting with Michail Ilyan at a resort hotel in the Lebanese mountains, and he too spoke of the scare headlines in the Western press. Sharing Malik's fears about the effect they'd have on Nasser, he cited adverse effects in Syria as well. Cairo's *Al Ahram*, Ilyan said, had just reported that Syria had concluded a still secret arms deal with Russia in 1955 and that equipment would soon be arriving at Syrian ports. Saying that he knew positively that such reports were untrue, Ilyan argued that they were creating pressure on the government to reach an agreement with the Soviets on the assumption that the West was arming Israel.

While still spuming Russian and Czech offers of military assistance, Ilyan said, Syria was finding it difficult to refuse a Russian delegation and a Czech invitation for Syrian officers to visit Prague. Particularly if, as the Western press had it, a Middle East war was imminent, it would be even harder to refuse proffered assistance. Ilyan and his conservative Syrian colleagues were worried, but he repeated his assurances that there had been no arms deal. And unless the press headlines created a crisis, he said, he was confident that none would be made. As for the refinery project, Ilyan said the prospects for a U.S. proposal looked good. There would be a cabinet shuffle shortly, and a member of his party would head the ministry, which would have responsibility for making a contract award.

Because I'd recognized several Iraqis leaving the hotel as I arrived to meet Ilyan, including General Ghazi Daghestani in civilian clothes, I asked Ilyan why he'd come to Lebanon. He replied that he was going to see President Chamoun, his old friend, and nothing more. When I asked about Abdul Jalil ar Rawi, the Iraqi minister, Ilyan said that he hadn't seen him for some time. In fact, he added, the Iraqis seemed to have forgotten about Syria now that the Baghdad Pact had been signed.

Knowing that Ilyan was very pro-Iraqi, close to the crown prince, I suspected that I'd caught him in a lie. My hunch was that he was playing several sides just in case things went badly in Syria, the Iraqis and Chamoun being two of the cards he was keeping close to his vest. And who knew, I thought, he might have more.

Visiting Damascus a week later, I met with Dick Funkhouser and told him what Ilyan had said about the refinery and the probable cabinet changes. Confirming that ministerial shifts seemed imminent, Dick then said Procon's area vice-president from London had visited Damascus and received government approval for his firm to bid. Preparing the tender, however, would take at least two months; it was certain that no U.S.-subsidy decision would be made until the start of June.

Now, in the last week of March, I was wondering what I'd do in the meantime when I received a cable instructing me to proceed to London, where Jim Eichelberger would join me from Cairo for talks with the British government. On the long flight from Beirut to London I had time to catch up on what the English papers were saying, and found it hard to take seriously the tone of their comments about developments in the Near East. The press was lashing out at the "communist-serving Nasser" and calling King Saud degrading names. The Syrians were portrayed as nothing more than tools of the other two. Anti-American remarks were also frequent: we'd turned our backs on our British allies and were in league with our "tools" the Egyptians and the Saudis, who had vowed to chase Britain out of the Middle East. Depressed at what I read, I suspected we'd be in for a rough time at the upcoming meetings.

Jim Eichelberger arrived the next morning and moved into the suite my OCB calling card had enabled me to get at the Connaught Hotel. When he told me that we'd be meeting with Britain's Secret Intelligence Service, I asked him, jokingly, if we might be asked to join the British in doing away with Nasser. He responded without a trace of humor. "If our British cousins had their way," he said, "that would be just the plan," and we'd been sent to see that no such thing took place. Our instructions in fact were to meet the SIS for exploratory talks and stall any decisions until Allen Dulles and Kim Roosevelt came over at the start of the next week. As for why I'd been called in as a participant, Jim said that I'd been described as Allen Dulles's top man in Syria. That I'd just come from there, and Eichelberger from Egypt, would add weight to the U.S. position that conditions in Damascus and Cairo were not grave enough to warrant serious covert action.

I then asked him if that meant that I'd be identified as a CIA expert and would have to put aside my OCB cover. "Of course," Jim replied; "the British already know your true status." There was nothing I could do, but I wasn't pleased. In an attempt to cheer me, Eichelberger said that liaison relationships between the CIA and SIS were both completely frank and quite secure. Pondering this, I asked if we might be expected to join in something nasty simply because the British and French were upset. He said that this wasn't probable, but could happen if only to keep our allies from running completely wild. Resigned to my fate, I decided that at least I'd find out how the much vaunted British intelligence service operated. And if a joint intelligence operation in the Near East were put in motion, I assumed, I'd know about it in advance.

Going to our meeting, we rode the Underground to St. James Park Station. As we emerged, Eichelberger pointed across the street to a block of nondescript offices and referred to them as the Broadway Buildings, headquarters of Britain's Secret Intelligence Service (SIS or MI6). Officially known as the Government Communications Bureau, these buildings had been described so well in spy novels that most Londoners knew just what they were. Passing through the main building's lobby, we crossed an alley to another entrance. There, an ancient elevator carried us to the top floor. Seated at a long conference table in a small room whose plaster walls showed evidence of rain damage were our six hosts, wearing the drab English suits with ample wrinkles and stains to which I'd by now become accustomed. There wasn't a James Bond type in the bunch, and most looked like ordinary clerks in spite of the SIS's reputation for recruiting only Oxbridge graduates.

George Kennedy Young, deputy director to Major General Sir John Sinclair (the "nameless chief" of MI6, known to all but a few in Britain as "C"), was in charge. A big man, tough-looking, he promptly informed us that we were gathered at British initiative as the result of a change in U.K. policy with regard to the Middle East. The details of this change had been communicated to Secretary of State Dulles by Foreign Secretary Selwyn Lloyd, and, he went on, Foster Dulles had approved of what Britain proposed doing. Our meetings, then, were to prepare a joint "intelligence appreciation" of the Middle East situation justifying the new British strategy. Thinking back to the Shuckburgh meetings in Washington, the British hints that government changes were necessary in Egypt and Saudi Arabia, I wondered if the foreign office might have abandoned hope for U.S.-U.K. diplomatic collaboration and given George Young and his colleagues free rein.[45]

---

45 George Young, whose SIS cover was that of a senior official (later undersecretary) of the Ministry of Defence, held graduate degrees from Yale and had served in the British Middle East Office in Cairo. At the time of our 1956 meeting, Sinclair ("C") and Young were arranging to send to Beirut, under journalistic cover, H.A.R. (Kim) Philby, just vindicated in Parliament of accusations that he had been a Russian KGB plant in the SIS. Having just recovered from the embarrassment of this scandal, SIS, even more than Eden's

Since I couldn't be sure what the new British policy involved, I was relieved to hear Eichelberger say that we were merely a fact-finding mission, not authorized to agree to any particular plans or proposals. Impatient, Young shrugged this off, implying that we were simply not privy to the plans of our own governments and agreements already made between Lloyd and Dulles.

Moving on, Young said that Egypt, Saudi Arabia, and Syria threatened Britain's survival. Their governments would have to be subverted or overthrown. Iraq was the central point of British support and area stability; Prime Minister Nuri as Said's position had to be strengthened as much and as quickly as possible. Turkey and Iran were considered allies, and might be of help in any British action. Since Nasser, dedicated to the destruction of Israel and now an out-and-out Soviet instrument, could not be stopped immediately, priority must be given to Syria, which was about to become a Soviet satellite. Because adverse Saudi reaction to what would be done in Syria was sure to follow, the overthrow of King Saud would have to come next. Then, before Nasser could use Soviet bombers to eradicate Israel, he would have to be eliminated. The fates of Jordan and Lebanon depended upon prompt action to overthrow Syria's government, Young warned, so no more than a month could pass before this was completed.

Thinking that I'd entered a madhouse, I listened as George Young said that this first phase—the plan for Syria—could be implemented with Britain's own assets, with or without U.S. approval. We could be of help, however, in containing Saudi and Egyptian reactions until, in phases two and three, King Saud and Nasser were removed. In any case, at this moment the British were not prepared to reveal operational details of their plans for Syria, but they wanted to have immediately the U.S. position on the

government, was determined to demonstrate its ability to solve Britain's problems in the Middle East. In 1976, retired, a banker, and running a private antispy organization, Young made headlines by charging that Edward Heath's Tory government had been penetrated by a KGB agent—an M.P. or even a minister—and that the current Labour government was also a KGB target.

entire British scheme—before Allen Dulles's arrival, and by cable. On this note the first meeting ended.

Back at our hotel, Jim and I agreed that what we'd heard was sheer lunacy, undoubtedly an attempt by Young to provoke us and elicit alternate CIA proposals for action. We decided, therefore, not to send any messages until we could obtain specific details of the SIS planning.

At each of the three subsequent sessions the British behaved acrimoniously. George Young was clearly distressed that we weren't sending back daily cables, and the SIS position grew more extreme as a result. For instance, Young blasted Kim Roosevelt and said that his boasting about returning the shah of Iran to power had soured U.S.-Iranian relations, adding that Britain's position in Iran was the strongest it had been in fifty years. As for Egypt, he said we'd created a monster in Nasser, the intelligence we'd passed on about that country he termed "pure rubbish," and he claimed that we should either accept the SIS's evaluation of the Egyptian dictator or come right out and say we thought Britain's reports were "phony."

Because I'd just been in Damascus, I was able to bait Young until he revealed his plans for the Syrian coup. Turkey would create border incidents; the Iraqis would stir up the desert tribes; and the *Parti Populaire Syrien* in Lebanon would infiltrate the borders until mass confusion justified the use of invading Iraqi troops. Already, Young said, they'd discussed all this with the prospective participants.

At our last meeting, Young asked that I summarize my impressions of Britain's policy and plans. Biting my lip to avoid saying that I thought total insanity had set in, I told him that it seemed obvious that Britain was counting almost entirely on the Iraqis to accomplish their ends in Syria and Saudi Arabia. As for Egypt, I doubted that Iraq had any more capabilities there than did the British: talk about unseating Nasser sounded very much like wishful thinking to me. With that, George shook his head and said I'd forgotten one thing—"the snipcocks."

I was baffled by what he meant, but Eichelberger whispered that it was Young's term for the Israelis, an appellation dating from the British struggle with the Zionist terrorists during the Palestine mandate.[46] George then flashed a smile, not at all apologetic, and produced what he called a "minute," a summary of our talks. He suggested that we take it back to our hotel for use in preparing a cable to Allen Dulles. If we didn't mind, he'd stop by in the morning to review what we decided to write. Although Young didn't know it, he finally succeeded in getting us to the point of sending an operational-immediate cable by his reference to joint plans with the Israelis. He might have said it deliberately, of course, but if it really represented British-government thinking, both the Dulles brothers would have to know that our plans for an area peace settlement were now in real trouble.

While drafting our cable, Jim and I thought it might sound alarmist, but, after all, what we'd heard bordered on insanity. Yet, the next morning when Young stopped by to read it, he termed it satisfactory, except for several additions I inserted to the message as he dictated: "Britain is now prepared to fight its last battle"; "no matter what the cost we will win"; the "situation in Syria has been discussed with Israel, but not in terms of getting their positive support"; and "we have to face the possibility that Nasser might close the canal, and would like to know how the U.S. would react to that." Asking for a carbon copy of my finished message, Young said that our meetings would be discussed in the British cabinet, and I added that before I sent the cable off.

As we shared a bottle of White Label, Eichelberger and I appraised what we'd heard. Because Jim had been a part of the Kim Roosevelt clique that had taken such pride in "inventing" a pro-Western Nasser, I wasn't surprised when he said that there was absolutely no evidence that the Egyptian president was a tool of the Soviets. But I couldn't fault Eichel-berger's view that we had yet to oppose Nasser's policies openly and that we'd be be better

---

46 Young's wife, Geryke (of Batavian-Dutch parentage), was then and remains an anti-Zionist activist in England. Since retiring, George Young has joined his wife in a movement called the Society for Individual Freedom, which lashes out at all Semites (Jews and Arabs), Asians, and American blacks as inferior to the Western "pioneers of civilization."

off trying to counter his actions in a way that would leave room to negotiate with him when he finally realized that he might be smothered by the hug of the Russian bear. In fact, I thought, if we stood back while Nasser discovered how many strings would be tied to his new Soviet equipment, he might just share our views of the dangers of communism—then we'd be on the common ground that was part of Sam Kopper's "apple-pie diplomacy."

As Eichelberger flew back to Washington to be available for questioning, I relaxed over the weekend until Kim Roosevelt arrived. Apparently somewhat annoyed when he greeted me, Kim said that our cable had broken up the tennis game he'd been playing at Allen Dulles's home. Secretary Dulles had been out of town, so, not wishing to take a chance by sitting on the cable, Allen Dulles had passed it to Under Secretary Hoover. Not familiar with what Foster Dulles had discussed with the British, Hoover had panicked and called in the British ambassador and demanded an explanation. Although the ambassador had denied there was anything to what we'd cabled, there were enough suspicions in Hoover's mind that Secretary Dulles would have to straighten it all out. Roosevelt kept telling me that he wasn't angry, but even if he wasn't, I was. I held my temper when Kim told me to return to Syria, that he and Allen would handle the British government from now on: I was sure I'd soon be vindicated; also, I wasn't at all sure that George Young had been bluffing.

That the sensationalistic British press and dire predictions of the British government were creating international havoc became apparent when I reached Beirut. In the U.N. Security Council, Russia accused the West of creating a war scare in order to justify plans for intervening militarily in the Middle East on the pretext of preventing war. Several days later, there were indications that Foster Dulles might indeed have accepted Britain's new policy without informing either President Eisenhower or Herbert Hoover, Jr. Referring to the possible use of U.S. troops to ensure peace in the Near East, Dulles said at a press conference that "although congressional approval would be desirable before committing our forces, we might send U.S. troops without this if an emergency arose when Congress was not in session."

The President reacted immediately with a statement denying any such probability.

All of this, combined with Hoover's reaction to my cable, caused me to wonder if George Young might not have been entirely serious when he'd told us of the Dulles-Lloyd agreement on policy. What came out of the Allen Dulles-Kim Roosevelt meetings with Selwyn Lloyd and the SIS would provide a clue regarding the question of whether the Dulles brothers were making foreign policy on their own. Far from convinced that a coup in Syria was either justified or possible, let alone a solution to problems there, I considered that any indication of the CIA's willingness to back Britain's plans to use the Iraqis in Phase One of their area scheme could mean that Foster Dulles was in fact considering going along with the British all the way.

Within days I found evidence to support my suspicions about the SIS's plans for covert action: the British press carried stories reporting a serious tribal clash on Syria's border with Iraq. Certainly, I thought, this could be a prelude to the Syrian "instability" Young had described as justification for changing the government in Damascus. Nonetheless, I feared that if I sent a CIA message suggesting this, I'd be accused of trying to corroborate my London cable. For the first time, then, I tried another route.

I'd found out in Washington that Secretary Dulles read the *New York Times* in his limousine while riding to work and that his key staff officers had learned to be as prepared to answer the secretary's questions about news in the *Times* as those concerning our ambassadors' telegrams. I then looked up Sam Brewer and decided to use him without explaining what was involved. Discussing with him the scare headlines I'd seen in the London papers, I acknowledged that I'd just been in England. He was aware that I knew the Iraqis, and my casual suggestion that they might be trying to stir up the Syrians had the desired effect: Sam left for Syria, and the next day's *Times* carried a front-page report of the border incident. I was certain now that some of our policy planners in Washington might read into it what had occurred to me.

Having found out how useful Sam could be, I established my own set of ground rules for dealing with the many reporters I saw at the Saint Georges bar. Through Brewer I'd already met a number of distinguished correspondents and columnists—Cyrus ("Cy") Sulzberger, Joseph Alsop, and Homer Bigart were three—and I wanted to retain their trust. Of particular importance to me, they had access to sources of information—the radicals, for example—who were beyond my reach because of my official cover. I decided, accordingly, never to attempt to discourage a story even if sensitive or covert activities might be involved. In return for my access through them to information, and as a quid pro quo for being provided an additional channel of communications to Washington, I'd furnish them with occasional leads.

CHAPTER FIFTEEN

THE TICKING CLOCK 1956

It was a beautiful spring in Lebanon, and when I was offered the use of the naval attaché's Ford convertible, I decided to combine a tour of the country with a long-overdue visit to Aleppo, Syria. Removed from the rumors, intrigue, and bustle of Beirut, most of the Lebanese population seemed nearly oblivious to the struggles going on about them. In the south, near the common border with Israel, a smuggling trade flourished. High-up Lebanese politicians controlled this traffic with Israel and were growing rich even as they denounced each effort to bring about peace between the Arabs and Israelis. Swinging east to enter the southern end of the fertile Bekaa Valley, I traveled through vast fields of hashish, one of Lebanon's unofficial revenue-producing exports. This, too, was controlled by politicians who, in their parliament, trumpeted the morality of Lebanon's role in the Arab cause.

After spending a day in the imposing first-century Roman-temple ruins at Baalbek, I cut back to the Mediterranean and visited the port of Byblos, where 5,000 years earlier Egyptian ships had loaded lumber. Climbing to the famous Cedars of Lebanon above, I watched skiers race, before I descended through Zgharta to the port of Tripoli. Roadblocks and rifle fire impeded my progress, but not until later did I learn that I'd been in the midst of one of Lebanon's most serious religious disputes: the Moslem Karami family were endlessly fighting the Maronite Christian Franjiehs in something like a Hatfield-McCoy feud. Among other rackets, gun running, dope smuggling, and extortion filled Suleiman Franjieh's family coffers. As I drove north to cross Lebanon's border with Syria, I was sorry to leave so beautiful a land but very glad indeed to escape its pervasive corruption.

The quiet and beautiful coastline of Syria was filled with the farms of industrious peasants. As I passed through the ports of Tartus, Baniyas, and Latakia, no attempts were made to interfere with my freedom, and there was not the slightest sign of the Russian ships and Czech aircraft and tanks that I'd been told in London were turning Syria into a virtual Soviet base. Pushing on, I reached Aleppo, Syria's second-largest city. Its broad avenues and sidewalk cafés hummed with business activity, creating an atmosphere unlike that of Damascus, which was heavy with political machinations. Finally, heading south, I traveled through Hamah and Homs, passing ever more convoys of trucks as I approached the capital. The trucks were filled with flag-waving, shouting farmers and Bedouins, all obviously happy, as if en route to a county fair.

Picking my way through the traffic, I finally reached the Hotel New Omayad, where all seemed normal, including Ilyan and his nargileh-smoking followers grouped in the lobby. Speaking with him that evening, I asked about the convoys of trucks. Was it a holiday? Laughing, Ilyan said that I'd witnessed the preliminaries of what the press and the Western embassies would report as a "spontaneous demonstration by the 'street' in protest against the government."

He then explained that the leftists, supported financially by the communists, organized these expressions of "popular discontent." "Would you," Ilyan asked, "if you were a tenant farmer, poor laborer, or simple camel driver, be happy to receive ten Syrian pounds, free food and transportation, and a day in Damascus?" In return, all they had to do was march in a parade, carry flags and banners, and repeat some slogans. The schools would be closed tomorrow as a "safety precaution," Ilyan added, and then I'd see where the pupils spent their holiday.

The next morning at dawn I awoke to the noise from the walled courtyard of the secondary school just across the street. As I pulled back the curtains, I saw hundreds of students organized into columns, marching in serpentine lines, each headed by an adult cheerleader seated backward on the shoulders of the man bearing him. First slowly and softly, the students rehearsed and the prepared slogans. Then the tempo and volume increased, and by the time I was dressed a great roar rose from the courtyard below.

Not sure when this mob would be loosed on the streets, I drove straight to the embassy. The demonstrations, Ambassador Moose explained, were expected to call for the ouster of Premier Ghazzi's conservative government, the recognition of Communist China, and arms from Russia for defense against the Israelis.

When I said that it all seemed artificial, Moose disagreed. This wasn't the first demonstration of this type, he pointed out, nor would it be the last. "The more they shout these slogans," he said, "the more they tend to believe them." What I'd seen, he continued, was how Arab public opinion was influenced and formed: not, as in the United States, by advertising, interest groups, lobbies, and political rallies; but the effect was much the same. Unfortunately, he concluded, even if we had had unlimited funds there was little hope here of organizing demonstrations based on such sentiments as "Peace now with Israel" or "Unify Syria and Iraq."

When I asked why the government didn't regard the demonstrations as the false manifestations they were, Moose pointed out that once people flooded the streets, anything was possible. The military dictatorships could always rely on the army to control things, but we'd urged Syria to return to constitutional civilian government, and it was now doubtful that the president and cabinet could count on the army's support much longer. The young leftist officers were becoming more powerful all the time, and their goals resembled the slogans of the demonstrations we'd seen today.

Not wanting to remain to find out if this would be the "expression of popular opinion" that the Syrian army couldn't or wouldn't control, I decided to return to Beirut. Crossing the Bekaa Valley, I stopped at the old French resort hotel at Shuturah for lunch. I was enjoying a small bottle of Arak and a *mezzeh* when I noticed a group of men engaged in intense conversation about thirty feet away. The center of attention was a man wearing the aba and kaffiyeh of the desert, and his face was so familiar that I turned away lest a further display of interest betray my knowledge. It was Colonel Adib Shishakly, the deposed Syrian dictator, who was supposedly living in Spain. His presence obviously signaled plans to change Syria's government, but the real question was for and with whom he was working. One thing seemed certain: the Lebanese government knew he was here. As for his sponsors, they could be Syrian, Lebanese, British, French, Iraqi, or Turkish—or combinations of these—and about the only thing I felt sure of was that the CIA wasn't involved. I paid my bill and made a hasty exit.

Zogby was just leaving his office when I dashed in to report Shishakly's presence. He had heard rumors that the ex-dictator was back, Zog said, and asked me to accompany him home, where he'd be meeting his liaison contact with the Lebanese sureté. If I came along, we could both hear the official Lebanese explanation of what I'd seen. When I protested that this would blow my local cover, Zogby calmly explained that he'd already informed the sureté's chief about me. Security, he said, was no problem; his liaison relationship was based upon complete frankness. I agreed to go along with Zog, but was far from pleased. This was the second of at least two instances in which the CIA had identified me as one of its own. Moreover, the Syrian press had speculated correctly in the *An Nasr* article, and I was willing to bet that the Egyptians now knew all about me. Also, if what I'd heard of Israeli espionage in Arab countries was accurate, Mossad, too, had my name in its files.

To my relief, Zogby introduced me to Emir Farid Shehab, head of the Lebanese sureté, as a high-level consultant upon whom our area embassies relied. Although this may have been done for my benefit, I was pleased that Zog hadn't claimed I was part of his station staff. Perhaps, I thought, if I continued to conduct my activities completely in the open, even Shehab would eventually discount the possibility that I was a clandestine operator.

Certain that Shehab's people had reported on my recent trip in a diplomatically licensed vehicle, I spoke of visiting Aleppo to investigate sites for our planned consulate in order to justify how I'd happened to spot Colonel Shishakly on my return from Syria. Shehab merely nodded his head and smiled. The Lebanese, he said, knew of the ex-dictator's presence but did not consider it significant. He was merely visiting old friends socially, Farid told me, and would soon return to Spain. The sureté was following Shishakly's every move, however, just in case he again became involved in politics.

When I asked Shehab how Syria would react if it knew, he dismissed my question as unimportant. Although Zogby seemed satisfied with what Farid had said, I wondered if it really made any sense. Colonel Sarraj's Syrian G-2 operatives reportedly knew in detail of the *Parti Populaire Syrien's* activities in Lebanon and, with Egyptian help, had penetrated the local government. All Syria had to do was close its borders, and economic paralysis would soon immobilize Lebanon's entrepot economy. It seemed to me that Shehab was overconfident—or possibly being deceptive.

When I found Sam Brewer at the Saint Georges bar, I joined him for dinner and described the trip I'd made up the Syrian coast. Hearing my account of having visited Syria's ports without seeing any sign of Russian activity, Brewer showed me the day's London *Daily Telegraph*, which carried a front-page story of daily Soviet shipments and a Syrian arms pact with the Czechs. I remembered that I'd been told that the *Telegraph's* man in Beirut was almost certainly a deep-cover agent of the British SIS. It all fitted in with the attitude I'd encountered in my London meetings. According to British intelligence, of course, Syria was headed irreversibly toward becoming a Russian satellite.

Again I thought Sam could serve a purpose while covering a legitimate news story. Obviously it would have been easier for him simply to write a story based on our conversation, but by now, Brewer had agreed never to quote me or use me as the sole source of any report. I decided, therefore, to tell him that I was tired of seeing our Damascus embassy's reports being shot down in the British press. This was all the bait Sam Brewer needed, so critical was he of the English papers; he'd be off to the Syrian port of Latikia the next day, he assured me. Just as I was congratulating myself on another opportunity for confronting Foster Dulles with evidence that he'd accept as more accurate than his ambassadors' telegrams or what the British alleged about the Near East, Sam Kopper breezed in, fresh off the private airline that Aramco operated between New York and Dhahran.

At lunch the next day with Kopper, I learned of a new Aramco plan for paying transit royalties to the four Arab states (Lebanon, Jordan, Syria, and Saudi Arabia) through which the oil-company's subsidiary, Tapline, carried crude from the Persian Gulf fields to the Mediterranean.[47] Now, Sam said, an American commercial organization would put to a test the claims of Arab solidarity and see if Arab brotherhood in fact went beyond common opposition to colonialism and the state of Israel. To do this, however, would require some previously absent honesty. Quite deservedly, Aramco had been criticized for selling abroad at huge profits and grossly understating these to the oil-producing and transit states. Now, for the first time, the oil company was prepared to admit that it was cheaper to ship by pipeline to the Mediterranean than to transport crude oil in tankers around Arabia and through the Suez Canal. There was, obviously, a profit factor in Tapline—it was hardly the "service organization" that the petroleum companies had long held it to be.

Now, Kopper explained, Aramco was prepared to disclose the savings derived from its Tapline operation and divide them fifty-fifty with the Arab states through which the pipeline passed. The four transit states themselves, however, would have to decide how to share the money. Saudi Arabia had the greatest pipeline mileage and of course also had the oil it carried. Lebanon, with only short transit mileage, had the pipeline terminus and a small refinery. Without Lebanon, the pipeline would go nowhere and be useless. Both Jordan and Syria permitted the pipeline to carry oil through

47   The Trans-Arabian Pipeline Company was organized in 1945 and has been known since as Tapline. Construction was interrupted by the Palestine War, and Syria and Lebanon withheld agreement to its completion until 1949, when, in November, the first oil was pumped to the Mediterranean. This foreign construction project established Bechtel Corporation in the role it now plays as the world's largest oilfield engineering and construction company.

their territories. Thus, even the distribution of the minimal fees Aramco had been paying left the oil companies with the burden of adjudicating four bitterly contested claims. As I heard all this, I agreed with Sam that the Arabs would have only themselves to blame if they could not reach an equitable formula. We concurred in predicting that it could take a year.

I then confronted Kopper with the accusation that his company was still being only half-honest with the Saudi Arabian and American governments. "What," I asked him, "about the purely artificial 'posted price' under which your parent companies sell oil in the Persian Gulf at the end of a pipeline for a price calculated to be equal to that of oil shipped from Texas to these Middle Eastern ports?"[48]

"Hell, we can't let the Arabs' oil be sold for anything less than it would cost to ship Gulf of Mexico oil out here—we're just protecting the American economy," came the answer.

"And I suppose you are protecting the taxpayers at home by charging the U.S. Navy two bucks a barrel for oil that you produce for ten cents a barrel in a field a few miles away from the navy's loading port at Bahrain?" I shot back.

"That's just good business; we aren't a charity organization," Sam replied.

---

48   The "posted price," or "Gulf-plus" system, was agreed on by the oil-cartel members in 1928. It involves a "phantom freight" charge based on the sales (not cost) price of oil produced on the Texas Gulf Coast plus the freight rate between the Gulf Coast port and the Persian Gulf oil terminals. Thus, if oil sold for one dollar a barrel in Texas, and the freight rate from there to Bahrain was twenty-five cents a barrel, the oil produced in Bahrain and sold there would have a "posted price" of one dollar and twenty-five cents—even though it actually cost ten cents a barrel to produce and royalty payments to the Bahrain government amounted to an additional twenty cents. More-over, the twenty cents the oil company paid in royalties could be used as a credit against the oil company's U.S. taxes for domestic or foreign operations. There were many more of these "gimmicks," and only the oil companies who devised them knew where and how they appeared on the company's operating-costs statements. Naturally, the OPEC members were pleased to carry on the price formulas the oil companies devised, and the first OPEC increase in 1973 to five dollars and eleven cents a barrel had as its base the three-dollars-and-one-cent price that the oil companies charged for oil which cost a mere twenty-five cents to produce, even in 1973.

I realized that this was getting a bit touchy, but I had to ask Sam one more thing. "What about every cent the oil companies make out here, being free of U.S. income taxes—is that patriotism to keep the IRS from having to work so hard?" The impish grin on Kopper's face as he shifted the conversation was, to me, an admission that oil-company honesty had its limits.

Ordered to return to Washington for consultations, I stopped in London en route to speak with George Young, now that I knew that British claims about a disintegrating Syria were as much propaganda as they were fact. The London station's liaison between the CIA and SIS, Dan Debardeleben, found that Young would be occupied all day in meetings, so I told Dan of some of the phony claims I'd uncovered and attributed to the British government's panic. What I heard was not reassuring. Amid expressions of hope that agreement might be reached to stop Soviet-bloc shipments of arms to the Near East, Debardeleben told me, Bulganin and Khrushchev had just made an official visit to Britain. The conference had quickly turned sour: the SIS had sent a frogman to examine the underside of the powerful Russian cruiser that had landed the Russian leaders. The frogman had disappeared, the Russians had protested the incident, and the SIS was again being accused of bad judgment. Dan's conclusion about all this was that we should be even more aware of the possibility that the SIS might now try to salvage its reputation by coming up with some coup or political-action operation in the Near East.

Back in Washington, I obtained my first clue about what had emerged from the Allen Dulles-Kim Roosevelt meeting with Selwyn Lloyd in early April. The State Department's Middle East Policy Planning Group had organized a new task force, this one designated "Omega." As I learned this, I thought of Alpha, which had concentrated on an Arab-Israeli peace agreement. Now we had Omega, with nothing between the two, and I wondered if it signified a final effort or last chance. Kim Roosevelt's people in the CIA were preparing a request for policy guidance from Foster Dulles. The subject was "Operation Straggle." I'd heard George Young use this code name and knew it was British: it was, I learned, the plan for a coup d'état in Syria. It was now all too clear that the Dulles brothers had bought at least the first phase of the SIS concept advocated in the London meetings, which was, I assumed, why I'd been called back to Washington.

That plans to undertake a coup in Syria were centered in the Department of State struck me as highly unusual. I'd expected to see papers referring to NSC policy decisions and instructions that the OCB coordinate carrying them out. Instead, it seemed, the decision had been made by the secretary of state, and the Omega planners were in charge of following through. State desk officers were drafting the department's position on the request for CIA guidance Kim Roosevelt had signed on Allen Dulles's behalf. One encouraging development was that Omega was chaired by a seasoned Near Eastern diplomat for whom I had great respect— Raymond Arthur Hare, former ambassador to Saudi Arabia and Lebanon. Rather than try to buck the CIA head-on, I decided to sound out the Omega Group's attitude by arranging to see him.

Our long conversation provided me an opportunity for expressing my views that there could be found in Syria a brand of true Arab nationalism, not simply the negative and expansionist type Nasser espoused, but one opposing both communism and colonialism. Acknowledging the possibility, Hare proposed that I prepare a paper on this theme. Then, referring to his knowledge of Saudi Arabia, he questioned the possibility of any Western-backed action in Syria being interpreted by King Saud as anything other than an effort to facilitate an expansion of Iraq's Hashemite dynasty, concluding that this might affect our access to Saudi oil.

Before the final Omega drafting session, I handed Ray Hare the paper I'd prepared. After reading it carefully, he complimented me on the points I'd made and concurred in my expressed fears that the British might be stampeding us into an ill-conceived operation that Syria's conservatives couldn't sustain. I now considered Hare an ally, especially since the CIA had done little to solicit my views and the whole purpose of my being in Washington seemed unclear.

I didn't attend the May 23 meeting with Secretary Dulles, but when Ray Hare showed me the policy guidance to the CIA that it had produced, I was relieved to find that no final approval of a coup in Syria had been given. Instead, there was to be a "probing operation" to determine what assets we might have to assist in a covert political-action program to strengthen Syria's government. Then Hare winked. "You're to be the 'prober,'" he said. "Now, go out to Damascus and come back with recommendations. I'd say you have two months at the most."

Then, to illustrate that his voice had been heard, Hare showed me Foster Dulles's instructions that both Britain and Iraq were to be told that we presently opposed any covert action in Syria on their part. These instructions not only challenged British plans to use their "tame Arabs," the Iraqis, in Syria, but also poured cold water on any hope of U.S. agreement to a coup in Saudi Arabia. Recognizing that Iraqi participation with the United States and Britain would be almost impossible to conceal and would drive Saud straight into Nasser's arms, the secretary of state's position was explicit: "No success achieved in Syria could possibly compensate for the loss of Saudi Arabia."

Although I'd again been tempted to break off my CIA assignment and go into the petroleum business, my conversation with Norman S. Paul the next day provided an incentive for me to stay on to see the refinery project through. At thirty-seven, Paul was about my age, but of a quite different background—he'd attended Yale, been a lawyer, and had an independent income. We had, however, worked together in formulating NSC policy papers and had twice been on missions to Egypt at the same time. Now he had replaced Roger Goiran in charge of the CIA's clandestine services in the Near East and Africa. His very presence in the CIA heartened me. To begin with, I'd no longer stand out as an exception among the senior old-boy–OSS clique that had direct access to Allen Dulles's ear. Furthermore, I respected Norm Paul's judgment and his understanding of the Near East. Particularly if covert political action were to play a part in American policy for the area—and I was far from convinced that it should—Paul could be trusted to make intelligent decisions. Archie Roosevelt would remain as Norm Paul's deputy. From what little I'd seen and heard of this one of the two CIA Roosevelt cousins, he seemed as professionally competent as the reports I'd read from his tour in Iraq as military attaché.

The real question was how much influence Paul would have on Allen Dulles, who was no stranger to the Middle East. The Allen Dulles-Kim Roosevelt operation to oust Mossadeq as Iran's premier had led to Roosevelt's becoming an assistant deputy director of the clandestine services and, *de facto*, the CIA's "Mr. Middle East." Beyond his personal relationship with Allen Dulles, Kim had free rein in planning for the area because of the preoccupations of his superiors and colleagues. Deputy Director for Plans Frank Wisner was busy exercising what he considered to be his mandate from Foster Dulles to liberate the people behind the "iron curtain"; Richard Bissell was absorbed in the U-2 spy-plane project; and Richard Helms was dealing with the CIA's Berlin Wall tunnel, which had just been discovered by the Russians. Finally, because there were few career officers with Near Eastern experience, Kim Roosevelt had been able to dominate CIA decisions for the area. The sole exception to this was James Angleton, who was responsible for liaison with Israel: he worked with Roosevelt because Allen Dulles insisted he do so.

Kermit Roosevelt was then still an enigma to me. Even if the fawning praise of his acolyte Miles Copeland put one off, it was nonetheless clear that Kim had developed contacts with many prominent personalities in the Middle East.[49] It also seemed, however, that having always operated at such high levels and having lived in the area only briefly during wartime, these facts plus his own privileged background might prevent Kim from empathizing with the aspirations of the people who would shape the destiny of the Middle East. In any case, I was certain that our tussle in London had not been serious. In retrospect, I wished that I'd insisted on staying on until Allen Dulles's arrival. The existence of

---

49 Copeland delighted in telling stories of Kim's relationships with world leaders. One involved Roosevelt's acknowledgement that he'd felt comfortable calling India's Nehru by his first name (Pandit) yet couldn't bring himself to address Pope Pius as Eugenio—although the Holy Father always called Roosevelt "Kim."

"Operation Straggle" as a part of U.S, planning led me to wonder if Dulles and Roosevelt hadn't agreed with the secretary of state to give the British the impression that we accepted their plans for the Middle East. From what Norman Paul could tell me, we hadn't yet agreed to the entire British package. There was, at least, too much CIA prestige invested in Nasser. To forestall the SIS plan to eliminate the Egyptian president, the CIA had, apparently, compromised with an offer to consider joining in a Syrian coup.

CHAPTER SIXTEEN

A NIBBLE ON THE BAIT

My business finished, I flew off to Beirut, via Frankfurt, intentionally skipping London. Presumably one of the Dulles brothers would convey the U.S. position on "Straggle" to Selwyn Lloyd or the inscrutable "C," but I had no wish to expose myself to George Young's wrath when he realized that we'd be delaying his plan for Britain's "survival."

Although anti-Western rioting in Jordan had subsided, Nasser's "Voice of the Arabs" broadcasts still incited Jordan's Palestinians, and precipitated, in March 1956, the dismissal of British General John Bagot Glubb (or Glubb Pasha, as he was always known), the man who'd built Jordan's Arab Legion into a crack fighting force. A senior Arab general had been named by King Hussein to replace Glubb, most of whose key British staff officers had been sent off to England.

Alerted to the possibility of further trouble in Jordan, I found *Time's* Abu Said a nearly prescient, always reliable source of information about that beleaguered kingdom. Usually available at the other end of his telephone were contacts in the army, cabinet, and palace—even the king; they often phoned him news still unknown in the capital of Amman. In this way I learned of King Hussein's appointment of a young officer to take over the Arab Legion, Lieutenant Colonel Ali Abu Nuwar, promoted overnight to the rank of major general. Nuwar would be coming to Beirut the next day, Abu Said told me, and hinted strongly that I should meet him.

Until then hesitant about becoming involved in matters concerning Jordan, I changed my mind when I realized that the new Arab Legion commander was probably unknown to the Amman CIA station. Although the CIA had a young officer (Fred Latrash) in secret contact with Hussein, I assumed that I might help the station in Jordan by evaluating the new commander's attitude toward the West. It all worked out quite naturally: Sam Brewer was going to interview Nuwar, and I sat in as a friend.

The general said he represented Jordan's "free officers' movement," which to me sounded suspiciously like Nasser's Revolutionary Command Council. A new and larger Jordanian army would be organized, Nuwar said, and would integrate all units of the national guard. Only fifteen British-army technical advisers would be retained, and the Anglo-Jordanian Treaty's terms would have to be clarified. If Britain refused to honor its commitment to defend Jordan in case of Israeli attacks, then the treaty would have to go. This, I thought, didn't augur well for peaceful Jordanian-Israeli borders, and the inexperienced young general sounded as if he were spoiling for a fight.

He had no worries about Britain's threat to end its subsidy to Jordan, Nuwar said, since the Egyptians, Saudis, and Syrians had already offered to match it. As for military equipment, there was a Russian offer to accept if the British stopped supplies. He was also sure, he told us, that the United States would provide arms if Jordan requested them. At that point Sam blew my cover as a casual observer, calling me the American area expert on such matters. Aware then that he'd unwittingly muffed it, Brewer hastened to end the interview, and we left hoping that Nuwar had missed what Sam had said. But later that night Abu Said called to say that General Nuwar wanted a private chat with me. At least, I thought, I'd be typed as a policymaker, or as an arms peddler at the worst, since nothing had been said about the CIA.

Nuwar's message to me was short and simple: he sought U.S. help in freeing Jordan from dependence on British arms supplies. I said I'd report this to Ambassador Mallory in Amman, the proper channel for a request to our government, but the general insisted that Mallory was too close to British Ambassador Duke. He urged me to discuss the matter personally with King Hussein, who'd soon visit Lebanon in order to drive in a sports-car rally. All this led me to believe that Nuwar was unaware of the CIA-Hussein liaison through Fred Latrash. I agreed to watch for the king's arrival, and that ended our conversation.

I spent the next week in Syria, beginning with a long talk with Ambassador Moose. Although he'd heard of the new Omega Group, Moose knew nothing about "Straggle" and Secretary Dulles's position opposing a joint British-Iraqi coup in Syria as likely to affect adversely U.S. relations with Saudi Arabia. Under the circumstances, I used Moose as the first target of my "probing operation," assuming that the Department of State would tell him of U.S. planning when it considered this appropriate. I then asked the ambassador if there were enough conservative, pro-Iraqi politicians in Syria to form and sustain, with U.S. and U.K. encouragement, a strong anticommunist government, not necessarily pro-West, but capable of eliminating the leftist-oriented army officers. From his hesitation, I sensed that Moose was of two minds. Without question, he was convinced that the American position in the Near East could not improve unless we withdrew our support for Israel until it agreed to make peace with the Arabs. Yet, mindful that his predecessor had been demoted for inflexibly expressing this view, Moose was reluctant to present it as the only solution to Syria's problems. He had, moreover, acknowledged that the Arabs had never agreed on terms for making peace with Israel; they'd like to see the state disappear, but they knew that they couldn't defeat Israel militarily. And, although the ambassador regarded Iraq's aspirations to merge with Syria as being British-instigated, he considered an extension of Nasser's influence among Syrians a far greater threat to the West. So, he finally concluded, a pro-Iraqi Syrian government was probably the only practical solution available.

I then suggested to Moose that another possibility existed: the Ba'ath party, which advocated a completely independent Syria. In my view, I said, although the Ba'ath was dedicated to socialism, it was basically a party of Syrian nationalists who could be expected to oppose communist domination as well as Western colonialism. For the ambassador, however, the Ba'ath was anathema: he insisted that its leaders, although they were members of parliament, were collaborating with the Communist party's parliamentary deputy. Since all three spoke vehemently against the West, he said, all served Russia's objectives no matter how they phrased their devotion to Syrian independence and nationalism. I'd hoped that Moose might have changed his view of the Ba'ath, but it was clear that he would not look with favor on any contacts I had with its leaders.

Speaking with Roy Atherton of the embassy's political section, I learned that he felt we were not encouraging the Syrians to solve their own problems. As the junior member of the political section, however, he was unwilling to buck Moose's position against contacts with the Ba'ath. He did manage to talk to the socialists at diplomatic functions and had concluded that their nationalistic objectives might be compatible with our goals, yet he could not meet them officially. He'd hoped that the CIA would make contact with them, but Vern Cassin had chosen instead to build relationships with lower-level Syrian conservatives and businessmen.

Continuing to make my rounds to appraise the situation in Syria, I met with Iraq's Minister Rawi, who was still optimistic that Ilyan and his conservative political colleagues would be able to agree and form a strong anticommunist government. As for Iraq's plans in Syria, Rawi merely shrugged his shoulders: he was so violently opposed to Iraq's Prime Minister Nuri as Said that he had long since despaired of any Iraqi government's being able effectively to support the pro-Iraqi Syrians. His government's adherence to the Baghdad Pact, Rawi felt, had made it impossible for even the Syrians most friendly to Iraq to advocate collaboration between the two governments. Meanwhile, he explained, a new anti-Israeli force was being organized in Syria: the Palestinian refugees. Colonel Shaham of the Syrian army was already starting to train cadres of these refugees, which might one day supplement the Arab armies. Personally distressed by this development, Rawi said it illustrated the need for us to emphasize peace between the Arabs and Israelis before the Palestinians themselves became a force to be reckoned with.

When I met with Turkish Minister Kural, I found that he still felt that the Syrians would have to save themselves, that intervention by Iraq and Turkey would produce anti-Western reactions throughout the Near East. And, he said, it would provide the leftist Syrians with the excuse they sought for demanding closer ties with Russia. Kural again deplored our failure to seek common interests with the Ba'ath. Speaking frankly, however, the Turkish minister complained that his views were less popular than ever in Ankara since Turkey and Iraq had joined in the Baghdad Pact.

On Kural's suggestion, and with Ambassador Moose's approval, I went to see Sir John Gardner, the British ambassador. Initially reluctant to criticize his own government's pro-Iraqi stance, he spoke more freely when I told him of Washington's view that any attempt by Britain to use the Iraqis to intervene in Syria should await a determination of the strength and will of pro-Western Syrian politicians. We wanted to know, I said, if, even with clandestine U.S., U.K., and Iraqi support, a truly independent and nonaligned Syrian government could survive.

At this point, Sir John answered that the British ambassador in Baghdad had already assured Prime Minister Nuri as Said that the United States and Britain would back an Iraqi coup in Syria. When I asked if he believed that such intervention by Iraq was feasible, he said resignedly that the foreign office seemed to listen more to Sir Michael Wright in Iraq than to him, when matters involving Syria were concerned. This reminded me that both Evelyn Shuckburgh and George Young had said that there was a consensus of Britain's ambassadors in the Middle East that a coup in Syria was needed. It seemed quite obvious that Sir John wasn't being listened to in London.

I'd been avoiding Michail Ilyan, wanting to hear the views of others, but now we met once again. Hoping to provoke a strong response, I told him that the U.S. government was greatly disappointed that he and other patriotic Syrians were still squabbling. After a long pause, Ilyan flicked his worry beads, shrugged his shoulders, and reverted to an expression I'd heard him use so often: "*Ya Ahmee*,"[50] Then, with a half-smile, he looked at me and said, "Mr. Eveland, we aren't as bad as your government seems to think." Because I now feared that he'd learned about possible British and Iraqi intervention and might sit back and let it play out, what he said next took me by surprise. The present weak, leftist-intimidated prime minister and his government, he told me, would soon be forced to resign. In their place would be a new coalition government headed by the Nationalist-party leader and including two men personally designated by Ilyan. One of them, Majd ud-Din Jabiri, would be named to head the ministry that would make the final decision on the Homs refinery.

All this news pleased me: if what Ilyan described took place, even the Ba'athist deputies would be unable to dominate the conservative majority in Syria's parliament. At least until this conservative coalition could be tested, there seemed to be the prospect of stability and control of the "street." I then asked Ilyan why, as a former foreign minister, he didn't take a post in the new government. "*Ya Ahmed*," he said, "I'm a Christian in a Moslem country. I can be much more effective behind the scenes."

As I left I extended my congratulations and told Michail Bey I'd be watching in hopes that a truly independent Syria might be possible. "This may be our last chance," Ilyan said, "so don't leave the area until we try it." I promised not to.

Back in Beirut, I reported Ilyan's predictions to Washington and my view that no externally induced coup was warranted, at least until the conservatives formed their coalition government and we saw whether it could be anticommunist and still survive. The first part of Ilyan's prediction to me was soon confirmed, when the prime minister and his cabinet resigned. Two weeks, however, then went by without a new government's being formed. Meanwhile, the caretaker government made two disturbing policy pronouncements with whose consequences its successor would

---

50   Literally, "O my uncle," a catch-all used in Arabic, like the English "you know." It can be anything from a fond greeting to an expression of frustration over the obvious facts' being ignored.

be saddled: Syria intended to recognize Communist China; and Soviet Foreign Minister Shepilov would be visiting Damascus in June. Perhaps these developments stimulated the conservatives, because the coalition government soon materialized as Ilyan had predicted, obtaining the parliamentary votes of confidence it required.

Meanwhile, I told Sam Brewer what Rawi said about the Syrian army's training Palestinian refugees. My hope was that Sam would write a piece for the *Times*, and he did. I wanted to remind Washington that the Palestinians were more than just starving refugees. We'd not challenged Britain's interpretation of refugee activity in Kuwait as communist inspired, but this wasn't the point. As Rawi had warned me, we needed peace between the Israelis and the Arabs before the Palestinians themselves became a force with which the area would have to contend.

The sounds of Lebanese police sirens brought me to my Excelsior Hotel balcony at midday, and I looked across to the Saint Georges entrance at the motorcycles escorting a sleek silver Mercedes sports car. Its gull-wing doors flapped upward and from within emerged a short young man wearing a sports shirt and slacks. It may have been in an unconventional manner for royalty, but King Hussein had indeed arrived to compete in a sports-car race in the Lebanese mountains. When Abu Said approached me later in the Saint Georges bar, he said that he could arrange for me to meet Hussein sometime during his visit and asked for one of my OCB cards. Agreeing, I thought I'd be able to gauge Abu Said's influence with Hussein, whom he supposedly knew well.

Although I'd anticipated a few days' delay while my credentials were verified, the confidence I'd acquired in Abu Said proved to be fully warranted in this instance. When I arrived at my hotel that evening, the concierge greeted me with unusual formality. I was handed an envelope bearing the crest of the Jordanian embassy and addressed to "His Excellency Mr. Wilbur Crane Eveland." Within was a handwritten message from Jordan's chargé d'affaires to advise that the king would receive me in his suite at nine the next morning.

Hussein's erect bearing reflected both pride and the British military training he'd had before he'd been thrust onto the throne. Radio Cairo's appellation for him, "Dwarf King," bore no relation to Hussein's actual appearance. As for courage, few monarchs had been so tested. He'd been a boy when he saw his grandfather King Abdullah shot down, and later his father had cracked under mental pressure and been institutionalized in Turkey. Finally, the odds on Hussein's survival were growing less attractive every day.

I opened our conversation with a reference to my conversation with General Nuwar and said that in the past I'd been involved in U.S. military-aid planning. Using the imperial "we," Hussein expressed his own interest in obtaining the best equipment for his army, without regard to its source. "We expect soon to discuss this with your people," the king said, and I interpreted this to be an indication that an approach to Ambassador Mallory would be forthcoming. Not wishing to antagonize yet another ambassador, I decided to leave it at that and quickly mentioned that my principal interests involved the Syrian situation.

King Hussein said that developments in Syria were threatening Jordan. Most dangerous of all the Syrian problems, he said, was General Shuqayr, the armed-forces chief of staff, because he and his senior officers were dictating to President Quwwatly the makeup of the Syrian cabinet. When I suggested that it might be better to have the senior officers doing this than the younger leftist-oriented officers, Hussein said that Shuqayr was now challenging the new defense minister and might find himself out of a job. Then the young procommunist officers would be able to take control of the entire country. As our conversation about Syria continued, I began to feel less sanguine about Michail Ilyan's forecasts.

Leaving Hussein, I went to the embassy to prepare a cable reporting my meeting with him. I suggested that since the king now knew me, I might serve as a channel of communications to him during his frequent visits to Lebanon. Zogby was pleased With this, since if my proposal were accepted, it would add to the Beirut station's list of "agents" and its position as a center of regional CIA activities. But he was literally elated over news in a cable from Washington that he handed me, which said that the Roosevelt cousins would be arriving in Beirut within a few days. I was to arrange that they meet Ilyan in Damascus, which meant I'd have to leave immediately to alert Michail Bey. Two other reasons for this high-level mission were given: meetings with King Saud in Jidda and with King Hussein in Amman. Thinking back now to my morning's conversation with Hussein, I wondered if this might not involve what the king had had in his mind when he said that "we" expected soon to discuss arms with America. I hoped, in any case, that this didn't mean Kim would be getting into arms aid and subsidies, as he had done in Egypt.

On July 1, 1956, my thirty-eighth birthday, Kim and Archie arrived. Ilyan had been delighted when I told him of the visitors we'd have. He'd always admired F.D.R., he said, and to meet his sons would be an occasion of great historical moment. I didn't feel like getting into the difference between F.D.R. and Teddy, so I let this comment pass. I wanted to convey to him only that the cousins were important.

Kim stayed at the embassy to speak with Ambassador Moose, but Archie came as scheduled to our meeting in Ilyan's hotel suite. Explaining that he'd served at our embassies in Iraq and Lebanon and was still with the Department of State, he said he wanted to hear Ilyan's assessment of the Syrian situation and of what the United States could do to help Syria retain its independence. With dozens of *Ya Ahmees* and worry beads spinning back and forth, Ilyan described Syria's political ills and concluded, to my surprise, that outside help would be needed if things were to turn out right. When Archie asked what assistance would be needed, Ilyan spoke of the massive Saudi, Egyptian, and Soviet spending. Unless the anticommunist Syrians could match this, he said, their cause was doomed.

Not the least bit fazed, Archie asked what would be needed to give the Syrian conservatives enough control to purge the communists and their leftist sympathizers. Ilyan responded by ticking off names and places: the radio stations in Damascus and Aleppo; a few key senior officers; and enough money to buy newspapers now in Egyptian and Saudi hands.

While Archie listened calmly to all this, I was on the edge of my chair. Ilyan was talking about nothing short of a coup d'état. Roosevelt probed further. Could these things, he asked Ilyan, be done with U.S. money and assets alone, with no other Western or Near Eastern country involved? "*Ma'aloom*," Ilyan replied and nodded gravely. I didn't have to interpret for Arabist Roosevelt, who knew as well as I did that this meant "without question." Archie then departed.

I now sat alone with a Syrian who was smiling like the cat who'd just swallowed the canary. My mind still racing, I felt obliged to tell Ilyan that Archie had of course only been asking hypothetical questions. I can't say that Ilyan looked convinced.

When I returned to the embassy to see Ambassador Moose, on the heels of Kim Roosevelt's departure, I found the ambassador looking more than usually pleased. Kim, he told me, had explained U.S. plans for involvement in "Straggle" and my own assignment to the probing activities Secretary Dulles had directed. To my surprise, Moose gave no sign that he felt I'd bypassed him by not telling him in advance of this.

As we talked, Colonel Molloy barged in with the news that General Shuqayr had been forced into retirement, just as King Hussein had predicted. A little-known general, Nizam ud-Din, had been named to be chief of staff. Moose thought this might work out, but the ever pessimistic Molloy shrugged off General Nizam ud-Din as a "knucklehead" and an easy mark for the army G-2, Colonel Sarraj, to push around. Hearing this, I asked if anything else had happened and learned that parliament had just subjected all Palestinian refugees to the Syrian-army draft. Bob Molloy considered this development to be favorable: the independent Palestinian force would have to be disbanded, he said. Not wishing to appear a skeptic, I kept to myself the other danger I could envision, namely that no matter how they received their military training, more Palestinians would acquire skill in the use of arms.

Back in Beirut I encountered another situation threatening to disclose my CIA affiliation. Zogby's wife, Helen, had decided to throw a cocktail party for the Roosevelts, and I was expected, with the station's staff, to help in entertaining guests. As I reviewed the list of prominent personalities invited, I saw Sam Brewer's name sticking out like a sore thumb. I couldn't believe it: so much for secrecy! Over drinks at the Saint Georges, Brewer showed me a story he'd just cabled: Kim Roosevelt, described as an assistant to Foster Dulles, and Archie, an aide to Assistant Secretary George Allen, were in Beirut, the story read, en route to Jordan on a Sate Department mission. When I told Sam that I'd just returned from Syria to find an invitation to Zogby's party for the Roosevelts, he immediately suggested that I accompany him. At least in this way my arrival would seem quite normal and set me off from the spooks assisting Helen Zogby.

I'd hoped to speak with Kim and Archie about Syria after the cocktail party, eager to learn what plans the government as a whole, or the CIA, had in mind. This conversation was postponed, however, until the Omega Group could meet in Washington to make a final decision, and I was to be called back at that time. Meanwhile, Kim told me, the Roosevelts would fly in the Damascus air attaché's plane to Jordan and Saudi Arabia "to avoid the publicity associated with commercial travel." As for Jordan, he said, the U.S. had plans to bolster Hussein personally, while the British would continue to handle arms supplies.[51]

---

51 Although I didn't then appreciate the magnitude of what was to follow, this was the start of a U.S. program to "beef up" Hussein and Jordan. Under the CIA's system of pseudonyms and cryptonyms, the first two letters designated the countries in which the agents or operations were located: "WA" for Syria; "CU" for Iraq; "SI" for Egypt; "PE" for Lebanon; and "NO" for Jordan. King Hussein was NORMAN, and Kim selected NOBEEF to disguise the program to subsidize the king personally. For years this name covered the multimillion-dollar payments until, in 1977, the press stumbled onto the cryptonym, which was then exposed in the world press as "No-beef."

CHAPTER SEVENTEEN

THROUGH THE GLASS DARKLY

Spending a night in New York on my way to Washington, I saw in the *New York Times* a report indicating that the U.S.S.R. was planning to work both sides of the Arab-Israeli dispute in competing with the West for economic influence. The story said that Israel and Russia had reached an agreement for the Soviets to supply the Israelis' petroleum requirements and to provide well-drilling equipment for oil exploration in the Negev Desert. Wondering what the Omega planners would make of this, I remembered that Alpha had sought peace agreements and that now Omega was concerned with coping with British assertions that overthrowing governments represented the only means of preserving the West's influence in the Near East. Hardly a peace-making course of action, to be sure.

Reporting to the Omega Planning Group's conference room in the State Department, I joined the State desk officers and CIA representatives in reading draft position papers relating to "Straggle." A covering memorandum informed the secretary of state of the results of the CIA "probing operation" that he'd authorized on May 23. This operation, I read, had produced the conclusion "that it was within the capability of the indigenous anticommunist elements within Syria, assisted by the United States and the United Kingdom, to arrest the rapid drift toward the left." Two possible obstacles were cited: the presence in Lebanon of former Syrian president Shishakly, who might attempt a coup of his own; and the Syrian leftists, who might try to take over the government.

A Department of State attachment rejected the original "Straggle" concept of a coup, advocating instead a gradual strengthening of Western-oriented groups in Syria with concurrent elimination of the leftist officers from the army. The objective would be "the establishment of a nationalistic government in Syria, free of charges of being a Western puppet, and yet prepared to follow a moderate pro-Western and anticommunist policy." To encourage this, I read, we should be prepared to offer economic aid without the formal agreement required by the Mutual Security Act. Although both Iraq and the United Kingdom would prefer stronger action, the United States believed that the Iraqis would have to be restrained, and no Iraqi troops were to be used in this plan. We would take responsibility for encouraging Shishakly's departure from Lebanon, and both Britain and Iraq would be asked to help block his return.

So far, so good, I thought. There would be no coup; responsibility for action in Syria would be ours alone; and, if the secretary of state approved, there'd be money for subsidizing the oil refinery and other economic-aid projects: an appropriate way to offset Soviet inroads into Israel while avoiding the kind of military-aid competition we'd lost out on in Egypt.

Also attached to the memorandum to the secretary of state was a paper prepared by Kim Roosevelt, "Next Steps in Connection with Operation Straggle." As I read I thought that the description of the CIA's "probing operations" might better be entitled "Bill Eveland's Discussions with Michail Ilyan and Abdul Jalil ar Rawi, including Archie Roosevelt's Thoughts on How Ilyan Will Save Syria for US!" Kim's enclosure suggested that I was the CIA's key to Syria and that all the things that Ilyan had told Archie should be done were now actual CIA capabilities. I was tempted to laugh, but remembering that I didn't have the slightest idea how coups were staged, I read on.

Kim's paper concluded by stressing the necessity of restraining the British and Iraqis, warning that unless they kept their hands off, not even the most pro-Iraqi Syrians would be able to work toward what had been defined as U.S. objectives. This point struck me as sound, and I could see no reason why we might not try to learn from Ilyan more about what he hoped to accomplish and how. What I thought, of course, didn't matter: Kim had signed his paper on behalf of the CIA, and the agency undoubtedly had capabilities of which I was unaware. The meeting concluded with the decision that the memorandum and its enclosures would be put before Secretary Dulles the next day.

As I left the conference room I sighted Miles Copeland pacing the corridor outside. His face ashen, he drew me over to a corner. "The secretary of state has gone mad!" he said. Copeland had just spoken with Ahmed Hussein, the Egyptian ambassador, who'd been meeting with Foster Dulles that morning to hear the American decision on financing the Aswan High Dam. Miles quoted Hussein as saying that Secretary Dulles had insulted Nasser, the ambassador, the Arabs, and Arab nationalism, and, in withdrawing the U.S. offer to finance the dam, had implied that the Egyptians were politically, morally, and economically bankrupt. Predicting that Nasser would react violently, Copeland claimed that Hussein had been authorized to convey Egypt's agreement to all terms imposed by the United States for granting the loan.

I did my best to calm Kim Roosevelt's frenzied protégé, but with little effect. I reminded Copeland of his management-consulting firm's report that unless Egypt could contain its population explosion the country would be in worse shape ten years after the High Dam was completed than it was today. Then I asked him if building this expensive structure should be Nasser's first priority. That wasn't the point, Copeland said: the Egyptian president's personal prestige was involved, and the dam was a political necessity. Put off by this, I argued that Nasser wanted us to do more than finance the dam: several abortive Egyptian attempts to overthrow the Sudanese government now threatened that country's cooperation in granting Egypt access to the Nile's headwaters; and Nasser now seemed to expect the United States to mend his fences with the Sudan. Undaunted, Miles continued to defend Nasser. Secretary

Dulles, he said, had acted entirely out of a belief that Egypt had recognized Communist China and mortgaged the Egyptian cotton crop to buy Russian arms just to spite the American secretary of state.[52]

Because neither of us really knew what had transpired during the Dulles-Hussein meeting, I suggested to Copeland that since Nasser now knew the U.S. position on the long-pending arms-aid and dam-financing requests, we might expect a hiatus during which relations between our two countries could be improved. No, he said, Dulles wasn't through: the secretary of state personally sympathized with Britain's plans to eliminate Nasser. Having just seen the Omega Group's recommendation that we oppose British and Iraqi action in Syria, I found this hard to believe and said so. Copeland then told me that Secretary Dulles was assigning Raymond Hare to Cairo to replace Ambassador Byroade and that Assistant Secretary George Allen would be relieved of his Middle East responsibilities and named ambassador to Greece. Although these moves were very significant, I didn't realize what they represented until Copeland told me that Allen's replacement as assistant secretary would be William Rountree. That made it clear that Foster Dulles was now clearing the deck of any independent thinkers and would take complete personal charge of the Middle East. Rountree, a former intelligence researcher, was then George Allen's deputy and had reputedly progressed in the foreign service by seldom making independent decisions, thereby immunizing himself against accusations of being wrong. None of this encouraged me.

52 Originally favoring U.S. aid for the dam—both to benefit Egypt and to tie up for ten years credit Nasser might otherwise use to buy Soviet arms—Secretary Dulles knew before meeting Ambassador Hussein that opposition in Congress and from Treasury Secretary George Humphrey made American funding impossible. A diplomatically worded rejection had therefore been prepared in advance of the meeting for Dulles to hand to the Egyptian ambassador. Arriving with Nasser's instructions to accept American credit terms, Ahmed Hussein's joking (but false) intimation that Russia had offered alternative financing provoked an emotional outburst from Dulles, who alleged that a bankrupt Egypt was now trying to blackmail the United States.

The next morning I went with Allen Dulles to meet Under Secretary Hoover. Foster Dulles had agreed that the CIA would subsidize the Homs refinery, putting up any money needed to ensure the award of the contract to an American firm, even paying the entire cost if this were necessary to keep the Soviet bloc from building it. But we could not proceed openly, Hoover said: it would have to appear that Exxon was providing the funds. Howard Page would coordinate this, on Exxon's part, with Procon, which would actually build the refinery. My instructions were to see the Procon vice-president in charge of their London office to be sure that the bid was completed as rapidly as possible. I would then inform Syria's minister of public works that Procon was prepared to underbid the lowest offer received from any other source.

I rode back with Allen Dulles to his office, where he handed me a copy of the memorandum his brother had approved concerning "Straggle." Glancing at the cover page, I saw that it appeared to be the same as the draft that the Omega Planning Group had prepared. Not having time to read it in full, I asked if I might take this copy with me. When Dulles agreed, I said, "Well, it seems that we've left 'Straggle' behind." He made no response, so I rephrased my observation. "We've gone back to the WAKEFUL concept of bolstering the Syrians' capability of helping themselves, haven't we?"[53]

"That's it, exactly," Dulles replied. "Will you stay on until we do that?" When I asked if he really needed me, Dulles replied that my contacts in Syria were important and that he also wanted my ideas on how we could be certain that Shishakly would leave Lebanon. Zogby would express the U.S. position to the Lebanese sureté, but Dulles had reservations about asking Ambassador Heath to take up this delicate matter with President Chamoun. At that point I said that I could approach Chamoun directly if this would help. Dulles enthusiastically urged me to do so.

Realizing that I'd in effect volunteered to stay on in the area for the CIA by bragging about my entrée to Chamoun, I decided to

---

53   WAKEFUL was the CIA cryptonym covering my assignment to help "stem the leftist drift in Syria."

ask for something in return. Sick of living in hotels and riding taxis over the mountains to Damascus, I requested authorization to rent an apartment and furnish it. I also wanted the CIA to purchase for me the Ford convertible I'd been lent by Ed House, the naval attaché who was being replaced in Beirut. Dulles agreed without hesitation. As I stood up to leave, he handed me a copy of a thick CIA message from Vern Cassin in Damascus. "Take this with you," the DCI said. "It concerns the present situation in Syria." As I packed these documents in my briefcase, Dulles placed a telephone call to Norman Paul, telling him that I'd agreed to return and what my terms were. I gathered that my willingness to go back to the Near East had been in doubt.

For the first time, I left Washington with a one-way ticket to Beirut. My decision to commit my future to that troubled area also marked the end of a marriage that had been in difficulty since Baghdad in 1950. Dismayed when I'd given up the security of the army, my wife, Marjorie, had returned to her career as a nurse, and we were now really beyond reconciliation. My son, Crane, was eager to attend a military school and would still see me on visits almost as often as we were together now. I'd give up my home in Virginia, then; the Near East would now be my home.

Landing in London the next day, checking in by phone with our CIA station, I then went to meet Procon's vice-president, who was full of questions. Disclaiming knowledge of financing arrangements for the refinery project, I urged him to expedite the tender to the Syrian government and to contact Howard Page for confirmation that other arrangements were in order.

When I returned to the Connaught, I found a message from the London CIA station saying that SIS deputy director George Young was even then on his way to the hotel to see me. Still exhausted and wanting to report with total accuracy anything he had to say, I suddenly remembered that I was carrying a pocket Grundig wire recorder from Walter Snowdon to Ray Close. Having always been fascinated with gadgets, I set about rigging it up.

Young soon arrived, all business, and sat down in a small armchair in the corner. Just feet away, I placed myself on the edge of the bed, under which my flight bag containing the activated recorder reposed, giving off nary a telltale whir. Young started by saying that now that Secretary Dulles had infuriated Nasser by turning down the Aswan Dam, it was imperative to change the government in Syria, whether or not the United States agreed to go along. I should know, he said, that Britain and the Iraqis were mobilizing their Syrian assets and that a coup would be implemented even if it took the entire Iraqi army to make it work. Accusing us of temporizing and claiming that Secretary Dulles had agreed to the plan months ago, Young harangued me for a half-hour, as if to ensure that every word was impressed on my mind. I responded by saying that I wasn't a regular CIA officer and was merely assessing the situation in Syria to be sure that action there didn't cost the West its remaining Arab friends. Young laughed. "You're the key man and you know it," he said. "Let's stop playing games and get the job done now!" After a few remarks about Kim Roosevelt's omitting London on his way back to Beirut, Young departed.

Now alone, I retrieved the recorder and played back our entire conversation. Pleased with myself, I fell into a deep sleep.

Landing in Beirut, I soon met Kim Roosevelt at Zogby's home. Vern Cassin was there, too, just in from Damascus. When I told Kim of George Young's irritation at not seeing him in London, Roosevelt said he hoped I hadn't met with Young. After I explained that the CIA's London station had set up the meeting, he sighed with resignation and asked for a full report. Pulling the recorder from my briefcase, I announced that I had, verbatim, the words that would demonstrate the foul mood Young and the British were in.

To my amazement, Kim snatched the recorder from my hand and exclaimed indignantly that I'd just breached all the rules of spycraft among allies. Worse, he said, it was perfidious. Finding this somewhat strange—what, after all, was the game that intelligence services played?—I suggested that we all listen to the recording. "That won't be necessary," Roosevelt said abruptly. "I'll inform Allen and Foster of what was discussed in London. Now let's get on with your work."

Angry at being treated like a mere courier, I pulled a London paper from my case and handed it to Kim. "If you read this," I said, "you will see that Iraqi King Faisal and Prime Minister Nuri as Said are coming to London to meet with Anthony Eden. Not a bad place and time to agree on an Anglo-Iraqi coup in Syria," I added.

Roosevelt made no response, and just then other area chiefs of station arrived to meet with him. Saying that I'd return later, I took my leave. I then called President Chamoun, reminded him that we'd met through Sam Kopper, and asked if he could see me. Not long afterwards, I was in his study in the presidential palace. Chamoun was wearing a safari suit and said that he'd been out shooting pheasants. Offering me one of his long, mono-grammed Cuban cigars, the president explained that he had few chances to relax at his favorite sport, given his responsibilities during these trying times. He then asked what I had on my mind.

Passing over one of my OCB calling cards, deliberately not specifying which of the brothers I meant, I said that I'd just left Washington, where I'd met with Mr. Dulles. The U.S. government, I said, had decided to provide encouragement to those Syrians who were concerned about the growing procommunist sentiment in their country. When Chamoun said he approved of this, I told him that we were aware that Colonel Shishakly was in Lebanon, that I'd seen him myself, and that his presence made it difficult for us to proceed with our plans. So long as the colonel remained in the area, I added, it would be difficult for us to maintain the impression that foreign powers were not involved in what would have to be an indigenous Syrian effort to straighten out their own country. The CIA, I told Chamoun, would be expressing the same views to Farid Shehab (of the sureté), but my call was to assure the president that the wish for Shishakly to leave represented America's position at the highest level.

Saying that Shishakly would depart Lebanon without delay, Chamoun added that he thought the United States, Britain, and Iraq had agreed that Shishakly's return to power would be a good thing. Not certain that it was yet true, I replied that the views of my government had now been made clear in London and Baghdad. "How about the French?" Chamoun asked. "They may never forgive me for this." Noting but not commenting on this remark, I said only that it would be to Lebanon's benefit to maintain neutrality in the area's power politics and intrigue.

Although I'm now certain that Chamoun must have thought me utterly naive, he had the grace not to say so. Instead, he called my attention to the constant plotting and subversion going on in Lebanon, particularly to the newspapers started up almost monthly as vehicles for Egyptian and Saudi-financed anti-Western propaganda. He could do nothing short of censorship to stop this, an action that even the West would criticize. Furthermore, even as the French had once acted as proconsuls in Syria and Lebanon, now Egypt's ambassador—an object of Sam Kopper's and my "apple-pie diplomacy"—was referred to as *le haut commissaire*. This was all distressing, the president said, and it would only get worse. The following year, 1957, elections to Lebanon's chamber of deputies would be held, and already radical Moslem candidates were collecting Egyptian and Saudi subsidies to buy votes. Chamoun said he would bring this to the attention of Ambassador Heath, since the delicate political balance of Lebanon could be disrupted by foreign intervention in these elections.

Agreeing that Heath would be the proper channel for this matter, I thanked Chamoun, saying, again ambiguously, that I'd inform Mr. Dulles of our conversation. After chatting about our friend Kopper, Chamoun addressed me as Bill and said that I'd be welcome to come to see him at any time. As I left, the president winked and urged me not to forget the coming year's elections.

Returning to Zogby's office, I kept my appointment with Kim Roosevelt. Now more friendly, since he needed something from me, he said: "We've decided to go ahead with WAKEFUL in Syria. Your man Michail Ilyan will be the key to the operation." Continuing, Kim explained that Ilyan would work behind the scenes to coordinate an indigenous Syrian program to mobilize and unify conservative political leadership. Anti-Western and procommunist factions were now strong, Roosevelt admitted; still, these were minority elements in the parliament.

Mindful of what Chamoun had told me, I asked Kim how Egyptian and Saudi intrigue and financial subsidies would be eliminated. To begin with, Kim said, King Saud now perceived the

Egyptians as a threat. He'd be seeing Saud on this trip to encourage him to recognize that the future of Saudi Arabia depended on U.S. support. As for the Egyptians, Roosevelt continued, Nasser had been stunned by our refusal to finance the Aswan Dam, which damaged Egyptian prestige in the Near East. Now that Egypt's president realized that the United States could be tough and was prepared to counter his disruptive activities, Kim claimed, Nasser would have to pay attention to his own serious domestic problems.

When I asked Roosevelt if he really believed that the Syrians were capable of cleaning up their own house, his response was one I found difficult to dispute: "We must at least give them an opportunity to do what Ilyan claims is possible." As for Saudi Arabia, he said, we'd never subscribe to the British SIS proposal to overthrow the monarchy there. "I have good reason to believe that Saud will do what's best for his country and our oil interests there," Kim said, "and there are now ways for us to control expenditures of Saudi money, without which our friend Gamal in Cairo will have to cut down on his subversive activities." That sounded new, but logical. "And will there be a coup to topple Nasser as the SIS proposed?" I asked. "Certainly not yet," Kim answered. "We'll watch him carefully and concentrate on creating a friendly bloc of Iraq, Syria, Saudi Arabia, and Jordan."

Roosevelt then introduced a new aspect of the role the CIA had in mind for me. Ilyan would obviously need money for countering anti-Western propaganda and encouraging those in the parliament and the army who feared communism. "We want you," Kim said, "to meet Ilyan and find out just how much financial support he considers necessary." When I asked how much detail was wanted, he said that I should get names, specific actions, timing, and so forth. "Through Vern Cassin's agents and other channels," Kim said, "we'll have the means to evaluate and monitor what Ilyan plans and actually does." The most important thing, I was told, was to find out how rapidly Ilyan could move and produce results—provided, of course, that he received something like the amount of money he wanted.

Before we parted, Kim said that he'd be making other stops in the Near East to arrange things, all of which would indirectly support what we wanted to accomplish in Syria. Now becoming secretive, Roosevelt told me that it would be just as well if I didn't know all of the details. He did say that there were ways of relieving the British-instigated pressure on Saudi Arabia from the Trucial Sheikhdoms on the Arabian Gulf. Also, both through our membership in the countersubversive committee of the Baghdad Pact and by using clandestine radio stations, to be set up by technicians flying out with CIA equipment from Washington, we would have new means of countering anti-Western propaganda in the Near East.

Now ready to leave for Damascus, I pulled out the papers Allen Dulles had handed me and read them carefully before locking them up in my office file. The long cable from Cassin turned out to be a summary written by Ambassador Moose on the Syrian situation. I immediately sensed something wrong: Moose didn't send his views to Washington through CIA channels. The style was undoubtedly the ambassador's, however, and when I checked the date-time group on the cable, it seemed to me certain that Moose had employed the CIA and Allen Dulles to reach the secretary of state before the Omega Group's recommendations were acted on. I now wondered what had taken place during Kim Roosevelt's conversation with the ambassador, at the time Archie and I were meeting with Ilyan.

As I read Ambassador Moose's conclusions, I saw that he began with his long-held view that modification of U.S. policy toward Palestine was the precondition of voluntary Syrian cooperation with the West. He knew, of course, that in a presidential-election year we'd never take a strong stand and demand concessions from Israel. This was pure Moose. But what followed was both quite new and startling. Ending his message, the ambassador expressed opinions that left me baffled: "Should consideration be given to cooperation with the West not dependent on Syrian willingness, Iraq would appear to be the most promising channel. . . . If, for example, Syria were to fall under a large measure of Iraqi control, the conditions for cooperation would be greatly improved. . . . In no event will the reorientation of Syria be easy or cheap."

This wasn't the Moose I knew. He obviously felt that the situation had worsened to the point that we might have to change things in Syria with or without its people's help. I could only hope that I'd find things less grim than Moose seemed to believe they were.

I then turned to the "Straggle" document. While the covering memorandum—rejecting the notion of a coup in Syria—read as it had in the meeting I'd attended, I soon discovered that the State Department's staff paper had been changed and Kim Roosevelt's paper eliminated: that is, all mention of the problems involved in restraining the British and the Iraqis, and the warning that their intervention would make it impossible for even pro-Iraqi Syrians to support our moves. Presumably, under this authorization, the secretary of state had agreed that we'd encourage Ilyan and his friends to counter the leftists and communists, and close our eyes if Britain and Iraq tried to arrange things another way.

Putting all this together with what George Young had told me in London, the defensive attitude Kim had first assumed in Beirut, and the sudden change in Ambassador Moose's thinking, I concluded that there must be parts of this story of which I was unaware. Still, my only job was to find out what Ilyan thought he could do to improve conditions and how much money he believed this would cost. This was not incompatible with what Allen Dulles had asked me to do in Washington, and after all, I had never been promised that I'd be privy to everything the CIA did.

CHAPTER EIGHTEEN

SUEZ AND THE BLUFF

Leaving on the morning of July 24, I drove to Damascus and, as usual, registered at the New Omayad. Ilyan would hear of my arrival, I knew, but this time I was reluctant to meet in his suite, which I assumed to be a target for bugging by the local sureté. Employing what I could remember of my counterintelligence training, I searched my room for listening devices. Finally, feeling fairly secure, I was ready to discuss money with Michail Bey.

When he arrived I pointed a finger at my ear and then turned up the radio to indicate that our talk would be secret and that the whining Oriental music would prevent any eavesdropper from hearing what we said. This conspiratorial beginning seemed to delight Ilyan, who drew his chair close to mine and hunched over with elbows on his knees. Head bowed, looking alternately at me and the floor, my coconspirator flicked his worry beads at a speed I thought might match that of the abacus clicking in his head to come up with a price tag for his operations.

Telling him I'd been back to Washington and now had word of American plans, I said that we were prepared to consider helping him and his fellow Syrians help themselves. But, I emphasized, we did not believe that Iraqi intervention would be beneficial, and opposed any consideration of using Iraqi troops. Ilyan seemed dismayed at this, but I held firm, asking what plans he had in mind, what support he'd need—short of the Iraqis'—and how long it would take to get results.

A good fifteen minutes of silence and worry-bead twirling followed as Ilyan stared intently at the rug on the floor. Finally, he made his proposal. "*Ya Ahmee*, it will take money—much of it and soon—to care for the press, the 'street,' key army officers, and others." When I asked him if the politicians too would want money, or if saving their country and their fortunes would be enough, Ilyan gave me a look I'd last seen when my mother had prepared to wash out my mouth with soap. "Mr. Eveland," Ilyan said, "we don't expect anything for ourselves. It's just those who have been offered dirty money to oppose us whom we'll have to buy off." Far from convinced that I'd met my first honest man in the Middle East, I said I'd have to assure Washington that no pockets would be lined with our money. I'd not meant to offend him, of course, I added.

Since getting down to specifics seemed impossible before we had a firm plan of action, I decided to try for an estimate of money and a time frame. After more silence, tongue clicking, and rustling of beads, Ilyan asked for "a half-million and at least thirty days." Since he hadn't said which currency he was referring to—about three Syrian pounds made a dollar—I deliberately chose the lesser possibility, saying that it would take time for the people who handled such things to collect that much Syrian currency on the Lebanese money market.

My ploy unchallenged, I then tried to get Ilyan to commit himself to a precise date by which he could have his plans, organization, and key people ready for action. "Can I safely inform Mr. Roosevelt that you will be fully prepared by the end of August?" I asked. This produced an eye-to-eye confrontation, accompanied by the characteristic Arab gesture of clicking the tongue and simultaneous lifting of the head which had at least three possible meanings: "certainly, without any question"; "if Allah wills it"; or, "don't be foolish, nobody can say for sure." I pinned this down to "certainly" by saying that there could be no thought of U.S. money until Ilyan provided a plan of action and a firm target date. Many other people would be involved in supporting his activities, I intimated, stressing the need for coordination and precise timing. Obviously taken aback at my suggestion that he and I alone would not be responsible for executing his operation, Ilyan asked whether I would approve his plan and bring the money myself. Now really extemporizing, I explained that I'd do neither; there were trained professionals for such matters, I said, and I'd arrange that they contact him. Meanwhile, I wanted Ilyan to set up an appointment for me with Majd ud-Din Jabiri, the new minister who'd evaluate the refinery bids and make the contract award. Disappointed but agreeing, Ilyan shook my hand and walked off down the hall, hands clasped behind his back, worry beads now limp, his head nodding toward the floor.

Back in Beirut the next day, I drafted what I hoped would be my first and last operational WAKEFUL message. The CIA had people trained to evaluate and supervise covert operations of the type Ilyan planned, I assumed, and, after reporting the money and time figures I'd been given, I offered to put the professionals in touch with Ilyan before I bowed out to watch the transformation of Syria take place. Now I wanted to arrange for the new perquisites I'd been issued to make my life more comfortable.

The Beirut embassy's naval attaché, Lt. Commander Ed House, was visibly upset when I called on him to arrange for the purchase of his car. His final days were marred by an unpleasant task he'd been instructed to perform on an urgent basis by Ambassador Heath. As I listened to Ed's tale, I had a lesson in the way that corruption in Lebanon could escalate to the point where an international incident threatened.

Periodically, the U.S. Sixth Fleet made "goodwill" visits to Lebanon both to provide reminders of American strength in the Mediterranean and to allow shore leave for its sailors and marines. For Beirut, where cabarets proliferated as the demands of tourists grew, fleet visits were a boon to the economy. European "artistes" were encouraged by their impresarios and local nightclub owners to supplement their incomes through after-hours activities entertaining affluent or companion-starved customers. Only Beirut's seamy red-light quarter was declared off limits to the navy, because of the high incidence of venereal disease there. Nonetheless, showing a liberty-bound sailor a map defining the part of town into which he was forbidden to venture was like waving a red flag before a bull.

During a recent visit by a pair of destroyers, the shore patrol, accompanied by Lebanese gendarmes, had raided a brothel. One of the American sailors had escaped through a window, colliding on the street with a Lebanese man and knocking him to the ground, breaking his leg. Although the sailor was never identified, the "union" to which the injured man belonged was powerful politically, and the Lebanese foreign ministry now demanded that the U.S. government pay compensation for the man's injuries and loss of income. Ed had just visited the victim in the hospital and paid all medical charges but was now faced with the task of calculating compensation for six weeks' lost earnings by a Lebanese pimp who controlled a string of five young prostitutes.

If all this seemed ludicrous, it was no joking matter: that paragon of Christianity Charles Malik was, as foreign minister, forced by political pressure to file a formal protest with the American embassy. The figures I volunteered on the going rates for cabaret girls were of no value to Ed; he was forced to calculate on another level, one involving "tricks" per hour, not per night. Instead, we negotiated the current sales price for a 1954 Ford convertible, duty paid, in Lebanon. As we concluded our transaction, I cursed Walter Snowdon and his CIA colleagues, whose objections to my diplomatic passport now cost the U.S. government the import taxes on the car and deprived me of the immunity from violations of traffic and other laws, to which the transfer of Ed's diplomatic license plates would have entitled me.

Now equipped with "wheels" of my own, I drove to the Saint Georges bar, reflecting again on how tired I was of hotel rooms. At the bar I bumped into Larry Collins of *Newsweek*, and luck was with me: he was giving up a small apartment, next to Sam Brewer's flat, and moving to a larger place. I could have his old place, Larry said, and we concluded the deal on the spot. Just as I was contemplating the prospect of finally living a normal life, I was called to the telephone at the end of the bar. It was Abu Said, who told me in an excited voice to come across the street to *Time's* penthouse office.

As I arrived I could hear a loud voice on the radio speaking Arabic. "It's Radio Cairo—Nasser," Abu Said told me. Most political speeches by Arabs are made in the classical language I'd studied, but I could scarcely make out a word of Nasser's harangue. "He's speaking colloquial Egyptian," Abu Said explained. "He's been going on for hours—he's in Alexandria—he's just taken over the Suez Canal!"

Finally switching off the radio, Abu Said explained that Nasser had said that compensation would be paid and transit rights guaranteed under the Constantinople Convention. One hundred twenty thousand Egyptians, Nasser said, had died building the canal. It belonged to Egypt. Now the canal's profits would be used to finance the Aswan Dam and the West could choke on its fury. Suddenly George Young's words in London came back to me: "We have to face the possibility that Nasser might close the canal, and I'd like to know how the United States would react if he did." Thinking of things closer to America, I remembered my days in Panama, and the tenuous hold we'd have on the canal if the Panamanians decided to nationalize it.

The question now was how the British and French, who owned the company formed in 1888 to operate the Suez Canal, would react. Abu Said explained that the Canal Company's rights were to expire in 1968, a date that had been reaffirmed in the Anglo-Egyptian agreement of 1954. It was rather unusual, I thought. Egypt was asserting its rights only twelve years early and still offering to pay the company it was taking over. Nonetheless, who knew what would follow?

Predictably, Britain and France treated Nasser's speech as a *casus belli*, nationalized Egyptian assets abroad, and ordered warships and troops to the Mediterranean to supplement those already based on Cyprus and Malta. The first U.S. official statement was critical but not condemnatory, and Russia urged restraint, warning that putting pressure on Egypt could have undesirable consequences. On the defensive after Arab criticism of its agreement to supply Israel with oil, Russia attacked "certain Israeli leaders" as having been abetted by "imperialist quarters" to threaten war against their "peace-loving neighbors."

Secretary of State Dulles had been in Peru when Nasser made his announcement, and the first moderate U.S. statement emerged from consultations between the President and Acting Secretary Hoover. When Dulles returned to confer with Eisenhower, however, the American position reflected British and French alarmism: Egyptian government funds in the U.S. were frozen; and the secretary of state left immediately for London to confer with his British and French counterparts.

Although it was ignored by the West's leaders, Nasser's formal statement claimed that the canal already belonged to Egypt and therefore in fact had not been nationalized. Rather, it was an Egyptian-franchised company—the Suez Canal Company—that he was taking over. This highly profitable private company, whose stock was traded on the Paris *Bourse*, had been created to run the canal and maintain it (at a profit), but the canal's profits were now claimed by Nasser to finance the dam project we had rejected. Britain itself had violated the provisions of the Constantinople Convention by denying to its enemies access to the canal during wartime, and Israeli ships had not been permitted to transit the waterway even while Britain and France controlled its operation. None of these things seemed to matter now to the frenzied Western powers. As subsequent events were to illustrate, the British and French were seeking a reason to bring Nasser down, and the Suez issue provided all the excuse they needed to try it. And even had Nasser now been willing to allow Israel's ships and cargos destined for that country to pass through the canal, the Israeli invasion of Egypt eliminated this possibility.

Now settled in the new apartment the CIA was providing, I felt more obligated than I had in the past to help the agency fulfill its basic mission, the collecting of intelligence. I was curious, too, regarding the effect of Nasser's actions on Michail Ilyan's plans to mobilize pro-Western forces in Syria, so I drove over the mountains to Damascus. Surely, I thought, the price for changing the political orientation of the Republic of Syria had escalated, and I expected Ilyan to open our conversation with a new estimate of costs. Instead, in near despair, he spoke of the futility of trying to change anything under the present circumstances. Although Nasser's speech had been impetuous, Ilyan said, the inflamed reactions of the British and French made him the hero of the Arab world, and now few politicians would dare speak out against him. Furthermore, Eden's characterization of Nasser as a blackmailing dictator plotting to ruin the West only worsened matters. "*Ya Ahmee*," Ilyan said, "the Arabs hardly see Nasser through Western eyes." I could understand this, but I wondered how many people in Washington did.

When the United States had abruptly withdrawn financing for the Aswan Dam, Ilyan said, people of the area saw only that Egyptians would be denied new farmland and water. Now that Egypt was going to use revenues from a canal it had owned since gaining its independence in order to build the dam, the West was calling Nasser another Hitler. Showing me the English and French newspapers he had with him, Ilyan asked me just what he could do with our money to convince the Syrian people that collaboration with the West to punish Nasser was in the interests of the Arabs. I had no answer. When I clicked my tongue and lifted my head like an Arab, Michail Bey knew just what I meant.

"And what," he asked me, "do you propose for slogans to bring the farmers from the desert to march on Damascus? Should they protest Russia's willingness to barter cotton for the arms that the West refuses to sell us for protection from the only enemy we can see and are affected by daily—Israel?" Another click of my tongue confirmed that I had no answer for this question either. Ilyan wasn't done, however. Both American political parties, trying to outdo the other during an election year, were advocating arms for Israel to counter Nasser's clearly legitimate actions. How, he asked, could we expect Syrian army officers to work with America to overthrow their government for seeking now from another source arms that the United States had denied them? "Mr. Eveland," Ilyan said, "I'm not sure any amount of money can help us unless you can restrain your allies and convince your politicians that maintaining peace in this area is the only way of keeping the communists out."

I feared that Ilyan had given up but asked him if an Egyptian-dominated Syria was his idea of what those who had fought the French to obtain independence now wanted. "Not at all," he replied. "We'd much rather unite with Iraq to form a stronger country capable of opposing both communism and an expansionist Israeli state." Tossing a *Ya Ahmee* at him, I explained that a merger with Iraq might lead Saudi Arabia to nationalize Aramco and ally with Egypt: in that case there'd be no oil, no canal. Acknowledging that this posed a dilemma, Ilyan then proposed a modified version of the old Greater Syria plan—Syria, Lebanon, and Palestine united, as they had once been. "Let Iraq and Jordan work together as Hashemite countries, and encourage the Lebanese to join with us, as your relative Charles Crane recommended before the French split up Syria."

Although all this sounded much like a Syrian Christian's version of heaven, it gave me a peg on which to hang my case for cooperation among anticommunist Syrians as an essential first step. Meanwhile, what I'd heard convinced me that trying to finance a Syrian coup would amount to throwing money away.

My report to Washington of what Ilyan had said went unanswered, and I interpreted silence as recognition that covert political action was no palliative for the present situation. Clearly, agreement with Britain and France on a realistic course of joint action was the objective the U.S. should seek in order to control the hysteria that had followed Nasser's speech. Meanwhile, the attention of the whole world was riveted on the area in which I was living, and being in the center of things wasn't a bad feeling at all.

In this period I tried to appraise my own situation. I'd now dealt with chiefs of state and international policies, and was involved in events that might precipitate a world war. The thought of returning to a routine existence appeared less attractive each day. Although working for Aramco in dusty Riyadh might offer a better future, more money, and security, I finally admitted to myself that I didn't want to accept their position. I'd face the future when it came, but right now I was "high" and didn't want to come down. Finally, thinking about staying with the government in Washington, it seemed certain to me that John Foster Dulles had assumed personal control of U.S. policy for the Middle East. As another member of the bureaucracy back home I'd have no real influence, even in the OCB job, but by remaining overseas I might be listened to. I'd see how this worked out.

As days passed, it seemed that the fate of the Middle East hung on the Big Powers' conferences, as diplomats shuttled in and out of London to formulate proposals and deal with those advanced by Russia. The heads of the Western governments ponderously deliberated the fate of Egypt and how the canal should be run, yet so remote were these maneuvers from the country involved that Arab views and realities seemed inconsequential. In fact, contrary to dire predictions, the canal continued to function under Nasser's control as if the Suez Canal Company hadn't been taken over. Had the site of these lofty deliberations about Egypt's future been Cairo, Nasser might well have attended them, but he'd made clear that he'd be damned if he'd travel to London to have the Big Three explain how his disruption of their plans threatened the future of Egypt. Under the leadership of India, usually siding with Russia's proposals, the states of the Third World who'd organized at Bandung began to use their influence in support of Nasser, in part because their economies depended largely on keeping the canal open.

In mid-September, another London conference of eighteen "concerned" nations was called to form an organization that Foster Dulles had devised and dubbed the Suez Canal Users' Association (SCUA), which was to run the canal on Egypt's behalf.[54] Neither Egypt nor Russia was enthusiastic about this; in fact, both wanted the U.N. Security Council to discuss the threat to peace posed by British and French troop movements into the Mediterranean, which portended an armed invasion of Egypt. Britain and France, meanwhile, had a plan for the SCUA to buy a tanker of oil and challenge Nasser to bar its passage through the canal. All of these

---

54   As an international lawyer, Secretary Dulles had examined the treaties under which Britain and France claimed Nasser's actions had been illegal and found that the Egyptian president had had every right to act as he had.

things were sustaining a crisis atmosphere, except in Beirut and the other Arab capitals, where life went on pretty much as usual. I began to wonder what part America had to play in this, other than as a peacemaker and the spokesman for American oil companies, who used the canal principally to ship their oil from the Middle East to Europe.

The extent to which naiveté and disregard of the political realities of the Near East had affected even the highest level of the U.S. government did not become clear to me, however, until I received a cable directing me to proceed to London to participate in what turned out to be a presidential "mission impossible." My orders were to contact David Newsom at our embassy and obtain from him details of a secret assignment in which we'd participate. I'd known Newsom since we'd served together in Baghdad during 1951–52, and now he was officer in charge of Arabian Peninsular affairs in the Department of State.[55]

When we met the next day, I learned that Newsom had arrived from Washington on a special-mission White House plane with Robert Anderson, who'd been deputy secretary of defense when I'd served in the Pentagon (and had saved me from having to tell the shah of Iran that we didn't believe his army was ready for modern equipment). Our mission, Newsom told me, was to fly to Saudi Arabia to meet with King Saud. This arrangement sounded pretty silly, I told him, suggesting that I might have been picked up in Beirut and saved the government money. Almost whispering as he explained, Newsom said that our mission was both delicate and secret; we'd dare not fly over an Arab country and would approach Saudi Arabia over Turkey and Iran. Continuing, Dave told me that Howard Page of Exxon had convinced President Eisenhower that King Saud held the key to solving the Suez crisis. We, Newsom explained with a sheepish grin, were to persuade Saud to induce Nasser to accept the SCUA plan for foreign operation of the Suez

---

55 Newsom occupies the position of under secretary of state for political affairs in the Carter administration. Prior to that he was in charge of African affairs and ambassador to Libya, Indonesia, and the Philippines.

Canal. When I pointed out that we'd just warned Saud that Nasser was trying to depose him and had allowed communism to spread in the Middle East, David smiled and said that Anderson had a plan that Page had developed. He'd fill me in later, he said.

Greeting us at Dhahran was Ambassador George Wadsworth, who'd flown across from Jidda to explain the formalities of a visit to the capital at Riyadh. There were no hotels there—without a royal invitation you just didn't come, and we'd be put up in one of the king's guest houses.

Settled in a guest house, we were summoned to the Royal Diwan, a huge rectangular hall, heavily carpeted and dominated by great chandeliers. Along one wall, at least fifty high-backed chairs stood empty; in their center was the throne. On it sat King Saud ibn Abdul Aziz as Saud, round glasses with thick lenses dominating his goateed face; he wore white robes, kaffiyeh, and gold agal. To his left sat the real power of the kingdom, Crown Prince Faisal, and, down further to the left, the royal counselors, led by Sheikh Yusef al Yassin, originally a Syrian, whose black beard and shifting eyes seemed to come straight out of "Ali Baba and His Forty Thieves."

Taking our places to the king's right, we received small handleless cups of strong, bitter coffee, each refilled, as soon as it was consumed, by a servant carrying a long-nosed brass pot. Dave Newsom, the ambassador, and I drank several rounds and then signaled an end to it by waggling our cups back and forth between our fingers. Beaming and nodding to the king as he drank, Bob Anderson was on his fifth cup before the ambassador intervened to cut off the flow. So far we'd sat in silence.

Wadsworth then explained through the interpreter that President Eisenhower had sent Anderson as his personal emissary to discuss a matter of extreme gravity. Briefed in advance, Robert Anderson extended the president's wish for good health, the kingdom's prosperity, and many sons (to a king who'd lost count of his hundreds of progeny!), as well as a long life. Throughout this, Prince Faisal stared straight ahead without the slightest sign of emotion (or betraying his excellent command of English). Sheikh Yusef's dark eyes examined us carefully, as if searching for hidden meanings.

Finally, Anderson got to the point, stating in ornate language that a misguided Nasser's nationalization of the Suez Canal [sic[56]] threatened to render Saudi Arabia's petroleum worthless. He was careful to add, of course, that Nasser was a good man and a great leader but was receiving bad advice from godless people. Given all this, in any case, our president advised that Saud should explain to the Egyptian president the way in which his actions were a threat to all Arab people. Still not briefed on Howard Page's scheme to use the Saudis, I wondered if the oil companies were going to threaten to stop buying Saudi oil.

At this point King Saud looked up from the floor, nodded his head gravely, and appeared to be waiting for Anderson to continue. But the key words—"rendering Saudi Arabia's petroleum worthless"—had already been spoken. They had not, however, escaped Prince Faisal and Yusef Yassin, who whispered to each other. Prince Faisal then muttered something into the ear of King Saud, who, as if suddenly enlightened, turned to Anderson and said that Nasser had done nothing more than claim what belonged to his people.

Ready for that one, Anderson assumed a fatherly tone and asked what good the canal would be if the world's shippers had no faith in it and had to seek alternate routes. That would prove more costly, and the king's oil would fetch less. Then both the Saudi and Egyptian people would be the losers, the Russians would gain, and the cost of defending the free world against communism would be higher. We might even have to devise means of meeting Western Europe's energy requirements from other sources. Furthermore, what Nasser was doing might provoke a war in the area and interrupt the flow of Saudi oil through the pipeline to the Mediterranean. (Good God, I thought, I hope Anderson's not going to hint that we had plans to blow up the Middle East's oilfields!)

"Your Majesty must understand," Anderson continued, "we've made great technological advances and are now on the threshold

---

56 Anderson seemed unable to understand that Egypt owned the Suez Canal and had no need to nationalize its own property. What Nasser nationalized was the Egyptian-domiciled, foreign-controlled Suez Canal Company.

of sources of power that will be cheaper and more efficient than oil." He concluded by saying that "it might become necessary for us to ensure that our allies are self-sufficient and free from threats of blackmail."

King Saud seemed not to have followed Anderson's remarks, but then a troubled look suggested that at least one basic point had gotten through—here was Robert Anderson, a Texan, talking as if oil weren't indispensable. All those Cadillacs and palaces might turn into mirages again. Getting more advice from Faisal and the sheikhs, Saud asked through the interpreter what the Europeans might use as a substitute for oil.

Fully prepared, Anderson uttered the words "nuclear energy" and then explained that despite massive expense, we now had the technology to convert Western Europe to nuclear power. There it was, I now realized. Howard Page and his colleagues had apparently convinced the President that not even the major oil companies would be blackmailed into charging more for their products.

A long silence followed, and then the king stood, to signal the end of our audience. As we bowed in departing, word was passed that we'd be expected at the palace for dinner just after prayers.

After naps we met again and George Wadsworth resumed his briefing about formalities. A dinner in our honor would be hosted by the king. As was the case each evening, perhaps 200 guests would be present. The food would be fine, the ambassador assured us: the king had an American chef. Campbell's tinned tomato soup was a royal favorite, after which we'd have whole-lamb and baby-camel dishes with mountains of rice. For those who found the prospect of drinking warm camel's milk unappealing, there would be fruit juices, too. The water's safety was doubtful: French drillers seeking oil had hit water instead, a bounty far more welcome than the black gold upon which foreign economies depended.

Soon we heard the call to prayers: "*Salaat! Salaat!*" The city became silent as muezzins in all quarters called out from their minarets, "*Laa ilaaha ilia Ilaah* (There is no God but Allah)," the first words of the prayers that all of Riyadh's 150,000 souls were uttering as they faced Mecca to the west.

When prayers were over, we walked through quiet streets to the pink-walled Naseryah Palace. Ugly in daytime, the mile-square palace compound was really a city within a city. Brilliantly illuminated with hundreds of bare neon tube lights, it appeared to house a gigantic carnival or country fair. As we entered the mammoth banquet hall, we saw that it was filled with princes, court attendants, and those—mighty and humble—who were visiting Riyadh to pay homage to King Saud.

As we took our seats near the king, the ambassador whispered, "Don't start eating until after the BBC!" And indeed that was the routine: the court crier appeared and in Arabic read off most of London's overseas news broadcast. After this, there came loud testimony to Allah's kindness and compassion. "*Bisim Ilaahi ar rahmaan ar rahim.*" Once this was said, we could eat.

As Wadsworth had predicted, there was no dinner-table conversation but food enough to feed an army. An "army" waited outside, in fact, to eat the leftovers—the women, children, retainers, and others not allowed in. Servants tendered rosewater to remove the grease on hands and fingers and then brought incense burners for each guest to hold under his kaffiyah in order to absorb the fragrance into his beard. Then the crier called "*Bakjkhir wa ruuh* (Take the incense and depart)." Dinner was finished.

Early the next morning Dave Newsom roused me to say that it was all over. We'd be dropping George Wadsworth off in Jidda and then flying over Africa to Rome and London. Once we were airborne, Newsom passed me a handwritten letter in Arabic and said it contained King Saud's answer to President Eisenhower; I was to translate it. Prince Faisal, it appeared, had done considerable reading on the subject of nuclear energy and rejected as impossible Anderson's assertions that we could provide Western Europe an alternative to petroleum. Rather than imply that Eisenhower had been duped, or, worse, had tried to pressure King Saud with a lie, Faisal had arranged an alternative means of terminating our mission so that we need not lose face by meeting the king again. Well after midnight, Anderson and Newsom had been taken out on the desert to meet Prince Faisal, who orally expressed his doubts concerning our nuclear capabilities and then handed them the message I held before me.

The Saudis said that punishing Nasser would have little effect on our efforts to keep communism out of the Middle East. The United States, they wrote, had to use its leverage to force Israel to repatriate or to compensate the Palestinians before there could be peace. Otherwise, war was imminent, and only the Soviets would gain. Finally, because the Saudis feared that Britain, France, and Israel were planning to attack Egypt, Faisal had insisted that a warning about this be delivered personally to President Eisenhower.

As I labored over my translation, I kept thinking that these simple people of the desert had caught us bluffing, and neither Anderson nor Newsom made any case to prove that this was wrong. Some day, I vowed, there would be a proper time and place for me to tell Howard Page how badly he had misjudged the Arabs with whom he'd dealt for years. I felt certain also that if I'd been called upon to deliver such a message as Aramco's representative in Riyadh, the Saudis might not have treated me so kindly, and I might even now be looking for a new job.

CHAPTER NINETEEN

THE DROP

When we arrived in London I found our embassy bustling with "experts" preparing for the third major-powers conference about Suez. In the U.N., the Security Council was debating Egypt's charges of aggressive troop movements by Britain and France and their counter-charges against the Egyptians for the "warlike" act of nationalizing the canal company. The British press was carrying crisis headlines predicting an imminent war. (I had the feeling that England must have been very much the same during the Munich crisis just before World War II. Anthony Eden, who had at that time resigned as foreign secretary in protest over Chamberlain's appeasement of Hitler and Mussolini, now raged in Parliament about Nasser as a Fascist dictator, and spoke as if the British government had no alternative to using force to bring him down.) It was a relief to leave this madness and return to the quiet of the Middle East.

Back in Beirut, I learned from Sam Brewer and his colleagues that the combination of the Suez crisis and the presidential-election campaigns was contributing to an atmosphere of hysteria in the American press as well. Criticizing his own paper to me for the first time, Sam said that editorials in the *New York Times* portraying Nasser as "the Hitler on the Nile" ignored factual reporting from the paper's seasoned correspondents on the spot. Kennett

Love, the *Times* man in Cairo, had found this so frustrating, Brewer told me, that he'd asked to be assigned to another area.[57] Then, to give grounds for his complaint, Sam showed me some of the cables he received daily from New York to advise which stories the *Times* had used and where they had appeared in the paper. One cable showed that a story from Tel Aviv describing Israeli claims that Egypt was about to start a war had been featured prominently on page one. By contrast, a story that Brewer had written about Arab fears that the F-84 fighters Canada had sold to Israel would be used to launch a preventive war had ended up inside the paper.[58] Dismayed by all this, Sam contended that pressure by Zionist groups and the paper's advertisers was now shaping the *Times*'s editorial policy. Sam sounded even more exasperated when he spoke of the favorable reporting from Egypt concerning Nasser's reforms by George Weller of the Chicago *Daily News* (whom we both knew well and saw frequently in Beirut). Despite a threatened boycott by advertisers, Sam said, Weller had received the full support of the management and the editorial-page staff.[59]

I began to hope, accordingly, that Secretary Dulles would be too busy to read the *Times*. That presidential candidate Adlai Stevenson might be reading the *Daily News* was indicated by a *New York Times* story I'd recently read, in which Stevenson was quoted as saying that there currently existed no imbalance between the armed forces of Israel and of the Arab countries. That was the situation as I'd known it in Washington, and all this talk about a war between the Arabs and the Israelis seemed complete nonsense to me and the many newsmen I knew in Beirut. That Britain and

---

57   Kennett Love's book *Suez: The Twice-Fought War* (N.Y.: McGraw-Hill, 1969) is a well-written and scholarly study of the 1956 Suez war and its aftermath.

58   The correspondent for the *New York Times* in Israel was Moshe Brilliant, an American who also worked for the *Jerusalem Post*, the English-language newspaper generally reflecting the views of Ben-Gurion's Mapai Party

59   When approached by a group of Jewish advertisers threatening to withdraw their accounts, the managing editor of the *Daily News* invited them to proceed, explaining that if their threat materialized, a front-page editorial naming the advertisers and their reasons would appear the following day. No accounts were cancelled, and George Weller continued to report news from Egypt as he saw it.

France might lose their heads and start one against Egypt was a possibility, though, and this did worry me.[60]

I was long overdue in following up on my request that Michail Ilyan arrange for me to discuss the Syrian refinery with Majd ud-Din Jabiri, the minister who'd make the decision, and I finally drove to Damascus to see him. Telling Jabiri that I'd just been in London and learned that Procon's formal tender was nearly complete, I explained that the U.S. government was prepared to encourage the American oil-company shareholders in the Iraq Petroleum Company to assist in ensuring that the Procon bid was successful. As an example, I suggested that it would be possible merely to submit a bid for the complete project for "X" dollars under the lowest competing price. "Would this be feasible?" I asked. When Majd un-Din expressed dissatisfaction with such a method, I proposed that if he estimated the lowest Soviet-bloc bid, Procon's price could come in a few thousand dollars lower. Again, Jabiri was unenthusiastic, although he indicated that he had a good idea of just what the other bids would be.

The more we talked, the less progress I made, until finally Jabiri said that there was no way he could award the refinery to an American company. Stunned, I asked what he'd do if we gave the refinery to Syria free of charge. That wouldn't do, either, he told me. The decision was no longer his. The Syrian government, he explained, had deliberated the whole question of foreign aid. Both American failure to finance the Aswan Dam and Western economic pressure against Egypt had produced a final decision—President Quwwatly would soon go to Moscow to close agreements for long-term loans. A refinery, to be dismantled in Bulgaria, would be shipped to Homs for a fraction of the cost of constructing a new one. Technicians to assemble, operate, and maintain the refinery would be furnished free as part of the arrangement.

---

60   An interesting footnote to history, which meant little to me (or presumably to Washington) at the time, was a story in the *New York Times* (September 14,1956) from Paris reporting a press conference given by a little-known leader of a minority party in Israel's Knesset, one Menachem Begin, urging an Israeli-French alliance against Egypt.

Trying somehow to salvage our offer, I reminded Jabiri (an engineer) that refinery technology was basically American, that from the Soviet bloc the Syrians would get only obsolete equipment. Furthermore, I said, there would be political strings attached to the Soviet offer. Jabiri replied that whatever they received would be adequate to handle Syria's offtake from the Iraq Petroleum Company pipeline for years to come.

As for the strings I'd spoken of, Majd ud-Din then lectured me for nearly a half-hour. Given the example of the Aswan Dam, it was clear to him that if Syria differed from the United States on an issue, there would always be the possibility that we'd change our minds and withhold completion of the project, in order to exert leverage on his country. Furthermore, because the West had responded so wildly to Egypt's nationalization of the Suez company, Syria simply wasn't willing to take the risk. "We have a canal, too," he said: "our oil pipelines. What if we decide to nationalize our pipelines as national assets? America has an interest in them, as well as Britain and France. Isn't there the possibility that Eden would be making the same threats about our cutting off Europe's lifeline? And, since you have an interest here that you don't have in the canal company, wouldn't America join its allies and threaten us with military action?"

Not waiting for my response, Jabiri concluded with a final blast. Every cent the United States provided Israel in economic aid, he charged, enabled the Israelis to divert other revenues to buy weapons for use against the Arabs. "The Russians," he said, "have never threatened us, either militarily or politically, and they are willing to supply us arms to defend our country.

If Mr. Dulles sees morality in that use of American aid, in his approach to Aswan, and in what is now going on in London, then we don't need your foreign aid, your advice, or your technicians!" With that, his face almost purple, Majd ud-Din walked off.[61]

---

61   In this same period, the Egyptian government announced that it would reject bids by Western contractors for new development projects in reaction to Western economic pressure over Suez. Instead, these contracts would go to "friendly" countries, the statement said.

I saw Ilyan briefly and told him how disappointed I was. "Let Majd ud-Din cool off," he said. "He doesn't want the Russians here, but he's trying to survive among the army officers who do."

Returning to Beirut, I reported all this to Washington by cable. A week later, I received word that the CIA had decided to support Ilyan in the plans he'd outlined to Archie Roosevelt. I myself was to obtain the funds he'd requested and pass them to Ilyan as soon as possible, with instructions that his program was to be implemented by October 25. This message from the CIA's headquarters was not a request; it was an order.

Harvey Armado, head of the regional finance office of the Beirut CIA station, was one of the busiest members of the staff. Beyond his fiscal responsibility for the administrative and operational activities of all stations in the Middle East, Armado worked under direct orders from Washington on worldwide financial transactions. Having no prohibitions on foreign-exchange transactions, Lebanon was an ideal location for such activities. There were no currency restrictions or controls, and money of every nation, including Israeli pounds, was traded there. With his own connections, Harvey employed the facilities of many of the hundreds of banks and money changers operating in Lebanon. In this way he could make even million-dollar transactions without drawing attention or risking their being traced to a single source. In addition, he received cash from Washington and other stations for laundering. Dealing as he did in a fluctuating money market, Armado could purchase currency at rates far below the official rates established in controlled-exchange countries and, by shipping these funds back to their country of origin, enable the local CIA operations and administrative costs to be paid for at black-market rates.

It was a huge operation. I'd often been in Armado's office, usually to be reminded by Harvey that my expense accounts were far overdue, and I'd more than once seen cash stuffed into diplomatic mail pouches for shipment. Also, I banked with a Palestinian, Yusef Beidas, who had in a few years moved up from changing money in an alley to operating the Intra Bank, and I had encountered Armado there from time to time. Although Intra was becoming one of Lebanon's largest banks, I was still taken directly to Yusef's private office, where he'd personally send out my checks to be cashed, the way he had done as a fledgling banker. It was possible, I thought, that Harvey's transactions had contributed to Intra's remarkable growth.

In any case, when I called on Armado to say I needed a half-million Syrian pounds, he hardly blinked. Did I need new money, old money, a mixture? Bundled or boxed? When I professed ignorance, Harvey suggested a combination of old and new Syrian bills from various banks in Syria, so that their Lebanese origin could not be traced from the bands on the bundles. "Give me two days," he said, "and I'll have it for you in a nice suitcase purchased in Damascus. Do you need a receipt when you turn over the money?"

"Hell, no," I answered. "I'll pass the damn stuff, but I don't want a piece of paper with an amount and a name on it. What if I get in trouble?" Nothing from my cable in Washington said that I needed a receipt, and after Jabiri's lecture I wasn't prepared to have Ilyan accuse me of holding a paper confirming what I'd paid him over his head for use at some later date.

I didn't have the slightest idea how to get the money to Ilyan, and Ghosn Zogby wasn't much help. If the CIA had a manual on this subject, he didn't offer me a copy. Zog merely suggested that I put the money in the trunk of my car and drive to Damascus. As for passing it to Ilyan, the Beirut chief of station was sure that Ilyan himself would have a suggestion. Possibly he'd pick up the suitcase in my room. "How in hell," I asked, "do I get a heavy suitcase full of money up to my room? The hotel lobby is usually crowded, and the doorman and bellboys fight over my bags the minute I drive up."

"You'll find a way," Zog said. "After all, didn't you start out in intelligence work fifteen years ago?" I wasn't sure whether his line was intended as a compliment or as a dig. I'd never had a classroom lecture on this kind of thing, let alone practical experience. Finally, I gave Harvey my car keys and asked that one of his boys put the suitcase of money in the trunk of the Ford—and not while it was parked in front of the embassy. When I reclaimed the vehicle later, I stared at its contents with awe but declined to spend the hours it would take to confirm that the half-million pounds were actually there.

I decided to make a daytime crossing into Syria. The officials were now so used to seeing me that a show of the white identity card I'd obtained from the Syrian foreign ministry (to prove that I was attached to the embassy in Damascus) usually sufficed. The benefit of having this card was that I was entitled to pass on examination by the immigration inspectors without needing to take my passport into the office and have entry and departure stamps placed on it and my name entered in a ledger. Although it conveyed no diplomatic status or immunity, the card cut time off going through the two border stations, and often the guards just waved me on through. The Ford convertible was an asset, too, just as I'd thought when I'd arranged to get it from Ed House. Who would believe that someone in such a conspicuous car was up to secret activities?

As I drove through the Bekaa Valley toward the combined Lebanese-Syrian customs examination building, my mind raced. What if I were subjected to a complete vehicle-and-baggage inspection, as sometimes happened? No story of shopping for brocade, Damascene silver, or Persian carpets would account for the huge amount of cash I was carrying. (Once more I cursed Walter Snowdon, Kim Roosevelt, and the whole CIA system for depriving me of the protection of a diplomatic passport and the license plates that would immunize my car against inspection—so much for security when I really needed it!) Although I'd filled two suitcases of my own with clothing and thrown them on the backseat, if I were told to get out of the car, the bag of money in the trunk would almost certainly be opened, and I was determined to avoid that at all costs. If it looked bad, I decided, I'd make a hurried U-turn back into Lebanon, shouting that I'd just realized I'd left my passport behind. Although this might arouse some suspicion, at least I'd be in Lebanese hands and able to demand that our embassy, or even President Chamoun, be contacted. Once in Syria, where distrust of Westerners was growing, I feared that I might come under the "plausible denial" disclaimer that the American government attached to all covert operations.[62]

The closer I came to the border, the more nervous I got. Why in hell, I kept wondering, was I risking my future to pass funds to a man who was still unaware that we'd decided to give them to him? By now, however, I was approaching the line of cars at the first border checkpoint. There was nothing to do but push on.

Spotted, praise Allah, by a customs inspector who remembered the zany American who drove a car with its top down in all kinds of weather, I was waved out of line almost before I'd fully braked to a halt. Still, I wasn't free from danger. There was always the risk of being stopped at the Syrian immigration post some three miles farther on in the foothills of the Anti-Lebanon mountain range. There too, to apprehend smugglers, a search could be made. But, as it turned out, my waving of the white identity card evoked nothing more than a laugh, and I was passed through the last barrier after merely slowing down.

Only one immediate danger then remained: being involved in an accident in the crazy Damascus traffic, where some drivers considered observing traffic signals to be a sign of weakness. So, like the little old ladies of La Jolla out for a Sunday ride, I entered the city cautiously, observing all traffic signs and creeping warily through intersections. I finally pulled up in front of the New Omayad and relaxed for the first time since leaving Beirut.

---

62   A provision for approval by the OCB of clandestine CIA operations was a declaration that the president and the secretary of state could plausibly renounce any U.S. involvement in the event that the operation aborted or its participants were exposed by a foreign country. Two outstanding examples of the fallacy of such procedures were the U-2 incident and the Bay of Pigs invasion. Although in both cases the president initially denied U.S. complicity (leaving our uninformed U.N. ambassadors loudly to protest innocence), the scope and international implications of these affairs later produced presidential admissions that the U.S. had sponsored them. Not so fortunate personally were the CIA agents captured on individual missions—such as the two held in Chinese prisons for nearly twenty years—who remained "nonpersons" in official U.S. eyes in order to avoid admissions of CIA guilt. When this practice was questioned by the Pike Committee in 1975, a high U.S. official replied that "covert action should not be confused with missionary work."

By now I realized that I was the "bag man" in a totally unprofessional CIA operation. No one from the Damascus station even knew Ilyan, nor did I have any means of making advance arrangements for a covert meeting. There was also the chance that he might not be in Damascus. Leaving the money in the trunk, rather than risk having the strange, heavy suitcase somehow arouse the suspicions of a bellboy who would alert the Syrian sureté, I instructed the doorman to remove the two bags in the backseat, then drove around the corner to park at the side of the building. If the money were stolen, I thought, that would have to be that, since I preferred taking such a risk to being questioned in jail.

Luck was with me, and I found Ilyan in the lobby. Waiting until we were able to talk alone, I told him in a low voice that I'd brought the money with me. But first, I said, I'd have to have the names of his key people, details of his plan, and assurances that a firmly anticommunist government would take over in Syria no later than the twenty-fifth of October. When I asked if the deadline might be a problem, Ilyan exuded confidence. Passing money in the hotel, however, was out of the question, he said: the employees were all G-2 informants, he suspected, and keeping that much cash in his suite would be too risky. We'd have to meet outside the city.

Michail Bey was still reluctant to name the people with whom he'd be working. I insisted that the organization furnishing the money would be unwilling to pass it over until they knew how it would be used and with whom. I bit my tongue as I told him of this improvised requirement. What if he refused? I'd have to return the money to Lebanon, where the frontier examination was far stricter. To my relief, Ilyan agreed to give me the names. He would not, however, commit them to paper. I'd have to memorize what he told me and send it on to Washington solely for the information of his friend Mr. Roosevelt. Making this promise didn't really bother me, since Ambassador Moose wouldn't want to know and Vern Cassin would in any case read my CIA message. Returning to my room, I saw that the Ford convertible was apparently undisturbed, so I took a quick nap, content that my risk would end after one more meeting with Ilyan.

At five Ilyan and I met again in the lobby. We'd discuss the Suez situations in the U.N. and London, he said, to cover the information that he'd wedge in as we spoke. It seemed obvious that he'd given some thought to this plan, such as it was, and was enjoying himself. The names he gave me were all those of senior colonels in the army who, he said, would use their troops to take control of Damascus, Aleppo, Homs, and Hamah. The frontier posts with Jordan, Iraq, and Lebanon would also be captured in order to seal Syria's borders until the radio stations announced that a new government had taken over under Colonel Kabbani, who would place armored units at key positions throughout Damascus. Once control had been established, Ilyan would inform the civilians he'd selected that they were to form a new government, but in order to avoid leaks none of them would be told until just a week before the coup.

For these men, Ilyan said, there were considerations more important than money. To guarantee their participation, they required assurance that the United States would both back the coup and immediately grant recognition to the new government. This, I argued, was a new condition, and I saw no way of meeting it. Ilyan, however, had come prepared with a solution. In April, he explained, President Eisenhower had said that no U.S. troops would be sent to the Middle East unless Congress approved the action. Couldn't the President repeat this statement, in light of the Suez crisis, he asked, on a specified date when Ilyan's colleagues would be told to expect it? Eisenhower's words would provide proof of U.S. support and American intent to recognize the new government in Syria once it had been formed.

The best I could do was agree to report Ilyan's request to Washington. Although I knew that cooperative reporters often asked "loaded" questions in order to enable the President to make a point, I had reservations that he'd become involved in such a plan, but I would try. I'd need at least a day to check it with CIA headquarters by cable, which meant that no money could be passed until I received an answer. Meanwhile, the damned money would have to sit in the trunk of the Ford convertible. Before parting, Ilyan and I agreed on where we'd meet and how he'd know what my answer from Washington had been.

As I composed a cable to send to Allen Dulles, I had little hope of success, nor was I convinced that failure would be a bad thing. Somehow, I had the feeling that the CIA wanted Ilyan to proceed, no matter what the prospects for success, and this new stipulation would impose a brake on what could turn into a disastrous operation. Encouraging a coup was one thing, and I was sure that some in the agency found that in itself to be satisfying, but I'd observed long ago that the United States had always been careful to ascertain that any new government had *de facto* control of a country before recognizing it. An initially successful coup in Syria could, without prompt recognition, start to falter, and the British might then send in the Iraqis, which would infuriate Nasser and provide him with ample grounds for alleging Western intervention. With the Suez issue commanding the world's attention, the U.S. would find it hard to avoid condemning any form of external military intervention. There was also the possibility that Ilyan's plans might be exposed and the U.S. role revealed. Although Britain and France might find this convenient for eliciting support of any military action they might try in the effort to bring down Nasser, I didn't want to think now of that possibility. Becoming famous certainly had its appeal, but not at the price of being tagged as the American who'd single-handedly tried to overthrow the government of Syria and been exposed doing it.

To my surprise, an affirmative response arrived from Washington the next day. A proper occasion for the requested statement would have to be found, I read, and Secretary Dulles might be the one to use the key words in a press conference. These days, the president was trying to stay out of the limelight on Middle East matters. If, however, Ilyan would accept Foster Dulles as a substitute, a restatement of Eisenhower's April statement on the use of U.S. troops would be given to the press between October 16 and October 18, which would provide the week's time to obtain civilian support for the coup. If Ilyan concurred, I was to turn over the money and return to Beirut.

Ilyan and I met in the lobby the next morning, and he agreed to accept Secretary Dulles in lieu of the President. We'd meet that night at ten o'clock, after I'd signaled that I was ready by checking out of the hotel promptly at six. We separated, and I then had time to kill. The day seemed interminable as I explored the shops on The Street Called Straight, then ordered brass trays and camel-saddle footstools to send home to friends. Using taxis, I frequently returned to the hotel to load my purchases in the Ford's trunk and to confirm that the suitcase holding the money remained untouched. Finally it was six, and I checked out with considerable ceremony in order to be certain that Ilyan would know of it. With two hours still to wait, I drove about aimlessly, doubling back occasionally to be sure that I wasn't tailed, deferring to all other cars to avoid any possibility of an accident. Then, following all the specifics of the plan that Ilyan and I had agreed on, I headed west up the Barada River toward Lebanon, passing the cutoff to Bludahn as I went.

Now the winding mountain road I'd traveled so often before made it possible for me to watch for the headlights that would betray any car in pursuit. Ten miles into the mountains, as instructed, I reversed my direction and checked the deserted highway over which I'd just passed. Coming back, at the Bludhan turning I swung left onto the casino road, which was steep, narrow, and winding—just right for me to be able to be sure I was alone. Finally I reached the old French gambling casino Ilyan had spoken of, which was dark—there was only a watchman's light inside. Turning around in the parking area, I drove back and found the side road that Ilyan had designated for our meeting place.

There was no sign of life anywhere, as my odometer showed me that I'd gone the two miles described as the point at which I should make a U-turn and pull off the road. Alone in the stillness, I took stock of my situation. I was frightened. My mind kept racing. I thought I heard noises. Was I just imagining things? Then, from behind, I heard dogs barking, and soon a swaying lantern came into view. It was a Bedouin camel caravan, I realized. Just before it reached me, I stepped from the car and pretended to relieve myself in the ditch. Too scared to do anything more, I simply hoped that they weren't robbers and shuddered with relief as the caravan passed out of sight and beyond hearing.

What seemed like an eternity was in fact only about ten minutes before a car's headlights came bouncing into view and the dark bulk of Ilyan's limousine showed that my wait had come to an end. Shocked to see that he himself was not driving, I demanded to know why he hadn't come alone. His answer was simple enough: he'd never learned how to drive. In any case, he said, he trusted his driver, Artim, as he would a brother. So, as America's candidate for changing Syria's government puffed complacently in the backseat on a long cigar, Artim and I transferred the suitcase, and finally the Chrysler went off in a cloud of dust.

Sighing with relief, I drove back to Beirut, gradually relaxing as the cold mountain air blew about me. When I arrived at my apartment, I poured myself a stiff drink, sat on the balcony, and stayed until the sun came up, still thinking that the suitcase I'd handled might have a profound effect on seven million Syrian lives.

CHAPTER TWENTY

FRIENDS AND ENEMIES

The Suez issue was still being debated in the Security Council, where Britain, France, and Egypt were being pressed by the United States and Russia to agree on a formula for Egyptian operation of the canal. Less than a month remained before our presidential elections, and the Eisenhower administration was being accused of favoring Egypt and the other Arab states at the expense of Israel. When Israel's army crossed the Jordan-Israel frontier, leaving forty-eight Jordanians dead, King Hussein requested Iraqi military assistance, which both the United States and Britain agreed was necessary to prevent the collapse of Hussein's government (which had withdrawn army units from the Israeli border in hopes of avoiding just such a clash). Israel, however, threatened to move up to the West Bank of the Jordan River if the Iraqis answered the Jordanian call. Then, just seven days after their first incursion, Israeli troops attacked Jordan again in what was described as a retaliatory raid.

If there had been any thought of having to contrive justification for a press conference to confirm to Ilyan that the United States approved a coup in Syria, Israel's actions in further exacerbating the tense Middle East situation made this unnecessary. Two days after Israel's second attack, Secretary of State Dulles described the raids as contributing to the "deterioration of the [Middle East] situation" and pledged that the United States would "assist" and "give aid to any victim of aggression" in the area. This, he said, was in keeping with the President's declaration of April 9, 1956. This final statement, of course, embodied the words Ilyan had requested to assure his civilian collaborators that the United States would promptly recognize a new anticommunist Syrian government.

It was now October 18, and I therefore assumed that Michail Bey's people would act within a week. There was nothing I could do but wait; presumably these things came off without any additional help. Even so, I found it difficult to believe that Ilyan could organize all this on his own. Since Iraq's army had been alerted and was reportedly preparing to move to Jordan, I wondered if America and Britain would continue to encourage this aid to Hussein, in consideration of Israel's threat to occupy a significant portion of Jordan. It all seemed like a jigsaw puzzle, and matching up the pieces was more than I could do. The British and French had refused to call off their military buildup in the Eastern Mediterranean, and I read CIA reports of more shipments of Mystère jets to Israel, French pilots staying behind to train Israeli crews. Our embassies in London and Paris, and their CIA stations as well, complained of a freeze of information from our allies. Certainly something was brewing, and I felt as if I were sitting in a tinderbox not knowing when or if it would explode.

Because of all this, Beirut was full of foreign correspondents. Hanson Baldwin, the *New York Times's* military expert, came in from Cairo to assess the pact being discussed that would place the Egyptian, Syrian, and Jordanian armies under the command of Abdul Hakim Amir, the young general I'd met with Nasser in 1954. Sam Brewer, Baldwin, and I were discussing this proposed command arrangement when I was called from our table at the Saint Georges. Artim, Ilyan's chauffeur, handed me an envelope from his boss containing news that the date for action had been changed to October 29. Without means of learning why the coup had been postponed, I could do no more than send a cable to Washington to advise of the change.

By now my nerves were frazzled; the continuing uncertainty about what would happen was getting me down. That evening Sam

Brewer introduced me to two visiting friends whose ability to view the world with humor was so infectious that the problems of the Middle East soon departed from my mind. John Lardner—a son of the famous Ring—I knew to be a talented sportswriter. His traveling companion, Walt Kelly, was the creator of *Pogo*, a comic strip I'd enjoyed for years. A bear of a man, Kelly soon impressed me with his political knowledge and his ability to lampoon pompous politicians. He was to do some radio interviews, one with Lebanon's Foreign Minister Malik, whom I arranged for him to see. When Kelly spoke of going to Egypt, I advised him not to, explaining that many correspondents had come to Beirut from Cairo, anticipating imminent war. I still couldn't believe that the world was on the verge of madness, I said, but on the other hand Britain and France were clearly ready for anything. As I heard my own words, I thought of George Young's suggestion that Israel would join Britain in bringing Nasser down, but I still felt that Israel's dependence on U.S. support and Foster Dulles's warning that we'd aid any victim of aggression would be adequate to keep the Israelis in check.

The next few days passed quickly, and by October 29 I was watching for any signs that the situation in Syria was about to change. I was having lunch with Kelly, Lardner, and Brewer in a garden restaurant when the shouts of a street newspaper vendor hit us by surprise. Explaining that extra editions of Lebanese papers were a rarity, I rushed to buy one in anticipation that news of Ilyan's coup was fresh off the presses. Returning, I read out the Arabic headline "Israel's Army Mobilized" and put the paper aside. Unable to explain my relief that the Syrian coup hadn't aborted, I passed off the news as just another example of the hysteria now pervading the area and added that it probably wasn't important at all.[63] Nonetheless, I used my three preluncheon martinis as a

---

63   Kelly and I later became very close friends, and my name and my son's appeared on the swamp boats Pogo poled through the Okefenokee Swamp. Walt's humorous account of the Beirut "extra" episode may be found in his *Ten Ever-Lovin' Blue-Eyed Years with Pogo* (N.Y.: Simon & Schuster, 1959), p. 196. Kelly died in 1973, however, without my ever revealing the cause of my anxiety on the day of this incident and during those following it.

pretext for excusing myself for a nap, then drove straight to the embassy to find out what our official reports had to say.

There, I found a state of nervous anticipation, although there was little hard news about exactly what Israel's mobilization protended. Army-attaché reports confirmed that Israel's reserves had been mobilizing for days and that the country's army was now in a state of full combat readiness. President Eisenhower had sent Ben-Gurion a stern warning against initiating hostilities, but Ambassador Eban had assured Secretary Dulles that Israel would not start a war. Now worried about the recent shortage of information from British and French intelligence, the CIA had alerted Egyptian Ambassador Hussein to inform Nasser that an Anglo-French attack on Egypt might be imminent.

President Eisenhower instructed the State Department to warn all nonessential Americans in the Near East that they should leave. That night Brewer and I drove Kelly and Lardner to the airport, arriving to find a confused mass of fire trucks and military vehicles swarming about the terminal. Syria had closed its air space, we learned; Lebanon feared an Israeli air raid; and the Pan American flight on which our visitors hoped to proceed to the Melbourne Olympics had been terminated in Istanbul. Amid all these signs of a possible war, we returned to the city to see what developed.

Before dawn, I was roused from my sleep by the persistent ringing of my doorbell. It was Michail Ilyan, his face was flushed with anger. "*Ya Ahmee,*" he said indignantly, "thanks to God I'm alive to see you and say what a terrible thing you and your government did." I was startled but understood all too soon what had happened. "Last night," Ilyan said, "the Israelis invaded Egypt and are right now heading for the Suez Canal! How could you have asked us to overthrow our government at the exact moment when Israel started a war with an Arab state?"

Ilyan, I learned, had tried to call off the coup but didn't know if his messages had been received. Most of his cohorts, he was sure, would believe that he'd been aware of the plans for Israel's sneak attack. Fearing for his life, he'd come to Beirut. My protests that I'd been ignorant of the Israeli plan fell on deaf ears. Over and again Ilyan lamented that his life had been destroyed, that he'd never be able to return to his own country. "Your Secretary Dulles," he said, "is a cruel man. He surely knew what would happen when he encouraged us to go on."

Trying to console Ilyan, I was utterly dismayed. Hadn't the CIA been created just to be sure we'd never be caught napping again, and what of James Angleton's vaunted liaison between the CIA and Israel's Mossad? But unlike what had happened at Pearl Harbor, this time it was our allies who'd deceived us. Obviously Britain and France had encouraged the Israeli attack and had their troops standing by in the event it bogged down. How cleverly timed, I thought. All three had decided to act during what Sam Kopper called our "silly season"—just before the presidential elections, when neither political party would risk losing the Jewish vote by criticizing Israel.

As Ilyan calmed down somewhat and I thought about what had happened, I asked him why he'd wanted the five-day post-ponement. He explained that Colonel Kabbani, under whom the new government was to have been organized, had told him that his people weren't quite ready. Was it possible, I wondered, that Kabbani was working for Britain? Had the British made him wait in order for Israel to complete its mobilization? I could visualize the British SIS using the Iraqis to set this up, leaving the United States and Ilyan as the scapegoats in the event the coup failed. Had Ilyan not attempted to abort his plan, had he been captured and confessed that he was financed by the CIA, the United States would have been in an even weaker position for condemning the Israeli invasion of Egypt. Perhaps Ilyan had been set up—by the Allen Dulles-Selwyn Lloyd agreement that the CIA would implement the coup in Syria—as a pawn the British hoped might be caught.

Exhausted, Ilyan said that he was going to the mountains to wait until he learned just how much he'd been compromised. As I watched him go, I kept asking myself if I, too, had been set up, if the United States had in fact collaborated with Britain and Israel. Of one thing I was certain, however: Archie Roosevelt knew no more about staging coups than I did—nothing at all, that is to say.

From Zogby's office, I sent an urgent cable describing my meeting with Ilyan and explaining the possibility that both he and I might be exposed at any time. Reading through embassy and CIA messages, I learned that Israel had announced that a preventive foray was in progress as a "security measure to eliminate Egyptian *Fedayeen* [commando] bases in the Sinai Peninsula." Meanwhile, in fact, we now knew that Israeli troops were approaching the Suez Canal. Demanding an emergency meeting of the Security Council, the White House had also urged the British and French to oppose the Israeli invasion but had received no assurances of compliance. It seemed certain that a war was developing and that we might all have to evacuate soon.

When I found Brewer, he was inundated with a flood of cables from New York asking him what was going on. Beirut airport was now closed. Unable to leave, Kelly and Lardner were enjoying the prospect of serving as war correspondents. *Timestringer* Abu Said, making frequent calls to Jordan and Syria, had learned that the Iraqi army was moving into Jordan. There were also arrests in Syria, he said, but he didn't yet have any names. The Lebanese army was mobilizing, he continued, and in Cyprus and Malta the British and French were putting out to sea in the direction of Egypt. This was the only hard news I could find; everything else was rumor.

The next day, the story began to emerge. Britain and France issued an ultimatum demanding that both Israel and Egypt stop fighting, and then—in a transparent ploy that defied credulity—in order to ensure Egyptian compliance, British and French warplanes wiped out Egypt's air force and its bases. Meanwhile, in the Security Council, both Britain and France vetoed the U.S. resolution demanding that Israel's troops withdraw from Egypt, leaving the United States and Russia joined in condemning aggression. Even as all this was going on, 20,000 Russian troops with tanks were entering Hungary to put down an uprising there that posed the possibility that all states behind the "iron curtain" would revolt. Finally, reports came that an Anglo-French force was preparing to land in Egypt.

As the diplomatic maneuvering continued—now in the General Assembly of the U.N., where vetoes had no power—it seemed obvious that Britain and France were either so ill prepared or so inept that they'd never reach their presumed objective, Cairo.

During this period, air service to Turkey resumed, most correspondents left for Cyprus and Egypt, and my life approached being normal, except for the constant suspense of wondering if my name would make the headlines in Syria's papers. Brewer's airmailed copies of the *Times* gave me some sense of the world's reaction to all this and of how these crazy events of the past week had affected America's position abroad.

The November 3 issue featured a "Man in the News" article reviving some memories. "A young, tough native Palestinian [Major General Moshe Dayan] "now commands the Israeli Army in action against Egypt," I read. When I saw that Israel's army had routed 30,000 Egyptian troops and gained control within ninety hours of the entire Sinai Peninsula and the Gaza Strip, I thought back on Dayan's proposal to Admiral Davis that Israel contribute to NATO as a small-arms supplier. This in turn made me wonder what we were actually achieving through our massive support of our NATO allies. Five days after the Suez campaign had started, the forces of our two mighty European partners were still milling about in confusion offshore Egypt, preparing to land. Surely, I thought, the buildup of British and French troops in the Mediterranean over the past months and the use by France of NATO equipment in North Africa and Indochina must have convinced Russia that the preservation of colonial influence by our allies enjoyed priority over Foster Dulles's exhortation that the West "roll back the 'iron curtain'" and liberate its captive peoples. Now confident that NATO neither could nor would interfere, the Soviets were continuing their brutal suppression of the Hungarian freedom fighters. Yet in Budapest, the *Times* said, poorly armed patriots still resisted the tanks of the Russian army. The hollowness of American political rhetoric suddenly struck me. Just five days before, on October 29, the White House had recommitted the United States to aiding any victim of aggression, but what were we doing to help the Egyptians and the Hungarians? Nothing: trapped now by the perfidy of our own allies, we could do little but make speeches designed to encourage peoples who had taken the United States at its word.

■ ■ ■

For years, Frank Wisner, the senior CIA deputy director, had worked on plans to help the Eastern Europeans liberate themselves. The first major CIA operation to free Albania had gone awry, and now Wisner was forced to watch helplessly as the Hungarians were being crushed.[64] One aspect of this tragedy had just touched me personally. The Hungarian crew members of a Bulgarian freighter had mutinied at sea and sailed their ship into Beirut in anticipation that the revolt in Budapest would be successful. The Lebanese authorities had referred these men to the American embassy and assumed that we'd request they be given asylum. I had interviewed the frightened seamen and cabled Allen Dulles about their plight, but he responded that they should be advised to return their ship to its rightful master. Dulles even failed to propose that we encourage the Lebanese to offer them safety. Two days later, I watched the tiny ship disappear over the horizon with its cargo of Hungarian patriots, now consigned to death or a lifetime in prison.

In the wake of Israel's invasion of Egypt, Syrian nationalists sabotaged the IPC oil pipelines. As Majd ud-Din Jabiri had told me so angrily, these conduits were Syria's canal, and the Syrians had demonstrated their determination to do with them what they chose. With thousands of barrels of crude oil now spilling onto the sand, the British, French, and American oil companies demanded some kind of punishment for Syria. At a critical juncture of the General Assembly debate on Suez, Foster Dulles had been taken seriously ill and hospitalized; Herbert Hoover was therefore acting as secretary. Presumably at the oil-companies' request, Hoover asked Allen Dulles about the possibilities of yet another American-backed coup in Syria. Although Vern Cassin relished this prospect, Kim Roosevelt, to his credit, termed such thinking foolish.

If one could believe what friendly intelligence services said,

---

64   Planned in liaison with the British SIS, the CIA's Albanian operation had ended in disaster when those sent to infiltrate the country had been captured and executed. After defecting to Russia, Kim Philby, the SIS's key man in Washington, who'd worked with Wisner, admitted his role in arranging that the Albanian government arrest the patriots who'd infiltrated their country to organize a revolt. When I next visited Washington, I learned that Wisner had been hospitalized with a mental breakdown. Later he took his own life.

there were reasons aplenty to justify a Syrian coup. Israel's Mossad claimed to have irrefutable evidence that Syria was becoming an armed Russian camp. The Syrian army, both the Israelis and Iraqis reported, was going to purge the civilian government and take over. Soviet jets, they said, were being shipped to Syria. But most ominous, I felt, was the information that two Syrian parliamentary deputies had been arrested and that warrants for another twenty-four had been issued. Michail Ilyan's name was frequently mentioned. The charges were "plotting with Iraq to overthrow Syria's government." Clearly, now, Ilyan would never be able to return. The army officers arrested in Syria, however, confessed to working for the Iraqis but never claimed U.S. involvement (if indeed they knew of it).

The CIA in Washington recognized that we had a moral obligation to Ilyan and instructed me to maintain contact with him. I was also authorized to speak to President Chamoun about our interest in Ilyan's safety and future. This I did, and Chamoun assured me that Ilyan could remain in Lebanon so long as he refrained from engaging in political activity against Syria.

Then, as if to reward me for not getting caught (a feat apparently synonymous with success in the CIA), I was granted greatly increased allowances. I had furniture built for a much larger apartment, bought a new car, and hired a chauffeur. There was clearly no success like failure.

CHAPTER TWENTY-ONE

UNCERTAIN SECRETS

The possibility that the press was exaggerating the extent of Soviet influence in the Middle East was a matter I'd raised earlier in Beirut with Turner Catledge, managing editor of the *New York Times*. Some of his editorial staff, and many of the Times's readers, Catledge had told me privately, felt that Sam Brewer was too pro-Arab, possibly playing down the threat of a substantial Russian presence in Syria. I'd assured Catledge that our embassies had no hard evidence to contradict Sam's stories, and suggested that the *Times* send out other reporters to ensure that its area-based correspondents were without bias.

I was pleased, therefore, when I saw that Pulitzer Prize winner Homer Bigart had been sent to Israel to cover the invasion of Egypt. Now that rumors of Russian technicians and equipment flooding Syria again abounded, I proposed to Brewer that he accompany me on a trip to Baghdad, in the hope that Catledge might use this occasion to send Hanson Baldwin or some other *Times* expert to investigate reports that the Syrian army had seized control of the country.

Direct flights from Beirut to Baghdad were still prohibited (Syria's air space was closed to Western airlines); this meant flying by way of Turkey in order to get to Iraq. I wanted to look into the extent of Iraqi involvement in Ilyan's coup planning, and I had to

attend to another fence-mending problem with Ambassador Gallman. Because Joe Alsop had unwittingly brought about my pre-
dicament, I found some satisfaction in asking Sam Brewer, who
had introduced us (and disliked flying), to share with me the difficulties of area travel in the wake of Suez.

My visits to the Arab capitals in the spring of 1956 had
involved a number of chance encounters with Alsop. Later, in
Beirut, we'd discussed the plight of the Palestinian refugees and
agreed to spend a week driving through Syria and Jordan to see
how these stateless people lived. In addition to having had pleasant
company, I was pleased when Joe's first piece filed from Jerusalem
highlighted the need for the United States to concentrate on Arab-
Israeli peace treaties before Soviet intrusions increased tensions
to the point of war. Although he'd frequently complained to me
about our lack of a consistent policy for the area, it was not until
his June 29 *Washington Post* column that he dealt with the issue
and cited my assignment in order to make his point. After noting
that flying the American flag was the only common policy of our
Near Eastern embassies, Alsop wrote of "an able young staff member" of the OCB—me!—"sent to rush from embassy to embassy in
order to synthesize viewpoints," and then concluded that "this had
little visible effect." The day I read this article in the Paris *Herald* I
was sure that a chorus of ambassadorial complaints would do me
in; instead, as acting secretary, Herbert Hoover sent me a message through Allen Dulles saying he hoped Alsop's piece would do
some good. Now, nearly six months later, I was braving Gallman's
bailiwick in hopes that his wrath had died down. By having Sam
Brewer's travel agent make hotel reservations for both of us, I was
free from dependence on embassy hospitality and able to cut short
my visit, should the ambassador be in a bad mood.

As it turned out, Waldemar Gallman and his principal aides
were preoccupied with explaining to Washington the embassy's
position on a local crisis and had little interest in seeing me or
discussing Syria. Hermann Eilts of the political section dealt with
Iraq's role in the Baghdad Pact, however, and his concern over what
the Iraqis had been caught doing in Syria was nearly as intense as

mine.[65] He perceived in the exposed Iraqi coup attempt additional ammunition for Nasser to use in branding the pact an "imperialist" scheme for dividing and controlling the Arabs.

The new CIA chief of station, Carlton Swift, tried to facilitate my mission by insisting that I stay at his home, then inviting General Ghazi Daghestani for a meeting there to discuss the Syrian situation. This not only associated me with the CIA but also resulted in an initial stand-off, owing to Daghestani's reluctance to criticize his own government in front of the newly assigned Swift.[66]

Eventually I managed to get Daghestani alone and learn the full story. Contending that he'd become involved in plans for a coup in Syria only to try to control Nuri as Said's wild plans for taking over the country with the help of the Iraqi army, Daghestani admitted that he'd been instrumental in bringing Colonel Shishakly to Lebanon. Authorized to finance Shishakly to lead a coup, Ghazi said that he'd paid the colonel a small sum, then withheld any further money when it became evident that he had no real following in Syria. Learning from the British that the Americans had arranged for Shishakly to be expelled from Lebanon, Ghazi told me, he'd assumed that the coup was a dead issue. Now he was sure that Anglo-Iraqi plans for Syria (agreed upon at the time the king and Nuri dined with Anthony Eden in London, when Nasser's nationalization of the canal company was announced) had proceeded under control of the Iraqi military attaché in Beirut. What all this had involved, Daghestani wasn't sure: arms had been smuggled into Syria; politicians and army officers had been paid; and, he

---

65 Eilts became American ambassador to Egypt in 1974, when diplomatic relations, suspended at the time of Israel's 1967 attack on Egypt, were renewed as a part of Henry Kissinger's "shuttle diplomacy." Highly regarded by President Sadat, Eilts continued to play a key role in negotiations for a peace treaty between Israel and Egypt.

66 Swift was well known to the Iraqis and the American press as the CIA's chief and, by meeting me at the airport, and insisting that I cancel my hotel reservations and accompany him home, did everything but hang a CIA sign around my neck in front of Sam Brewer. I therefore later told Sam that Swift had conveyed a message to me from the OCB requiring that I cut my trip short and return to Beirut.

suspected, Britain and France might have induced the Israelis to attack Jordan, just to provide an excuse for the Iraqi army to move to Jordan, to be used later in supporting a Syrian coup.

It was clear that Ghazi was disgusted with the intrigue carried out by the royal family and the prime minister, and, like Ilyan, he now believed that the British had used the Iraqis as a diversion to their major plan of eliminating Nasser. "And how about Ilyan?" I asked as casually as possible. "Do you believe he was involved?"

"You financed him," he said, smiling, looking right at me. Arguing wouldn't have helped, I realized, and if Ghazi knew this much I was sure that he had concluded that America had been another pawn in the overall Anglo-French strategy. Although I couldn't be sure who had fooled or used whom, one thing was certain: the invasion of Egypt had culminated in a total fiasco, militarily and politically, leaving Nasser, in the eyes of most Arabs and Third World people, an even greater hero.

Deciding to leave the next day, I accepted Ghazi's offer to book me on Iraqi Airway's nonstop flight to Beirut. Authorized by the Syrians only that day, it would be the first overflight by an Iraqi aircraft since the Suez invasion, and would enable me to get home without spending the night in Turkey. We'd just entered Syrian air space when our plane abruptly slowed and then banked to the right. Through the window I could see two Syrian jets far too close for comfort. Our pilot then announced that he'd been refused permission to return to Baghdad and ordered to land at Damascus. The only other non-Arab passenger, an Englishman, sat across from me, the diplomatic pouch handcuffed to his wrist showing that he was a courier with a bag full of documents that the Syrians would no doubt love to read. Since Syria had severed relations with Britain and France over Suez, this now sweating man would have no embassy to help him in Damascus. Identifying myself as an American official, I volunteered to have Ambassador Moose call the British embassy in Beirut and seek assistance. Then, startled, I remembered that I'd made detailed notes on my conversation with Daghestani about the abortive Syrian coup and had these notes in my briefcase. Suddenly I was frightened; I might be in real trouble too.

The plane was soon down, and, surrounded by soldiers, we were led into the transit lounge. Finding an immigration official I'd known well in the past, I showed my white identity card and asked to phone my embassy. Treating me as a complete stranger, this man with whom I'd once joked, as he routinely cleared Eric Johnston's flights from Damascus directly to Israel, now replied curtly, "All telephones are out of order." He then ordered me to open my briefcase. Before landing I'd transferred my notes to my jacket pocket, so I complied immediately, exposing a collection of newspapers and a book. At that moment he spotted a box I'd left on a bench, which contained two kittens I'd been given in Baghdad after I'd complained about mice in my new apartment. When I explained that the box contained nothing but cats, the inspector expressed disbelief and tore it open. Angry and embarrassed, he stomped off without ordering the body search I had feared. For the moment I was safe.

Suddenly I saw a way out. An Air Jordan flight to Amman had been announced, and among the passengers waiting to board were two *Life*-magazine staffers I'd known for years. When they started walking to the men's room, an idea hit me—so, too, did the stomach cramps I feigned as I doubled over in mock pain. A soldier standing guard nearby eyed me suspiciously, then reacted instinctively to my curses about "*my'ya min an Nahr Dijla*," a warning that if one who'd drunk water from the Tigris River didn't find a toilet, someone else would have to clean up with a mop. The soldier, bless him, waved me to the men's room.

Once inside, I asked the *Life* team to call Ambassador Mallory the minute they landed and urge him to telephone or radio Ambassador Moose and ask him to rescue me. Excited at the prospect of saving a captive diplomat, my friends agreed immediately and proceeded to their plane. Now in the safety of a closed-door stall, I sent a rushing flood of water to drown the finely shredded remnants of evidence that, at a minimum, the U.S., British, and Iraqi governments had been involved in an attempt to overthrow the country in which I now found myself. Although relieved, I was still far from certain that my name on the airline's passenger list might not also be found in the Syrian army's G-2 files.

Allowing time to be sure that the flight had reached Amman, I again asked the officer to let me call the embassy. To my surprise, he took me to a telephone, and I soon spoke with Ambassador Moose, who, laughing, said that someone was on the way to get me and drive me on to Beirut. It seemed, the ambassador told me, that the Syrian foreign minister had already intervened to guarantee my freedom. What better evidence could there be, I thought, that the civilian government was still in control.

Back in Zogby's office, I sent a cable to Washington to report my experience and, assuming that the *Life* team might have filed a story, to urge that the Department of State be alerted in order to protect my cover. Going to the Saint Georges for a drink, I found myself surrounded by correspondents, who concluded from my story that Syria was in the hands of the communists.[67] It was quite the opposite, I contended: my release by the foreign minister proved that the conservative government could countermand an attempt by the Syrian air force to express displeasure with Iraq.

Later I read in the *New York Times* articles to substantiate the opinion I'd formed. Turner Catledge had sent Kennet Love (from London) and Hanson Baldwin (from New York) on separate trips to Syria. In their stories, each described Syrian government and army officials as being open and cooperative. Neither writer found any evidence of Soviet-bloc arms shipments since the Israeli

---

67 Among the correspondents there was Kim Philby, then writing for the *Observer* and the *Economist*. In 1977 I learned from CIA records that my innocuous personal contacts with Philby and his wife had been subject to CIA surveillance, in the United States and abroad, and that my mail had been opened under the illegal CIA/FBI mail-intercept program. Since activities of this type, directed at American citizens, have reputedly been abandoned, I wrote to Philby as a lark. What follows is part of Kim's reply: "I remember an occasion at the bar of the Saint Georges when you argued that Syria (Abdul Hamid Sarraj and Co.) had not gone roaring commie. I knew that you were quite right, but I could hardly tell you how I knew, could I? And now the wheel has come round full circle, with the Americans getting their fingers burnt in the good ole li'l M.E. For your personal information, I was always against too close an involvement; the region just ain't stable, as you will readily agree!" (Moscow, November 1, 1977)

invasion. There were, they wrote, no Soviet jets or Russian technicians; less than half the army's equipment had been obtained through commercial deals with the Czechs; and to them the army seemed underequipped. Colonel Sarraj, the head of intelligence, did hold the balance of power, they found, but he was not a dictator and probably would never be one. Furthermore, concerned with Western reaction to the pipeline sabotage incidents, the leftists now feared the prospect of the United States breaking diplomatic relations: with only the Soviet bloc to look to, Syria would lose the bargaining power it now enjoyed.

Although there had been no answer to my cable informing the CIA that I'd been forced down over Syria, friends soon sent me clippings from the press about the incident. Sure enough, the *Washington Star*, carrying the first report, wrote that the Department of State denied they'd ever heard of me. The next day's *Star* and *Washington Post* gave the story greater space, and the *Star* quoted a State Department spokesman as saying that I "was studying problems of coordinating the work of our Middle East missions." I couldn't help wondering which story Joe Alsop had read and how he'd reacted to it.

Next, further exposing the cover I'd devised to disassociate myself from the CIA, Ghosn Zogby's driver proudly showed me the new DeSoto that the chief of station had purchased to replace his standard embassy Chevrolet. It was identical to my new sedan, apparently Zog's way of demonstrating that I, too, had CIA status. Adding this to Carlton Swift's blooper in front of Sam Brewer; the State Department's initial disclaimer; and Daghestani's knowledge that the CIA, through me, had financed Ilyan, the CIA itself had within a single week blown my OCB cover sky high four times.

Called back to Washington for consultation, I saw Michail Ilyan before I left. Fortunately, Lebanon had informed Syria that neither he nor the other fugitives would be extradited. Furthermore, during the trials in Damascus no mention had been made of American involvement or my association with Ilyan. Even so, I was certain that going back to Syria was far too risky and wondered what the CIA had in mind for me now.

When I met with Allen Dulles I told him what Daghestani had said. Listening attentively, Dulles puffed on his pipe and complimented me but in no way indicated whether he already knew about British and Iraqi involvement in the Syrian coup attempt. Perhaps he simply thought that given Suez, Anglo-American relations had had enough stress to last awhile. Also, as before, he was loath to discuss the policy implications of data presented to him. Always, he reminded me, our job was merely to collect information. The president and the secretary of state, he said to me more than once, would use it as they saw fit.

As I heard this, my mind went back to the cable I'd sent from London in April, describing George Young's warnings and predictions, and to our agreement later to become involved in Britain's "Straggle." It seemed to me certain that this business of "merely to collect information" was simply a device Allen Dulles used when he didn't wish to speak further. And, finally, I thought that if the CIA had indeed done the job for which it had been created and objectively collected intelligence information, there wouldn't have been an Anglo-French-Israeli invasion of Egypt.

Dulles then told me that his brother was preparing a dramatic new program for dealing with the Middle East crisis. Arrangements had been made, he said, for me to sit in on the planning for this at the Department of State.

As I started to leave, Dulles asked me about having been forced down in Syria. The State Department, he explained, had been caught unprepared when questioned by the press about my official status, a problem inherent in my not being a career CIA officer with official cover documented in the Department of State's *Foreign Service List* and *Biographical Register*. Then, after receiving my assurances that my new living accommodations and allowances were satisfactory, he reminded me that I would have greater official and career protection if I applied for permanent status with the CIA. Expressing my thanks, I dodged his offer by saying that I'd give it some thought once my family affairs were settled. Going through the mandatory processing and training at "The Farm" did not appeal to me, and I knew that some personnel specialist might decide that the agency's area-rotation program dictated my being sent far from the Middle East.[68] Furthermore, the infighting for promotion and status I'd seen in the CIA appalled me. I had all I wanted for the present and could always quit if things changed. I'd worry about a pension at some other time.

During the Christmas holidays, I had time to reflect on what had happened to the West's position in the Middle East since I'd become involved with the CIA two years before. Clearly, we were far worse off than we'd been when I traveled to see Nasser in 1954, and the Egyptian president's influence and popularity had grown by leaps and bounds. Worse, our losses were not confined to the Middle East—events there had badly shaken the Atlantic alliance, and NATO's future was now in doubt.

I thought back to George Young's warnings, which in April had sounded paranoid, and to how the next seven months had demonstrated that Britain's obsessive determination to "fight its last battle" had in fact consigned that nation to being a second-rate power, no longer a real factor in the Middle East. In retrospect, it

---

68   "The Farm" is the CIA's training facility, situated on nearly 500 acres of land near Williamsburg, Virginia, and operated under the guise of an army installation called Camp Peary. There, all career trainees receive their initial indoctrination and instruction. Advanced training is provided for future covert operators of the clandestine service (DDP) and the paramilitary Special Operations Division. In a segregated, highly guarded section, foreign defectors are held for interrogation and possible infiltration later into unfriendly countries. Before leaving for overseas duty, personnel slated for assignments under official cover are integrated into the Department of State's records systems, their training and headquarters duty usually written up in terms of their being "analysts" for one of the military services. Designated as foreign-service reserve (FSR) or staff (FSS) officers, their names appear in the *Foreign Service List* and *Biographical Register* along with the names of regular foreign service officers (FSOs) and genuine FSR and FSS personnel having no affiliation with the CIA. By a simple examining these unclassified publications (available from the Government Printing Office and most public libraries), anyone can trace with little difficulty the careers of agency personnel operating under official cover. This technique has been employed by foreign newspapers and authors like Philip Agee, who have exposed CIA officers abroad, just as, we must assume, Russia's KGB had done for years before Agee joined the CIA in 1957. Belatedly, publication of the *Biographical Register* was suspended in 1977.

was clear that Britain and France had dealt with Nasser as if they were peevish children instead of as the great powers they'd once been. First, contending that Egypt couldn't be trusted to keep the Suez Canal open, they'd had all European ship pilots withdrawn, just to make sure this prophecy came true. Then, after the canal continued to operate normally, those dependent upon it as a life-line had sent in troops to "secure" their access, with the result that the wreckage-clogged waterway was now closed to traffic of any kind. Great Britain was now wracked by political dissension, faced with the threat of economic collapse, and Anglo-American relations were at their lowest ebb in years. Finally, in addition to failing to topple Nasser, it seemed that Anthony Eden had ended his own political career.

British and French participation with Israel in the invasion of Egypt had made a travesty of the 1950 Tripartite Declaration, and that once useful device for keeping the Arabs and the Israelis apart could now be written off as void. In the United Nations, however, the United States and Egypt had agreed on resolutions providing for insulating the Suez Canal's operation from the politics of any country and forming a new commission to negotiate a Palestine settlement between Israel and its Arab neighbors. Both were conditional on the withdrawal of all foreign troops from Egyptian soil; arranging for this was the task the United States faced next.

With Secretary Dulles still ailing, President Eisenhower turned to Treasury Secretary George Humphrey, in whom he had great confidence, to use America's economic weapons with our allies. Humphrey didn't suffer from a lack of ammunition, nor did he have any political or diplomatic compunctions about employing what he had available to him. To begin with, our allies and Israel had guessed wrong in assuming that Eisenhower wouldn't risk his reelection by opposing the Israeli attack on Egypt: the President had prevailed without difficulty at the polls. It was winter in Europe, and an emergency U.S. program to relieve the oil shortage there was predicated on the withdrawal of British and French troops. France presented no problem—Russian threats of intervention to assist Egypt had proved as effective in getting the French moving as had the U.N. resolutions and the need for U.S. economic aid. Moreover, Humphrey was one of those who believed that access to U.S. financial support was not a right but rather a privilege to be earned by those assisting America in achieving its foreign-policy objectives. In the end, it was Britain's absolute dependence on U.S. loans that enabled Humphrey to compel Anthony Eden to recognize that British forces must be withdrawn if the United Kingdom were to survive.

That left Israel. Premier Ben-Gurion remained obdurate, refusing to withdraw a single soldier until he was guaranteed freedom of navigation in the Gulf of Aqaba and security from Egyptian raids launched out of the Gaza Strip. The secretary of the treasury had cards in his deck to deal with all sides of these questions as well. Clearing and reopening the Suez Canal would cost at least $40 million (more than the total U.N. annual budget), and there was no doubt that both U.S. financing and engineering skill would be needed. Egyptian assets of $40 million, frozen by the United States after the nationalization of the Suez Canal, had still not been released, and gave America leverage with Nasser. Finally, the newly elected administration was in a strong position to resist domestic Zionist pressure and stop foreign aid to Israel.

As 1956 ended, I wondered if the State Department meetings I'd be attending might deal with plans for inducing Egypt and Israel to make peace. If so, a near disaster might be turned into an advantage. Just contemplating the dilemma the United States would have faced in having to choose between loyalty to its European allies and a U.S. commitment to oppose aggression in the Middle East made me uneasy. Clearly, albeit tragically, Russia's invasion of Hungary had extricated the United States and enabled us to employ the U.N. General Assembly (where vetoes didn't apply) to separate the combatants and to condemn aggression from any quarter.

The sands of time were running down the hourglass, and it seemed certain that we couldn't permit the Arab-Israeli problem to put us in the same position again. Developments within Israel leading up to the Suez invasion, however, had dealt a death blow to the peace overtures made a year earlier by Foreign Minister

Moshe Sharett.[69] Since the Qibya massacre, Israel had increasingly employed armed retaliation to deal with the border incidents that had formerly been adjudicated by the U.N. Mixed Armistice Commissions. Now a full-scale military operation had been launched and the prospects for peace seemed even more remote. The Russian bear already had its nose under one corner of the Arabs' tent, and unless the United States sponsored a major peace initiative, offers of Soviet arms and even Russian military advisors might prove irresistible to Israel's Arab neighbors.

Complicating all of this, Israel had alleged its "right" to expand at any time in the future its pre-1956 borders. Before the Knesset on November 7,1956, Premier Ben-Gurion had declared [Egyptian] Sinai to be historically a part of Israel and had proclaimed that the 1949 armistice agreements and boundaries were "dead and buried and will never be resurrected." To the Arabs, Israel's expansionist aims had been confirmed by force of arms.

---

69   In his diary *[op. cit.]* Sharett writes that Ben-Gurion had ousted him from the cabinet because he would have been an obstacle to the [Sinai] campaign. Out of the government and on a mission in Asia when the war broke out, Sharett was profoundly shocked, and his one-line diary entry read: "We are the aggressors!" Later Sharett wrote: "In the midst of taking stock of the gains and losses of this war it is quite obvious to me that I am one of its casualties."

CHAPTER TWENTY-TWO

THE EISENHOWER DOCTRINE

The January 2, 1957, meeting to review Secretary Dulles's dramatic new program for dealing with the Middle East crisis was convened in the third-floor conference room of the Bureau of Near Eastern, South Asian, and African Affairs. The Alpha and Omega Planning Group conferences I'd previously attended had been held upstairs on the same floor as the secretary of state's office, and this shift in venue struck me as significant. Certainly, interagency discussions were not involved this time: I was the only outsider among the desk-level officers from State; and, as I watched Bill Rountree, Dulles's compliant assistant secretary, arrive to preside, I had the feeling this group had been assembled merely to refine and endorse views already settled in the mind of John Foster Dulles.

Before us on the table were copies of a draft of a speech prepared for President Eisenhower to deliver to Congress. The Arab-Israeli problem was mentioned only in an aside; the main burden of the speech was that Russia had long coveted a foothold in the Middle East and that America was willing to give military and economic assistance to the states of the area, "many, if not all" of which "are aware of the danger that stems from international communism."

I was shocked. Who, I wondered, had reached this determination of what the Arabs considered a danger? Israel's army had just invaded Egypt and still occupied all of the Sinai Peninsula and the Gaza Strip.

And, had it not been for Russia's threat to intervene on behalf of the Egyptians, the British, French, and Israeli forces might now be sitting in Cairo, celebrating Nasser's ignominious fall from power. Predictably, none of the career officers at the table had any substantive comments to offer as we read the draft. Present only as an observer, freshly reminded by Allen Dulles that the CIA never became involved in policy, I merely listened; apparently the President and secretary of state had decided that this was what the Congress and the American people should be told. Mindful of my limited access to Washington's inner secrets, I sat back, soon became bored, and let my mind wander.

Secretary Dulles, I saw, obviously had some of the President's idiosyncrasies in mind when he drafted the address. Thinking perhaps of his boyhood in the Midwest, Eisenhower liked the term Mideast, and I sighed as it popped up all over the speech. And the word "now," which the President used frequently for emphasis and in order to gain time to collect his thoughts, started no fewer than ten sentences on the first three pages. Struggling to remain alert, I penciled in a dozen extra "now"s.

Then, apologizing for being late, Stuart Rockwell, Rountree's director of Near Eastern affairs, entered the room and took a seat next to me. He also took my copy of the draft speech, on which I'd been doodling, since there weren't enough to go around. Later, when Bill Rountree asked Rockwell for his comments, Stuart opined that the speech was fine except that "the secretary had used too many 'now's this time." Hearing this sage observation, seriously delivered in the cultivated voice of an aspiring ambassador, I could contain myself no longer and broke out laughing. The redfaced Rockwell glared at me as his subordinates' pencils roamed the text seeking to make appropriate deletions. And that was about it. So much, I thought, for the capacity of Secretary Dulles's Middle East advisers to criticize or provide guidance.[70]

---

70   Stuart Rockwell eventually became our ambassador to Morocco. He was returned to Washington in the mid-1970s to become deputy chief of protocol under Shirley Temple Black, and during that period I met him socially and reminded him of this episode. He acknowledged that I might have played a small role in refining the final text of the Eisenhower Doctrine.

What I'd seen turned out to be known as the Eisenhower Doctrine. After much debate, Congress passed a joint resolution authorizing the President to spend up to $200 million for military and economic aid to the states of the area and to commit U.S. troops to any nation requesting our assistance to repel "armed aggression" from "any country controlled by international communism." The ambiguity of these phrases bothered me: did a full-fledged army have to be the aggressor; and could a local communist party take over a country with impunity? Apparently President Eisenhower himself wasn't certain that Foster Dulles knew what these phrases meant. In any case, employing that magic formula of an ambassadorial commission to bestow instant wisdom, he anointed a just defeated Republican congressman, James P. Richards, with these credentials and pronounced him "Special Assistant to the President for Middle Eastern Affairs." Ambassador Richards, the White House announced, would soon leave for the area—apparently to find out what the governments in the Middle East *thought* Eisenhower had said and to try to convince them of the advantages of "adhering" to the doctrine. Almost immediately, Egypt, Syria, and several North African states let us know that they failed to perceive any dangers from "international communism" and suggested that Richards go elsewhere.

That Lebanon and Iraq considered the doctrine useful, however, became apparent at the United Nations, where I was sent to meet with the foreign ministers of those states, Charles Malik and Fadhil Jamali. There, too, I encountered Sam Kopper, now busy with Aramco's plans for welcoming King Saud, who was to address the General Assembly at the invitation of Secretary General Hammarskjöld. Soon sharing Sam's suite at the Waldorf Towers (where Ambassador Lodge lived and many of the delegation heads stayed), I was once more in the center of the U.N.'s activities.

Returning to the hotel in the evenings, we had to pass through noisy picket lines protesting U.S. pressure on Israel to withdraw its troops from Egypt. One night Kopper came in late and woke me, excited about a new and ominous development. In response to Zionist pressure, Mayor Wagner had authorized a spokesman to announce that New York City refused to welcome King Saud;

in fact, the city would not turn a single traffic light red to facilitate the travel of "this monkey" from his ship to the U.N., the statement to the press said. Although Sam was a member of the mayor's U.N. Hospitality Committee, his efforts that night and all the next morning to reach Wagner to warn that this slight might cost the United States both the USAF's Dhahran airfield and the Aramco oil concession proved fruitless. Adlai Stevenson was out of town, unreachable by telephone, so Kopper called Eleanor Roosevelt, who agreed to see him. Sam brought me along, and we listened as this distinguished opponent of discrimination expressed her personal outrage but admitted that there was little she could do on her own.

Because the U.S. government had much more at stake in this than Aramco did, I telephoned Allen Dulles, and he authorized me to do anything I could to help avoid an international incident. A reserve officer in the navy, Sam was also deploring the effects of a cutoff of Saudi oil on our fleet and the defense of Western Europe when a solution occurred to the two of us simultaneously. Wondering why I hadn't thought of it before, I grabbed the telephone and placed a call to the colonel who'd replaced me in Defense and was now chief aide to the assistant secretary, ISA. The king's party and Ambassador Wadsworth were en route from Naples on the S.S. *Independence*, and I was assured immediately that the navy could take the group off at Ambrose Light, where the pilot boarded, and transport them by destroyer to the Brooklyn Navy Base. Spurred on by Kopper, I then proposed that a military-police and shore-patrol escort be assembled to use *their* red lights to deliver the king to the U.N. A return call confirmed that this too would be done; in fact, I was told, the President had now become involved personally and would be sending the *Columbine* to fly the king to Washington, where Eisenhower would break precedent and appear to welcome Saud. Obviously the President couldn't order Mayor Wagner to change his mind, but even though Sam Kopper wasn't aware of it, the head of the nation's largest city had just been outwitted by a crazy CIA coup—the only one I ever enjoyed, and possibly the only one that really served the interests of the United States in the Middle East. Later that evening, Walter Cronkite stopped by for a drink, chuckled over the story of our triumph, and—bless him—agreed not to broadcast it. (Those were the days before TV "anchorpersons" dabbled in Middle East peacemaking.)

King Saud handled the situation with great dignity, saying to the press that he was here not to visit New York but in response to an invitation by the U.N. With him was young Prince Mashur, a cripple since birth who was to be treated at Walter Reed Army Hospital in Washington, and pictures of this engaging child in Arab dress soon took over the front pages of most American newspapers. The outpourings of sympathy, letters, and lollipops for Mashur from children across the country infuriated the Zionists, however, and criticism of Saudi Arabia for refusing to allow Jewish airmen to serve at Dhahran soon found front-page space in New York's newspapers. The real truth was that Dhahran had long been considered a hardship assignment, and it was so difficult to induce men to serve there that civilian contractors had been retained to reduce the number of uniformed personnel needed. The king had left for the United States with plans to remove all religious restrictions on service in his country, but, as Secretary Dulles later pointed out, Mayor Wagner's snub to Saud resulted in the monarch's refusal to lift his country's ban on Jews.

The important point was that Saud's visit had been timed to permit the United States to negotiate a five-year extension of the Dhahran agreement. Back in Riyadh, Crown Prince Faisal (who had himself once been spat on by Zionist demonstrators at the U.N.) now suggested that it would be easier for all concerned if the United States simply evacuated the base. Saudi Arabia, he reminded us, was constantly being attacked by Nasser's propaganda outlets as one of the Arab countries still "occupied" by foreign troops, and the nominal rent Saudi Arabia received for the base hardly compensated for Nasser's plotting to overthrow the monarchy. In the end, the Saudis were pacified, but the Zionists' campaign cost us dearly: to show our continued goodwill, we agreed to construct new civil air facilities and a terminal at Dhahran and, furthermore, promised Saudi Arabia that we'd sell it additional military hardware.

· · ·

The simultaneous visits of King Saud and Iraqi Crown Prince Abdul Illah gave them an opportunity to reach agreement on matters of common concern. Both now recognized that Nasser's brand of Arab nationalism threatened all monarchies. Moreover, the growing affinity between Syria's leftists and Nasser made it desirable for Iraq and Saudi Arabia to oppose jointly the Syrian and Egyptian trends of looking to Russia for support. Because this was a context in which covert CIA planning and funding could contribute to the objectives of the Eisenhower Doctrine, Allen Dulles and Kim Roosevelt approached the royal visitors with offers of aid. Abdul Illah insisted on British participation in anything covert, but the Saudis had severed relations with Britain and refused. As a result, the CIA dealt separately with each: agreeing to fund King Saud's part in a new area scheme to oppose Nasser and eliminate his influence in Syria; and to the same objective, coordinating in Beirut a covert working group composed of representatives of the British, Iraqi, Jordanian, and Lebanese intelligence services.

As the major source of all funding, however, the CIA insisted on overall leadership. Kim Roosevelt would now be opposing Nasser, whom he'd once backed to lead the area. As symbols of U.S. dominance, two new cryptonyms were pulled out of the hat: SIPONY (against Nasser, whose cryptonym was SIBLING), and WAPPEN (to deal with Syria). There would be no more talk of "Straggle," the Iraqis were told (this being the SIS name for what I'd originally been sent out to start in Syria as WAKEFUL). Yet, as it turned out, nothing the CIA did could induce the SIS to abandon "Straggle." Furthermore, the CIA gave Vern Cassin in Damascus a chance to try WAKEFUL again, to prove that I'd been a complete amateur. Professionals, it seemed, should do better.

Having promulgated this doctrine, President Eisenhower now found himself on weak ground in attempting to persuade the Arab states that the United States would oppose aggression in the Middle East: in spite of repeated U.N. resolutions and U.S. pressure, Israel still refused to withdraw its troops from Egypt. Finally, an Afro-Asian resolution calling for sanctions against Israel gained enough support in the General Assembly to ensure its passage.

Washington was in a dilemma: on one hand we were trying to dramatize the dangers of armed aggression by "international communism" and were condemning Russia's actions in Hungary; on the other, even personal letters from Eisenhower to Ben-Gurion proved unable to dislodge the Israeli aggressors firmly entrenched in Egypt. In an article in the *New York Times* (February 10, 1957) Dana Adams Schmidt summed up the manner in which the "entire membership of the United Nations" challenged the United States: "It's up to you. The right kind of word from you and Israel would fall into line. Then we wouldn't need to go through with this resolution." In the end, the President found no alternative to going over the heads of Israel's supporters in Congress and the Zionist lobby and appearing on national television to appeal for support from the American people.[71]

By the time I returned to Lebanon, the Richards mission to sell the Eisenhower Doctrine had arrived. Already Charles Malik had proposed to President Chamoun that Lebanon be the first country to "adhere." While Chamoun wasn't initially enthusiastic, he accepted Malik's assurances that we would bolster Lebanon's poorly equipped armed forces and agreed to go along. The Iraqis and the Libyans did the same, and largely for the same reason as did Lebanon. Jordan and Saudi Arabia also endorsed the doctrine (King Saud, like King Hussein, now had a personal subvention to assist in opposing "international communism").

Later, in April, there was an attempted coup in Jordan when King Hussein rejected proposals for union with Egypt and Syria,

---

71 On February 20, 1957, the President referred to stipulations Israel had set for agreeing to withdrawal and said that the United States had no alternative to voting for sanctions against Israel unless it abandoned all preconditions and immediately left Egyptian territory. For the United States to agree otherwise, Eisenhower said, would undermine the entire U.N. Charter: "No nation," he said, "should be allowed to occupy foreign territory and be permitted to impose conditions on its own withdrawal." On March 7, 1957, after 125 days of occupation, Israeli forces completed their exit from the Gaza Strip. As Eisenhower had cautioned, however, Israel's refusal to comply with the U.N.'s orders that territory captured from Egypt, Jordan, and Syria in 1967 be relinquished has undermined the effectiveness of the U.N. as a peacekeeping force in the Middle East.

and, contending that Jordan was menaced by "international communism," President Eisenhower ordered the Sixth Fleet into the eastern Mediterranean. Congressional questioning, however, resulted in the sober conclusion that the coup's leader—General Ali Abu Nuwar, backed by Palestinians—wasn't exactly a communist, nor were Egypt and Syria indisputably under communist control.

That major changes had occurred in the Beirut CIA station became evident in my first meeting with Ghosn Zogby: an "empire" had been created while I'd been away. Zogby's office, he told me, would now coordinate the multinational intelligence-planning group that would implement WAPPEN and SIPONY. Moreover, now that President Nasser was considered by Kim Roosevelt to be beyond salvation, Beirut would be the regional center for directing all covert activities: his "deep cover" staff would be greatly augmented; there would be a large program to produce films and propaganda material; and undercover men sent out by the new Defense Intelligence Agency (DIA) would come under Zogby's supervision and control.[72] This wasn't the self-effacing man who'd urged me two years before to supplement his meager staff. Sighing now under the weight of his new responsibilities, the chief of station made it clear that the professionals had taken over. Although I seemed to have been shunted aside, I was in fact relieved, since I'd never regarded myself as a covert operator and had no desire to learn the skills of spycraft. But knowing the CIA's area chiefs of station and regarding them as novices, I couldn't help wondering how this new clandestine offensive could help much. To the best of my knowledge, Zogby had seldom ventured out of Lebanon, but he'd have responsibilities for operations in places he'd never even seen.

In any case, the station chief told me, I was to maintain contact with Ilyan and wait for further orders. Although I had no objection

---

72   Assigned to work under "deep cover" in Zogby's new propaganda organization was David Atlee Phillips, who later published *The Night Watch*, subtitled "25 Years of Peculiar Service" (New York: Atheneum, 1977), an impassioned defense of the CIA.

to being well paid and comfortable, doing nothing didn't offer the satisfaction of being a part of a new U.S. policy for the area, which was why I'd returned. I'd wait and see, and if nothing challenging came up, I'd return to speak again with Allen Dulles.

When General Nuwar took refuge in Syria after the failure of his attempt to overthrow Hussein, Kim Roosevelt came screeching out from Washington, and the WAPPEN and SIPONY planners descended on Beirut to decide what should be done to prevent a communist takeover in Syria. Since Roosevelt was staying again with the Zogbys, their well-known top-floor apartment became the clandestine planners' conference site, and this gave me ample reason to stay away. So obvious were their "covert" gyrations, with British, Iraqi, Jordanian, and Lebanese liaison personnel coming and going nightly, that the Egyptian ambassador in Lebanon was reportedly taking bets on when and where the next U.S. coup would take place. If the Russians were really interested, their agents needn't rely on Egyptian or Syrian intelligence to find out that the CIA chief in Beirut had been elevated in status.

CHAPTER TWENTY-THREE

CANDIDATES AND COUPS

Once Roosevelt departed for Saudi Arabia, Zogby asked me to attend a late-night planning session at his home. Ghazi Daghestani was there, looking a bit embarrassed at being caught in the Iraqi coup planning he'd described as foolish when we last talked in Baghdad. Colonel Radi Abdulla, King Hussein's representative, also looked sheepish; he, Abu Said, and I had lunched that day, and Radi had expressed praise for the Palestinians who'd backed General Nuwar's attempt to overthrow the king. The Emir Farid Shehab, Lebanon's sureté chief, sat silently in a corner, glancing nervously at his wrist watch. "Where in hell is George Young's man?" Zogby demanded, speaking of the SIS officer sent from London to represent Britain's interests in the scheming. Just then the doorbell rang, and a moment later the SIS officer reeled into the room, as drunk as a lord. Apologizing for neither his lateness nor his condition, he took over the meeting. Teams had been fielded to assassinate Nasser, he informed us, and then rambled on about the bloody Egyptians, who'd planned to turn the Middle East over to the commies. His voice trailing off, he finally sank into his chair and passed out. That ended the meeting. As I left, completely disgusted, wagging heads and shrugging shoulders accompanied the farewell handshakes I exchanged with the plotters remaining behind.

Norman Paul and I had an arrangement that I decided to use at this point. A personal letter sent by pouch to Washington evoked a cable ordering me to return to headquarters for consultation about my future activities, and I boarded the first plane leaving Beirut.

During my meetings with Norm Paul, I mentioned my misgivings about all the intrigue being plotted in Beirut and opined that it appeared to me that the U.S. had resorted to a shotgun approach to diplomacy by turning loose amateur clandestine operators who might run amok at any time. Not disagreeing, Paul explained that these activities were beyond the scope of his division and now emanated from a triumvirate consisting of the secretary of state, Allen Dulles, and Kermit Roosevelt. It appeared, Paul told me, that Foster Dulles had really wanted the British and French attack on Egypt to succeed. Dulles now feared that both NATO and the Baghdad Pact would be seriously weakened unless changes in the governments of Egypt and Syria could be effected to show the world that eradication of their "proCommunist" regimes had been the real object of the Suez invasion. As the hero of the Iran coup, Kim Roosevelt had been charged by the Dulles brothers to work with the British to bring down Nasser without further delay. Roosevelt now spoke in terms of a "palace revolution" in Egypt, Norm said, and then acknowledged that he was relieved not to be involved in trying to find revolutionaries who fit that category these days.

There was some other planning going on at lower levels of the State Department, Paul told me. One result was an OCB decision to support the recommendation of the American ambassador to Lebanon that the U.S. authorize the expenditure of CIA funds to oppose anticipated Egyptian and Syrian intervention in Lebanon's forthcoming parliamentary elections. We had little time to prepare for this, Norm acknowledged, and Zogby would be away on leave during the period, so I was to deal personally with President Chamoun, to try to assure that such funds as might be authorized were first well justified and then used as effectively as possible. Laughing, I accused Paul of joking, and then explained that the only thing I knew about the Lebanese parliament was that its deputies drove cars with low-number license plates. His request was serious, Paul assured me, since it was the first covert political-action operation for which he'd be completely responsible, and he didn't want it to turn into a spending spree.

Ambassador Heath, I learned, was already claiming that massive U.S. funding would be necessary to offset what the Lebanese government claimed to be large subsidies paid by the Egyptian ambassador to the opposition candidates, and Zogby's reporting supported Heath's estimate. For this reason, Norm had arranged that the clandestine services assign an "election specialist," Van Deluer, to be sure that the operation would be handled professionally. When I asked if Van Deluer knew the Near East and Lebanon, I was told that he didn't but that it didn't matter, since Paul had been assured that financing a campaign was pretty much the same thing no matter what country was involved. Just as I was thinking about the prospect of three totally unqualified people messing about in a foreign election, Norm said that sending Van Deluer out had another purpose. The ambassador's recommendations could override those of the Beirut CIA station, Paul feared, but Heath would be less likely to challenge a man sent from Washington with previous experience in foreign elections. Because I admired Paul and his judgment, I agreed to return and assist in any way I could. Perhaps, I thought, this operation had been approved on the sensible grounds of assisting an existing government to remain in power and to preserve the independence of Lebanon.

Back in Beirut, I received a personal cable advising that Sam Kopper was dead of a heart attack. When I broke the news to President Chamoun and Charles Malik, I shared their sorrow at the loss of a good friend who'd worked hard to seek justice for all of the people of the area, Jews and Arabs alike. When I'd seen Sam in New York the week before, I'd finally confided that I was working with the CIA. He'd surmised this, Sam told me, but he didn't believe that CIA ties would preclude a good future for me in government or business. He himself, he said, was becoming increasingly disenchanted with oil-company diplomacy and was thinking of other things. We'd made plans to work together. Now he was dead at forty-three, far too early, and I'd miss his sage counsel, his help, and his sense of humor.

Lebanon's parliamentary elections were to be held in June. The country was divided into four election areas, and, to enable the police and army to maintain order at the balloting places, voting would take place on four successive Sundays. The 1957 elections would have particular significance because the parliament chosen would vote in 1958 for the new president of the republic. In theory, then, the political orientation of the deputies elected would indicate the degree of popular support for the pro-Western (actually pro-American) Chamoun regime. But that, as I already knew, was not the way things worked in Lebanon. In designing the country's constitution, the French had invested the president with virtually unlimited authority in foreign affairs; he could negotiate and sign treaties, referring them later to parliament for confirmation, with the power to dissolve the chamber of deputies should they not comply. There was, too, the National Covenant (unwritten, having the force of law, under which the complex groupings had been arranged to secure political, religious, and feudal-dynastic balance). Under the covenant, a Christian majority in Lebanon was presumed, although no census had been taken since independence, and the president would always be a Maronite Catholic. The Sunni Moslems traditionally provided a prime minister; the Shi'ite Moslems, the president of the chamber of deputies (parliament). Control of these three positions meant, in effect, control of Lebanon's international posture, and majority support by the parliament was, although desirable, not even essential to the government's domestic policies.

The only man in the Beirut station whose knowledge of Lebanese politics impressed me was Ray Close, and I went to him for advice about what we faced in dealing with the elections. To Close, the issues boiled down to the question of whether or not the benefits Lebanon might gain from adherence to the Eisenhower Doctrine could offset the emotional appeal to Lebanon's Moslems and young Palestinians of Nasser's brand of Arab nationalism. Charles Malik, Close explained, had pushed ratification of the doctrine through parliament by claiming to have Secretary Dulles's personal assurances that the United States would furnish Lebanon with "unlimited" economic and military aid. Ray acknowledged that he didn't know what the United States planned to give the country, but he was certain that unless some dramatic evidence of U.S. aid became apparent immediately, we'd be unable to offset Nasser's appeal without spending a great deal of money.

Before Zogby's departure for leave in Europe, a preelection strategy meeting was convened in Ambassador Heath's office. Large-scale financial intervention in the elections by Egypt, Saudi Arabia, and Syria seemed to be taken for granted. Although Heath appeared to want both to select the candidates we'd support and also to dole out the money to elect them, he knew that he'd have to forego handling the money. He would, however, be the overall strategist, and he hoped for a 99.9 percent-pure pro-U.S. parliament. As an example, he cited the seven deputies who had resigned (certain that secure constituencies would reelect them within a few months) in protest over Lebanon's adherence to the Eisenhower Doctrine and said that they were to be defeated as punishment no matter what the cost. With both the president and the new chamber of deputies supporting American principles, Heath argued, we'd also have a demonstration that representative democracy could work in the Near East. It might even be time, as his wife had suggested, to propose that women be elected to the chamber in order to show how modern Lebanon really was.

Heath assumed that I would deal directly with President Chamoun and obtain his recommendations about the funds needed and to whom and how they'd be dispensed. Zogby then surprised both the ambassador and me, proudly announcing that he'd "recruited" Prime Minister Sami as Solh and assured him that all CIA funds to support Moslem candidates would be passed by Zogby's deputy to Solh. Heath had no objections, but I was incredulous. Because I saw them often, the president and foreign minister were listed by Zogby as CIA "agents," and now he'd added the prime minister to the list. The CIA's liaison with King Hussein in Jordan had been supplemented when the chief of station there "recruited" the prime minister. If the CIA blanketed the rest of the Middle East the same way, we'd soon be out of key politicians for CIA personnel to recruit. What, I wondered, were our ambassadors supposed to be doing? And if Washington really believed all this nonsense, we could in theory close down our embassies, use safe-house meetings to direct foreign affairs, and substitute personal subsidies to our "agents" for conventional foreign aid.

When Ambassador Heath kept me behind in order to speak privately, he said that he wanted Charles Malik to run for parliament so that he could both vote and speak regularly in support of Lebanon's pro-American alignment. I was asked to convey this view to Chamoun and to encourage Charles to file as a candidate.

During my meeting with Chamoun, the president explained that it would be extremely expensive to defeat the deputies who'd resigned—their family positions, patronage, or political stature had always allowed them to win handily. Instead, our funds should be used to support candidates in evenly divided districts where winning a hotly contested election could be important in supporting the government's policies, and, he stressed, a victory would be less vulnerable to accusations of Chamoun's own intervention. As for channeling funds to Moslem candidates through the prime minister, the president considered this impractical, since a duplication of effort might occur and the effect of our money dissipate. Instead, before each area election, he and I could review the slate of candidates in order to discuss those deserving of support and the amount needed to ensure their election. Chamoun also opposed the notion of Malik's running for office and had told Charles so on a number of occasions. His opponent had been well entrenched for years, Chamoun said, and he was not anti-Western. In any case, the president didn't need a tame chamber of deputies. Overkill, he explained, would leave him open to charges of intending to amend the constitution so that he could succeed himself in 1958. For all these reasons, Chamoun said, Malik should not be a candidate, and in any case he should not detract from his international reputation by associating with ordinary Lebanese politicians dependent upon corruption for their following.

I reported Chamoun's position on Malik to both Heath, who shrugged it off without comment, and to Allen Dulles, with a hint that a message from the secretary of state discouraging Malik might end the matter. As a result, the ambassador received a telegram from Foster Dulles containing instructions for the embassy to do everything possible to discourage Malik from running. The night of the deadline for the registration of candidates, Chamoun called me to the palace to complain that Ambassador Heath was still encouraging Malik to run. Disbelieving, I went to the Maliks' apartment and learned that Heath had never passed on the secretary of state's position. For two hours I sat as a friend with Charles and Eva as they debated their future, then sighed with relief when they decided that Malik would not be a candidate. Fortunately, he'd about run out of time in any case, since the midnight deadline to file was only a half-hour away.

Just then the ambassadorial Cadillac, flags flying, screeched to a halt on the street below. In came Ambassador Heath, who, resplendent in black tie and white dinner jacket, hauled the foreign minister away in urgent conversation. Outranked, I sat with Eva until Malik emerged to announce that he was off to register his candidacy. Watching this, I understood one reason why John Foster Dulles seldom trusted and often ignored his ambassadors.

Tensions mounted as the elections approached, and in order to prevent interference with the voting, the government closed the borders with Syria and expelled Syrian nationals. Anti-Western riots broke out, with five fatalities in Beirut, and the car of the embassy's army attaché was smashed. Then, in response to Heath's urging for evidence that adherence to the Eisenhower Doctrine paid off, the initial shipment of U.S. military equipment arrived on the first day set for the voting. It consisted of thirty-seven shiny Jeeps!

Tension also prevailed at the strategy meetings, in which Van Deluer tried to maintain control of CIA election-fund spending. Overruled by the ambassador, the CIA's election expert finally conceded that some Moslem candidates might be financed by Zogby's deputy through the prime minister. Ray Close and Gene Trone also prevailed with arguments to make payments directly to the agents they handled who were also running for parliament. Then, totaling these requirements and adding them to the list Chamoun had given me, the ambassador used his sensitive channel to the Department of State and asked for a major increase in the initially authorized election fund. Unbeknownst to Heath, Van Deluer promptly sent a CIA cable to say we had adequate money, and then provided me with a summary of the candidates the United States was supporting for use in inducing Chamoun to cut down his own spending. As a capstone to this comedy of errors, Ambassador Heath had come to the palace to insist that Chamoun use previously earmarked funds to assure Charles Malik's election.

Throughout the elections I traveled regularly to the presidential palace with a briefcase full of Lebanese pounds, then returned late at night to the embassy with an empty twin case I'd carried away for Harvey Armado's CIA finance-office people to replenish. Soon my gold DeSoto with its stark white top was a common sight outside the palace, and I proposed to Chamoun that he use an intermediary and a more remote spot. When the president insisted that he handle each transaction by himself, I reconciled myself to the probability that anybody in Lebanon who really cared would have no trouble guessing precisely what I was doing.

So obvious was the use of foreign funds by the president and prime minister that the two progovernment ministers appointed to observe the polling resigned halfway through the election period. There was also large-scale fighting in northern Lebanon, and many were killed and wounded during the voting. By the end of the third week the government's plurality was so great that consideration was being given to creating a senate to provide seats for defeated candidates of stature. A second, more substantial, military-aid shipment arrived just before the government's landslide victory was finally announced, and one might have expected the results to be interpreted as a vote of confidence in the Eisenhower Doctrine. Instead, the opposition press and Radio Cairo cited Chamoun's victory as proof that he intended to change the constitution so that he could stay on as president.

In the end, the principal Moslem opponents of the government were soundly defeated, and Charles Malik won by a wide margin. Bombings and shootings still plagued the country, however, and when the embassy announced a $15 million commitment of military and economic aid to Lebanon, Chamoun called me to the palace. He anticipated increasing problems, he told me. Three former prime ministers would soon be indicted, and the president wanted our arms shipments to be expedited: if there were more trouble and rioting, he'd need them. While Ambassador Heath seemed more pleased with the election results than Chamoun was, one matter bothered him. He'd learned of Van Deluer's cable opposing more funds and now swore to see that Van Deluer's CIA career ended.

During the heat of the campaign, Chamoun had shown me evidence that Syrian arms were being smuggled into Lebanon and that much of the violence could be traced to Syrians backed with Egyptian funds. The immediate goal of this activity, obviously, was to influence the election. At the time, however, I'd wondered if Syria and Egypt might not be responding to Lebanon's role as a haven for political refugees they'd condemned and those plotting coups against them. In addition to Zogby's WAPPEN and SIPONY planning, I knew, Vern Cassin of the Damascus CIA station was simultaneously moving ahead with his own version of a WAKE-FUL coup. While describing his new plan in the Beirut CIA station, Cassin had looked at me tolerantly, then winked at Zogby and explained that it would be a thoroughly "professional" operation. Kim Roosevelt, he said, had arranged that Howard Stone be assigned to Damascus from Khartoum, just to be sure that the "engineering" was done by a "pro." After that meeting Zogby had explained that Howard ("Rocky") Stone was already, at thirty-two, a legend in the CIA's clandestine services as the man who'd helped Kim Roosevelt replace Iranian Premier Mossadeq in 1953. Then, perhaps to impress on me that I was an amateur, Zogby confided that Roosevelt's Iranian coup had been executed with a mere $10,000 and six or seven career CIA agents, including Stone.

I'd been too busy to give attention to the plotting in Syria, and my first indication of what Cassin's operation involved came from Arthur Close who, with Stone, had come to Beirut on a secret and risky mission. Now, Close told me, it was the CIA that was in contact with former Syrian president Adib Shishakly, and by supplying a false passport they'd brought into Lebanon Colonel Ibrahim Husseini, who'd been Shishakly's chief of security and was now the Syrian military attaché in Rome. Art Close's unenviable task was to transport Husseini (a moose of a man) in the trunk of an embassy car across Syria's border so that he might meet secretly with Cassin's key Syrian agents and provide assurances that Shishakly would come back to rule once Syria's government had been overthrown.

This time the coup was exposed before it ever got started. Syrian army officers assigned major roles simply walked into Colonel Sarraj's G-2 office, turned in their money, and named the CIA officers who'd paid them. Although Cassin, Close, and most of the station's staff had been protected by using cut-outs to make contacts, Stone and another career CIA officer (Frank Jetton) were caught red-handed and declared *personae non gratae*, and written up as such in the press. So too was Colonel Bob Molloy, the army attaché who'd always wanted some intrigue and had finally found it. Once escorted to the Lebanese border, Stone and Jetton had been spirited off to Beirut airport and flown back to Washington.[73] Molloy, however, had a different story to tell, and I agreed to bring Sam Brewer around to enable Molloy to unburden himself. His account of how he'd run his Syrian motorcycle escort off the road as they approached the frontier with Lebanon had a certain flair, and I listened with interest. But then Molloy spoke of standing beside his car, shouting to the fallen rider that "Colonel Sarraj and his commie friends" should be told that Molloy would "beat the shit out of

---

73   During trials held in Damascus during February 1958, ten Syrians were sentenced for their participation in the CIA plot and given no more than short prison terms, perhaps owing to the coup attempt's having been such a farce. Ex-president Shishakly, Colonel Husseini, and two others who'd escaped from Syria got life terms *in absentia*; Husseini was cashiered from the army, of course, and lost his Rome attaché job. But as evidence that the CIA rewards failure, Stone and Jetton ended up on top of the career ladder. By 1971, Stone had become chief of station in Rome—one of the agency's most coveted jobs—and by 1976, Jetton (who'd meanwhile moved on to Kinshasa, the former Belgian Congo, site of the CIA' attempt to assassinate Patrice Lumumba) held the number-two job in Paris.

them with one hand behind his back if they ever crossed his path again." I now understood another reason why Syrian-American relations were strained to the point of breaking.

One of the Syrians condemned for complicity in the 1956 coup that I'd helped finance through Ilyan was gunned down in Lebanon, and the Lebanese sureté now attributed an attempt to bomb the American embassy as revenge for the CIA's attempt to overthrow the Syrian government. Michail Ilyan, staying in the Lebanese mountains, called me to see him and said that in remaining he risked assassination. He had decided to move to Turkey, where he'd been promised round-the-clock bodyguards. When I reported his plans to Washington, I was instructed to go to Istanbul and arrange for Ilyan to have liaison with the CIA base there.

We'd expelled Syria's ambassador to the United States and recalled Ambassador Moose to Washington for "indefinite consultations" in feigned outrage over accusations that the CIA had been caught trying to overthrow the Syrian government. Depending on how matters worked out, therefore, we might have to close our embassy in Damascus, and Ilyan still had valuable contacts in Syria through whom we might keep apace of developments there.[74]

When I reached Turkey, my mission was extended to include what turned out to be an extremely relaxing assignment, although, I later learned, it infuriated the career chiefs of CIA stations in Ankara and Baghdad. King Faisal of Iraq, having completed his

---

74   Ambassador Moose never returned to Syria, and our embassy staff was cut to the bone. Vernon Cassin was transferred to Amman to be chief of station, where he "handled" Prime Minister Samir ar Rafai, and then moved on to Washington before assuming a "deep cover" post in the Middle East. Arthur Close and the rest of the Damascus CIA staff were returned to Washington; Close later served as chief of station in Tunisia and Libya.

In late December 1957, Charles W. Yost was assigned as ambassador to Syria, but within months Syria joined Egypt to form the United Arab Republic, downgrading our embassy in Damascus to the status of a consulate general under Ambassador Hare in Cairo. In 1967 President Johnson sent Yost to Cairo with assurances that Israel wouldn't attack Egypt—he was there when the Six Day War began! Yost later performed brilliantly as our ambassador to the U.N., and he now contributes perceptive articles about the Middle East to major U.S. newspapers.

education and now installed on the throne, was ready for marriage, and a suitable young girl from the Turkish nobility was being sought. Accompanied by his uncle, Crown Prince Abdul Illah, the king was ensconced on the royal yacht, anchored on the Sea of Marmara within sight of my hotel balcony. We assumed that Ilyan would resume contacts with the Iraqis, a process I was to monitor, as well as to remain available to receive any news Iraq's royalty had to pass on about conditions in Syria. For two months I acquired a fine tan and dutifully relayed reports from both Ilyan and the crown prince that most Syrians would prefer living under a Hashemite monarchy. The crown prince was looking for a throne, and Ilyan was a man without a country. It was hard to view their appraisals of political possibilities as much more than wishful thinking.

CHAPTER TWENTY-FOUR

THE PHILBY CONNECTION

After I returned to Beirut I saw President Chamoun frequently, our meetings often lasting late into the night. Committed now to a state visit to Greece in November, he'd made his plans before realizing how the election results and events in Syria would lead to the deterioration of Lebanon's internal security. There would be serious troubles in 1958, Chamoun feared, and he wanted Washington to understand why.

A number of the government's supporters in parliament now sided with the opposition in protest over the one-sided election, the president told me, and then admitted that he himself had lost control over the distribution of our subsidy payments. Prime Minister Solh, however, had conducted a campaign to defeat the government's Moslem opponents, and this, Chamoun said, became possible when we decided to channel funds directly to the prime minister. The traditional deputies who'd been defeated had also been humiliated before their constituencies and now vowed to bring down the president before the end of his term. Worse, Egypt and Syria were still sending arms into Lebanon, and Chamoun claimed that Russian guidance was becoming more evident all the time.

Then the president bluntly criticized America's actions: our aborted coup in Syria, our use of his country for plotting against other Arab states, and our too visible role in the elections all exposed his government to justifiable criticism from the area's radicals. The fears of Syria's young army officers were very real to them, Chamoun assured me, for whether the CIA had any actual capabilities or not, American power was something these people regarded with awe. As an example, he told me, Colonel Sarraj had invited General Serov, the chief of Russia's security services, to come to Damascus to reorganize Syria's intelligence organization. That this happened in the immediate wake of the exposed American coup planning should illustrate that the CIA's own actions had brought the Russian KGB into Lebanon's neighboring state and, he added, prompted the radio broadcasts now beamed from Moscow encouraging the overthrow of the Lebanese government and rejection of the Eisenhower Doctrine.

For all of these reasons, then, Chamoun said, he was giving serious consideration to Charles Malik's recommendation that the Lebanese government ask for a postponement of Ambassador Heath's transfer to Saudi Arabia. In spite of his anger over Heath's role in the Lebanese elections, the president now regarded it as too critical a period for us to bring in a new, and possibly inexperienced, chief of mission, and I was asked to stress this point with Mr. Dulles.[75] Then, as I prepared to go, Chamoun asked me to tell Washington that the U.S. government owed him 75,000 Lebanese pounds, the amount he'd paid out to reimburse Charles Malik's opponent for his campaign expenses. We'd also authorized payment of the same amount to Malik during his campaign. The price,

---

75 I'd been urged by Heath, who said that his wife's health could not tolerate life in Saudi Arabia, to discuss this matter with Chamoun. Certain that changing ambassadors would be a mistake at this juncture, I'd avoided bringing up the subject with the president for fear that Heath's case would suffer from "overkill." The ambassador's deputy had induced Zogby to recommend Heath's retention in a message to Allen Dulles, and I knew Malik was pressing the same point in personal letters to Washington. While in the Pentagon I'd become involved in Heath's similar efforts to avoid a transfer to Lebanon from his post in Indochina: a message from the chief of the host government and one from the head of our military mission (alleging that our military posture in Southeast Asia would suffer if Heath departed) had infuriated Foster Dulles.

then, of a relatively easy (and not very influential) Greek Ortho-dox seat in parliament—one that should not even have been con-tested—came to 150,000 Lebanese pounds ($50,000).

Secretary Dulles had transferred to the Syrian situation a por-tion of his anger over Nasser and Egypt, and he no longer bothered to deny reports that the Syrians had fallen under Russian control. Instead, Dulles implied that our embassy in Damascus was now not free to transmit information about the dangers in Syria. Then, as if to make certain that the things he feared were real and to induce President Eisenhower to announce his alarm as well, he sent Deputy Under-Secretary Loy Henderson on a trip to the Middle East. After speaking with Iraqi, Turkish, and Lebanese offi-cials—and without ever visiting Syria—Henderson returned with the gloomy forecast that we might even now have a communist satellite in Syria.

I soon found myself in the position of having to fuel the sec-retary of state's anger. Early one morning the Iraqi and Turkish ministers to Syria, Rawi and Kural, drove to Beirut to see me and report what they considered an ominous development. They said that a new chief of staff, Afif Bizri, had taken over the Syrian army, and he was suspected of being a communist sympathizer. Early that morning, and without any advance notice, Bizri, Colonel Sarraj, and a Ba'athist cabinet minister had flown off to Cairo. In Rawi's opinion, this was a sure sign that a union between Syria and Egypt was imminent. The Russian presence in Syria was also increasing, Kural said, referring to the courtesy visit of two Soviet vessels to the port of Latakia. All this I reported to Washington without comment, although I was tempted again to emphasize what Chamoun had told me about the Syrians' really fearing an American power play to change their government. Was it really surprising, I wondered, that Sarraj had turned to Russia for advice, or that some Syrians were willing to consider sacrificing their country's independence for the strength they perceived in a union with Egypt? I decided to use restraint, nonetheless, fearing that anything I might say along these lines in a CIA message risked being interpreted as sour grapes and a deliberate slap at Vern Cas-sin's coup attempt. It was becoming clearer to me, however, that the West's own mistakes had opened the door of the Middle East to Russian influence.

If it was frustrating to hold back reports of my views, Sam Brewer faced another kind of problem in filing his reports from Lebanon, one that he described with humor and resignation. As an example of the workings of the Lebanese mentality, Sam told me, all stories he sent by cable were now subject to long delays imposed by censorship to delete any mention of the Lebanese security forces' effort to maintain order. References to the increasing number of bombings, killings, and protest strikes were proscribed in journalistic cables as well. Sam had therefore resorted to telephoning his material to the *Times*, where, uncensored, it was published in New York and in an international edition printed in Amsterdam. Daily air-freight shipments of the European edition were now first taken to the censorship office, where any offending parts of Brewer's stories were excised with scissors before the papers were released to news dealers. Incoming personal mail, however, was not examined, so Sam received by airmail untouched copies of both *Times* editions carrying in full the same stories he'd dictated from Beirut. This was indeed the crazy place I'd been warned of when I first landed in Lebanon in 1950.

If Sam could smile at the strange maneuverings of the Lebanese, he had less to laugh about when he spoke of his family life. Even before his wife and daughter joined him, the Brewer apartment had become my second home; I was always welcome for a drink, a meal, or just a chat to let off steam. Eleanor Brewer was a tall, attractive woman, artistically inclined and intelligent, but quite uninterested in political developments in the Near East. The same age as I, she was also a native of the state of Washington, which provided us with common ground, and I was often invited to visit when Sam was absent on a story. Little Annie Brewer, age eight, was a blond, blue-eyed sweetheart, and I frequently stopped by just to help her with her homework. But it was obvious too that the marriage had its problems, at least for Eleanor, who early on complained to me that Sam thought of nothing but work and that she no longer felt herself a part of his life.

None of this would have been remarkable, except for a favor Sam asked of me in September 1956. Ordered by the *Times* to cover an out-of-town story, Brewer wanted me to accompany Eleanor to the Saint Georges to keep an appointment Sam had made to welcome to Beirut a fellow newsman with whom he'd worked during the Spanish Civil War—Harold Adrian Russell ("Kim") Philby. Although neither Eleanor nor I had ever laid eyes on Sam's friend, I was glad to go along because the name Philby meant something to me for two reasons.

Kim's father, St. John Philby, was a great Arabist whose books I'd bought and studied. His association with Charles R. Crane in obtaining Aramco's original oil concession had piqued my interest in my family background and led me to learn more about Crane's career and his role as one of Woodrow Wilson's principal advisers on the Middle East. As for Kim, I knew that he'd been the top British intelligence officer assigned to Washington when, in 1951, he was forced to resign on suspicion of having facilitated the defection of two senior British diplomats (Donald Maclean and Guy Burgess) to the Soviet Union. Certainly Philby had been in a position to alert the traitors that they were about to be arrested by MI5 in England, and General Walter Bedell Smith, then head of the CIA, had demanded that the SIS recall Kim once the defectors had surfaced and acknowledged long service as Russian spies.

Then, in 1955, a member of the British Parliament charged that Philby had been the "third man" in the Maclean-Burgess defections and accused the Tory government of a cover-up to avoid embarrassment. In the end, Foreign Secretary Harold Macmillan had unequivocally cleared Philby, nonetheless giving assurances that he'd never again be used for intelligence work. Now employed by the London weeklies the *Economist* and the *Observer*, Philby had arrived in the midst of the Suez crisis to make his Middle East headquarters in Beirut. With him, as Eleanor Brewer introduced herself, was St. John Philby.

The Kim Philby I met that day with Eleanor looked nothing like a former spy. Quiet, polite, and physically unprepossessing, Kim was then forty-four. Staying at the time with his father in a mountain village, he visited Beirut infrequently, until St. John returned to live in Riyadh (having been expelled for a period after the death of King ibn Saud). As might be expected of a man who'd been unemployed for five years, Philby avoided the Saint Georges barroom and, instead, took to frequenting the Brewers' home, where I saw him often. A heavy drinker, he spoke with a stammer, which seemed to abate as liquor relaxed him. By then I'd read some of Kim's articles and found him to be a talented writer, although Sam told me that he suspected Philby was still with British intelligence. This, I assumed, might have accounted for Kim's frequent travels to Egypt and Syria, and I'd been fascinated by Philby's accounts of conditions in Aleppo and the Syrian desert, where few correspondents then ventured. If Philby still had SIS connections, Zogby and Kim Roosevelt gave no hint of knowing it when I'd mentioned how frequently I encountered Philby at the Brewers'. (Zogby was first introduced to Philby at a party Sam and Eleanor gave in honor of Walt Kelly and John Lardner.)

Later, on my next trip to Washington, Allen Dulles asked me what I knew about Philby and then explained that Kim had once, figuratively speaking, had the keys to the CIA's safes. The question was whether he'd ever used them and, if so, who'd received the information. Then, laughing this off, Dulles said that he suspected that the British might still be using Philby as an agent, in spite of what Macmillan had promised. Almost as an afterthought, he suggested that I mention Kim to James Angleton, the agency's deputy in charge of counterintelligence, who had once worked closely with Philby in London and Washington. I did try to speak with Angleton about Philby but was brushed off as if he already knew everything I might say. As Bob Amory (the deputy director for intelligence) later told me, Angleton was in a foul mood, embarrassed that his contacts with Mossad had produced nothing but denials that Israel was planning to attack Egypt.[76]

---

76   All intelligence services devote tremendous efforts to ensuring that their secrets are protected from the enemy's using a high-level officer as a "mole" or double agent. Seeing to the constant loyalty of all CIA personnel was one of the primary responsibilities with which James Angleton was charged. It is ironic, therefore, that after Angleton was dismissed by William Colby, Angleton himself was investigated on the possibility that he might have been a "mole."

Back in Beirut, I saw less of Philby, and I had no reason to seek him out. By then tired of Kim's passing out and spending the night, or returning from outings with Eleanor, both of them showing signs of heavy drinking, Sam had banned Philby from the Brewer household. Now, Sam told me, Philby and Eleanor had said that they were in love and wanted to marry, and Brewer had just agreed to a Mexican divorce. Eleanor and Annie, he explained, would be sailing to the States in a few days, and he hoped I'd come to the ship to say good-bye, for Annie's sake. I said I would, and I did. After Eleanor left, I learned that Kim and Sam's wife had been keeping secret rendezvous in the homes of Brewer's friends for months.

CHAPTER TWENTY-FIVE

GATHERING STORM

My report on Chamoun's concern about Heath's replacement had attracted the attention of Allen Dulles, and he sent a message advising that the secretary of state would be attending the NATO foreign ministers' meeting in Paris and had agreed to see me. Arriving in France, I was referred by the embassy to Stuart Rockwell, who'd accompanied the secretary in order to advise him on Middle Eastern matters. Greeting me coolly, Stuart complained of being late for a meeting but condescended to let me walk with him to a ministerial session. The chill November winds of Paris seemed warm by comparison with the icy glance Rockwell shot me when I mentioned Chamoun's name to explain why I'd come. There on the crowded sidewalk he berated me, the CIA, and Allen Dulles for having gotten the U.S. involved in financing the Lebanese parliamentary elections and inducing Charles Malik to run. Saying that he deplored the vast CIA expenditures in Lebanon, Rockwell told me that now we'd have to spend even more money in the 1958 presidential elections.

Stunned, I didn't know how to counter this criticism of a project that had, after all, originated in the Department of State and had then been turned into a fiasco by Ambassador Heath in Beirut. As for the presidential elections, I was startled to hear Rockwell speak as though he thought Lebanon's president would be elected by popular vote. Deciding to avoid intruding something so mundane as fact into our conversation, I simply said that Secretary Dulles was expecting me to discuss Ambassador Heath's transfer. That wouldn't be necessary, Stuart replied impatiently. A new ambassador, Robert McClintock, had been named and proposed to the Lebanese government. Seeking an opinion about potential successors to Chamoun, I mentioned several prominent names. None meant anything to Rockwell; such matters were handled by his Lebanon-desk officer, I was told. Then, making it clear that the secretary of state would have no time to see me, Stuart strode off and left me to my thoughts. I remembered something about McClintock's having been rushed out of Cairo by Ambassador Caffery for intervening in Britain's Suez Base negotiations. Not promising, I thought, but the ambassadorial question had obviously been settled. My trip wasted, I called Cy Sulzberger at the *New York Times* office and accepted his offer of lunch.

Sulzberger brushed aside as "witch hunting" Foster Dulles's preoccupation with the elusive specter of "international communism" and his fears that Syro-Egyptian unity might result in a Soviet-armed anti-Western military bloc outflanking NATO and the Baghdad Pact. Suggesting that our own ill-advised intervention in Syrian affairs risked bringing about a military confrontation with Russia, Cy reminded me of an interview that Khrushchev had granted to Scotty Reston of the *Times* during October, in which he accused Secretary Dulles and Loy Henderson of pushing Turkey into war with Syria by massing troops on their border. Although Sulzberger was gracious enough not to mention Vern Cassin's aborted coup attempt, I was sure that he suspected that the game of "brinksmanship" in which Dulles was now engaged with Russia had evolved out of the CIA's attempt to change Syria's government. As I left for the airport, Syria was very much on my mind, and I decided to stop off in Istanbul to see Michail Ilyan before returning to Beirut.

The sight of an El Al Constellation as I took off from Orly turned my thoughts to how our quest for an Arab-Israeli peace agreement had been subordinated to coping with diversionary crises. The 1956 Suez invasion had undoubtedly escalated Arab animosity toward Israel, but a year had passed since then. Whether or not the Russians had been bluffing with their threats to rain down rockets in order to stop the attack on Egypt was something we'd probably never know, but the news that the Soviets' Sputnik had been sent (on October 4, 1957) circling the earth at 18,000 miles an hour had both impressed the world with Russia's technology and also caught the West—including the CIA—napping. At that time the United States had been engrossed in dealing with the threat Foster Dulles perceived in "international communism" subverting and controlling the Arab states. A contingent of Egyptian troops had been sent to Aleppo, Syria, and we'd countered this by airlifting tanks and artillery to Jordan in response to King Hussein's claims that Nasser planned to overthrow the Hashemite monarchs (in Iraq and Jordan). We'd also expedited American arms shipments to Lebanon, Turkey, and Iraq following Deputy Under-Secretary Henderson's return from his "investigation" of the Syrian threat. Surely none of this activity had escaped Israel's notice. Israel had also adhered to the Eisenhower Doctrine and might be expected to ask for American arms to defend against the two Arab states (Egypt and Syria) that we were now branding as Communist dominated. Perhaps my encounter with Stuart Rockwell had colored my perceptions, but nothing Washington was doing in the Middle East made the slightest sense to me.

Even my three years of exposure to the CIA's thinking hadn't conditioned me to believe that a Communist bent on the West's destruction lurked behind every tree. If the Soviet threat to the Middle East was really military, I conjectured, why in hell didn't we face up to defending the area on those terms? My Pentagon training had taught me that defense pacts were the answer; but I knew, too, that not a single state we were arming in the Middle East—with the possible exception of Turkey—could withstand for more than a few hours an attack by the Russians. Our arms shipments were in fact dividing the Arabs into rival camps, straining economies that should have been devoted to improving the lot of the people, and providing the Russians with targets of opportunity they could never have devised on their own. If we continued this way, I feared, the Russians might be invited into the area to assist the states whose policies we opposed, rendering our "northern tier" defense line as weak as a rope of sand.

A rough landing at Istanbul jogged my thoughts back to the mission I'd devised for myself there. Although there were few CIA operations I could influence, being a nonprofessional, I suspected that Ilyan might be the key to one that hadn't yet gotten off the ground. Fearing that he was now working with Turkish intelligence to spark a revolt in Syria, I wanted to stop his planning. Although I was confident that Washington would support me, I wasn't at all sure that Justin O'Donnell, who headed the CIA station in Ankara, would feel the same way. His station's efforts to send agents across Russia's border had been spectacularly unsuccessful, and I had an idea that O'Donnell might enjoy working with his Turkish counterpart on the relatively easy task of organizing penetrations of the poorly guarded Syrian frontier to the south. Whether the CIA might be involved in this was something I didn't want to discuss with Ankara, however, because Allen Dulles's instructions that I maintain liaison with Ilyan and Iraq's royalty had irritated O'Donnell from the start. He was one of the senior members of the CIA's career "establishment," and outsiders like me just didn't deal directly with the boss in Washington and survive—not in O'Donnell's scheme of things.

Ilyan at first denied having encouraged the Turks but finally admitted that he'd prepared plans at their request and saw no reason why the U.S. should want them halted. I explained to him that we were now dealing with a situation that far transcended events in Syria. Secretary Dulles had responded to Khrushchev with a warning that a Russian attack on Turkey would force the United States to honor its NATO and Eisenhower Doctrine commitments and come to Turkey's aid, I reminded Ilyan, and added that Dulles had made it clear that this would not be a "defensive operation," with the Soviet Union as a "privileged sanctuary." We couldn't afford to get caught again, I emphasized to my now startled Syrian friend, because Turkish intervention in Syria could mean the start of a global war. It was difficult for me to demand that a man who'd lost his possessions and country now forget them, We, of course, had been at least partially responsible for his exile. In the end Ilyan agreed to accept my advice, but I doubted he'd confide in me again. He'd surely find the Turks, Iraqis, and British more receptive.

As I flew back to Beirut, I thought about Syria and what had happened since I'd first arrived there two years before. The embassy I'd reported to at that time now had no ambassador, and only a skeleton staff survived. Although I'd had nothing to do with it, we now had a consulate in Aleppo. I pitied Roy Atherton, who'd been moved there from Damascus to work with once friendly Syrians who now considered America an enemy. They had enough evidence, unfortunately, to convince them that Woodrow Wilson's promises of "unmolested opportunities for autonomous development" were also as fragile as ropes of sand. Still clinging to the hope that Washington possessed wisdom of which I was unaware, I was nonetheless convinced that what the CIA had tried to do in Syria was in a large measure responsible for conditions in that country—and probably also responsible for the game of "brinksmanship" with Russia in which Foster Dulles was now engaged.

Back in Beirut, Zogby brought me up-to-date on WAPPEN and SIPONY planning. Both, he said, would be left dormant until we could assess the damage done by Vern Cassin's attempted coup in Syria and decide if our efforts to arrange an Arab-Israeli peace settlement could be revived after the first of the year. Pleased, I was even more gratified by the last part of what Zogby had said. Thinking that perhaps the new planning group that Secretary Dulles had created (Gamma) had made progress that I didn't know about, I asked Zog for details of the proposed peace settlement. He couldn't discuss them with me, he said; they were too sensitive. With that, chills ran down my back. Remembering Kim Roosevelt's visits to the area and the charges that Nasser had leveled against King Hussein, I feared that the CIA had again become involved in the peace-settlement business. Earlier in the year Egypt's semiofficial news agency had carried a story alleging that Jordanian Foreign Minister Samir ar Rafai had met with Israeli Premier Ben-Gurion. Then, just weeks ago, the Egyptian newspaper *Ash-Shaab* had accused King Hussein of negotiating with Israel in exchange for a $30-million U.S. payment. I wondered if we were going to put

Hussein on every Arab's "hit list" and expose him to an assassination like the one he'd witnessed as a young boy when his grandfather, King Abdullah, had been killed.

Then I relaxed as Zogby continued and passed on some news he'd received from Washington indicating that the CIA might be giving up planning Middle Eastern coups and peace-settlement efforts. Kim Roosevelt had resigned, I was told, and would now become a vice-president in Gulf Oil Company's Washington government-relations office, with Middle East responsibilities. Archie, Kim's cousin, had been assigned as CIA chief of station in Madrid. Miles Copeland and Jim Eichelberger were leaving to form an independent consulting company in Beirut, it would have Gulf Oil Company as its initial client. My first reaction to all this information was that Kim Roosevelt, Copeland, and Eicheberger had conjured up new deep-cover assignments with the oil company and would remain as active as before, simply wearing other hats. But it might also mean that a sinking ship was being deserted, and I wondered if I, too, should look for a lifeboat.[77]

Now resigned to accepting what he seemed to consider "exile" in Saudi Arabia, Ambassador Heath was preparing to depart. Soon a cable arrived advising that the Department of State wanted an estimate of CIA budgetary requirements in anticipation of "probable" U.S. involvement in the Lebanese presidential elections. Zogby confirmed my suspicions that Ambassador Heath was behind Washington's thinking and said that our departing envoy even had his own nominee to become the next president of Lebanon: Jawad Bulos, a man whose chances for election as a parliamentary deputy had been so slim that President Chamoun had opposed wasting money to support him.

---

77   From 1958 to 1964 Kim Roosevelt directed Gulfs Washington office and made many trips to the Middle East. That Gulf secretly channeled funds to Beirut, Italy, and other places concerned with its Middle East activities was disclosed before the U.S. District Court for the District of Columbia (Civil Action No. 75–0324) on December 30, 1975.

I met with Chamoun a few days later to find out what factors would be involved when the parliament elected a new president in July 1958. Not wishing to introduce the subject of money, I merely asked what Chamoun thought of Jawad Bulos as a future chief of state. Snorting a rejection of Bulos as a possibility, the president indicated that he knew very well who'd put this idea in my head. Referring to Ambassador Heath, Chamoun said that in spite of the "Malik affair," he'd intervened in an effort to postpone Heath's transfer; Washington had decided otherwise, so we could put the former ambassador's views aside. Now Chamoun had accepted Robert M. McClintock—with whom he'd had a passing acquaintance at the U.N. during the Palestine debates—and ensuring that our new ambassador was fully briefed on America's position toward Lebanon was the most important task at hand.

At our urging, Chamoun reminded me, he had associated Lebanon with the Eisenhower Doctrine at a time when neutrality in the East-West struggle for influence in the Middle East would have been an easier, and possibly wiser, course. Sustaining Lebanon's pro-American position had not been easy: most of Lebanon's politicians and religious leaders believed that their country's interests would be better served by their remaining aloof from inter-Arab and global conflicts. The results of the recent parliamentary elections had introduced another issue with which both Chamoun and America would have to contend. Accusations that the voting had been rigged to permit the president to seek a second six-year term of office were being made by the country's Egyptian-backed Moslems and Palestinians, supported by Radio Cairo's calls for Chamoun to resign immediately. For these reasons, the president warned me, there was simply not enough time to enable our new ambassador to settle in and learn the intricacies of Lebanese politics before recommending to the State Department what the U.S. position on the presidency should be.

As part of a lengthy lecture on the rudiments of Lebanon's political system and constitution, Chamoun pointed out that he had himself been instrumental in amending the Lebanese constitution to prevent the reelection of an incumbent president. The question of presidential succession had been tested only once, by

Chamoun's predecessor (Lebanon's first postindependence chief of state), who'd renewed his term and then been driven from office for corruption. Now, in order for Chamoun to become eligible for a second term, the constitution would have to be amended by March 23, 1958 (six months before the next president would be installed in office). The president believed that he could get the necessary votes to do this, given the composition of the new parliament, but he wasn't sure he wanted to try, and he'd never run without the embassy's assurances that the United States thought he should stay on. That, then, eliminated the consideration of CIA money: I knew Chamoun well enough by now to know that he'd ask for funds if he'd need them. We'd already "bought" him a parliament, and that was enough—possibly too much, I now feared.

As I prepared to leave, I said I could see great advantages to the president's simply announcing that he'd refuse a second term, since he'd thus deprive his opponents of an issue and have time to select his successor. It was an idea he was giving thought to, Chamoun told me as he walked me to the door. His wife, Zelpha, who'd by then joined us, made it clear that she and their sons wanted Chamoun to do exactly this. They'd then be able to relax with a normal home life and enjoy watching the presidential aspirants tear themselves apart. Shaking my hand, the president became serious and said that Lebanon's survival as an independent country was the only thing he wanted and that he'd always be active on the political scene. To be effective in this role, he'd have to retire from office with dignity, and I was reminded that America's decisions might have a lot to do with his achieving this.

Chamoun's parting words contained a challenge: "Why don't you fly back to Washington and urge that your government's decision be formulated and brought here by McClintock when he presents his credentials?" This, I knew, meant arguing against the concept that a presidential appointment endowed its recipient with great wisdom. I decided, however, to try it.

Arriving in Washington at the height of the Christmas season was not a propitious action unless one had been called back to deal with an international crisis, and tiny Lebanon wasn't expected ever to qualify in that category. To begin with, I was told by Assistant

Secretary Rountree's office that Ambassador McClintock had been thoroughly briefed. He was away for the holidays, and then he'd sail for Beirut to arrive in early January 1958. When I asked State's Lebanon-desk officer what our position on the Lebanese presidency might be, he reminded me that the election wouldn't be held until July and that we'd have plenty of time to decide before then. Allen Dulles was tied up and couldn't see me, but Norman Paul and I found an audience with Richard Helms, who'd now added Kim Roosevelt's responsibilities to his own. Helms admitted frankly that he knew little about the Middle East, but complaining that he'd been saddled with a legacy of the area's aborted operations, he was eager to hear about the CIA's funding of the Lebanese parliamentary elections. As I ticked off the problems we'd had with the embassy, Helms asked that I summarize my position in a memorandum and include my recommendations concerning future U.S. policy toward Lebanon.

Now without a family in Washington, I spent Christmas Eve typing up a fourteen-page report on what I'd learned about Lebanon and my views about how the United States should deal with the coming presidential election. The issue as I described it was not just what we should do about Lebanon, but how what we did there would affect our position in other states of the area. Nor should the U.S. position be based on Chamoun's views alone. That a Maronite Catholic would be the next president was not in question, for even the most antigovernment politicians had a stake in preserving this provision of the National Covenant, under which all faiths and sects benefited. The question, rather, was whether any Maronite president could sustain Lebanon's pro-American orientation without support from two key coreligionists—the commander of the armed forces and the Maronite patriarch. Chamoun appeared to have the backing of General Fuad Shehab, whose military forces were predominantly Catholic, but Shehab was not noted for being forceful and he'd also once enjoyed the status of heading Lebanon's government during a presidential crisis. Chamoun was at odds with the patriarch, who'd broken with the president over the Eisenhower Doctrine, holding that the church could not survive a conflict with Arab nationalism. Although presumably pro-American—he'd been a pastor in New Bedford and Los Angeles and, for a time, an American citizen—the patriarch saw Lebanon as a mediator between the Arabs and the West.

Also important were the leaders of the government's opposition, I wrote, whom I feared Washington tended to think of as entirely Moslem, forgetting that what we'd done in the elections had alienated many Christians who'd previously sympathized with America's Middle East policies. By highlighting the cleavages within Lebanon that our own actions had produced, I hoped to discourage thinking that support of a Chamoun bid for reelection would either unify Lebanon or enhance that country's position with its neighbors.

I'd also learned that we still counted on Lebanon, with Chamoun's permission, for planning to implement WAPPEN and SIPONY to change the governments in Syria and Egypt. Worse, there was still a WAKEFUL program, meaning that in addition to scheming with friendly intelligence services, we were still thinking about yet another unilateral CIA crack at Syria. I dealt with this in my report by drawing attention to the probability that we'd not be able to use Lebanon for such purposes under a successor to Chamoun. As I wrote these words, I hoped that we'd consider Lebanon's future on grounds more lofty than the convenience of having a place in which to plan coups.

Concluding my report, I urged that U.S. policy for Lebanon be defined without delay. We had to decide almost immediately if we would support Chamoun's reelection or announce our neutrality concerning the presidency. I believed that Chamoun was sincere in saying that he'd not run again without our blessing: if we encouraged him to try we should be prepared to stick with him; switching positions in the event of trouble could prove disastrous to America's position in the Middle East. In any case, I wrote, there would be no need for covert funding to facilitate another term for President Chamoun.

As 1957 closed and I flew back to Beirut, I decided that I'd made my last attempt to influence U.S. policy in the Middle East by working for the CIA. I'd see through the presidential election in Lebanon and then search for other opportunities to put to work what I'd learned.

CHAPTER TWENTY-SIX

SHOWDOWN

A cable from Allen Dulles awaited me in Beirut. Ambassador McClintock, it said, was "sympathetic to the agency" and had been briefed about my relationship with Chamoun and my area responsibilities; there should be no problems, Dulles predicted confidently. Soon afterward, Robert Mills McClintock, then forty-eight, took up his second ambassadorial assignment, while Washington hoped that it would prove less controversial than his first in Cambodia. In Phnom Penh, as in Cairo, he'd had a problem adhering to the protocol that governed relations with the chief of state, and King Suramarit had suggested that McClintock be replaced. At our first meeting, the ambassador greeted me cordially—we discovered that we were both Washingtonians, he from Seattle—and he urged me to continue my relationship with Chamoun during this period of transition.

Settling in with his wife and Golly, their miniature poodle, McClintock soon moved the chancery into a gaudy pink eight-story apartment building, a not altogether felicitous symbol of the American presence in Lebanon. With the arrival of foreign-aid experts to administer shipments arriving under the Eisenhower Doctrine, the building was soon filled to capacity; now the smallest country in the area had the largest American embassy and staff. Quickly dubbed "Rapid Robert" around the chancery, McClintock differed from some of his colleagues in that he didn't believe that diplomacy was the art of postponing the inevitable as long as possible. Rather, as a man of direct action, he often forced events instead of waiting for guidance from Washington.

Beirut, meanwhile, was quiet, but the country was still tense. Three Syrian political refugees were murdered, further straining relations between Syria and Lebanon. Then, in mid-January 1958, President Quwwatly begged Nasser to implement and lead the federal union that the Syrian and Egyptian legislatures had endorsed in vague terms the previous November. This prospect alarmed Washington and created new Lebanese fears of being directly exposed to an Egyptian frontier. My cable to the CIA commenting on this development characterized Shukri Quwwatly—the man who'd fought so hard for Syria's independence from France—as having established himself in history as the first Syrian who had willingly given away his country's sovereignty.

At the suggestion of Allen Dulles, and with Ambassador McClintock's encouragement, I left for Ankara, where the Baghdad Pact foreign ministers were to meet. I'd serve as a liaison between the area's CIA stations and the secretary of state, reporting reactions to the imminent union of Egypt and Syria. When I'd tried to see Secretary Dulles in Paris, Stuart Rockwell had turned me away, despite the fact that Allen Dulles had notified his brother that I'd been sent to see him. This time Assistant Secretary Rountree offered to pass my messages to the secretary but said that Dulles was obviously too busy to spare me any time. Then, after I'd handed Rountree an "eyes only" cable from Allen Dulles to his brother, describing the Soviet attitude toward the union, Rountree returned sheepishly to announce that he'd been instructed to say that John Foster Dulles wanted to see *me personally*, not just a piece of paper! My big moment had finally arrived.

When I walked into his office, Dulles was on a long leather sofa, one leg stretched out to relieve the gout from which he suffered constantly. He looked worn and appeared still to be recovering from the major surgery he'd undergone the previous October.

"Ah, Eveland," he said, "my brother has spoken highly of you. What do you make of Nasser's plan to take over Syria?"

What a beginning, I thought. I was going to have to start by disagreeing with him. "Sir," I said, "I don't think Nasser is up to anything. The Syrians have come to him because they're afraid the Russians will take them over, or that we'll either encourage the Iraqis to do so or ourselves attempt to stage another coup. Nasser has never set foot in Syria, and the only commodity Syria can contribute to Egypt's economy is apricots." I knew I was treading on dangerous ground but was still under the impression that I was being paid for expressing my opinions. The secretary did not seem displeased.

We then spoke about when the union might take place, and I said that it could happen within days. "What do the Russians think about it? They must be behind it," Dulles observed and then paused, as if not expecting nor wanting an answer.

Again, despite this illustration of the secretary's obsession with the idea that the Soviets were intent on taking over the entire area, I had to risk disagreement. "What we hear in Damascus and Cairo," I said, "is that the Soviets have taken no public position, although we assume they agree with the Syrian Communist party's opposition to the union and would prefer to divide the Arabs and deal with each state individually." To that I added Allen Dulles's advice that open opposition by us or by the Baghdad Pact states would probably give fresh impetus to the union.

Foster Dulles then asked, his tone of voice still encouraging me to be frank, why I thought that statements of opposition would prove counterproductive. "Sir," I replied, "I'm certain that Nasser still has doubts about taking responsibility for Syria. Our Cairo station quotes him as being caught by surprise. If he has any doubts, our public condemnation might just cause him to join the Syrians to spite us." Thinking, then, of the Aswan Dam turndown and the Suez Canal Company nationalization, I knew that I was really testing "to the brink" the patience of a man whose subordinates appeared to believe that he'd never countenance an argument or a hint that the secretary's past judgments had fallen short of infallibility.

Dulles snorted, apparently ambiguously, and then told me to keep up the fine work I'd been doing. He might not have liked what I'd said, but he'd let me present my position and I'd emerged unscathed. In the end, the secretary ignored the exhortations of the pro-Western Middle Eastern states that he deplore Syria's move toward Egypt, and not a word of opposition to the proposed union was voiced publicly in Ankara.

Dulles's response to urging that the United States announce full membership in the Baghdad Pact was awaited with intense interest by all its members. I'd learned that U.S. opposition to this proposal hadn't changed: we were still trying to do a balancing act in order to appease both anti-Pact-Arab and Israeli sensibilities, while holding out to the Moslem members of the alliance the presumed advantages of the CIA's participation in its countersubversion committee as a bulwark against covert encroachment by forces of "international communism." It seemed to the Pact members and to journalists in Ankara, however, that Foster Dulles was thoroughly enjoying keeping the word on tenterhooks.

In his speech to the closing session, Secretary Dulles managed to obfuscate the issue of U.S. membership in the Pact. Instead, he extolled America's commitment under the Eisenhower Doctrine to come to the aid of the Baghdad Pact nations with armed force, if necessary, to resist aggression by a communist-controlled country, and then announced a U.S. grant of $10 million to improve radio and telephone communications among the Middle East members—subject to the approval of Congress. Sam Brewer was in a tizzy trying to complete a story he'd prepared, leaving for the lead paragraph the critical issue of whether America would join the Pact as a full member. Collaring me at our hotel, Sam implored me to tell him if Foster Dulles's reference to the Eisenhower Doctrine had meant that we were joining the Pact with a full commitment to its defense. No, I told Sam, the secretary had meant to say just the opposite: our pledges under the Doctrine obviated the need for membership. For the first time, Sam used my own words—"meant to say"—in a *Times* story, and I appeared as a "qualified source."

All this was foolish, I thought, as I reflected on the U.S. position. Without question, Foster Dulles himself was universally credited with the original suggestion to form a Middle Eastern alliance as a barrier to Soviet expansion southward. Our reluctance to become a founding member was ascribed originally to fear of losing the friendship of Egypt. At the present the State Department doubted that the Senate would approve U.S. membership unless some special agreement to defend Israel were also given. This, of course, would upset the Arab states: in fact, Nuri as Said, heading the Iraqi delegation, had unsuccessfully urged that the final communiqué reflect Arab views advocating a state for the Palestinians. From Nasser, however, our refusal to join had not evoked a friendly response. Whether we joined was unimportant to him, since we'd conceived this vehicle for drawing Iraq away from the Arab fold. To the Moslem Pact members, U.S. indecision was an indication that we might not come to their aid if Russia were to invade one of them. The British, meanwhile—having admitted to us that the Pact's value was solely political—were now furious with Foster Dulles for leaving Britain as the only nonindigenous member.

The formation of the new United Arab Republic of Syria and Egypt was announced on February 1, 1958 (the day after the Baghdad Pact Council meeting ended). By the time I returned to Beirut, McClintock was settled in, now dealing directly with Chamoun, and he'd decided that we should encourage a constitutional amendment to permit the president's reelection. Undaunted by having been in Lebanon for just a month, Rapid Robert was proving himself a man of action, although I now questioned the wisdom of his quick judgment.

Called back to meetings in Washington, I found that the CIA guard in the Middle East was indeed changing. Norman Paul, in full control with Allen Dulles's support, had brought in Gene Milligan (from Karachi) to take over Archie Roosevelt's responsibilities as head of the Near Eastern Division of the clandestine services.

When Paul, Milligan, and I met with the director to discuss Lebanon, Dulles told me that I was to reestablish direct communication with Chamoun and assure him, although I'd been relieved of the role by McClintock, that the secretary of state wanted it that way. It was possible, Dulles said, that given the prospect of serious trouble in Lebanon we'd want Chamoun to announce that he would not seek another term. Although this was not yet our policy, he wanted me able to pass on word without forcing the ambassador formally to reverse his previous position. Before we parted, Allen Dulles said that I should feel free to direct critical messages to him personally, especially if they differed from McClintock's telegrams and if I felt that the secretary of state should know my views. This was a liberty, I learned, not common in the agency, although I'd taken it sparingly before. Because Allen Dulles said this in front of Paul and Milligan, I intended to do just as he suggested.

During March and April, clashes between government forces and outlaw bands led by Moslem opposition leaders—principally the three defeated former prime ministers and the Druse of Kamal Jumblatt (also defeated for parliament)—grew more frequent and serious. Criticism of U.S. failure to supply the aid Malik had predicted the Eisenhower Doctrine would bring was used against the government by those usually supporting it; anti-United States feeling was growing. When Lebanon announced it would seek a $230 million U.S. loan for development projects over the next six years, Ambassador McClintock promptly called in the press to say that no aid increase was contemplated.

The relationship between McClintock and Chamoun was showing strains, and the ambassador's dealings with Foreign Minister Malik were far from cordial. If this Mutt and Jeff jousting could be viewed as humorous, it was sadly out of place, with new problems appearing every day. Soon both the president and the foreign minister were calling me to discuss matters of U.S. relations, an arrangement with which the ambassador seemed quite content: he'd by now "discovered" the government's opposition leaders and was seeing them regularly, a procedure that violated the basic precepts of diplomacy.

A new form of indirect U.S. involvement in Syria occurred in early March 1958, in a style so crude that it was greeted with humor throughout the area. In an effort to block the formation of the United Arab Republic (UAR), King Saud had sent Syrian G-2 Sarraj three cashier's checks, amounting to more than $5 million, with assurances of U.S. recognition of an independent Syrian republic to be headed by Sarraj as president. Handing photocopies of these checks to the Damascus newspapers, Colonel Sarraj sent along a statement publicly rejecting Saud's offer and confirming that the funds now resided in the treasury of the new UAR. Although the U.S. government obviously declined to make any comment, I wondered if this might not have been Kim Roosevelt's final effort to pull off a Syrian coup after all.[78]

On May 8, a procommunist, antigovernment newspaper publisher, who had just been released from jail after attacks on Chamoun, was murdered. Our CIA sources reported that this might have been arranged by the increasingly active Russians in order to create a rallying point against the government. The president showed me police reports that tended to confirm this theory, and gave me solemn assurances that none of his supporters had been involved.[79] No matter who was responsible, the assassination set off a round of violence. The USIS library in Tripoli was sacked in rioting that took 35 lives and left over 200 persons wounded. After making a protest to Malik, McClintock employed the right of any U.S. ambassador and ordered an American-flag vessel into Tripoli to evacuate Americans, although none had been harmed. The USIS library in Beirut was gutted, the IPC pipeline branch to Tripoli cut, and a Belgian diplomat posted to Damascus arrested at the frontier with a car full of automatic weapons and ammunition

---

78   In 1964, after relinquishing his throne to his brother Faisal and moving to Egypt, Saud reportedly acknowledged to Nasser that he had spent 12 million pounds sterling ($33.5 million) of American money in escapades of this sort. In his book *Dulles* (New York: Dial Press/James Wade, 1978), Leonard Mosley alleges that Kim Roosevelt offered the ruler of Abu Dhabi $90 million of CIA-Aramco-Saudi money in return for conceding a strategic oasis (Buraimi) to Saudi Arabia. The ruler refused, by that time aware that his sheikhdom would one day be a major oil producer.

79   Although the Beirut CIA station had no knowledge of this, Kim Philby had by now moved into the rebel-held Basta quarter of Beirut, presumably emerging from time to time to provide the British SIS with reports of anti-Western activities by the government's opponents. Because he was now estranged from Sam Brewer I had no reason to see Philby, nor was the CIA station ever queried about his activities. With hindsight, it now appears easy to speculate that he may well have been the key KGB agent directing Russian subversion throughout the Near East during this period—a task he may also be performing from the comfort of a dacha outside Moscow today.

for the Lebanese rebels. All this the antigovernment press attributed to Chamoun's supposed plans to amend the constitution. In any case, the embassy warned all Americans to stay off Beirut's streets.

By May 12, armed rebellion had erupted in Beirut. Opposition leaders called upon Chamoun to resign or face a civil war, and he declared a state of national emergency. When queried by the press, the U.S. embassy said it saw involvement both by the communists and the new UAR; Secretary Dulles then announced that he, too, perceived "international communism" behind what was happening in Lebanon. Two destroyers of the Sixth Fleet were dispatched to posts just over the horizon to stand by for an evacuation of U.S. citizens. McClintock then asked Washington to give him authority to order all Americans out should this seem wise, and his request was granted.

For the next week the ambassador's office resembled a command post, and he seemed to enjoy communicating with the navy and U.S. military headquarters in Europe as much as he did sending crisis telegrams to Washington. Police equipment, to help quell rioters, was airlifted to Beirut's airport; tanks and other heavy equipment, under the Eisenhower Doctrine, were sent by air and sea from army stores in Germany; the Sixth Fleet announced that it was doubling its amphibious marine strength and beginning "routine" maneuvers with the British fleet in the central Mediterranean; and huge USAF transports flew to Europe to help evacuate Americans from Lebanon should the need arise. Barricades went up and fires broke out all over the city, and the U.S. embassy was threatened, but the major fighting was in the mountains just above the airport, where Kamal Jumblatt fielded an army of 2,000 Druse and sent the army of the republic scurrying from the first major engagement of the war. Scattered bands roamed out from the Moslem districts and either hit random buildings or simply fired guns in all directions: soon each Lebanese who owned a gun was joining in the firing, usually straight up into the air. At the border, the five customs guards who caught the Belgian diplomat smuggling arms were gunned down at their posts. Closing the Lebanese-Syrian border and deporting 12,000 Syrians didn't stop infiltration from the UAR: the mountain trails had been used for years for smuggling, now to the end of supplying the rebels.

In Washington, President Eisenhower and Secretary Dulles briefed congressional leaders on what they saw as a communist-inspired uprising in Lebanon, fueled by the UAR to the brink of a civil war. As I read the text of the president's press conference of May 14, I couldn't help thinking back to Stuart Rockwell and his Lebanon-desk officer, who'd casually suggested that we'd deal with the issue of Chamoun's successor when the time for elections arrived in July. Now the President, Secretary Dulles, the NSC, and the Joint Chiefs of Staff were meeting almost daily to evaluate the possibility that the Lebanese situation might bring the U.S. into another confrontation with Russia.

Ambassador McClintock called in the press to announce U.S. determination to help the Lebanese government maintain internal security, but his words had little effect on the rebels, who now refused to settle for anything short of Chamoun's immediate resignation. Throughout this period the ambassador frequently summoned Zogby and me to his office. He loved an audience, and having us there to dictate telegrams was a partial reflection of McClintock's disdain for the deputy chief of mission he'd inherited from Heath.

One afternoon McClintock called Zogby, a secretary, and me to the residence and commenced to dictate a top-secret, eyes-only telegram to Secretary Dulles, while his Chilean wife, Elenaita, passed around cups of coffee. This was too much for the staid career foreign service secretary, who demanded that the ambassador wait until his wife left the room. McClintock then announced that he'd bestowed the highest government security clearance on his wife the day she took the wedding vows in Santiago. I reflected sadly that my cover status had gone out the window, now that I was spending nearly every evening in the palace with the president to review the developments of the day. I'd almost commuted there during the elections, and these new nightly visits made it clear that I was the principal U.S. contact with the man the rebels were threatening to run out of town. There were few secrets in Lebanon, of course. Zogby's favorite agent, Samir Souki, often went to the palace in search of news, and frequently Zogby knew before I told him the next morning whether I'd stayed beyond midnight—so too, presumably, did Souki's close friend the Egyptian ambassador.

In a vow he would keep to the letter, Chamoun told me that he would never leave the palace until the rebellion subsided or a new president of Lebanon had been elected by constitutional means. A month earlier, I'd suggested that he might ease tensions by making a statement renouncing a move for reelection. Chamoun had snorted and suggested that I look at the calendar: March 23 was a month behind us, and no amendment to permit another term could legally be passed after that date. Obviously, as he had pointed out, the issue of the presidency was not the real issue; renunciation of the Eisenhower Doctrine was what his opponents wanted. Now it was May 21, and I asked whether the president wouldn't see Sam Brewer and make this point clear. Chamoun had Sam and all members of the press who could be located come to his bedroom later that night; there he issued a press statement that he'd never resign but that after the last day of his legal term of office he'd leave voluntarily, as provided for in the constitution. That wasn't enough, I knew, but as a very proud man, Chamoun refused ever to go beyond that point in dealing with the press.

Although fighting continued round the clock in the country and bombs planted in the city were supplemented by firing most of the night, life resumed a semblance of normality. Tanks were now arriving by military airlift, and Charles Malik said that he was taking the matter of UAR intervention before the U.N. Security Council to have it condemned as outright aggression and to seek a resolution demanding that it be stopped. This sent the Arab brethren into a frenzy, and an Arab League meeting in Cairo was called to settle matters within its house. That night, on Washington's instructions, I went to the palace to ask that the U.N. request be postponed until the League had its chance to bring things to a halt. Chamoun agreed, reluctantly, reminding me that Egypt had always dominated the Arab League—"that group from which antisomething resolutions flow at will," the president called it—and that it was illusory to expect the UAR to condemn itself.

By this time most foreign businessmen in Beirut had moved with their families to Athens or Rome. Then the American Community School closed after a bomb threat, and most of the remaining U.S. citizens departed. A day of seemingly incessant street firing had carried on into the night when I next saw Chamoun, and the sound of bomb blasts nearby in the city center interrupted our conversation several times. As I started to leave, near midnight, the president signed and handed me a piece of paper, which he described as Curfew Pass Number One. "From tomorrow night onward there'll be a dawn-to-dusk curfew," he said, "and I enjoy your company, so you've lost any excuse to stay home." Two nights later a stray bullet passed through my car's right front window. As he drove me home, my chauffeur, William, said his mother in the mountains had contracted a "serious illness," and I never saw him again.

It was an eerie feeling to be often driving the only civilian car on Beirut's streets, but my routine of going to the palace in the evening and reporting the results in a postmidnight cable from the embassy continued. What I was doing was far from illegal; as for danger, my best protection was the openness with which I operated. There was little sense to being secretive, and the bartenders at the Saint Georges usually greeted me with a whispered "How's the president? Tell him we're still behind him." My friends in the press discreetly asked no questions, giving no indication that they considered what I was doing to be unusual. Nor did I feel that I was performing a CIA mission: Ambassador McClintock and Chamoun were no longer friendly, and a white-and-gold DeSoto driving from the embassy to the palace was, in principle, no different from the ambassador's calling on the legal head of the republic in his black Cadillac with flags flying. There was, however, a difference in the attention Rapid Robert would have attracted. Early on, he'd requested that a police motorcycle escort, preceded by a machine-gun-mounted jeep, always accompany him about the city (the only such concession Chamoun had authorized for a foreign envoy). America's popularity with many Lebanese was ebbing, and we were certainly better off not having the U.S. presence heralded at night by the piercing whine of motorcycle sirens.

■ ■ ■

In early June I was instructed to fly to Washington before the U.N. Security Council heard Lebanon's complaint (filed after the Arab League had, predictably, failed to act). At Allen Dulles's request, Norman Paul gave a dinner at his residence, at which I was the guest of honor, and the director came along with all the CIA's top brass. I was treated like a hero—the man who braved Beirut's embattled streets each night.

I was asked repeatedly why the Lebanese army couldn't control the fighting and whether the U.N. could help with an observer force to stop the smuggling of arms and money from Syria. By way of explanation, I first referred to an article in the *Times* by Hanson Baldwin saying that Lebanon's army might split along sectarian lines if ordered into serious combat. I then quoted Chamoun as saying this had been just what the chief of staff, General Shehab, wanted to hear as an excuse for not committing the army to fight. Relations between Chamoun and Shehab were no longer cordial. The general had aligned himself with the Maronite patriarch, whose statements proposing that Chamoun take "a vacation" had further split the country. The president suspected that Shehab was just waiting for all factions to beg him to save the nation, as he'd done in 1952 by becoming an interim caretaker (although there had been no fighting then and corruption was the issue). This time, Chamoun had told me, General Shehab was seeking election to the presidency as his prize. As for U.N. observers, they could be effective if they were given authority to go where they wished without army interference. Chamoun was eager to have them and had agreed to let them roam the country at will.

The next day Allen Dulles saw me in his office and confided that Ambassador McClintock was suggesting that I might be turning too pro-Chamoun. Apparently Acting Secretary of State Christian Herter wanted to talk with me about it. "Answer any questions Mr. Herter asks," the DCI told me as we drove to the State Department, "but avoid getting into personality problems or saying anything that would make McClintock look bad." With that

I was on my own, since Dulles said he had to go on to the White House for a meeting.

Secretary Herter received me cordially, moving from behind his desk with a cane and then joining me on the sofa to which I'd been gestured after we'd shaken hands. He then opened the conversation with a shocker. "We've good ambassadors and bad ones," he said, "and I'm afraid that the one you are working with has let his job go to his head." I wasn't sure of this remark's implications, so I waited to hear what followed. In effect, Herter told me that Secretary Dulles was becoming weary of McClintock's constant crisis telegrams. Furthermore, the tripartite ambassadorial meetings with his British and French colleagues over which the ambassador presided tended to convey the impression that U.S. foreign policy was being made in Beirut.

Christian Herter then asked my views of the crisis. I said I believed Chamoun could weather his term provided the U.S. held to the position that it would support him. My point produced no indication of disagreement or a possible change of policy from Herter. He told me to keep up what I was doing in seeing the president, and then assured me that my efforts were both noted and appreciated by those following the situation at home, including President Eisenhower. Later, Allen Dulles gave me a similar send-off, after agreeing that I might stop off in New York to see Charles Malik at the U.N., where the Security Council was preparing to hear Lebanon's case.

Four days after I'd left, I landed again in Beirut.[80] In my absence, the government had announced that parliament would meet on July 24 to elect a president to replace Chamoun, and there was hope that this might pacify the rebels. Just the opposite came to pass, however, and concerted efforts to capture Beirut and drive Chamoun from the palace were mounted with increased support from Syria. The army repulsed an attack on the capital, and a column of 500 men smuggling arms from Syria was shot up by the

---

80   Prior to the introduction of jet aircraft on trans-Atlantic flights in 1959, in-the-air flying time between Beirut and Washington averaged twenty-three hours. In addition were six intermediate stops and a night in London.

air force, dashing the hopes of the rebels to win the war before the Security Council could send a force to stem external intervention. Israeli border police also cooperated with the government by capturing smugglers from Syria and turning them over to the army as prisoners, but street fighting still raged in Beirut after the U.N. announced the names of its three head observers. The United States now warned Americans against traveling to Lebanon for any reason.

Tanks ranged the streets of Beirut on June 16, the day the first member of the three-man team of U.N. supervisors arrived. He was an Ecuadorian, Galo Plaza y Lasso, whom both McClintock and Sam Brewer had known before. Chamoun asked that I arrange for Galo Plaza to come to the palace the evening of his arrival, and McClintock agreed. Sitting with the president for two hours while he waited for Galo Plaza to arrive, I finally called the ambassadorial residence and learned that he had located a local gambling club and decided to spend the night there instead. This far from auspicious beginning was further marred when, that night, the radio carried news of U.N. Secretary General Hammarskjöld's decision to fly to Cairo to find out from Nasser just what Lebanon's problem might be. The arrival of the other two supervisors with about ninety observers provided little encouragement that things would improve.[81]

The U.N. observers soon reported that rebel forces denied them access to more than 11 of the 172 miles of Lebanon's frontier with Syria, so Galo Plaza decreed that his men would remain billeted in Beirut's hotels and move out only when the Lebanese army

---

81 The second senior member was an Indian civil servant, Rajeshwar Dayal, who'd represented his country in Moscow and just completed a three-year term as ambassador to three iron curtain countries. Dayal found in Druse rebel leader Kamal Jumblatt a fellow mystic, with whom he communed in various yoga positions while discussing what Chamoun was doing wrong. The military member was a Norwegian named Odd Bull, and the press soon dubbed this general "the Queer Steer." Galo Plaza, the forty-nine-year-old son of a deceased Ecuadorian president, had attended USC to play football before stepping into his father's presidential shoes at the age of thirty-eight. Later he became head of the Organization of American States in Washington.

reported evidence of UAR infiltration—providing the experienced smugglers a good hour or two to disappear in the mountains before any U.N. force could arrive in territory they'd never seen before. The U.N. chief rejected as biased both the army reports of intervention and prisoner interrogations passed to him by Chamoun, sending to New York only those from U.N. observers, with the result that Galo Plaza was soon able to support his conclusion (reached in advance) that Syrian infiltration was very small-scale.

The CIA's technicians had installed in my bedroom a short-wave radio, enabling me to communicate with sets installed in the sleeping quarters of the ambassador and Chamoun, as well as with the embassy's command post and one of the navy destroyers positioned offshore. Always, then, I was in the thick of this chaos, except when I'd take refuge in a cabana I had at the beach. Zogby had given me a pistol for my protection, a .22 automatic with a silencer (an assassination weapon). Late at night, looking out from my apartment balcony at the deserted street and the peaceful sea below, I'd take pot shots at the arc lamps on the road down in front. Sometimes I'd score a hit, only the shattering glass made a sound.

I wasn't the only odd bird in Beirut. Ambassador McClintock, obviously under great pressure, had a beach house to which he sometimes would go to swim. When I was at the shore relaxing and heard sirens shrieking, I'd look up to see the embassy Cadillac racing toward the sea, Golly the poodle yapping in the front seat, eager to retrieve his master. I'd take this as a signal that my rest time was over and that I'd better get back to the chancery for a dictating session.

Then, one day, a gasoline-filled truck was run down the hill toward the palace on the theory that it would explode as one huge Molotov cocktail. The truck hit a car short of its objective, fortunately, and by the time I reached the presidency, convinced because of the smoke plumes that it was burning, I found Chamoun up on the roof with his hunting gun, looking for someone to emerge from the burning truck's cab. Several nights later Chamoun, his wife, and I dined alone at the palace. As I left, Zelpha handed me a large case containing the family jewels and asked that I store them in the embassy's safe. She and her husband, she told me, had determined never to leave the palace, but she charged me with ensuring that their boys receive the jewels in the event that she and the president were killed. I was moved to tears as I walked to my car. Cabling Washington to report what I'd been given, I wondered how this would be interpreted. Bravery? Or cowardice? To me, in any case, Chamoun had become a symbol of Lebanon's independence, and I was sure that history would prove me right.

I was called to one of McClintock's tripartite-ambassadors meetings the next day and learned that British naval units were joining the ships we had anchored out at sea. The poor French ambassador, however, found himself unable to offer protection to the country France had created and once ruled. The Algerian situation had nearly destroyed the capacity of the French government to rule. "I don't know who's leading my government," the French ambassador said, "and I can't even be sure where the seat of government is. I can offer nothing, but I hope that this will change." For once, I thought, the French were doing something right about Lebanon. The appearance of French forces, of course, would only provoke resentment and certainly fuel the fires now burning.

When I next saw Chamoun he handed me a document in Arabic that, he said, had been signed by all members of his government, both Moslem and Christian. He now had full authority, he explained, to request the landing of U.S. troops under the provisions of the Eisenhower Doctrine and as provided for in Article 51 of the U.N. Charter. He planned to use it only if there were no other hope, he assured me, particularly if the army refused to fight. He wanted me to notify Washington that he held this authority (valid under Lebanon's constitution), so that there need be no delay were he to invoke it. When I spoke later to McClintock, he agreed that we'd need some sort of showdown between the president and General Shehab before we could land troops in Lebanon on the premise that the army was unable to defend the country.

Secretary Dulles responded to press leaks about Chamoun's authority to request outside help with a restatement of the U.S. position of willingness to help Lebanon protect its independence. Upset by this, Dag Hammarskjöld took off for Lebanon to confer with his U.N. observers and to "confirm" that no threat to the republic's independence existed. Some American papers wrote that the United States was heading for a second Suez or for war. After Eisenhower hedged on what Foster Dulles had said, declaring that any U.S. military action would depend upon the judgment of the U.N. observers and Secretary General Hammarskjöld, Chamoun demanded a clear statement of American policy and told me he didn't intend to mince words with Ambassador McClintock. I cabled Allen Dulles, asking that his brother make our position clear, and suggested that the Hammarskjöld mission was simply an example of stalling. By this time telegrams were flying in all directions, including one from Cabot Lodge at the U.N. predicting that any help from U.S. forces in Lebanon Would provoke a Soviet attack and global war. Poor President Eisenhower, I thought, trying to keep both Lodge and Foster Dulles happy.

The next day, a long, top-secret telegram to the ambassador from Secretary Dulles arrived with instructions that McClintock "urgently meet with President Chamoun" and pass to him a lengthy message clarifying what President Eisenhower had meant to say. As the ambassador's secretary typed out the text to be handed to the president, I was given a copy of the Dulles telegram to read. It was the damnedest mess of weasel-worded statements I'd ever seen, and I wasn't too surprised to hear McClintock say that I'd been designated to hand the typed copy to Chamoun, "since the two of you are so close." I had no real choice but to take on this unpleasant task, but before going we tried to figure out what Foster Dulles had really said to Chamoun.

At the start, he seemed to say that Lebanon had caused our problem by going to the U.N. in the first place. Presumably a direct appeal to the U.S. under the Eisenhower Doctrine would have produced American troops if Chamoun had requested them. That this wouldn't go over with the president was certain, and I knew it wasn't true. Next, Dulles wrote that Eisenhower's words "should in no way be interpreted as meaning that we would require the concurrence or recommendation of the [U.N.] Secretary General prior to military assistance to the Government of Lebanon," and "we continued ready to take exceptional measures on behalf of the country without any reference to any other source." Chamoun would snort at this; he had a copy of Eisenhower's full statement, which said just the opposite.

The secretary of state then assured Chamoun of the U.S.' full confidence in him personally as "the symbol of Lebanon's determination to defend its independence." Finally, Dulles expressed confidence that Chamoun could himself solve all Lebanon's problems and that he'd do so without delay, for, Dulles wrote, were we to land troops it might amount to a propaganda victory for Nasser and diminish the West's status in the Arab world. In conclusion, the secretary wished Chamoun good luck in his efforts and assured him that he'd have our full backing in solving Lebanon's problems and safeguarding its independence by means other than the use of U.S. troops.

When Chamoun read this, he handed the text back to me. "It's of absolutely no use," he said. "Keep it as a souvenir to remember me by, Bill." (I did.)

Back at the embassy, I realized that McClintock now regarded Chamoun as washed up and expendable. The ambassador, it seemed, was thinking of a deal with General Shehab that he might arrange and come out of looking brilliant. McClintock told me that seeing Chamoun was all my job now and that he'd refrain from making contact with him until Hammarskjöld returned from Cairo with Nasser's plans on how to settle the situation in Lebanon. Meanwhile, the British ambassador told me that as far as his government was concerned, Chamoun was still the key to any solution but that talks were being held in London with Nuri as Said of Iraq, and he hinted at the possibility of an Iraqi-Lebanese defense agreement. Clearly, all the wheels kept turning.

At this point the difference between McClintock's objectives and mine were reflected in the American press. *Time's* bureau chief, John Mecklin, had long resented my friendship with Sam Brewer and finally accused me of handing Sam leaks. I told Mecklin that he was wrong but declared that if I were to leak secrets, I'd certainly choose a daily paper rather than a weekly magazine. Mecklin reported this incident to the ambassador. The upshot was that while the *New York Times* printed stories about Chamoun's having done everything possible to satisfy the rebels on the issue of a second term as president, *Time's* next issue described the Lebanese president as a worn man who cowered in the palace waiting to be bailed out by the U.S. Sixth Fleet. *Time's* view was clearly McClintock's, one he really wasn't sure was correct, since at the least he'd never visited the palace after curfew.

President Chamoun now decided to put General Shehab on the spot. He'd order the army to take full combat action against the rebels until it could no longer fight without threatening to disintegrate. The full cabinet approved the president's taking this position. In the event Shehab refused, Chamoun had a replacement in mind, a man he'd described as a professional soldier rather than an aspiring politician whose family name entitled him to command of an army. I was to explain Chamoun's plan to Secretary Dulles and, if possible, to President Eisenhower, and ask assurances of U.S. support with troops in case the army revolted or suffered a major defeat.

En route to Washington, I stopped in London to see CIA station chief Bronson Tweedy, at Allen Dulles's request. Tweedy told me, to my distress, that the story of the Chamoun family jewels' being kept in the American embassy was the talk of the foreign office and the SIS, but at least the incident seemed to have made the British understand that Lebanon's president was truly threatened. Speaking further with Tweedy, I learned that the Anglo-Iraqi talks had involved discussing the possibility of using Iraqi troops on Syria's frontier and in Jordan if the Lebanese crisis didn't ease. Following the formation of the UAR, the Hashemite monarchs of Iraq and Jordan had declared a union, and the Iraqi army would probably be able to move to aid King Hussein without too many complications. To put Iraqi troops on Syria's borders or to move troops into Syria to relieve the pressure on Lebanon, however, would undoubtedly have grave consequences.

Allen Dulles was waiting to be picked up by his brother and go to a White House meeting when I arrived at the CIA's headquarters. Dick Helms had been talking with the director, and he was asked by Dulles to take me to lunch and discuss the situation in Lebanon. So, in the director's limousine, Helms and I drove off to the Occidental Restaurant, which, he explained, was where J. Edgar Hoover and most senior people in the spy business liked to have lunch. At the end of a long, pleasant meal and conversation, Joe Alsop stopped by and insisted that I attend a dinner he'd arranged for that evening.

Alsop had assembled a gaggle of notables for dinner, among them Dean Acheson, Bill Bundy (Acheson's son-in-law, who was deputy to Bob Amory, the CIA deputy director for intelligence), and Dick Bissell (head of the clandestine services). After dinner Joe presided over the men gathered for coffee and brandy—the women were off in a group of their own—and, turning to me, brought up the crisis in Lebanon. "Wil-baar," he said, "you're just back from there: should we land troops or shouldn't we?" I tried to duck the question by asking Alsop his opinion, hoping for one of his famous ten-minute orations, but he kept me on the spot. Nothing I could say would be right, and given the audience of top-level CIA people, I wished I could disappear as I took time carefully to trim and light one of the long Cuban cigars Chamoun had given me for the Dulles brothers. It was Dean Acheson who came to my rescue. "Joseph," the former secretary of state said, "perhaps Wilbaar would prefer not to discuss his thoughts with you newspaper people." Joe conceded the point, and as the ladies returned, I felt Acheson's hand on my shoulder. It turned out he wanted to know what I thought our response should be if Chamoun asked for help. Transforming myself into a diplomat's diplomat, I replied, "Sir, if I worked for you, would you want me to answer that in this garden?" Acheson smiled and let me go.

The next morning Allen Dulles and I drove to his brother's home. As we went, Dulles asked if I'd had recent contact with Miles Copeland in Beirut. I said I hadn't seen him but had heard from Chamoun that Miles, accompanied by some pro-Western Lebanese politicians, had called on him and offered to use Copeland's close relationship with Nasser in order to mediate the crisis. Dulles laughed. Copeland, he said, had reported that Chamoun had rejected the offer, saying that Bill Eveland had advised the president to stand firm and resist resignation should this be Nasser's price for calling off the rebels. Apparently Chamoun had also said that although Ambassador McClintock favored such a compromise, he considered my advice sounder. By this time we were in the driveway of the secretary of state's vine-covered, Tudor-style home. "Just express your views as you see them," Allen Dulles told me, "and don't be afraid to speak frankly." Then, apparently trying to bolster me further, he said, "I showed Copeland's message to my brother. His reaction was that Chamoun had been right in his perception of both you and the ambassador."

Joining and welcoming us, the secretary said he'd been roused at night to send a telegram to McClintock, and handed me a copy to read. For months, Dulles said, Ambassador McClintock had been dispatching NIACT (night action) telegrams marked for the secretary's personal attention. This was annoying, Dulles complained, both because of the hour when the telegrams were received and because McClintock had usually already taken the action that he requested permission for "in the absence of instructions to the contrary." Now, apparently, the ambassador had pushed the secretary too far, proposing in another NIACT telegram that he meet with Druse rebel leader Kamal Jumblatt to arrange a cease-fire. Dulles's message in reply had denied the permission in no uncertain terms, declaring that ambassadors dealt not with rebels but with legal governments, adding that these were the U.S. government's final instructions on the subject.

As we got down to business, Allen Dulles explained that I'd flown back to answer questions about Chamoun's plan to commit the Lebanese army and his request for help if this failed. But, evidently tired of talking and thinking about Lebanon, the secretary abruptly said that he'd heard I was on friendly terms with the Iraqi crown prince and with Prime Minister Nuri as Said. Nodding my head, I wondered where this was leading.

The secretary of state then explained what was currently annoying him. It seemed that the British—Selwyn Lloyd, specifically—were determined to force full U.S. membership in the Baghdad Pact and had importuned its Moslem members to call a rump session in Turkey on July 14. There they would vote to disband unless the U.S. joined the Pact as a regular member. Worse, knowing that Dulles planned to send Christian Herter to the Pact's

London meeting later that month, Lloyd had arranged the meeting in anticipation that an ultimatum from all the Pact's members might persuade the U.S. to join in order to save the alliance from disintegration. All this, Secretary Dulles said, he could handle if necessary, but Lloyd had timed this tactic "in full knowledge that Janet and I would be off at that time spending our regular vacation at Duck Island on Lake Ontario and that I might not hear of it in time." He wanted me, he said, to fly immediately to Ankara, corral every head of government I could, and make it clear that the U.S. would not tolerate attempts at blackmail.

I looked at Allen Dulles, who only nodded. I had a new and important mission but had yet to get a moment to discuss the assurances I'd flown thousands of miles to obtain for Chamoun. It was now Saturday, July 12. I'd have to fly all weekend to arrive in Turkey by the date of the Pact's rump session—another of those four-day round trips that left little time for sleeping. As Allen Dulles and I started to walk out, his brother called us back. He had still another assignment for me. Britain and Iraq, Dulles now knew, had agreed to move Iraqi army units into Jordan along the Syro-Iraqi border. They were planning to do this, the secretary was sure, as part of a British move to demonstrate that America alone couldn't cope with Nasser's rebellion in Lebanon and that Britain could save the situation by using the Iraqi army to divert the UAR's attention from the Lebanese civil war. Describing this as pure madness, Foster Dulles said it would be suicide, "just like Suez." I was to speak on his behalf to the Iraqis and remind them that their U.S. military equipment could be used outside Iraq only with our permission, which we were emphatically now denying them.

As I rode back to CIA headquarters with Allen Dulles, I thought of the flap the secretary had made about British plans to interfere with his vacation. I ventured the suggestion that Foster Dulles might embarrass Foreign Secretary Selwyn Lloyd and expose his tactics more effectively by appearing unexpectedly at the London meetings. He could announce at its opening session, America's decision to shun full membership in the Pact and then, turning his chair over to Herter, simply fly to Duck Island to join Mrs. Dulles. The director sat silently for a few minutes, then put his hand on my knee. "No, Eveland," he said, "this is something special; it's a vacation my brother and Janet have counted on for a long time."[82]

Why, I then wondered, couldn't our ambassadors in Iraq and Turkey do what I'd been assigned to do? Perhaps the secretary considered Ambassador Gallman in Baghdad to be too much under the influence of the British ambassador. Still thinking I'd need some credentials to prove to our ambassador in Ankara that I spoke with authority from the secretary of state, I asked the DCI if a State telegram might be sent to Ambassador Warren to advise him that I was coming, and why. He was away on leave, I was told, but arrangements would be made to inform his deputy chief of mission. Trouble; I could sense it. The deputy was not a strong man. I wouldn't be able to count on him for backing if the embassy were questioned as to my right to get tough with the Baghdad Pact leaders on the issue of blackmail. Justin O'Donnell, the CIA chief of station, would love to tear me up in such a situation, and I wasn't about to get into a contest with him about my right to again invade his parish. Mentioning this to Allen Dulles, I received his assurances that he'd send a personal message to O'Donnell, supporting me.

Events moved faster than I did. As my plane from New York to Rome was preparing to land, the pilot announced that the flight's final destination, Baghdad, had been canceled. Passengers going there would have to debark in Ankara. There had been a revolution in Iraq, he said. Half-awake, sure that our pilot was wrong and thinking of the fighting in Lebanon, I went to the cockpit. A set of earphones convinced me that the BBC broadcast to which they were tuned was indeed announcing the overthrow of the Iraqi government by pro-Nasser army officers. Troops marching through Baghdad had seized the capital in the early-morning

---

82   John Foster Dulles underwent surgery in February, 1959, and in April it was announced that he'd resign as secretary of state and become a special assistant to President Eisenhower with cabinet status. By May 1959 Dulles was dead, a victim of the cancer for which he'd been operated on during the Suez Crisis of 1956.

hours, arrested the royal family, it said, and were now in complete control of the government. I could now scratch one of Foster Dulles's missions, and possibly both, off the list. When I arrived in Ankara that evening there'd be no Iraqi crown prince to hear me pass on the secretary's warning about moving troops to Jordan and Syria. Blast the British, I thought. Their passion for countering Nasser in Syria had backfired and might have cost them their "tame Iraqis." In fact, the question of whether the Iraqi revolution would spread and enable Nasser to bring down Iran and the whole Baghdad Pact was now the most important matter for me to discuss with its chiefs of state.

Undoubtedly overwrought by reports from Iraq before he reached his office Monday morning, Allen Dulles had not, as it turned out, sent O'Donnell a cable about my mission. Disbelieving, yet apprehensive about challenging what I told him, the Ankara CIA chief shrugged me off as if hoping that I'd stick my head in a noose this time. The next four days I met daily with the Baghdad Pact chiefs of state from Iran, Pakistan, and Turkey. Turkish Foreign Minister Zorlu knew me, made my appointments, and welcomed having an American official willing to spend time with these leaders. Rumors abounded, initially giving hope that the Iraqi royalty and Prime Minister Nuri as Said had escaped and were making their way through the mountains to Turkey, but as time passed even this wishful thinking abated.

Nasser's radio, which had for months been inciting the Iraqis to rise up against their government, now hailed the revolution and congratulated its leaders. So, too, did the Russians. That the Syrian army—it was now commanded by Egypt's Field Marshall Abdul Hakim Amer—might move into Lebanon was considered a major threat by Chamoun, who finally used the authority he'd handed me a month before to call for U.S. troops. The U.S. response was immediate. After asking for an emergency meeting of the Security Council, President Eisenhower addressed the Congress and the American people to advise that the Sixth Fleet had been ordered to land marines in Lebanon. As each new piece of news arrived at the embassy, I relayed it to the frantic Moslem chiefs of state. In a vain hope that the Iraqi leaders might somehow have survived, the Pact leaders moved from Ankara to Istanbul, and I accompanied them. The shah of Iran was more concerned than the others were. He'd been touring Europe for weeks, and fearing that the Iraqi revolt might encourage the Moslem mullahs and other critics he had silenced to rise up against another monarch, wasn't sure that he could safely return. I volunteered to cable Allen Dulles to get a CIA estimate of conditions in Iran and soon learned that in Dulles's opinion the shah's place was in Tehran. Rushing to give the shah this report, I caught up with him just as he was walking to his private aircraft at the airport. Message in hand, I caught him at the plane's steps and told him what I'd learned. Thanking me, he said that he had already decided to return to his country, no matter what the CIA recommendation might be.

On July 17, President Eisenhower announced that he was sending Deputy Under Secretary of State Robert Murphy to Lebanon, and I wondered accordingly what my new role would be. I'd received no instructions from Washington as to what I should do next and was almost certain that Murphy had been sent out because Chamoun and McClintock were at odds with each other. Should this be the case, I'd be needed, and I was sure that the president of Lebanon would want to have me there. Assuming that military-operational traffic was taking precedence over all but the most urgent messages the CIA and the Department of State might send, I decided to take a chance on using the telephone to get through to Washington. Placing a call to Norman Paul at his office, I waited hours at my hotel for it to come through. Larry Lisersohn, of the CIA base in Istanbul (Ilyan's contact), was giving a cocktail party, and I'd promised to stop by, so I had my call transferred to Larry's residence. It came through minutes after I arrived. Telling Norm where I was, I asked what he wanted me to do. He seemed surprised, saying that Allen Dulles had sent an urgent personal message three days before, instructing me to return to Beirut at once, and that both Secretary Dulles and Robert Murphy had approved of this. When I informed Lisersohn of the purpose of my call and what Norm had told me, Larry apologetically reached in his pocket and handed me a cable he said he had been intending to give me. Looking at the operational immediate-precedence message, I saw that it was dated precisely three days earlier—July 16—and I couldn't help wondering whether Justin O'Donnell had considered this his revenge for my intrusion, but I said nothing about it.

Getting to Beirut was easier said than done. All commercial and nonmilitary aircraft had been banned from the eastern Mediterranean by the Sixth Fleet. Lisersohn said he was under strict orders from O'Donnell not to assist me. Trying Foreign Minister Zorlu, I arranged to charter a DC-3 belonging to Turkish National Airlines. It would cost me about $2,500 for the three-hour trip, I learned. Despairing of any help from the CIA, I went to my old friend the consul general and found that the sight of Foster Dulles's name in my cable was all the authority he needed to give me the money.

Chartering the aircraft in my own name would, I knew, make O'Donnell furious, so I devised another solution. The Istanbul Hilton was crawling with frustrated foreign correspondents seeking a way to get to Lebanon, and I soon spotted one I knew and liked. Colonel J.V.J. Slade-Baker was based in Beirut for the London *Sunday Times*, so I made him a proposal. I'd get him to Beirut if he'd not tell his colleagues about it. In fact, I said, I'd give him the money to pay for the aircraft I'd arranged to charter if he'd proceed to the field immediately and book the flight under his own name.

I rendezvoused with Slade-Baker at the airfield later, and we were soon off, leaving O'Donnell and his crew to wonder where I was. As we approached Cyprus, a formation of U.S. Navy jets intercepted us, and our captain called to me for help. Getting on the mike, I told the jets that I was a White House staff member under orders to meet the president's personal envoy in Beirut. That worked, and we went on. En route, we passed over an enormous armada, and Air Transport Command troop carriers dotted the sky as we neared Lebanon. We landed safely, and I was pleased with myself—more complacent, I now know, than if I could have foreseen the extent to which O'Donnell and his career "establishment" brethren would use this incident to brand me a security risk to our country.

CHAPTER TWENTY-SEVEN

DEATH OF A DOCTRINE

Within the ten days I'd been away, Beirut had been transformed into an American military base. The port area was crammed with support ships augmenting the naval armada offshore. Khaldi International Airport, south of the city, resembled a military airfield in wartime; its adjacent beaches were littered with landing craft offloading supplies for the ten thousand marines and airborne troops who'd arrived within forty hours of President Chamoun's call for help. Yet, except for convoys of cargo trucks snaking their way toward supply dumps at the foot of the nearby mountains, there were few signs of the combat units I'd expected to see. They, I assumed, would be helping to disarm the rebels who had tried to unseat Lebanon's government.

I soon learned, however, that our men had strict orders to avoid engagements with armed Lebanese. Instead, the American troops were bivouacked discreetly in olive groves on the airport's fringes or on the city's outskirts, within easy distance of the port. With tanks and artillery pieces protected by revetments, their sights zeroed in on the rebel strongholds, our combat formations were positioned to defend against an attack. Only if the Nasserite forces broke out of their redoubt in the midtown Basta district, or if Kamal Jumblatt's Druse fighters (now commanded by former Syrian chief of staff Shawkat Shuqayr) descended from the hills just above the airport, were our troops to respond to gunfire. Otherwise, they were to remain inconspicuous, ready to be airlifted elsewhere should the Middle East situation take a turn for the worse. Strange. This didn't sound as if we'd landed to support Chamoun and his government; instead, actually we'd established a beachhead for moving inland to other countries.

Out of the terminal, I found Beirut as I'd known it. Cabbies fought for our luggage, their fares now sky high. This was hardly surprising. My landlord had tried to raise rents for those of us remaining once the other tenants had been evacuated. As we drove into town, our driver pointed out other incongruities. Huge claims were being filed by olive-grove owners for damage our troops had caused to trees whose life expectancy was allegedly never less than 100 years. Pepsi and 7-Up umbrellas on the beaches sheltered vendors who prayed that fresh waves of marines would land. And, having suffered through the curfew, cabaret owners now advertised dawn-to-dusk floor shows in the hope that Lebanon's troubles would quickly subside and the troops be turned loose on liberty. It was all evidence of typical Lebanese ingenuity: entrepreneurs had quickly diagnosed means of 'turning a fast piastre' no matter what might evolve.

As we passed near the presidential palace and approached the American embassy, we saw signs that our troops might mean business. Replacing the obsolescent Lebanese tanks, the most modern U.S. behemoths and troop-filled armored personnel carriers now stood guard. Instead of the lackadaisical local tankers who used to flirt with pretty girls, grim-faced GIs, armed to the teeth, appeared prepared to repel the rebels whose forays had formerly gone unchallenged. Entering the embassy was no longer easy: my White House calling card didn't impress the major in charge. For the first time since I'd shown them to Brewer and Kopper, I had to produce my Department of State cover orders. Then I learned that Deputy Under Secretary of State Robert Murphy and Ambassador McClintock would be unable to see me that day. They were meeting with the military commanders; appointments with local politicians had been arranged for after that, I was told.

■ ■ ■

Ghosn Zogby briefed me on the events in Iraq precipitating our decision to land troops in Lebanon, although hard information was scarce. Our embassy and CIA station had been caught totally by surprise in Baghdad. Generally aware that the Iraqi army planned moves to Jordan and Syria's frontier, U.S. diplomats were sleeping when the coup occurred; so too, unfortunately, was General Ghazi Daghestani. The 3rd Division troops he commanded had engineered the takeover of the government and the murder of Iraq's royal family and Prime Minister Nuri Said. How ironic, I thought: Ghazi had become literally a victim of the Operation "Straggle" he'd helped the British to plan. Moreover, he symbolized Nuri as Said's belated recognition that survival of his system of government—indeed, of the monarchy itself—depended upon entrusting younger men with government positions and control of the army's key units. As Iraq's liaison with the British SIS, Daghestani was to have accompanied the king, the crown prince, and Nuri to the rump session of the Baghdad Pact that Foster Dulles had instructed me to attend. Unaware that one of his brigade commanders, Colonel Abdul Karim Qassim, had just been proclaimed head of a revolutionary Iraqi government, Ghazi was arrested at his home just hours before the royal party was due to fly to Turkey.[83]

"Who is Qassim?" Zogby asked me. "Did you ever hear of him?" It seemed that Qassim and the plotters he led were unknown to our embassy or to members of the military advisory mission we'd had in Iraq for three years. The name meant nothing to me. Qassim could have been attending staff college in England during my tour in Iraq, or, more likely, had just not been on the never changing entertainment lists passed from attaché to attaché. This illustrated a fallacy in the rules set out for U.S. training personnel: they

---

83   In a showcase trial, broadcast in a circus atmosphere over Iraqi TV, Daghestani testified with great dignity (unlike Chief of the General Staff Rafiq Arif, who confessed "wrongdoings" in a plea for mercy). Admitting Iraq's participation, with the British SIS, in "Straggle," Ghazi justified his contacts with Syrian ex-dictator Shishakly and Ilyan's plotters by telling how this controlled and frustrated Nuri's plans simply to annex Syria by force. His death sentence commuted, Daghestani, released from prison moved to England, where I saw him several times prior to his premature death from a heart attack.

were enjoined to avoid any semblance of collecting intelligence or passing on what they learned to military attachés or to the CIA. Such standards of "fair play" were a joke to the British, who had no qualms about penetrating the Iraqi government at every level, by any means. Yet that Britain, too, relied on "tame informants" was evident from the torching of its embassy and the coup that had caught London by surprise.

None of this mattered now, Zogby philosophized: the streets of Baghdad were filled with mobs and vigilantes, and no Americans dared venture out. Two U.S. citizens had been dragged from their hotel and brutally murdered. One was a senior executive of Bechtel Corporation (George Colley), the other a visiting CIA officer, Eugene Burns, operating under cover of the American Friends of the Middle East.[84] As for who was behind the Iraqi revolution, Zogby explained that pro-Nasser officers had plotted it; radios Damascus and Cairo had greeted it warmly (as had Russia's Arabic broadcasts beamed to Beirut); and the CIA had good reason to believe that Moscow had orchestrated the overall plan. Then, intimating that he couldn't tell me "all that [he] knew," Zogby pointed out that Nasser, who'd been visiting President Tito, had flown straight to Moscow as soon as the coup's success had been assured.

Nasser's Moscow trip had for me another implication, however, and I envisaged a C. L. Sulzberger piece in the *New York Times* citing the Egyptian president's flight as an example of how little I (and American diplomats) knew about what went on in the Near East. I'd been dead wrong when Sulzberger and I had discussed Nasser and the Russians a few months earlier.[85] Now, it seemed

---

84　It was ironic that Burns, using for cover a CIA front organization set up partially to counter Zionist propaganda in the U.S. against the Arabs, should be killed by an anti-American Iraqi mob. The bodies of Colley and Burns were never recovered, in spite of repeated U.S. representations, which, of course, could not reveal Burns's affiliations with the CIA.

85　During March 1958, Sulzberger described to me his interview with Nasser and predicted the Egyptian leader would shortly take a trip to Moscow. Having followed CIA messages (Operation SIPONY) forecasting that Nasser would be ousted any day, I jokingly bet Cy that the Russian trip would be canceled. It had, however, taken place in April, and I'd sent my check for ten

clear, the press could write with total accuracy that no American in the Middle East or Washington had predicted the Iraq coup (as Allen Dulles later confirmed in testimony before congressional committees). Again the CIA had been plotting when it should have been listening.

When I asked about rumors I'd heard in Turkey that McClintock had tried to stop the U.S. landing, Zogby said he'd seen little of the ambassador during my absence. Secretary Dulles's order prohibiting contacts with the rebels had infuriated McClintock: he attributed it to me. Then, after requesting again that I be kept in Washington, the ambassador had been notified by Dulles that I was en route to Turkey and would return to Beirut. That the Iraqi revolt might encourage the Lebanese rebels to overthrow their government appeared less important to the ambassador than his belief that Chamoun's request for troops rebuffed McClintock's efforts to resolve the local crisis. Denied access to the rebels, the ambassador apparently turned to General Shehab in a last-ditch effort to thwart the U.S. landing. Zogby knew that Secretary Dulles had telephoned to order McClintock to stop interfering. As to just what had caused this, Zogby suggested that I ask my friends in the press: some of the things he'd heard seemed too ridiculous

---

dollars to Sulzberger in Paris, thus becoming an "example" in his book *What's Wrong with U.S. Foreign Policy* (New York: Harcourt, 1959). It has since been revealed that teams fielded to assassinate Nasser had been abruptly called off by Allen Dulles. The Dulles brothers had taken literally President Eisenhower's remark that he hoped "the Nasser problem could be eliminated." Later, finding that Eisenhower had merely meant "improved U.S.-Egyptian relations," Foster Dulles ordered his brother to bring the CIA's operation to a halt. Then, to ensure that the CIA and other intelligence services involved (British, French, and Israeli) understood this change in American policy, the secretary of state called in the press to emphasize U.S. confidence in "getting along with Nasser." Another "example" in Sulzberger's book was the U.S. ambassador to Saudi Arabia, Donald Heath. His telegram to Washington quoting the Saudi "Master of the Royal Garage" in describing King Faisal's foreign policy had been leaked to Cy, who considered it a classic example of the activities of the type of ambassador upon which the U.S. relied for information. Enraged, Heath demanded a full investigation of this "critical breach of security"; the "culprit," however, was never discovered.

to believe. Zogby's own position was now intolerable: he had to show Deputy Under Secretary Murphy communications intercepts that the ambassador was not allowed to see. It was now clear how delicate my position with the ambassador might be. Having received a copy of Allen Dulles's message confirming that both his brother and Murphy had concurred in my returning to Beirut, Zogby laughed off my expressions of apprehension and described McClintock as being too busy to care what I did. Fascinated with an opportunity to deploy ships and troops as admirals and generals did, the ambassador now spent much of his time on the Sixth Fleet's command ship. In McClintock's eyes, Chamoun was now a "has-been" and the U.S. would select his replacement, as well as a caretaker government to serve until the end of his term. Under these circumstances, Zogby assured me, I probably could see the "lame duck" chief of state whenever I wished.

Still not convinced that I was of any value under these circumstances, I headed for the Saint Georges to find out from the press what had really happened in Lebanon since I'd left.

This foreign correspondents' Mecca seethed with activity: new reporters, arriving daily by land and chartered aircraft, complemented the local hands and those who'd accompanied the navy in combat fatigues, eager to follow troops into battles that hadn't materialized. New brands of journalists had also appeared: women reporters, detached from society and fashion stories; and television's nightly newscasters, such as David Brinkley, accompanied by camera crews to capture footage for flights by special planes to the United States. The eyes of the world now focused on this tiny republic, especially since Khrushchev had assured Nasser that Russian "volunteers" would be sent should U.S. troops dare enter the Syrian province of the U.A.R.

Conspicuously absent was *Time's* John Mecklin: his (and McClintock's) predictions that we'd never respond to Chamoun's plea for help had resulted in John's assignment to Tehran to prepare a cover story on the shah, and so he'd missed the landing.

Expecting a landing, the visiting press corps had taken positions, drinks in hand, on the Saint Georges terrace, where, scanning the sea, they missed what went on directly behind their backs. Doubting that the marines would storm ashore through cabaret row (Zeituni) and the posh hotel district, Sam Brewer and his local colleagues headed instead for the sandy beaches 180 degrees to the south, where Beirut's airport could be secured as a primary military target. Hills obscured this area and its seaborne approaches from the sight of the hotel: a lone naval officer returning his boat to the Saint Georges marina was the only uniformed American the visitors saw until *Newsweek's* Larry Collins arrived to explain that the landing was over.

As the American fleet sailed toward Lebanon, McClintock huddled with General Fuad Shehab, now suddenly recovered from the "illness" that had prevented him earlier from ordering his troops to support their government. Springing into a fighting posture of leadership, the general described his no longer lethargic troops as being united in their determination to fight to the last man in repelling any foreign invasion of their country's sacred soil. Still confident that he could personally resolve the crisis, McClintock had summoned his naval attaché and charged him with putting to sea in a small pleasure craft in order to turn back the first wave of marines "by command of the American Ambassador to the Republic of Lebanon." The hapless lieutenant commander had complied, up to the point of conveying his orders to a grim-faced Marine colonel in a tank-and-troop-laden LCT who barely paused to hear the message. Leaving the attaché to churn in the wake of passing ships, the marine shouted back that *his* commander-in-chief was a man called Eisenhower who was even then informing the world that a landing *had* taken place. Then, voice trailing off, the colonel employed an appropriate Marine Corps phrase to explain where McClintock might appropriately "stick his embassy." (In his telephone call to McClintock, Secretary Dulles bluntly reminded the ambassador of Eisenhower's position and actions, adding that Murphy was flying nonstop from Washington [in a USAF KC-135 jet tanker] to be certain that McClintock didn't misunderstand.)

Unopposed, welcomed by bikini-clad bathing beauties and soda-pop hawkers, the marines scrambled ashore and occupied the airport at which our army airborne troops from Germany had started to land. Now the obdurate General Shehab headed a force of twenty-three Lebanese army tanks at the city end of the mile-long dual highway from the airport. There, at the roundabout dubbed Watermelon Circle (for the vendors who had swarmed in to sell Americans their fruit), Shehab was determined to prevent a single U.S. soldier from entering the city's confines. Flags flying, the ever present Golly yipping with excitement in its front seat, the ambassadorial Cadillac sped McClintock to the airport to prevent this confrontation.

Four-star Admiral James Lemuel Hollaway, Jr., had just been named to command America's first peacetime unified military attack force. Arriving at the airport by helicopter from his flagship, the *Taconic*, the admiral headed the seventy-six-ship, 35,000-man Sixth Fleet offshore, which now joined the 10,000 marines and airborne soldiers on the ground to challenge any opposition by Shehab's 8,000-man Lebanese army (which was dispersed throughout the republic). The American troops had brought with them atomic-armed rockets; the Sixth Fleet's Skyraiders could carry A-bombs from Lebanon to Moscow; the U.S. Air Force Tactical Air Command, at nearby Adna, Turkey, stood by to provide either conventional or atomic troop support; and, alerted worldwide in the air, were the thermonuclear bombers of the Strategic Air Force. With all this behind him, impatient to get on with his orders to ensure the survival of President Chamoun's government and protect Lebanon from foreign attacks, Hollaway was understandably unmoved by the breathless ambassador's description of the Lebanese miniforce confronting the Americans. Nonetheless, at McClintock's urging, the admiral agreed to *parler avec le grand general*.

Shehab spoke virtually no English; his wife was French. But Holla-way's French would be termed "fractured," at best. McClintock interpreted for the military commanders. The admiral, known in the navy as "Lord Plushbottom" and to the press as "Lord Jim," greeted the nervous Shehab with the puzzling announcement that he conveyed greetings from their mutual friend Lord Mountbatten. Perhaps interpreting this as a hint that the British navy was not far behind, the general recanted his prediction that U.S.

troops, advancing in force, would attract fire from the Lebanese army, and agreed to accept soldiers into the city in single file. Hollaway agreed to the compromise, provided this proceeded "tooty sweetie." The Battle of Watermelon Circle was averted: behind the ambassador, the admiral, and Golly (in the Cadillac), U.S. troops moved into Beirut. General Shehab then returned to his seaside home at Juniyah Bay, north of Beirut, to brood over his future.

Robert Murphy was alone in the ambassador's office when I returned to the embassy. During a friendly conversation he told me that he'd been briefed by Secretary Dulles and his brother, in front of President Eisenhower, regarding the role I had played in Lebanon. There should be no trouble in my continuing, Murphy assured me; also, he was aware of the personality clash between McClintock and Chamoun. Then, smiling frequently, the deputy under secretary of state described his first encounter with General Fuad Shehab.

Fluent in French, Murphy had no need for McClintock to interpret when they called at the home of the still-undaunted Lebanese general. His people, Shehab had warned him, were restless, resentful, and determined that Chamoun should resign and U.S. troops leave at once. Otherwise, the general could not be responsible for the consequences. For fifteen years his officers had acted behind his back; now, he feared, they might revolt and attack the American forces. He'd listened patiently, Murphy told me, and then escorted the general to a window overlooking the sea. Pointing to the supercarrier *Saratoga*, swinging at anchor on the horizon, the President's envoy had quietly explained that just one of its aircraft, armed with nuclear weapons, could obliterate Beirut and its environs from the face of the earth. To this, Murphy quickly added that he'd been sent to be sure that it wouldn't be necessary for American troops to fire a shot. Shehab, he was certain, would ensure that there were no provocations on the Lebanese side. That, Murphy told me, ended the conversation. It now seemed that the general had "regained control" of his troops.

Just then Ambassador McClintock joined us. First a glare, then a brief smile, welcomed me back. Explaining that they were due at a meeting, the ambassador proposed that he and Murphy leave. Dashing back briefly to collect Golly, McClintock shot me a glance that left the impression that for me to see Murphy privately again would be difficult and that my days in Beirut might be limited.

I'd no sooner reached home than Chamoun's voice on my shortwave radio called me to the palace. It was a welcome-back meeting; Lebanese politics were hardly mentioned and the president was in a good mood. He'd be able to complete his term, Murphy had assured him, and that was all Chamoun claimed to want. The family's plans for a fall boat cruise dominated our conversation.

My next radio summons from Chamoun came the next afternoon. Going to the embassy, I met with Murphy and McClintock to discuss whether I should see Chamoun. When Murphy asked what the president might want, I said I had no idea, and described the previous night's conversation. The ambassador commented snidely that Chamoun undoubtedly wanted to know Murphy's real mission and whether McClintock was being replaced. I discounted this, describing the association I'd had with the president for over two years. It was Murphy's decision that I should see Chamoun, but he said pointedly that we should confine our discussion to intelligence matters and that I should then report back to him. It seemed clear that Murphy was giving me little latitude.

As I started to leave, Murphy said that an American woman reporter had interviewed Mrs. Chamoun and, in a subsequent meeting with Mrs. McClintock, had apparently quoted Mrs. Chamoun as saying that the U.S. had "erred in not following Eveland's advice." I assumed that she had been referring to my opinion that if McClintock had confined his official contacts to ones with the chief of state to whom he was accredited—leaving his army attaché to deal with General Shehab—the Lebanese crisis never would have reached its present stage. Once the ambassador had started seeing the general on an almost daily basis, Shehab's sense of himself as savior of the country had so ballooned that he refused to see even the minister of defense, to whom he was supposed to be entirely subordinate.

As Murphy recounted Mrs. Chamoun's remarks, and given the restriction he was placing on me, I felt that McClintock might have been distorting the nature of my relationship with Chamoun. Feeling the need for prudence, I obtained Zogby's promise that he'd be present when I reported to McClintock and Murphy on my discussion with Chamoun.

At the meeting, the president complained that Shehab was not utilizing the presence of American troops to free the Lebanese army to disarm the rebels. Chamoun didn't expect U.S. troops to do this, but it would be impossible for anybody to govern Lebanon, when most of the population held illegal arms. The commander of the gendarmerie had agreed to collect the weapons if the army refused. Would we, to permit this, provide the gendarmerie with M-1 rifles? I reminded Chamoun of McClintock's repeated public statements that he would stop all U.S. aid to Lebanon should he learn that our equipment was being put into the hands of forces not directly under Shehab's control. Under these circumstances, I could offer no encouragement. Nor did I have an answer when Chamoun showed me a new Russian rifle, presumably part of a large shipment from Syria to the rebels that had been intercepted by the gendarmes the previous night. All I could do was agree to report his request to Murphy.

Zogby and I had just joined Murphy and McClintock to describe my meeting with Chamoun when the president's voice came over the radio in the ambassador's adjacent bedroom. There was heavy fighting nearby, Chamoun said, and he wanted Admiral Hollaway to instruct the U.S. tank commander to fire in case of an attack on the palace. Grabbing the microphone, Murphy told Chamoun we'd come immediately and then dispatched me to go with McClintock to see him.

Chamoun was very agitated when we arrived. One-third of his country was still under rebel control, he said, and fighting in parts of Beirut was now heavier than it had been before U.S. troops had landed. He'd ordered that presidential elections be held in eleven days, but now the rebels had announced that they'd refuse to accept any president elected unless U.S. troops departed. This, Chamoun said, was just what General Shehab wanted. The presence of

U.S. forces would allow the elections to be held, and Shehab now indicated he would "reluctantly" accept if he were chosen. Once voted in, although Chamoun's term would not yet have expired, Shehab would demand the departure of our troops to permit him to assume office. Nonetheless, Chamoun insisted, unless we made the Lebanese army disarm the country as a condition of our support of Shehab's election, nobody, including Shehab, would be able to govern a country of armed militias.

When McClintock asked Chamoun if he wanted more troops around the palace, Chamoun calmly refused. "I'm not what matters now," he said. "It's a question of whether Lebanon will be able to survive without law and order. Gentlemen," he continued, "you can't have it both ways. President Eisenhower's speech said you were here 'at the request of a friendly government to help preserve its independence and to preserve law and order.' Yet, since the day you arrived, Mr. Ambassador, you've done nothing but meddle in our internal politics, and now Mr. Murphy is doing the same thing—this, with a total of six months and six days combined experience between you in one of the most complicated societies in the Middle East. Either do what your president sent troops here to do and support this country's elected government, or stay out of our affairs and move out to sea to watch what happened in Iraq take place here, too!"

Red-faced, McClintock sat silently and then launched a bombshell that caught me completely by surprise. "Mr. President," he said, "you had better read President Eisenhower's speech again. Our President said we were aiding Lebanon to stem 'aggression from without,' but he didn't say it was communist, and you can't prove that it was. So, the only justification for our landing of troops was the protection of American lives and property. Under these circumstances, you'd better get your house in order while we're here, or I'll recommend that we move back out to sea, just as you suggested." Chamoun made no reply: it would obviously have precipitated an argument, and I doubted he considered McClintock a worthy opponent. What did bother me, however, was that the ambassador had said in so many words that we hadn't landed under the provisions of the Eisenhower Doctrine. Eisenhower said we had, and Congress had supported him under this authorization. What in hell was this, I wondered, a revival of gunboat diplomacy? As we shook hands at the door, Chamoun put in one more word: "You might read again the document I handed Bill, authorizing me to call for the troops you landed. It mentioned the Eisenhower Doctrine, and if Nasser and the rebels had known—as you've just told me—that the doctrine had no meaning, this building would now be rubble and my family and I would be buried in it!" Finally, alluding to Communist influence, Chamoun picked up the Russian rifle behind his desk and suggested that the ambassador tell him where in the Western world this might have been made.

Nothing was said until we reached the embassy gate. Hoping to cut the chill, I finally told McClintock that it seemed we now had too many cooks in Lebanon's kitchen and that it might be a good idea if I bowed out for a while. "That's a damn good idea, Eveland," McClintock rejoined; "why don't you pack up and leave tomorrow?"

"Fine," I agreed. "I'll include your request that I be transferred at the end of my cable to Allen Dulles describing tonight's conversation." As I moved toward my car, the ambassador called me back to apologize, saying that I'd done valuable work and that he wanted me to remain. When we joined Murphy and Zogby inside, the ambassador reported that Chamoun had merely been nervous, "as always," and proposed that we send a few more tanks to guard the palace. With a fatherly smile, Murphy suggested it would be better if I didn't see the president again, since I appeared to stimulate new requests for American help. That suited me fine: I didn't want to be party to giving Chamoun the impression that what he said was being heeded or reported. It was obvious that my days in Lebanon were ending; how to leave town gracefully was the only question that now concerned me.

Allen Dulles's urgent cable the next morning solved my dilemma. The secretary of state was going to London for the Baghdad Pact meeting and had asked that I join him there, provided Murphy and McClintock concurred with my being absent for three days. Expanding a message I'd drafted to propose my withdrawal, I explained to Dulles it was unlikely I'd be able to enlighten his brother about what Murphy and McClintock were planning. A return cable from the CIA director quoted the secretary of state as expecting me unless Murphy objected. The ambassador (who successfully isolated Murphy from me) encouraged my trip to London; so did Zogby, saying he'd already recommended me for a "top-drawer CIA medal and a well-deserved months' rest in the U.S."

As I departed, flying over American troops who'd landed just ten days before, I saw mortar bursts and artillery salvos in the mountains above them, stark evidence that Lebanon's rebels still were defying the government. I found it hard to believe that we'd accomplished anything at all. The Moslem members at the Baghdad Pact session I'd be attending had all now recognized the new Iraqi regime: we'd be hard pressed to claim that a communist-dominated Iraq justified keeping troops in Lebanon. The best that one could say—thanks to the U.S. and British troops occupying their countries—was that Camille Chamoun and King Hussein still headed their governments. No Arab state east of Suez could any longer be called pro-Western in the sense we'd once envisioned. The time for redefining America's objectives in the Middle East seemed to be now at hand. I thought back to Raymond Hare's conclusions when he'd served on the Alpha Planning Group: transit rights and access to oil were all we had the right to ask or expect.

If Allen Dulles's cable had rescued me from my troubles, getting our troops out without losing face seemed the best we could hope for—assuming, of course, that Foster Dulles agreed with Ambassador McClintock's explanation to Chamoun of why we'd landed there in the first place.

While U.S. policymakers pondered whether the Iraqi coup had been instigated by the Communists and deliberated about what to do with our troops in Lebanon, the Russians lost no time in seizing the initiative. That indecision and policy conflicts plagued our embassy was common gossip in Lebanon; undoubtedly, it was well known in Moscow as well.[86] Lebanon's rebel leaders now suspected that the Eisenhower Doctrine was a "paper tiger," and the next moves of the Soviets indicated that they had reached this conclusion as well. In what President Eisenhower branded "ballistic blackmail," Soviet Premier Khrushchev first proclaimed Russia's nuclear capabilities and then demanded an urgent five-power (Britain, France, India, Russia, and the U.S.) summit conference, under the U.N.'s aegis, to defuse the Middle East crisis.

A message from Allen Dulles awaited me in London, urging that I speak frankly to his brother about Lebanon in the "broad context of our overall Mideast policy and our position at the proposed U.N. summit." (I was asked not to engage in discussing "personality problems," since the secretary of state had "considerable background" in these.) Then, as a harbinger of what might lie ahead, this message dealt with the possible desirability of a "solution involving arrangements for troop withdrawal [from Lebanon] prior to [the U.N.] conference." This, Dulles had cabled, "was a risk which must be taken in light of [the] overall world situation."

There it was in black and white in front of me: our troops had been in Lebanon exactly ten days, but now it seemed almost certain that a policy decision to remove them only awaited Foster Dulles's approval. Yet, knowing Allen Dulles pretty well by now,

---

86   Banner headlines in *Blitz* (a leftist New Delhi newspaper often used for attribution purposes by the anti-Western Middle East press) claimed to reveal details of "Suezcide Number Three—The Eveland Plan" to turn the Arab states over to Israel. The article told of a "first-class embassy row between Ambassador McClintock and Middle East CIA Chief Eveland," in which I prevailed after the Dulles brothers sent out Robert Murphy to back me. The "Eveland Plan" was said to be set for implementation the spring of 1959, or before. Written by R. K. Karajia, an Indian journalist based in Cairo, the same story appeared in his book *Arab Dawn*, published December 1958 (pp. 244–248). It has since been established that Kim Philby maintained close contacts with Indian correspondents in the Middle East capitals. That Philby lived in Beirut's rebel-held Basta during the 1958 fighting, emerging from time to time to frequent the Saint Georges and other press hangouts, lends weight to the possibility that Kim was active in propaganda guidance (his first specialty with British intelligence) for the Soviets, if not a major contributor to Russian strategy in the Middle East while he lived there.

I detected a challenge to alter the U.S. position if I could produce enough ammunition to support my case. Bill Rountree posed the usual "too busy" obstacle to a possible appointment with his boss. Undeterred, I went directly to Jerry Greene, Dulles's personal aide, and secured the promise of a meeting as soon as the last Baghdad Pact meeting closed. Meanwhile, I decided to play through CIA channels the card Chamoun had handed me during our meeting just before I left.

Both Murphy and McClintock were avoiding me that morning, when my last-minute summons from the president arrived. Zogby agreed that I should keep the proposed appointment, and we sent a joint cable to Allen Dulles to explain the circumstances involved. The CIA director and State Department both approved my decision and asked that I report from London what Chamoun had had to say. Now, in a ten-page operational-immediate cable, I outlined details of the strategy Chamoun intended to use. It seemed almost certain that General Shehab would be elected president by parliament on July 31. Anticipating the general's demand for a U.S.-troop withdrawal immediately after he'd been named, Chamoun planned to announce his own resignation instead of remaining in office until September 23 to complete his term. Thus Shehab would face the prospect of trying to rule a rebellious country. The uncollected arms promised new fighting by pro-Nasser Moslems to oust Shehab, and even the threat of a full-scale war. Otherwise, Shehab would have to request Chamoun to stay in office and agree that American troops should remain. In this case, the president hoped Murphy and McClintock might consider more seriously the need for Lebanese forces to disarm their country to avoid the disintegration of Lebanon, which Chamoun predicted was certain if Syrian-supported private militias continued to operate at will. The thing that had convinced me that Chamoun was completely serious was his repetition of a theme he'd used many times before: with the growth of his country's Palestinian-refugee population, the slight majority that the Christians had held during the 1940s no longer obtained, as most everybody knew. Thus, unless Shehab could take office under U.S. protection, constitutional changes to make Lebanon a Moslem-governed country would become the armed rebels' minimum demand.

The CIA station chief, Bronson Tweedy, read my message, of course, and immediately repeated its contents to the secretary of the British cabinet, exactly as I'd hoped he would. I might not be able to see Foster Dulles immediately, but having Harold Macmillan, Britain's prime minister, do the job for me was something I didn't mind. The attention I'd sought materialized immediately: both Macmillan and Dulles were basing many decisions (their positions at the U.N. summit and their planning to withdraw troops from Lebanon and Jordan) on the assumption that Chamoun would remain in office until the expiration of his term, I was told; my advice on what might induce him to do so was sought by both the CIA station and the British SIS. As an immediate result, McClintock was instructed to assure Chamoun that we'd assure his peaceful succession by the newly elected president, and Murphy was told to leave for Cairo immediately after the elections to try to persuade Nasser to call off the Lebanese rebels.

But before I could really savor my moment of glory and discuss Middle East policy planning with the American secretary of state, Nikita Khrushchev intervened with what appeared to be either second thoughts or Soviet indecisiveness. In messages flashed to Washington and London, the Soviet premier decided to withdraw his summit-meeting proposal and brandish ballistic bombs again. My meeting with Foster Dulles was only fleeting; he was leaving for the airport to return home to discuss with the President what our next move would be. Gaunt, obviously worn out, and limping from his gout, Dulles greeted me briefly: "Sorry, Eveland. I'll see you in Washington; meanwhile, we've assured Chamoun that U.S. troops will remain."

Back in Washington, I learned that the secretary of state was preparing a speech that President Eisenhower would deliver before the United Nations. It had been decided to make a token withdrawal of one battalion from Lebanon in advance of the President's announcement that we'd pull out our forces once peace had been restored in the country (and Chamoun's term completed), provided that in the interim the U.N. sent more observers to ensure that law and order would prevail after we left.

When I suggested to Allen Dulles that this really meant that the Eisenhower Doctrine had died—a fatality attributable to world opinion and Russian threats—he didn't dispute my point. Instead, perhaps sensing that I'd prefer to be away when the President delivered his "funeral oration," the DCI proposed that I take the "well-earned month's vacation" Zogby had recommended before I left Beirut. Dejected, but nonetheless pleased that for the first time in three years I didn't have an airplane flight ahead of me, I accepted his offer on the spot. Not wanting to remain in Washington where I'd be exposed to the machinations of Middle East politics, and having a month ahead before my son, Crane, was due back at military school, I boarded a train with him to visit relatives in California. On the trip, we had a chance to get to know each other again.

Returning to Washington, I met with Norm Paul, who said that CIA chief O'Donnell in Turkey was so furious that I'd chartered the flight to Lebanon that he'd demanded my permanent exclusion from the Middle East. The next day I met with the Dulles brothers to discuss my future. Believing that we'd let President Chamoun down, Foster Dulles suggested two remedies, both of which would involve me. I soon gathered that the secretary had not forgotten Ambassador Heath's intervention in the Lebanese parliamentary elections (especially his role in inducing Charles Malik to run), and that he was also irritated by yet another telegram from Ambassador McClintock urging that I not return to Lebanon lest this be interpreted locally as evidence that the United States still believed Chamoun should complete his term.

Under the U.N.'s system of geographically rotating the presidency of the General Assembly, the Arabs were entitled to provide a candidate for election in the fall. A year before, Dulles had assured Malik that the United States would back him, but now Bill Rountree was arguing, with what the secretary described as "specious reasoning," that Malik's entry into Lebanese politics should disqualify him. Rountree also claimed, apparently, that the presence of U.S. troops in Lebanon spoke against our support of a man from an "occupied state." Led by the Egyptians, the Arabs had named a Sudanese alternative candidate whom Rountree wanted us to endorse. At Foster Dulles's urging, the President had told Ambassador Lodge that the U.S. delegation should do everything possible to ensure Malik's election. I was to go to New York and assure Malik that America's position would not change.

The secretary then asked me if I'd like to return to Lebanon. Because of O'Donnell's attitude, I answered that I thought I was entitled to go back to collect my personal belongings, although just when didn't matter a lot. At that point, Foster Dulles smiled and referred to the weather: a sea voyage home in the spring when the ocean was calmer was the thing he said he'd want if he were I. Both the timing and mode of travel suited me perfectly, and I waited to hear what he proposed I do until then. Getting me back to Lebanon before Chamoun's term expired was what Dulles wanted, adding that he'd inform McClintock that I'd return before September 23. As to when I'd leave Lebanon permanently, the decision was mine. Once I'd decided when to take the boat trip, I should tell the ambassador of my plans. Allen Dulles nodded as he heard this, then said he'd send a message to McClintock, through Zogby, saying that he "was convinced that [I] had a continuing capability to provide an important service to the CIA and U.S. government in the Middle East and that [my] base of operations should be Beirut."

Charles Malik's election to the presidency of the General Assembly came off by a comfortable margin: a U.S. victory, as the press described it. Bill Rountree stood behind me as the vote was declared official. "I hope that you're happy now that your man is elected," he said as he walked off. Although I was now sure that the Dulles brothers supported me, carrying out their orders was undoubtedly adding to my list of enemies within the career State Department and the CIA. I wondered how long I could survive under such circumstances.

That I still had good friends became evident when I met Charles and Eva Malik in the delegates' lounge to convey my congratulations. They invited me to share with them their first ride in the limousine to which Malik's new office entitled him, and we left for the Harvard

Club for a private victory dinner. Awaiting us there was Walt Kelly with a bottle of Malik's favorite, Jack Daniels Black, with which we toasted John Foster Dulles as a statesman who'd kept his word. At that moment, I missed Sam Kopper: his friendship and introductions had done much to make possible this occasion on which I could say that two of the men most prominent in world affairs knew and respected me. As for being able to return to the Middle East to face America's changed position there, I could thank Kelly and his sense of humor for being able to accept with some equanimity Pogo's famous discovery: "We have met the enemy, and he is us!"

How little we'd used the presence of our troops to insist that Lebanon put its own house in order became evident when I met with Chamoun after he'd turned over the presidency to General Shehab. The Lebanese army was still inactive; thirty people had been killed during one night's fighting in Beirut; efforts to form a cabinet were floundering; and although the rebels had taken down the barricades in the Basta, the government was not collecting illegal arms. Disgusted, Chamoun had moved to a resort in the mountains, the USAF had flown ex-Prime Minister Sami Solh to safety in Turkey, and sureté chief Farid Shehab had been sent off to Africa as an ambassador. Even with everything still going their way, the rebels themselves were now quarreling about who would be in the new government. Now *they* were protesting that Ambassador McClintock was interfering in Lebanon's internal affairs.

Just before all U.S. troops departed, agreement was reached that one of the former rebel leaders would become prime minister. He advised our embassy that Lebanon would accept an offer of U.S. economic aid in order to repair the damage done by the civil strife—a figure of $100 million was suggested. Now, it seemed, we might be trying to "buy peace" in Lebanon. Washington finally settled on $10 million as a grant, and as the check was handed over the new prime minister announced that Lebanon no longer supported the Eisenhower Doctrine, that it would shift from a pro-Western to a neutralist position on foreign affairs.

Wanting to get away from the absurdities of Lebanese politics, yet enjoined by Foster Dulles to remain until spring, I considered traveling within the Near East. Under present conditions, however, there were few places I could go. We no longer had an embassy in Syria, and I was almost certainly viewed with suspicion in both parts of the UAR. Iraq was risky, especially since each day the trials in Baghdad exposed more documentation of plots against Syria—there was good reason to fear that my name might surface. And, having sent troops to Jordan, the British were back advising King Hussein, even though CIA funds were supporting him. Deposed King Saud, meanwhile, was in Cairo, detailing his past intrigues, so that Saudi Arabia was another country in which my now exposed CIA affiliation could make me unwelcome. I did travel once to Istanbul, at the request of the Dulles brothers, but my presence antagonized the CIA station, and I declined a further proposal that I spend more time with Ilyan and the Iraqi refugees who'd congregated in Turkey.

Returning to Beirut and marking time, I tried to remain inconspicuous and avoid involvement in the political maneuvering that was still going on. In February 1959 Foster Dulles underwent another operation. Soon it was announced that he was terminally ill of cancer and would be relinquishing his office. In a remarkable display of bipartisan support of this now dying man, a movement started in Congress to urge that he continue to guide our foreign affairs. In April, Dulles was named a special adviser to the president, with cabinet status. Chamoun sent for me the day he learned of Dulles's condition. An old man in the Lebanese mountains had discovered a remarkable cure for cancer from a substance made of apricots. A bit embarrassed yet entirely sincere, the former president asked me to cable Allen Dulles with an offer to provide this "miraculous" substance as a last-ditch effort to save the man whom Chamoun had considered a friend since they'd worked at the U.N. together during 1947 on the Palestine issue. With thanks, the Dulles family declined Chamoun's gesture, and the DCI's message suggested that I might now want to leave the Middle East and come home.

On the day of my departure, I found that I was not really sad about leaving what was left of America's position in the Middle East, just over eight years since I'd met my first American minister to Lebanon. By chance, my passage home was booked on the *Excalibur*, the refloated ship upon which I'd been shipwrecked on my first voyage to the Middle East. If this ship could be salvaged, I thought, as I watched Beirut disappear into the horizon, perhaps the American position in the area could be, as well. I doubted that I'd have any part in this, however; I was eager to find a new challenge to meet. What it would be, I had no idea, nor was I much concerned as I went below to stateroom 127—the same one my family and I had occupied that day in July 1950.

Just out of Naples we received word by radio of John Foster Dulles's death. It was May 24, 1959. When we landed, I jumped ship, left my effects to follow by sea, and boarded a plane in Rome.

On May 26 I stood in the Bethlehem Chapel of the National Cathedral in Washington. It was late at night and only a military honor guard kept silent vigil alongside the flag-draped casket. Tears came to my eyes as I realized how privileged I'd been to have met this man whose inflexible principles had both shaped world events and affected the lives of millions of people. Whether this had been good or bad didn't then seem important.

When I walked out into the cool of the night I knew that it was time to plan my own future. It seemed certain that only the unique relationship between the Dulles brothers could have enabled cryptodiplomacy to play such an important role in U.S. foreign relations. If this were so, an era had ended; so had any justification for assignments such as I'd been given.

CHAPTER TWENTY-EIGHT

ON THE OUTSIDE LOOKING IN 1959–1974

President Eisenhower and Secretary of State Christian Herter inherited a foreign-service cadre that for six years had been conditioned to respond to Foster Dulles's personal Middle East policymaking. Most of these ambassadors and advisers instinctively blamed communist subversion for the anti-Western sentiment in Arab Asia; only a few urged prompt action to deal with the basic cause of the Arabs' bitterness—the Arab-Israeli conflict. As a result, President Eisenhower's idea of visiting Egypt to improve Arab-American relations was discouraged on the grounds that the domestic political necessity for a concurrent stop in Israel would offset any gains he might make with Nasser. This was not the time for peacemaking, the President's advisers argued. Instead, the United States should exploit the emerging conflicts between Arab nationalism and communism, and also acquire evidence of Soviet subversion in the Middle East for use in a showdown with Kruschchev when he and Eisenhower met in Paris in May 1960.

Allen Dulles was a strong advocate of this position. Congressional probers had quizzed him as to why the CIA had failed to predict the coup in Iraq and about how Nasser had been able to capitalize on the Lebanese revolution and emasculate the Eisenhower Doctrine. Unwilling to criticize his brother's policies or to acknowledge that the CIA had helped to establish Nasser as a symbol of Arab nationalism, Dulles unhesitatingly attributed the Middle East's problems to Russia. He vowed to use every asset available to his agency to check the spread of communist influence.[87]

It was under these circumstance that Allen Dulles and I met to discuss my future. The weary man I faced spoke with a candor I'd

---

87   There was a kind of ambivalence to Foster Dulles's position on the dangers of communism in the Middle East. Initially, he was among the advisers who recommended that President Truman extend immediate *de facto* recognition to the provisional government of Israel for fear that the preponderance of East European Jews in Palestine, and the key role that Czechoslovakian military equipment had played in the defeat of the Arab armies by the Zionists, might lead the new Jewish state to adopt a pro-Soviet foreign policy. (Russia extended *de jure* recognition to Israel three days after it proclaimed its independence, seven months before this was granted by the United States.) In dealing with Israel during the 1953–54 period, Dulles and Assistant Secretary Byroade stressed the Arabs' fears that expansionist Zionism was a greater danger than communism, and they urged a prompt settlement of the Arab-Israeli conflict as the most effective means of keeping Russian influence out of the area. At that time, the CIA's liaison agreement with Israel's Mossad was based on joint activities to liberate the people behind the iron curtain, and between themselves, the Dulles brothers considered this the best way of stemming the spread of communism worldwide. Israel's indigenous intelligence assets in the Soviet-controlled countries were vastly superior to the CIA's, and the U.S. was understandably influenced by Israel's assessments of Russian intentions in the Middle East. Israeli reports that Nasser was negotiating an arms deal with Czechoslovakia, combined with escalated attacks by Israel against Egyptian forces in Gaza and Sinai, resulted in a self-fulfilling prophecy and enabled the Israelis to portray the Arabs as falling under Soviet domination. This same pattern evolved later in connection with Israel and the Soviet arms offers to Syria, and had much to do with the CIA's decision to send me to Damascus. Thus, in Israel's own national interest, the obsession of the Dulles brothers with the cold war was a development to be encouraged in preference to an Israeli agreement to comply with the U.N. resolutions requiring repatriation or compensation of the Palestinians as the first step in an overall Arab-Israeli peace settlement. Once the Egyptian-Russian arms agreement was concluded, Israel became an ally—first with Britain and France, then with America—in using armed force to combat the "Russian-dominated" Arabs. The Dulles brothers-CIA cold-war strategy therefore enabled Israel to relegate the Palestinian issue to secondary status until the 1967 war provoked the formation of the PLO and the threat of its "terrorism" became the central theme of Israel's refusal to relinquish its occupied territories and accept the establishing of a Palestinian state for the refugees.

never encountered in him before. Once again he offered me career status in the CIA and also proffered several liaison positions with chiefs of state in Southeast Asia for my consideration. Instead of accepting, I expressed interest in the emerging nations of Africa, suggesting that lessons we'd learned in the Middle East would be valuable in dealing with the Africans' aspirations to rid themselves of the fetters of colonialism.

Dulles responded positively, saying that my preferences would fit in with recent CIA planning. Norman Paul's Near East and Africa Division was being split up, and Paul had been offered the post of chief of station in Rome. A new African division of the clandestine services would be formed under Bronson Tweedy, with whom I'd had frequent contacts in London. The director proposed that I stay on, travel through all Africa, and provide him, personally, with recommendations for enhancing America's position there. The prospects of a roving assignment, an "eyes-only" communications relationship with Dulles, and a continuing contract status were tempting. I accepted. There was one administrative problem involved: our diplomatic missions in Africa had relatively small staffs, so that providing official cover for a man of my salary level would be difficult. A "deep cover" assignment with legitimate business backing would be a solution to this problem, and Dulles told me to meet with Thomas Karamessines (in charge of arranging cover positions with private industry), who would work out something.

Dulles then embarked on a soliloqy concerning the CIA's responsibility to strengthen its anticommunist operations by any means available. He referred to my involvement in the 1956 coup planning in Syria and pointed out that I'd not been exposed because the agency had only helped finance an essentially indigenous political-action operation. Michail Ilyan had, after all, been sentenced to death as an Iraqi agent. Financing friendly intelligence services was a classic intelligence technique, Dulles continued. Regrettably, he said, our joint operations with the Iraqi, Lebanese, Jordanian, and Saudi Arabian governments had revealed that their people were rank amateurs.

We sat in silence as I watched his now familiar pipe-filling, tamping, and lighting ritual. "I guess that leaves Israel's intelligence service as the only one on which we can count, doesn't it, Eveland?" were his next words. My expression must have betrayed surprise, for Dulles added, "Not against the Arabs, of course, but against our common target, the Russians." There was nothing new about this collaboration, he told me: the CIA and Israel's Mossad had worked jointly to monitor developments within the Soviet Union and Russia's satellites and, even before the Egyptian-Czech arms agreement, the Israelis had warned that Russia had plans to arm the Arabs. After the 1956 Suez war, Prime Minister Ben-Gurion had refused to withdraw his forces from the Sinai and Gaza until the United States agreed to provide Israel with means to protect its population centers from attack by the Russian ballistic missiles that, Israeli intelligence reported, would soon be furnished to Egypt and Syria. The CIA had therefore been secretly authorized to help Israel acquire the capability of retaliating against possible attack by advanced weapons in the hands of the Arabs. Since then, Dulles continued, the CIA and Mossad had jointly monitored Russian arms shipments to the Middle East and had also mounted combined operations against Soviet influence in the Egyptian and Syrian intelligence services. Now that Iraq had been taken over by anti-Western elements, access to Israel's network in the Arab countries would be even more useful to the CIA. For all of these reasons, then, the director concluded, Norman Paul's replacement would coordinate intelligence operations in the Middle East with James Angleton's counterintelligence-counterespionage division (in which liaison with Israel's Mossad was maintained.)

In my view, relying on Israel's reports about Soviet activities in the Arab states and the quantities of arms they obtained from Russia for possible use against Israel was remarkably like depending on a fox to guard the henhouse. As for the CIA's role in facilitating Israel's development of advanced weapons, this certainly contravened the intent of the Mutual Security Act by sacrificing America's ability to control Israel's use of any weapons acquired or developed with U.S. assistance.

But Allen Dulles's good wishes for my future in Africa made it clear that our meeting was over and that my role in the Middle

East had ended. In any case, Dulles had estimated that it would take me at least a year to become familiar with Africa and to be able to provide useful information. I hoped that this indicated that in Africa the CIA would stick to its mandated role of collecting intelligence, instead of resorting to the "quick cure" coup attempts that had cost the United States so dearly in the Middle East. I'd had enough of that kind of remedy.

Thomas Karamessines had opened the CIA's first station in Greece and remained there to build it into one of the agency's largest. Then he'd been brought back to headquarters for promotion (later becoming head of the clandestine services under Director Richard Helms). Receiving me coolly with a reference to having heard about me from his colleague in Turkey (Justin O'Donnell, my old nemesis), Karamessines nonetheless performed like a man who'd been instructed by Allen Dulles to comply with an order to assist me and not ask questions. The agency had close connections with Howard Hughes, Karamessines told me, and I was sent to Los Angeles to meet with the CIA agent in charge of liaison with the Hughes organization. Within a week I was in Culver City taking familiarization flights in the new Hughes two-place helicopter. The plan was to have me open a sales office in Nairobi, flying (myself!) over Africa's jungles to sell this new Hughes aircraft.

From my CIA contact I learned of an international heavy-construction company through which the agency had placed deep-cover people in the Far East and Pacific. Thinking of my grandfather's days as a road-builder, not convinced that forty-one was the right age at which to start out as a pilot, I arranged to be taken to nearby Alhambra for a meeting with Allen Vinnell, founder of the corporation bearing his name. The two of us got on well, and by the end of the meeting he invited me to name my overseas location and provide a list of services that the Vinnell Corporation could furnish to support my mission (all costs of the arrangement to be reimbursed by the CIA).

In those days, travel across Africa was difficult: Rome's airport served as a gateway for flights to most African capitals and to the

Middle East, where Vinnell had construction projects. Karamessines approved my proposal that I set up an office in Rome and report to headquarters through the station there. Everything I asked for was agreed on without question; as one of Allen Dulles's personal projects, getting me out of Washington appeared to be the objective.

The African division was still being organized: if it had any priorities in Africa I wasn't told of them, nor was I given the names of CIA personnel assigned there. In some ways this arrangement pleased me. I'd not have to worry about chiefs of station disclosing my association with the CIA, as they had done in the Middle East. But what if I ended up in an African jail, accused of spying? As in 1955, I made my own cover arrangements. Vinnell authorized a corporate resolution appointing me a vice-president and even had the air force issue me an ID card with GS-18 civilian rank (in connection with the company's contract to maintain the USAF base at Dhahran).

Accompanied by my new wife, I started out 1960 living in Rome. I then toured the east and west coasts of Africa for five months to establish contacts, addressing progress reports to Allen Dulles each time I returned to Rome. Other urgent matters demanded the director's attention. During May, the agency's U-2 spy plane was shot down over Russia, and the Eisenhower-Khruschchev summit meeting collapsed as a result. Also, during the first half of 1960, the CIA's top-priority planning was directed at Latin America. The objective was to remove the threats to democracy perceived in the activities of Fidel Castro and Rafael Trujillo.

Finally, in July, it became Africa's turn to receive crisis attention at the top levels of the Eisenhower administration. Two months earlier, my travels had taken me to the Belgian Congo, where John Tomlinson, a friend of mine from the Beirut embassy, represented America's interests as consul general in Leopoldville. During luncheon at his residence, Tomlinson spoke of Belgium's enlightened form of colonialism and predicted that the colony's vast mineral resources would provide opportunities for heavy-construction companies. He urged me to return later on a longer visit to meet with colonial-government officials. My next trip to the Congo took place under circumstances far different from those that John Tomlinson had foreseen. Urgent instructions from Allen Dulles ordered me to report to the CIA's chief of station and offer my services. By that time Tomlinson had departed the country, as had the Belgians, including the civil-service corps and officers of the Congolese army. On June 30, 1960, the Congo declared its independence from Belgium and, to the surprise of the U.S. government, the Belgians simply went home.

The airport at which I landed was filled with USAF transport planes bringing in U.N. forces to restore order, and evacuating civilians fleeing in panic, leaving behind all their possessions in a country now wracked by tribal and provincial conflicts. Public-service and transportation systems no longer functioned, rendering Leopoldville nearly deserted during the day and a scary place at night. Staying in my hotel until the CIA contacted me was the only safe thing to do, but this posed another problem. Except for foreign correspondents (many of whom I knew from the Middle East), I was the only American guest registered. My story that I'd just dropped in looking for new contracts to build highways, dams, and airports was patently transparent.

Overnight, our consulate general had been elevated to embassy status. A new ambassador and CIA chief had just arrived, but neither had served before in the Congo. As inexperience was no impediment, the embassy and CIA officers quickly agreed that the Congolese situation posed a major threat to America's "national security." It was, they concluded, a classic communist effort to take over a new government, and Patrice Lumumba was consolidating the power of anti-Western forces. Whether Lumumba was a dedicated communist or merely a trained Soviet agent wasn't really important, I was told: Lumumba had to be stopped quickly or the Congo would become another Cuba. I'd waited a week to be briefed on this estimate, so I wasn't a bit offended when I was told that the CIA's professionals (led by Bronson Tweedy with six months on the job) had the Congolese problem well in hand and that my services wouldn't be needed. My comments and views had not been solicited, but I was offered help in finding a plane out of town. So much, I thought, for my new role as Allen Dulles's personal adviser on Africa![88]

The next day I boarded an evacuation flight for Ghana and proceeded on to Italy. When I arrived home I learned just how foolish my mission to the Congo had been. Sam Brewer (there to join his daughter, Annie, who now lived in Beirut with Kim and Eleanor Philby) had talked to the reporters who'd preceded me from the Congo. All were convinced that I was now the CIA's top man in Africa. Vinnell's executive vice-president was concerned about his company's reputation, and I was chided for having made the Leopoldville trip. In order to enable me to avoid similar assignments in the future, he'd flown in from California with a company directive that assigned me responsibilities for the company's Middle Eastern projects and for developing new business with the petroleum industry. Although this was just a device to enable me to justify trips to the Middle East, I decided to spend more time on Vinnell's business in hopes that I'd be considered for legitimate employment when my CIA contract expired.

The friends I'd made in the petroleum industry over the years now proved to be useful, and I soon negotiated contracts for the Vinnell Corporation in the oil fields of Libya and Iran. The company then proposed that I leave the CIA and become a bona fide vice-president. Accepting, I informed the agency that I'd not be renewing my contract in 1961. To preserve my clearance for classified information and availability for future assignments, the CIA continued me on its rolls as a consultant (an unpaid "independent contractor").

---

88   The Senate's Church Committee Report on Assassination Plots revealed that Richard Bissell and Bronson Tweedy were at the time of my visit discussing means of assassinating Lumumba. Allen Dulles then cabled the station chief that removing Lumumba was an urgent priority. He authorized the station to take action should a favorable opportunity arise. The President then accepted Dulles's view that eliminating Lumumba was essential, and a CIA expert was sent to the Congo with a special poison for this purpose. In the end, the Congolese announced Lumumba's death in Katanga province in January 1961, before the CIA could find a means of reaching him. In this same period, the CIA was trying to drug, discredit, or do away with Castro and Trujillo, using the Mafia in Cuba and arming the dissidents who finally killed the Dominican dictator.

My respite from the Middle East and its politics had lasted only a few months, and for the next fifteen years developments in that turbulent area affected nearly every aspect of my life. No longer isolated from reality by the error-forgiving cocoon that sheltered our politicians, bureaucrats, and diplomats, however, I lived daily with the effects of America's failures—including those of which I'd been a part.

The discovery of oil in Libya during the late 1950s set in motion a chain of events leading to the formation of the Organization of Oil Producing Countries (OPEC), the Arab oil boycott of 1973–74, and, finally, the West's belated recognition that the economies of both the industrial and the underdeveloped nations of the world were at the mercy of thirteen oil-producing states. These reversals in long-established patterns were triggered by the Libyan Petroleum Law of 1955, which was specifically framed to encourage small oil companies—the so-called "independents"—to compete for concessions against the cartel of the seven international petroleum giants that had controlled the world's oil supplies for thirty years. The American members of the cartel (Exxon, Mobil, SoCal, Texaco, and Gulf) considered the Libyan law a double-edged threat to their monopoly. First, new oil shipped by the independents from Libya to nearby Europe would upset the system under which the "majors" produced Middle East crude for a dime a barrel, then transported it via their own pipelines and tankers to subsidiary refineries for eventual sale at their company stations in a captive European market. Second, the antitrust exemptions and U.S. tax-free royalty payments that the American cartel members had been granted in the name of "national security" might be threatened if the myth that only the majors had the marketing capacity to deal in Middle East oil were exploded. In self-defense, the large U.S. companies scrambled for Libyan concessions. They hoped that by rushing these fields into production, they could induce the independents to sell their unrefined Libyan oil to the cartel at bargain prices.

There were good reasons for the cartel to believe that this strategy would succeed. In 1955 the American members had

relinquished a 5 percent interest in their Iranian-consortium ownership to a small number of independents (largely to justify U.S.
antitrust exemptions and preserve income-tax benefits). Thus,
some cooperation was due in return. Indeed, in the wake of the
1956 Suez crisis, America's major and independent oil companies
had cooperated—in a criminal conspiracy to gouge the public.
The Department of Justice acquired documentary evidence that
twenty-nine oil companies had colluded to increase prices on the
spurious premise that closing the Suez Canal had created a world
oil shortage.[89]

By 1958, however, cheap oil from the Middle East was a glut
on the market. Russia also had a surplus and was selling low-cost
oil to Europe, taking up 16 percent of the Italian market, where
Libya's production would normally go. Cheap gasoline was plenti-
ful in the United States, causing the petroleum lobby (fronted by
Lyndon Johnson) to oppose either imports of or reductions in the
price of Middle Eastern oil.

Suddenly, providence (wearing the kaffiyeh of Arab nationalism) provided the oil cartel with an alternative to curtailing
production in Iran, Saudi Arabia, and Kuwait. The 1958 Iraqi revolution portended nationalization of that country's oil fields, even
acceptance by the new military government of Russian offers to
assist in opening up new fields. In fact, a principal justification for
the revolution was that the Iraqi monarchy had allowed the cartel to produce only a fraction of the country's known oil reserves
(Iraq was capable of exporting more oil than Iran). Now it seemed
possible that Iraq's oil might fall under Russian control and be lost
to the West.

Although they had been dismayed by the nationalization
of Iran's oil industry seven years earlier, the founding members of the cartel were relieved by the possibility of the Iraq oil

---

89   Originally filed by the government in Alexandria, Virginia, the criminal antitrust case against the oil companies was mysteriously transferred to
Oklahoma City. There, Federal Judge Royce A. Savage dismissed the charges
and shortly became a vice-president of a principal defendant—the Gulf Oil
Corporation.

production's being suspended. There were no pleas for the CIA to oust the Iraqi revolutionaries (international opposition to the U.S. landing in Lebanon made it clear that moving troops to take over the Iraqi oil fields would have provoked a serious threat of war by Russia). Instead, led by Howard Page (America's "oil statesman"), the cartel settled in to protracted negotiations that would keep Iraqi oil off the market for years. It appeared that this oil was not vital to America's national security—certainly not to the extent of sabotaging Iraqi oil wells to deny them to Russia (under the U.S. policy—NSC 5401—I'd overseen in the OCB just three years before). The decision to stall negotiations was made not in Washington but in the boardrooms of the same American oil companies that the Truman and Eisenhower administrations had exempted from criminal antitrust prosecution on the grounds that they were "bulwarks against communism," "instruments of U.S. foreign policy," and "the protectors of the interests of the free world." Later, the Department of State obligingly warned all interested American independent oil companies to stay out of Iraq. State even intervened with the Italian and French governments to protest plans by their national oil companies to reach agreement with the Iraqis and permit this oil to be loosed on the world market.

By 1960, Libyan oil was about to reach the production stage. The cartel recognized that, even with Iraq down, disposing of their vast holdings of oil would require reductions in the world price of crude oil. Unilaterally, Exxon announced a cut destined to cost the Middle East producing countries millions in royalties they'd anticipated to operate their governments. The other cartel members' interlocking directorates and banking arrangements obliged them to follow suit.[90] Meanwhile, the oil-producing countries had

---

90   Either through major-oil-company membership on the boards of large banks, with whom their competitors also bank, or by having directors on oil-company boards nominated by their competitors' banks, thirteen of the largest American oil companies have at least one interlocking directorship with a competitor or its bank. This discourages competitive pricing and borrowing practices. The control by the Rockefeller family, its trusts, foundations, and controlled corporations, of four of the largest oil companies was shown on

started to organize in self-defense: they sought advice from Venezuela, which in 1948 had forced the oil companies to split their profits fifty-fifty with the government. I attended the Second Arab Petroleum Congress in Beirut in October 1960, when the oil industry learned that the exporting countries had organized to fight the cartel with one of their own. Controlling as they did 80 percent of the world's oil reserves, the three largest Arab oil-producing states, together with Iran and Venezuela, announced the formation of the Organization of Oil Producing Countries. OPEC was an acronym with which the oil companies and the world would have to reckon from that day onward.

Initially the oil cartel pretended that OPEC didn't exist; later, when Iran and Libya demanded higher prices, the cartel sought to use the organization to negotiate a uniform price for oil worldwide (again retaining John J. McCloy to obtain an antitrust exemption to permit a united front). This didn't work: the oil companies couldn't collaborate among themselves, and soon their governments were unable to back them effectively.

---

the only occasion (in 1938) when the Securities and Exchange Commission was able to trace the family's beneficial interests. The Rockefeller holdings provided effective working control of Exxon, Mobil, Standard of Indiana (now controlled by British Petroleum Company), and SoCal. Furthermore, the Rockefellers' Chase Manhattan Bank's directorships provide entree to the boards of other competing oil companies by the family. Astride all this sat John J. McCloy, who at the same time represented the oil cartel in its requests for antitrust exemptions and has advised every president from Roosevelt to Nixon on the propriety of the Department of Justice granting the exemptions. The importance of all this today is that in order to preserve their control of oil supplies and pricing through these arrangements, the oil companies have avoided the dilution of centralized control that would result from offering new equity participation (issuing new stock) to finance their expansion. Instead, they borrow from their banks and use inflated profits to finance new exploration and production.

For all these reasons, then, the oil companies view the Carter administration's windfall-profits tax as a regrettable but welcome alternative to being forced to comply with the antitrust laws or divest themselves of the horizontally integrated ownership of subsidiaries that enable them to control and profit from each stage of their operations: that is, from exploration through production, transportation, and refining to retail sales.

The companies then devised new accounting methods, accepted whole or partial nationalization, and climbed into bed with the OPEC members in order to salvage every cent of profit they could make. By 1973 the companies were quite willing to create another spurious oil shortage, and they remained (profitably) mute while an outraged world branded the Arabs as the villains. So much for oil-company patriotism, or for anything other than selfish concern about the American economy. As for the role of the companies as "instruments of foreign policy," their diplomacy did produce one result that the avaricious "statesmen" of the industry hadn't envisioned: the formation of OPEC provided the Arab oil-exporting countries with political and economic weapons capable of eventually forcing the United States to make efforts to resolve the Arab-Israeli conflict.

We'd failed to anticipate or deal with the causes of the Iraqi revolution. Worse, the U.S. government's secret involvement in the 1967 Arab-Israeli war and failure to insist that Israel implement the Security Council resolutions that ended it deprived America of diplomatic relations with Iraq, Syria, and Egypt, whose governments became increasingly hostile to U.S. foreign policies. But this was only the beginning of our estrangement from other formerly friendly governments in or near the Middle East area.

Working in Libya, I saw first hand the factors leading to the overthrow of that country's monarchy in 1969 and the emergence of yet another radically anti-Western regime. Oil-company greed, internecine rivalries, and subornation of corruption sowed the seeds of this further loss of American influence. Mustafa Ben Halim, Libya's second prime minister, was the force behind the drafting of the Libyan Petroleum Law of 1955. Wisely anticipating that the independent oil companies would be more inclined than the cartel's members were to discover and produce Libyan oil, Ben Halim did much to ensure that an American group operating under the name of Oasis (Continental, Marathon, and Amarada) received choice concession areas. Suddenly a rich man just after negotiating the first exploration concessions (and a renewal of the USAF air-base agreement at Wheelus Field[91]), Ben Halim prudently elected to allow members of the royal entourage to share in the spoils. When he became Libya's ambassador to France, Ben Halim, his greed still unsated, organized from Paris a near monopoly of all engineering and construction activities ensuing from Libya's by then well established oil discoveries.

Although I'd negotiated Vinnell's Libyan contract, I was faced with a dilemma: we could neither form the requisite Libyan company nor obtain work permits for our people without "special arrangements." When I met Mustafa Ben Halim, I learned how business was done in Libya. The formula was forthright and simple: Ben Halim or one of his brothers shared in the contract, with payments for this "service" to be made (illegally, under Libyan law) in a foreign bank account. In return, Vinnell was entitled to work and bid for new jobs against its (Ben Halim-sponsored) competitors. This arrangement produced "joint ventures" among longstanding antagonists such as the construction industry had never known before.[92] When the time came in 1965 to negotiate new or relinquished oil concessions, however, Ben Halim's brand of graft now seemed relatively "minor league." The cartel had failed to break the independent oil companies' hold in Libya, and new entrants in the concession race offered huge side deals for acreage. Four years later, when Colonel Moammer Gaddafi overthrew the

---

91 I was serving in the Office of the Secretary of Defense when the base agreement was negotiated, and had assigned to me as an assistant a Republican-party fundraising stalwart, who as a reserve officer handled this matter and then became our ambassador to Libya. With Pan American Airway's Washington lobbyist, Sam Pryor, and an independent oil man, Wendell Phillips, Air Force Secretary Harold Talbott became involved, through Ben Halim, in a Libyan oil concession. Later, President Eisenhower removed Talbott from office because of another impropriety.

92 Traditionally sponsored by Senator Lyndon Johnson, the Texas firm of Brown & Root was confident of receiving a major portion of the oil companies' pipeline and related engineering work. CIA director John McCone's old business associate Steve Bechtel also claimed this work. As a "partner" of both firms, Ben Halim resolved this problem by having the two companies join to complete jobs for which they'd normally have been rivals.

monarchy, neither the oil companies nor Washington should have been surprised—but they were, once more!

The shah of Iran, meanwhile, to compete with his Arab neighbors and compensate for new Libyan production, demanded that the cartel members increase Iranian oil exports. Although we built roads into vast new oil fields, the Iranian consortium's agreement nonetheless enabled the cartel's members "legally" to agree not to raise productive output and to continue their control of the world's oil supply and prices. As a sop, the shah was promised that more Iranians would be trained and given management positions in the southern oil fields. Soon the better-educated Iranians began to siphon off graft from the contractors to the oil companies, and a new breed of oil entrepreneurs emerged. At Ahwaz, in the center of the oil fields, I mobilized a contract to train the first Iranians to operate and maintain the equipment on which the exploration and production of oil depended. This also brought me back into contact with the CIA.

John Foster, a colleague from CIC days in Europe, was now deputy chief of the CIA station in Tehran. From him I learned why Vinnell had failed to obtain U.S.-government-financed contracts to construct airports at Tehran, Meshed, and Hamadan. Another forthright and simple formula was the answer: to win these contracts, one had to have as a partner the shah's twin sister, Princess Ashraf, and she'd been committed to another company long before—this was a "personalized" form of U.S. foreign aid!

Nonetheless, there was a way in which Vinnell could become involved in a U.S.-government project, and Foster broached this with me. The vital production, refining, and export aspects of Iran's oil production were largely located in the Province of Khuzistan. Its capital was Ahwaz, where Vinnell's new contract was centered. The population of Khuzistan was, however, more Arab than Persian; the natives considered themselves much closer to their neighbors and relatives in adjacent (then hostile) Iraq than to the people of the north and in Tehran. Of all the CIA personnel at the Tehran station, only Foster feared that one day the Khuzistanis might rebel against the shah's dictatorship and welcome the Iraqis to take over control of Iran's oil.[93] Foster was certain that the CIA could provide technically qualified linguists to augment Vinnell's training program. In this way the Tehran station could monitor signs of dissatisfaction in Khuzistan, since the CIA's principal agents worked in Tehran or near the Russian border. Confiding to Foster my previous relationship with the agency, I agreed to his proposal provided his men only collected intelligence and no political-action operations were allowed. On my next trip to Alhambra I cleared this arrangement with Allen Vinnell, then stood by to see what the CIA's plans would be.

To my amazement, I learned that the CIA now considered me a security risk; further contacts with me by agency personnel were proscribed. More amused than angry, I pressed Foster for an explanation. A half-dozen drinks of White Label were necessary to get him to tell me, and when it came out I had trouble believing what I heard. I "had compromised [my] affiliation" with the CIA during the period I'd served them in the Middle East.[94] Thinking of the station chiefs who'd boasted of having me under their supervision at that time and the lengths to which I'd gone to contrive the official cover the agency's petty jealousies had denied me, I was thoroughly disgusted and told Foster so. More than a decade passed before I ever knowingly contacted a CIA man in the field again.

What value might have accrued through a friendly relationship between me and the agency was obviously something for the CIA to decide. But in at least one matter—that involving the activities of British spy Kim Philby and his defection to Moscow from Beirut the night of January 23, 1963—I could have been a useful source of information.

---

93   Since the flight of the shah into exile, the Islamic government of Ayatullah Ruhollah Khomeini has had problems controlling the Khuzistan province, putting it under the governorship of the area's naval commander in a move to ensure the continued flow of oil on which Iran's economy and stability are dependent.

94   In 1977 I obtained a partial response to my Freedom of Information and Privacy Act requests of the CIA. Most documents were denied to me on grounds of "national security"; the few I received were heavily censored. The genesis of my "security risk" status does appear several times, however. Justin O'Donnell (and later his career CIA colleagues) never forgave my 1958 call to Washington from Istanbul to ask what I should do about Secretary Dulles's instructions and whether I should proceed to Beirut.

My second wife, Mimi, was also close to Sam and Eleanor Brewer. She'd known of Eleanor's budding romance with Philby long before Sam or I ever had a clue (Mimi's first real knowledge that I worked for the CIA will come when she reads this book). After the Philby marriage, Eleanor suggested that she and Kim spend Christmas at our home in Rome. Thus, the man who later surfaced as one of Russia's most damaging spies and his wife took their belated honeymoon in a CIA-subsidized apartment.

Traveling frequently to Tehran during the next few years, I stopped off in Beirut to visit the Philbys on many trips. And in the days after Kim's unexplained disappearance in 1963, I comforted a distraught Eleanor, who confided her fears that Philby had defected (Sam Brewer soon arrived to fetch Annie in fear that Eleanor might also go to Russia). Later, after the Philbys were reunited in Moscow, Eleanor came out to spend the summer with Annie. While staying in our home she called Kim to arrange for her visa to return to Russia, and I waited with her at the airport until the plane on which she left took off.

Dating from the day in 1956 when I accompanied Eleanor to the Saint Georges bar in Beirut, where she first met Philby, I had good reason to have access to him at any time. If anyone in the CIA had cared, I could have tried to find out what the truth of his life really was. The simple fact is that the Russian KGB's most successful penetration of the British SIS and the CIA thus far disclosed was detected only when it was too late, when Philby put his escape plan to use and announced that he'd "come home" to Russia.[95]

---

95   Kim Philby's presence in Russia was not confirmed until seven months after he left Beirut, when the news appeared in the Soviet press. By then, the Western intelligence services had explanations of his defection ready. The British SIS, the CIA, Israel's Mossad, and Germany's Gehlen organization all claimed a part in having discovered Philby's KGB connections. The "official" British leaks imply that Kim was allowed to defect in order to save Britain's government from embarrassment. The CIA was reputed to have had agents swarming the streets of Beirut at the time Philby elected to leave. Somehow they failed to find him, although I'd talked with him a few days earlier and he'd been at home until just a few hours before failing to join Eleanor at dinner with a British-embassy official.

After the Bay of Pigs fiasco, Allen Dulles was eased out and replaced by John McCone. Richard Bissell was another casualty of Cuba (and the U-2 incident), and thus Richard Helms moved up to head the clandestine services. By this time, the old OSS cadre had taken over most of the key CIA positions, and the covert operators soon discerned the prospect of a vast new "empire" in Indochina (where Justin O'Donnell was sent to be a chief of station). But the agency was not yet ready to give up on the Middle East. Walter Snowdon, who'd first briefed me on "stemming the leftist drift in Syria," ended up as chief of station in Damascus. Syria had seceded from Nasser's United Arab Republic, and in the CIA's eyes it was time for yet another attempt to overthrow an independent Syrian government. Caught in the act, Snowdon was expelled from the country. Eugene Trone, with whom I'd worked in the Beirut station, had moved on to Egypt and there fell victim to Nasser's displeasure. Since the early 1950s, Kim Roosevelt and the Cairo station had listed three prominent Egyptian newsmen as key CIA agents: Muhammad Hussanein Heikal and the Amin brothers, Mustafa and Ali. In a game Nasser knew of and willingly tolerated, Roosevelt would first see the Egyptian president, then contact these press "agents" to confirm that what Nasser had said could be reported as pure gospel. Trone carried this relationship too far, however, moving from intelligence collection to a proposal for political action. Plans for Mustafa Amin to bring down Nasser went awry, with the result that Amin was convicted of spying for the CIA and sentenced to life at hard labor. Protected by diplomatic immunity, Trone and his colleague were allowed to leave for "consultation" in Washington.

Only in Jordan, of all the Arab states, did the CIA's influence remain strong—so strong, in fact, that Washington had to recall an ambassador who was unwilling to defer to the custom that the CIA provide America's principal liaison with King Hussein (in return for a multimillion-dollar subsidy of CIA funds for the monarch). No longer was Lebanon available as an area center for the agency's plotting: as a concession to the politicians we'd defeated by subsidizing the 1957 elections, President Shehab had disbanded the country's intelligence-police service. Tom Karamessines proposed Greece as the ideal alternative, which fitted in well with James Angleton's solution: coordinated CIA-Mossad operations in Athens to cover the entire Middle East and Africa.[96] As it had done when the CIA was exposed in a 1960 operation in Singapore, the agency turned over most of its intelligence responsibilities in the Middle East to Israel.

As Allen Dulles told me before my departure for Africa, this shift in U.S. policy toward collaboration with Israel was not without precedent. Early in his administration, President Kennedy had tried to repair American-Arab relations, principally by efforts to induce Nasser to mold his brand of Arab socialism along more constructive lines within Egypt. But the Egyptian president was immersed in external problems: Syria's secession from the UAR; quarrels with the Iraqi Ba'athists; and a full-scale war in Yemen. In 1962 Kennedy approved the first sale to Israel of purely defensive weapons. Later, in a meeting with Foreign Minister Golda Meir, he became the first U.S. president to state publicly that America regarded Israel as its "ally" in the Middle East.

Other, more subtle forms of American assistance to Israel were devised, which I first encountered in bidding on construction projects for Vinnell. With the exception of the petroleum work I'd negotiated for the company, Allen Vinnell concentrated his overseas efforts on U.S.-government-financed projects. Although these were far less profitable than oil-company business, there was a major advantage to contracts financed by the American government: only bona fide U.S. firms were allowed to bid; all materials and equipment for the jobs had to be of American origin, shipped, whenever possible, on U.S.-flag vessels. No exceptions were allowed.

I worked with Vinnell's estimators to bid large contracts of this type in Africa and the Middle East. Five airfields in Ethiopia and

---

96   The press has reported that the CIA subsidized Mossad's African operations with annual payments of $80 million from secret funds. Most African states have cut diplomatic relations with Israel, and Congress is reportedly trying to determine the extent to which Mossad has spent CIA funds in the United States.

secret communications sites in Turkey and Iran were first awarded to our company, then, on Washington's orders, given to a firm that was neither American nor qualified to build the projects. The Reynolds Construction Company, we learned, was actually Israeli, but neither our embassies nor our lawyers were successful in protesting what was obviously an administration decision to ignore the requirements of foreign-aid legislation.[97] Thus deprived of profits on contracts financed with U.S. taxpayers' money, Allen Vinnell decided to stop bidding future aid projects in my area, and I was moved from Rome to take over the company's Washington office.

But that was only the commercial side of bending laws in favor of America's new "ally." The political and military implications were far graver in the end. President Johnson approved the first sale of "offensive" weapons to Israel (a bit difficult to reconcile with U.S. laws limiting the use of American equipment to self-defense). The objective was to provide the Israelis with clear military superiority over the combined Arab armies. Preoccupied with America's military problems in Vietnam, fed up with Nasser and the Arabs in general, Lyndon Johnson wanted no part of Middle East fighting and was persuaded that a strong Israeli army would prevent it. One result was evident. America's decision only whetted the Arabs' appetite for more weapons, and soon a full-scale arms race was on.

Using its own funds, the Saudi Arabian government embarked on a huge new communications-development program that included airports and highways. Vinnell's interest in this work kept me on airplanes, and I spent more time in Middle East hotel rooms than at home in Washington. This led to a new arrangement, under which I represented Vinnell on an annual consulting-fee basis, which left me free to accept retainers from other firms in

---

97   Owned by the powerful quasi-govemmental Histadrut labor organization in Israel, the firm of Solel Boneh retained President Truman's former special counsel Clark Clifford—the man who'd urged U.S. recognition of Israel even *before* the formation of the state was announced—to convert it into an "American firm" to do U.S. foreign-aid work. The corporate charter of the defunct Reynolds Ball Point Pen Company was obtained, and its name was used by Solel Boneh as a front for bids prepared in Haifa and mailed from New York.

the petroleum and engineering industries. With Beirut again my headquarters, I was concluding a large water-desalination contract with the ruler of Abu Dhabi on the morning when the 1967 war erupted. The contract depended on the shipment of materials from Europe, and with the Suez Canal closed again it couldn't be implemented. Nor could I return to Beirut, where the airport was closed and Americans already evacuated (for the first—*and only*—time in recent history, the Department of State voided U.S. passports for travel to the Arab states and Israel). Flying to New York via the Far East, I stayed with Sam Brewer, now a *Times* correspondent at the United Nations. There I listened to the debates that brought about a cease-fire and eventually (five months later) produced the Security Council resolution condemning Israel's acquisition of territory by force, ordering the Israelis to withdraw to their prewar frontiers, and enjoining the Arabs and Israelis to reach a peaceful settlement of their differences.

As the years passed, though, neither Presidents Johnson nor Nixon fulfilled their promises to the Arabs that America would insist that Israel return to its 1967 borders (with minor adjustments) and revoke its annexation of Jerusalem and its environs. Aware of the means by which President Eisenhower had induced Israel to give up territory captured in 1956, I was convinced that more than domestic politics and pressures by the pro-Israel lobby were involved in the reluctance of two disparate U.S. administrations to insist that Israel comply with the Security Council's legally binding orders. From friends I'd made in the CIA, knowledgeable journalists, and news stories that the U.S. government has never refuted, I was able to piece together a pattern pointing to American connivance in Israel's 1967 attack on Egypt. Joining this with what Allen Dulles had told me in 1959, I devised an explanation of why the U.S. government has never been able to demand Israeli compliance with the U.N.'s dictates. Like Britain and France in 1956, America had been party to starting a Middle East war, then lost control of it.

President Johnson's annoyance with Nasser was well known to James Angleton, who was a man searching for vindication after the defection of Kim Philby and eager to show that the CIA's liaison with Israeli intelligence could assist the U.S. in achieving its objectives in the Middle East. Using the same line of reasoning that had motivated Anthony Eden in 1956, Angleton concluded that Gamal Abdul Nasser was responsible for the West's only problem in the area. If Nasser could be eliminated and the Egyptian army defeated without overt major-power assistance, the Arabs would be left with no alternative to making peace with Israel. Another avid subscriber to this thesis was Angleton's Israeli contact in Washington, Minister Counselor Ephraim Evron.[98] The government-to-government channel between these two permitted Angleton to deal with top officials of Israel's ministry of defense and intelligence services, without involving Foreign Minister Abba Eban or the U.S. Departments of State and Defense. Evron arranged that Angleton meet with the heads of Israel's military and intelligence services, former General Moshe Dayan, and key Israeli politicians to discuss the feasibility of an attack on Egypt with the objective of toppling Nasser. The Israelis were interested but unwilling to carry the conversations further without evidence that Angleton was acting with White House approval.

In those days Israel's military encounters were largely with Jordan and Syria. U.S. Ambassador Goldberg, speaking at the U.N., described an Israeli attack on Jordan as far surpassing "the cumulative total of the various acts of terrorism conducted against the frontiers of Israel." Israeli jets ranged into Syria as far as Damascus, and air engagements between the two country's air forces led to ground fighting near the Sea of Galilee. Again friendly with Syria, Nasser reacted with fiery speechmaking, finally threatening to cut Israeli shipping lines to the Gulf of Aqaba. Next, he demanded that the U.N. troops occupying the key position at the Gulf's entrance be withdrawn. To the surprise of the world (and probably Nasser), Secretary General U Thant complied, ordering out the U.N. forces in Sinai that had separated Egyptian and Israeli troops since 1956.[99]

---

98   Evron was appointed Israel's ambassador to the United States in 1979.

99   Before ordering the U.N. Emergency Force from Egyptian soil at Nasser's request, U Thant offered to place the force on the Israeli side of the border—an offer that the Israeli government, exercising its sovereign rights as Egypt had done, had turned down.

Angleton and Evron now had the ammunition they needed to support their theory that Egypt might cut off Israel's "lifeline" unless a preemptive Israeli attack could be mounted.[100] To confuse things further, the Russians passed word to Nasser that Israel was preparing to launch a war against Syria.

In an attempt to defuse the situation, plans were made to send Vice-President Humphrey to meet with Nasser, and Egypt's vice-president readied himself to fly to Washington. Ignoring his own government's discussions with Angleton, Israeli foreign minister Abba Eban visited London, Paris, and Washington to express Israel's fear of war. The Israelis would never attack Egypt unless Nasser attacked first, Eban assured President Johnson (just as Premier Ben-Gurion had promised President Eisenhower when Israeli armed forces were mobilizing to invade Egypt in 1956).

Next, King Hussein placed his troops under Egyptian command, leading Israel to claim that a three-front war was imminent unless it was possible to soothe Nasser's bellicosity. At this point, President Johnson authorized Angleton to inform Evron that the U.S. would prefer Israeli efforts to lessen the tension but would not intervene to stop an attack on Egypt. This American position stipulated that there must be no Israeli military action against Jordan, Syria, or Lebanon.

By then, top officials in the Pentagon had been briefed on the Angleton discussions with Israel. Long concerned over the possibility of Russian intervention in Vietnam, the military now worried about Soviet reactions to renewed fighting in the Middle East. Under orders from the Joint Chiefs of Staff, the U.S.S. *Liberty* was rushed to the waters off Israel's shore to permit this sophisticated communications-monitoring vessel to follow the fighting should the Israelis attack Egypt. The *Liberty* wasn't sent alone, for an

---

100   Israel alleged that access from the Red Sea to the Israeli port of Elat (at the head of the Gulf of Aqaba) constituted that nation's vital "lifeline" and implied that Nasser's threat to block the gulf's entrance would imperil Israel's survival. This charge fails to take into account Israel's nearly 150 miles of Mediterranean coastline and its ports, including Haifa—one of the largest and best in the eastern Mediterranean—from which Palestine was sustained for centuries.

even more important reason. Stationed below her was the Polaris nuclear submarine *Andrew Jackson*, for the Pentagon knew that the CIA had aided Israel in acquiring a nuclear capability.[101] Moreover, the U.S. had provided the Israelis with missiles, to which atomic warheads could be attached. Thus, in case a bogged-down Israeli army decide to use ballistic missiles to win a war against the Soviet-equipped Egyptian army, the U.S. was in a position to warn both Israel and Russia that the introduction of nuclear warfare would produce instantaneous retaliation.

On June 1, 1967, Moshe Dayan, the architect of Israel's 1956 invasion of Egypt, was appointed minister of defense, an almost certain signal that war was imminent. Early on June 5, Israeli jets swept down on Egyptian, Syrian, Jordanian, and Iraqi airfields. Over 400 aircraft were destroyed on the ground and in brief skirmishes over Arab capitals, giving Israel complete air superiority for its ground attacks to take the Suez Canal, the West Bank of Jordan, and the Golan Heights of Syria. Message intercepts by the *Liberty* made it clear that Israel had never intended to limit its attack to Egypt. Furthermore, we learned that the Israelis were themselves intercepting communications among the Arab leaders. The Israelis then retransmitted "doctored" texts to encourage Jordan and Syria to commit their armies in the erroneous belief that Nasser's army had repelled the Israeli invaders. To destroy this incriminating evidence, Moshe Dayan ordered his jets and torpedo boats to destroy the *Liberty* immediately. Disabled in international waters, the American ship remained afloat to carry 34 dead and 171 wounded (70 percent of its crew) into the harbor at Malta.

As for the attack on the defenseless *Liberty*, the Israeli government claimed that the converted freighter had been mistaken for an Egyptian warship. A U.S. naval board of inquiry found that the daylight attack had been unprovoked and deliberate. Then the U.S. government shrouded the entire *Liberty* matter in secrecy under a cloak of "national security" considerations, where it remains even now. Individual claims of compensation for the ship's dead and

---

101　See Anthony Pearson, *Conspiracy of Silence* (London: Quartet Books, 1978).

wounded were paid by the U.S. government, supposedly on behalf of Israel. Even moves by Congress to stop all aid to Israel until $7 million in compensation for the *Liberty* was paid succumbed to White House and Department of State pressure. Why? Defense Minister Dayan had stated his government's position bluntly: unless the United States wished the Russians and Arabs to learn of joint CIA-Mossad covert operations in the Middle East and of Angleton's discussions before the 1967 fighting started, the questions of the lost American ship and how the war originated should be dropped. That ended the U.S. protestations!

All of this again illustrated the price America has paid for engaging in covert operations with other intelligence services. Although we'd not been exposed in trying to overthrow the Syrian government in 1956, Israel's concurrent invasion of Egypt (in concert with Britain and France) had left the United States unable to come to Hungary's aid when the Russian invasion began. A potential revolt of the countries behind the "iron curtain" was crushed. We'd condemned our NATO allies for starting this war, but in the end the United States couldn't abandon them or come to the aid of the people Foster Dulles and the CIA had promised liberation from Soviet control.

Then in 1967 we'd closed our eyes while Israel started a war and the U.S. remained impotent to stop its spread to Jordan and Syria. Also crippling America's hand was the agreement of which Allen Dulles had told me in 1959: the CIA's collaboration with Mossad left us exposed to blackmail and established Israel as the first nuclear power in the Middle East. Nearly 425,000 Palestinians had been driven from their homes and forced to live with the refugees of the 1948 war.

By then a new generation of Palestinians had emerged. Born of refugee parents and generally better-educated than their fathers, they'd grown impatient with the oratory of Arab politicians vowing to reclaim Palestine. Israel's denunciation of the 1949 armistice agreements and annexation of Jerusalem provoked a coalescence of Palestinians determined to act on their own behalf. In July 1968, the Palestinian National Covenant was adopted. It pledged to recover for the former owners all territory occupied by Israel since 1947 and to expel by force all Jews who had immigrated to Palestine since that year. Now counterpoised—and seemingly impossible to reconcile—were the Palestinians' claim to all of Britain's World War I mandate as a national homeland and the Israeli-Zionist Law of Return and Covenant, offering a homeland and citizenship to all the world's Jewry.

Between 1969 and 1973 Secretary of State William Rogers doggedly pursued a course of traveling personal diplomacy, attempting to negotiate interim agreements between Israel and its neighbors based on the 1967 Security Council resolution. Each attempt failed when Israel adamantly refused to associate the return of conquered territory with the rights of the Palestinian refugees. There was no such thing as a Palestinian, Premier Golda Meir asserted[102]: the refugees should live in Jordan or be absorbed by the other Arab countries. Meanwhile, militant Palestinians escalated terrorist attacks against Israel and its citizens and property abroad, which produced increasingly ruthless Israeli attacks on Palestinian commandos as well as on the states and civilians who offered them haven.

President Nixon's national-security adviser, Henry Kissinger, viewed the Middle East's problems as irritating distractions to his press-heralded effort to end the Vietnam war and to improve U.S. relations with Russia and China. Persuaded that a heavily armed Israel was the key to Middle East stability, Nixon replaced Rogers with Kissinger as secretary of state, and the U.S. peace offensive was allowed to die. Once more the world's strongest power employed weapons shipments as an alternative to the tough diplomacy required to prevent an outbreak of hostilities. America's position toward the Middle East had always involved domestic political considerations, and by then the exposure of the Watergate scandal had crippled the Nixon administration. The CIA, under Richard Helms, was preoccupied with the Watergate cover-up and with (falsely) denying its own involvement.

---

102   An odd statement for a woman who had once traveled on a Palestinian passport.

Just then, Anwar Sadat (who'd taken over after Nasser's death in 1970) surprised Kissinger and the CIA by ordering 18,000 Soviet military and civilian advisers to leave Egypt. Still in the throes of the Watergate Scandal, Washington was again caught off balance when Sadat launched (with Syria) his 1973 attack to reclaim territory captured by Israel in 1967. King Faisal of Saudi Arabia had warned Aramco's president that this war was imminent and cautioned that an oil boycott should be expected if the United States came to Israel's aid. The CIA's sources discounted the king's prediction, but the oil cartel was more perceptive than the American government was. Since the beginning of 1972 the oil companies had sharply increased Middle East oil production in anticipation that an embargo in that area would justify higher prices. The massive airlift of U.S. military equipment to enable Israel to retain its occupied territory resulted in an Arab boycott of petroleum shipments to the United States and its armed forces overseas. It also left NATO incapable of defending Western Europe, and the U.S. unable to fight a global war by conventional means.[103]

Finally, Henry Kissinger considered the Middle East ready for his diplomatic talents. He then picked up the same interim-settlement approach he'd caused Secretary Rogers to abandon (leaving the question of the rights of the Palestinians to be discussed later). And, as in the early days of the Eisenhower administration, Egypt, and CIA channels of communications to its president, became the keystone of American diplomacy with the Arabs. We'd come full circle, back to the 1954 days of my first affiliation with the CIA.

---

103   Later, when the chairman of the Joint Chiefs of Staff stated publicly that U.S. military assistance to Israel had jeopardized America's defense capabilities, he was accused in the press of being anti-Semitic and reprimanded by President Ford for his frankness.

CHAPTER TWENTY-NINE

DENOUEMENT IN LEBANON 1975

Though the Lebanese armed forces had not participated in the Arab-Israeli wars, the indirect effects of this fighting severely damaged the country's economic and political stability. The need to evacuate families in times of trouble led many foreign firms to abandon Beirut as a regional commercial center. When Kuwait made huge withdrawals from Lebanon's Intra Bank (to induce the country to accept more Palestinian refugees) the bank failed, and the collapse of the Lebanese economy was barely forestalled.

Nasser then summoned the commander of the Lebanese armed forces to Cairo to meet with PLO chief Yasser Arafat. There Lebanon reluctantly agreed that Palestinian commandos might operate in the southern Arkoub district, with direct access to Syria (the source of their supplies and training) and Israel. King Hussein's ban on commando raids from Jordan into Israel led to a PLO attempt to unseat the monarch. When this failed, the Palestinian guerillas fled to Lebanon. By now over 400,000 refugees lived in that country. Not enough of them were Christians, however, to avoid their fragmenting Lebanon's delicate religious balance. Worse, the political feuds stemming from America's meddling in Lebanese internal affairs during the late 1950s left a series of increasingly weak central governments reliant on an army that had never been able to control the country, let alone keep the Palestinians in their assigned areas.

During these troubled times, my business activities expanded to Southeast Asia and the North Sea area, where new offshore oil fields had been discovered. The jet age made round-the-world travel commonplace, and I "commuted" to Beirut from Singapore, Houston, and London.

In 1970 I flew into Beirut unaware that the presidential election was to be held in a few days. The American ambassador had gone off to Jordan (to give the impression that the United States was not interested in the election.) Still, I was greeted at the Hotel Saint Georges as if the CIA had sent me to endorse former president Chamoun's intimation that he would seek election to save Lebanon. As it turned out, Chamoun was only testing his support (which proved to be strong among Moslems as well as Christians), and he withdrew at the last moment. By a single vote, Suleiman Franjieh, the semiliterate warlord whose family had long dominated northern Lebanon through corruption, became the new chief of state.

As time passed, Lebanon became a battlefield in a senselessly escalating war that had no international status. The country's sovereign territory was repeatedly invaded (including attacks on midtown Beirut and aircraft at its international airport) by Israel's commandos, army, and air force, seeking to eliminate the Palestinian commandos who'd become refugees as a result of earlier Israeli conquests. These raids were not directed against Lebanon or its innocent civilian casualties, the Israelis contended, but rather against the "nonexistent Palestinian people" whom Israel refused to recognize. Nor could the tiny Lebanese army repulse the far superior Israeli forces that breached at will the frontier between the two countries: the border defined in the 1949 armistice agreement no longer existed, Israel claimed. The day after 3,000 Israeli troops, led by tanks and covered by jet aircraft, moved fifteen miles into Lebanon, the PLO complied with the Lebanese government's orders to evacuate all commando bases in the south of the country. Israel's air force then bombed targets deep inside Lebanon, some of these north of Beirut. The concepts of "hot pursuit" and retaliation for provocations were abandoned by Israel: former chief of staff Chaim Herzog pledged that the Palestinian guerillas would be attacked wherever they were in Lebanon and Syria. And by now there were at least ten separate Palestinian commando and terrorist organizations operating without central control, they often fought among themselves.

The Arab-Israeli wars of 1956, 1967, and 1973 had commanded the world's attention, but the killing and destruction in Lebanon became merely common fare for newspaper readers. The Security Council's repeated condemnations of attacks against Lebanon were rejected and ignored by Israel; the international organization was now branded as anti-Israeli by the very state beholden to the U.N. for its existence. The Palestinian guerillas' acts of international terrorism were also condemned in Security Council resolutions, which had little effect on the activities of the Palestinians, now intent on drawing the world's attention to a people who had no recognized status. "Aggression" and "terrorism" were the operative words in these resolutions, but innocent civilians were the victims in both cases. The bombs and bullets of the Palestinians struck down women and children who had nothing to do with making war. So too did the rockets and antipersonnel bombs launched from Israeli jets, tanks, and artillery pieces. As this went on, Henry Kissinger was negotiating the future status of a strip of Egyptian desert 225 miles south of Lebanon's border. It seemed a strange priority: there was no fighting there. Nor were there any Palestinian refugees: their fate, and that of Lebanon, would be dealt with later in Kissinger's approach to Middle East peace.

Since 1969 Alfred L. ("Roy") Atherton, Jr. (with whom I'd served in the embassy in Damascus), had been the Department of State's key adviser on Arab-Israeli matters. We'd met again in 1972, when I sought information concerning the possibilities of a peace settlement between Israel and Jordan that would have facilitated a business venture in which I was then engaged. From Atherton I learned that Secretary Rogers had abandoned his efforts to induce Israel to return to its 1967 borders. Instead, King Hussein (the beneficiary of multimillion-dollar CIA subsidies) had received President Nixon's support for a plan under which

Israeli-occupied Jordan would become part of a United Arab Kingdom, with Hussein as its monarch and East Jerusalem as its capital. Although this concept would have provided a home and nationality for the Palestinians, they, the Arab states, and Israel all rejected King Hussein's plan. Claiming that no single Arab leader had the right to negotiate with Israel or speak on behalf of the Palestinians, Egyptian President Sadat angrily severed diplomatic relations with Jordan (and they were not resumed until a year and a half later).

When I next saw Atherton, in 1974, he was being referred to frequently by Secretary of State Kissinger as "my Mr. Middle East." Promoted to assistant secretary of state for the area, Atherton accompanied Kissinger on his worldwide travels to enable the secretary personally to make every decision affecting his new step-by-step approach to a Middle East peace settlement.[104] Meeting with Atherton in Washington, I was encouraged by the confidence he expressed in the prospects for a comprehensive peace agreement between the Arabs and Israel. The Russians had been brought into the negotiating process again at the U.N.-sponsored Geneva conference, and there were now provisions for the Palestinians to have a voice in determining their own future. So far, Israel, backed by its powerful lobby in the United States, had impeded progress at Geneva by opposing a role for the Palestinians, but it now seemed possible to overcome this obstacle. President Nixon had resigned, and President Ford, free of personal involvement in the Watergate scandal, could now deal with the domestic political aspects of forcing Israel to relinquish its conquered territories and recognize

---

104   Atherton was continued in this key position by the Carter administration, which extended his service as principal Middle East adviser to three secretaries of state. During the era of the Carter Camp David summit negotiations, Atherton acted as ambassador-at-large to the Middle East, until he was appointed ambassador to Egypt and replaced by "super-ambassador" Robert Strauss (who reported directly to President Carter). The continuity of U.S. policy afforded by Atherton's familiarity with the arguments by which both the Arabs and Israelis had forestalled peace suffered as a result. But by then, both Sadat and Begin dealt directly with Carter, and the Department of State's role in the negotiations was more symbolic than practical.

the PLO (as spokesman for the Palestinians) in the interests of world peace.

I'd then been hired by one of America's largest refinery and petrochemical-engineering and construction firms to become its representative resident in the Middle East. My company was involved in a huge project contemplating a pipeline from the Gulf of Suez to Damietta, on Egypt's Mediterranean coast, where a large refinery would be constructed. This concept was a key element of Henry Kissinger's plan for inducing Israel to give up the Sinai (Abu Rudeis) and Gulf of Suez oil fields it had captured in 1967. To be financed by a consortium of American and Arab banks, the pipeline-refinery project would be self-liquidating, enabling the United States to demand Israeli withdrawal from the Egyptian oil fields without offering the huge grants of American aid that had been made in return for previous Israeli concessions. By allowing oil destined for Israel to flow through the interior of Egypt, President Sadat would be breaking ranks with the other Arab states' oil boycott of Israel, and the possibility of this costing Sadat the Saudi Arabian financing that supported the Egyptian economy was what I'd come to discuss with Roy Atherton. If King Faisal objected to the pipeline-refinery project, Kissinger's peace offensive would be impaired, and my company would be wasting time and money doing the engineering work that the banks required for funding.

At this point another familiar name from my past appeared as the key to this project: that of Kamal Adham, the brother of King Faisal's (only) wife, who had been my neighbor in Beirut for years. As one of the king's closest advisers and as head of Saudi Arabia's intelligence organizations, Adham was, Atherton confided, the man who had conveyed to Kissinger and the shah of Iran Saudi Arabia's agreement to allow Israel's oil requirements to be supplied through the proposed pipeline and refinery. In fact, I was told, Faisal had given tacit approval to a separate peace settlement between Israel and Egypt as a first step to a comprehensive Arab-Israeli peace settlement. Delighted to learn of these prospects, I prepared to resume permanent residence in the Middle East in the hope that this would coincide with the start of the era of peace there for which the world had waited so long.

My company's plans called for me to spend much of my time in Saudi Arabia, and I now felt that fate had always intended that I end up in a position similar to the one Sam Kopper and Aramco had offered me twenty years earlier (in 1955). In the meantime, Saudi Arabia had undergone a remarkable change. A huge ($40 billion) U.S.-engineered development program was directing oil revenues into transforming the desert kingdom from the conditions of its ancient past to being a bustling modern society. Young Saudi government engineers, holding advanced degrees earned abroad, were courted by major-oil-company presidents with offers to build and finance refineries and petrochemical complexes for processing the oil whose ownership by Saudi Arabia was no longer questioned. All of this portended dramatic changes in the world's economic and marketing systems. To bolster the sagging dollar, Saudi Arabia, Iran, and other oil-exporting states were now large holders of U.S. Treasury offerings—partners, financially, in the future of the domestic economy of the United States. That it had taken the 1973 war to force us to face up to our dependence on the Middle East was clear evidence of America's failure in this area. For the first time, I was sure that the U.S. government could obtain public support for any measures necessary to settle the Arab-Israeli conflict. Our delay in dealing with this issue had produced other problems, however: the fall of the regimes we'd built up as bulwarks against communism illustrated that neither arms sales nor industrialization projects alone could ensure the survival of governments that supported the West's policies despite public sentiment favoring neutrality in conflicts between the superpowers.

I'd be able to rely on a man who'd advised me in the past to help me understand the changes in Saudi Arabia. Raymond Close, the young case officer with whom I'd served in Beirut, was now the CIA's chief of station—working with Kamal Adham to develop a Saudi Arabian intelligence service to protect the monarchy. I wrote Close to tell him that I looked forward to joining him and informed him of my company's plans.[105]

Then, as I had done in 1950, I packed and shipped ahead everything I owned. There would be no shipwreck to disrupt my plans this time: my effects and I were traveling by air. At the age of fifty-six I was returning to the Middle East to stay.

On the night of March 21, 1975, my plane touched down at Beirut International airport. The newspapers I read after landing suggested just how fateful the next twenty-four hours might be. Since early March, Henry Kissinger and his airborne State Department had shuttled between Israel, Egypt, and Saudi Arabia in quest of another interim settlement to replace the 1974 disengagement agreement that the secretary of state had negotiated to end the Egyptian-Israeli war. Even as I landed in Lebanon, Kissinger's plane was being readied for a flight from Aswan, Egypt, to Jerusalem, where the fate of America's year of "shuttle diplomacy" would be decided. The previous day the secretary of state had left Riyadh with King Faisal's promise of support for the U.S. peace initiative. Then, from Anwar Sadat, Kissinger had wrested final concessions, including Egypt's agreement to the state of "nonbelligerency" upon which Israel's agreement to further withdrawals from Sinai and relinquishing of the oil fields had been conditioned. The moment of truth would start as the sun was setting to end the Jewish sabbath on March 22: if the Israelis really wanted peace, this was their chance to prove it.

My next days were filled with reunions with old friends I'd not seen for years. Driving around traffic-clogged Beirut, I selected an office in one of the new skyscrapers dotting the city's horizon and visited the new hotels erected to accommodate the commercial

---

105 After six years as chief of station, Close "retired" from the CIA in 1977 to become a business partner of Kamal Adham and to expand Saudi Arabia's foreign-intelligence service—a development the U.S. government described as "unusual" but satisfactory to both countries. The letter I wrote to Close was immediately cabled to CIA headquarters and I've never received a reply. In the copy I obtained through the Freedom of Information Act, Close's comments were deleted for "national security" reasons.

and tourist trade that the prosperity of peacetime would bring. The press reported that the American secretary of state had left Jerusalem abruptly without issuing a communiqué. I was too busy to pay this much heed. Surely, I assumed, Kissinger had gone back to Washington to clear with the president and Congress the terms of the final agreement before making them public.

The Saint Georges was the scene of my daily luncheon meetings. As always, the press corps gathered at the bar for drinks. There I first faced the shock of reality: an eerie silence filled the room as we heard the news flash announcing King Faisal's assassination. *Time's* Abu Said took me outside to sit on the terrace. "It's all over, Bill," he said; "the Palestinians have given up on Kissinger, and with this news they'll take matters into their own hands." I refused to admit that my hopes for peace had been shattered. I even placed a bet with my Jordanian friend that the information with which Roy Atherton had cheered me was more reliable than the pessimistic forecasts Abu Said received from his Palestinian contacts. Then came the news that Kissinger had admitted the failure of his step-by-step diplomacy. This development actually encouraged me: instead of secret deals and concessions being made in order to obtain an interim agreement between Israel and Egypt, the Geneva conference would be reopened and the entire Arab-Israeli problem (including that of the Palestinians) discussed under the world's scrutiny.

Two days later, I was advised in a telex message from California that my job had been terminated. This made no difference in my plans for a new and challenging project. Thousands of Americans were needed to execute the huge new development projects planned for the Middle East, and only by providing new boarding schools to educate dependents could qualified engineers and technicians be induced to leave the United States. For months I'd been making contacts with educators to confirm the feasibility of providing such a facility. Now on my own, I found Arab backers willing to finance the construction, staffing, and operation of a combined secondary school and junior college to be situated in Lebanon. Chosing a suitable location was my next task.

■ ■ ■

We were just abeam Juniyah Bay when Sheikh Fuad al-Khazen called me to the bridge of his yacht. His hand pointed high to the east at the domed Maronite patriarchy, then swept northward along Mount Lebanon. There, Sheikh Fuad told me, his people had lived for centuries in the protection of the rocky heights, beneath the snow-covered ridges that gave Lebanon its name—"the land of white milk." Later, anchored at the ancient port of Byblos, we enjoyed a typical Lebanese Easter Sunday luncheon and spoke of the Bekaa Valley, the fertile land beyond Mount Lebanon. Politics and smuggling had spoiled the valley, my host lamented; in addition, it was too close to the trouble brewing in Syria to risk educating children there. In Sheikh Fuad's opinion, there could be no better place for a new boarding school than on Mount Lebanon. We'd go there in a few days, he promised, to see the patriarch and arrange for a long-term lease of the land.

The next week, over dinner at their home in the mountains, Charles and Eva Malik listened intently to my description of the land I'd arranged and the boarding school I'd secured the funds to finance. Indeed, the former foreign minister said, he'd be happy to lend his name as an international statesman to sponsor the school; as an educator, he would help recruit the faculty, even become its director if that would help it get started. "Of course you've discussed this with Camille Chamoun," Malik said as we finished. I hadn't, I admitted. I was reluctant to bother the former president until my plans were more advanced. Impatient, Charles insisted that he and Eva accompany me down the hills to the Hotel Phoenicia: there, where I was staying, Chamoun's followers were honoring him at a banquet.

As we drove down to the brilliantly illuminated city, the former international statesman expressed his reservations about Henry Kissinger's step-by-step peace negotiations: in Malik's eyes, the secretary of state had sacrificed America's bargaining leverage by agreeing to massive arms shipments to Israel in return for nothing more than its agreement to return a small fraction of occupied Sinai. Unless we returned to Geneva, where Russia could influence the Syrians and the Palestinians could be represented, there would be no comprehensive or lasting peace settlement, according to Malik.

Also, he reminded me, as a result of the Egyptian-Israeli agreement, the combined Arab states had authorized the PLO to speak for all the refugees, and the U.N. had recognized the PLO's status. This would not have happened in October 1974 if Kissinger had kept America's promise to Syria and Jordan that Israel would be made to return their territory; now Lebanon was forced to play host within its own borders to a new, quasi-sovereign entity, he concluded.

When we reached the podium in the banquet hall the guest of honor greeted us warmly. In response to Malik's whispered question the former president said, "Tomorrow's Sunday, Bill; be at my rue Verdun office at five in the afternoon and I'll be waiting."

Chamoun never arrived. There was not a sign of activity around the street-level office, but I waited for an hour just in case he was delayed. When Charles Malik called for a report of the meeting, he was dismayed to learn that I'd missed the former president and said that he'd make another appointment. A return call set this for Tuesday, April 8, 1975.

Armed men outside the building and in its hallways eyed me suspiciously as I was ushered into Camille Nimr Chamoun's private office. With him was his son Dory, now a political understudy. While shaking hands I said I regretted having missed connections on Sunday; this evoked no comment. I then proudly described my plan to build a school to help repay Lebanon for the lessons it had taught me. The seventy-five-year-old statesman appeared preoccupied while I talked and during the long pause that followed while I awaited his reactions.

"You may have learned something, but your government certainly hasn't," was his first comment. "Remember the rebels your ambassador objected to my disarming while the marines were here in 1958? Well, they're still out there roaming the country as if they owned it, and they damn near do. Then one of my spineless successors let Nasser talk him into accepting the Palestinians Israel chased out in the 1967 war. They're now armed and dictating government policy to a corrupt and weak president: the same man I refused to have in parliament in 1957.

"There'll be trouble, Bill, and I suggest that you put off your school project for a while," he concluded. All of this sounded ominous, all too reminiscent of the warnings I'd heard in the past, but because Chamoun offered no further details, I wasn't sure what kind of trouble he meant. Of one thing I was certain, however: this silver-haired man whose middle name meant "tiger" knew every pulse of Lebanon's heart, and if there was to be trouble, he'd be in the thick of it.

As I drove down the Corniche to my hotel, I looked up to the top-floor American embassy office in which I'd once prepared cables to warn Washington of impending trouble. Tempted, briefly, to barge in and report what I'd heard, I dismissed the idea as being no longer practical. Now led by yet another ambassador transferred from Indochina, the embassy staff would think of me as just one more I-told-you-so Arabist crying wolf.

Five days later (Sunday, April 13, 1975), as I prepared to join friends for dinner at the Phoenicia's rooftop restaurant, a call came from my old friend Abu Said in *Time's* office just across the street. There had been trouble in town, he warned me, and I should not venture out of the hotel: a busload of Palestinians had been shot up by Christian-led militiamen; vengeful fighting was sure to follow. Just before midnight, as we tarried over drinks and viewed the harbor, the sky was illuminated by rockets that arced from the mountains toward the city and its port. Next, the staccato chatter of automatic weapons rose from the street below. Back on my balcony, now facing the southeast, I could look to the mountains from which the salvos of rockets were being launched. This was the Druse stronghold, scene of some of 1958's worst fighting, although then the artillery shells had been exchanged between mountain outposts without damage to the city, and the sporadic firing on the streets had come from rifles and pistols. I sat up all night, and with the dawn came my awakening to the implications of my conversations with Camille Chamoun, Charles Malik, and Abu Said.

Fearing that the Palestinians might soon usurp control from Lebanon's weak government and operate with impunity throughout the country, the leaders of the private militias had decided to stage a showdown. Clearly, Chamoun and his fellow militia commanders had concluded that the PLO must be brought under control and kept away from Israel's borders, lest Lebanon become, for the first time, a major battlefield in a full-fledged Arab-Israeli war. The failure of Kissinger's step-by-step diplomacy had raised the storm flag that triggered the fighting raging around me. Now eager to divert attention from its government's refusal to withdraw from Sinai, Israel might be expected to use the stepped-up terrorism by the frustrated Palestinians as justification for using American-supplied military equipment to launch large-scale attacks on PLO bases throughout Lebanon. Worse, Israel might even invade the country to dramatize its constant demands for "secure and defensible borders," or on the pretext of saving Lebanon's Christians. Chamoun had often mentioned his fears that the Israelis wanted a partitioned Lebanon, where Christians shared with the Jews their isolation in a sea of Moslems.

As time passed, the Hotel Phoenicia became untenable. Although I was tempted by the Maliks' pleas that I join them in the safety of the mountains, I moved up the hill to the new Holiday Inn. Abu Said telephoned frequently to report on the status of the fighting and to advise when it was safe to be on the streets. The periods of calm became less frequent, but, increasingly restless, I discovered that a dash through two hotel garages and down a short street would enable me to reach the Saint Georges with little risk of exposure to the firing. Most of the hotel's guests had departed, but a few friends still congregated to exchange rumors of a cease-fire and to speculate about the future.

An unexpected arrival was Joe Alex Morris, Jr., of the *Los Angeles Times*. We'd been friends since the mid-1950s, and as we reminisced I complained of the tendency of foreign correspondents to portray the Lebanese fighting as a simple religious feud and to overlook the fact that both Christians and Moslems served in the militias now fighting to bring the Palestinian guerillas under control.[106] Agreeing, Morris pointed out that Lebanon was

---

106   Morris continued to report on the Lebanese revolution until be became the first American press casualty of the 1979 Iranian revolution. He was shot and died while covering the events following one of the CIA's major failures: not predicting the overthrow of the shah of Iran.

now plagued with additional refugees from Iraq. These were the Kurds, who'd been left to the "mercy" of the Iraqi army after the U.S. withdrew from the Nixon-Kissinger agreement with the shah of Iran for providing (CIA) arms for a Kurdish revolt against the Baghdad government. This, I knew, had been Archie Roosevelt's CIA operation.

One evening I encountered Howard Page, Exxon's "oil statesman," sitting alone in the Saint Georges barroom. By then retired, Page had been caught in Beirut while attending the annual meeting of the American University board of regents, which he headed. An opportunity I'd long sought had finally arrived, and I gladly accepted Page's invitation to join him. After referring to my 1956 presidential mission to King Saud, I asked, "Howard, how could you have conned Eisenhower and Foster Dulles into believing that we could threaten Saudi Arabia by alleging that the West would stop using Arab oil and revert to nuclear energy unless the Suez Canal was opened?" A sheepish grin and a shrug of his shoulders preceded his reply: "Bill, it would have been a great ploy if the Saudis had used our warning to frighten Nasser." Unable to do more than shake my head, I drank up and departed. This was the man who'd long been accepted by the U.S. government as a leading expert on energy and Arab politics. Still, he seemed unable to understand that our being made to look like fools before the future King Faisal might have had something to do with creating the doubts that many Arab leaders now had about America's wisdom, power, and integrity.

Just how valuable Saudi Arabia considered its oil resources became apparent during a conversation I struck up with a stranger at the Holiday Inn a few days later. My interest was sparked by hearing a man at the bar boast loudly that he represented the largest American contractor in Saudi Arabia—the Vinnell Corporation. After identifying myself as a former vice-president of the company, I was told that under a contract with the Saudi government, Vinnell had hired a retired U.S. general and recruited Vietnam veterans to form an army of mercenaries charged with guarding the kingdom's oil-production facilities against sabotage and foreign attack. Moreover, the man was quite open in bragging that the Vinnell Corporation had secured the contract by paying a multimillion-dollar fee to a Saudi agent. This shocked me. I'd parted with Allen Vinnell (who died in 1970) over the issue of how to bid for the huge road- and airport-construction jobs in Saudi Arabia: a joint venture I'd arranged with the country's largest contractor had been spurned by Vinnell as "going native." As for paying a "fee" to buy a contract, I'd been criticized for years after making the oil-company-required arrangement with Ben Halim's brother in Libya to enable Vinnell to work in that country. Remembering how corruption had brought down the Libyan royal family, I wondered how long it would be before the rulers of other newly rich oil-producing states suffered a similar fate.

Large-scale corruption was another symptom of Lebanon's illness. Never immune to accepting payoffs to facilitate commercial transactions, Lebanese businessmen considered bribes an operating cost. But the huge "agent's fees" and payments to government officials flowing from the industrialization projects underway in Saudi Arabia, Iran, and the United Arab Emirates of the Persian Gulf had increased the greediness of President Franjieh who had now purchased "respectability" and had carried corruption to the top level of the Lebanese government. I'd visited Beirut six months earlier to investigate a proposed oil-refinery project. In no time I learned that the key to success was a million-dollar payment to Franjieh's son, Tony. I was told that the president, with just over a year remaining in his term, was determined to ensure that the members of his family became millionaires before he left office. But when fighting broke out and Lebanon desperately needed leadership, President Franjieh had first taken "sick," then retreated to the countryside. Stubborn or not, Camille Chamoun, the man who'd refused to leave his midtown palace during the 1958 revolution, now led the most effective fighting force endeavoring to restore law and order to the Lebanese republic.

There was no doubt that a revolution now engulfed Lebanon. The new skyscraper office buildings had been taken over for purposes of directing fire from the city's outskirts, and gun battles crept closer to the Holiday Inn, as a contest for the hotel district and the nearby port area began. It was not until loud explosions below a crimson sky brought me to my balcony to watch Beirut's port go up in flames that emotion finally overwhelmed me. My thoughts went back twenty-five years to the day I'd first entered Lebanon's peaceful harbor, and I sat up all night reviewing what had gone wrong since then: the many lost opportunities to arrange an Arab-Israeli peace settlement; the defense alliances and government leaders we'd concentrated on building up instead; and our covert intervention in the internal affairs of Middle Eastern countries. I was now in the midst of a disintegrating country where hundreds of people were dying daily as a result of what my own government had done or had *not* done, and I realized that my personal sense of guilt had deluded me into hoping that some miracle wrought by Henry Kissinger would bring peace to the Middle East.

Ignoring all the lessons I'd learned in the past, I—like most Americans—had been mesmerized by the illusion that America could barter a small strip of Egyptian desert for billions of dollars worth of aid and sophisticated weapons for Israel, and start the Middle East on the road to a lasting peace. But there was no fighting in Sinai—in Jordan, Syria, or Israel either—and I couldn't believe that the most powerful nation in the world would sit idly by while Lebanon burned to ashes. Landing troops (as we'd done in 1958) was obviously no longer possible, but what better reason than the prospective destruction of Lebanon could exist for reconvening the Geneva conference and joining with Russia to settle once and for all the Arab-Israeli borders and the question of a homeland for the Palestinians? Israel couldn't survive without American aid and political support; Egypt was now dependent upon Saudi Arabia and America for economic survival; Jordan didn't really have any options if the U.S. and Saudi governments endorsed a peace treaty; and the Russians would be faced with the choice of bringing the Syrians into line or admitting that the Soviet Union preferred instability in the Middle East. As for Libya, Iraq, Algeria, and the other militantly antipeace states that had no common borders with Israel, let them scream their lungs out in protest. With the future of the Palestinians settled, they'd be forced to pay attention to the problems of their own countries. I didn't know it then, but Kissinger and his advisers were considering this at that very moment as America's first option.

Then, on April 30, 1975, President Ford announced our evacuation in defeat from Vietnam. With this added to the Watergate scandal and the threat of New York City's bankruptcy, it seemed clear that Henry Kissinger's diplomacy had been as much a media spectacular to divert the world's attention from America's other problems as it had been a reasoned search for peace. Motivated initially by the energy and economic crises caused by the 1973 war, Kissinger's piece-by-piece tactics constituted no overall strategy and had been used always in the hope that the Palestinians might somehow disappear.

The secretary of state admitted to Roy Atherton that it had been a major blunder to rescue Israel with massive military-aid shipments without first extracting a promise that the Israelis would accept a U.S.-guaranteed peace settlement with the Arabs in return. He acknowledged too that strengthening Israel so that it would not have to negotiate from a position of weakness had brought on the breakdown of the March 1975 negotiations: by then the Israelis bluntly told Kissinger that they were strong enough to refuse to make peace with the Arabs except on terms completely acceptable to Israel (and these excluded any homeland for the Palestinians).

But assuming that Henry Kissinger might have profited from his errors provided me little comfort when I thought back to a conversation I'd had in Washington a few months earlier with a man who'd been a special assistant and close confidant to Presidents Eisenhower and Nixon. When I had asked him whether President Ford would support Secretary Kissinger or Treasury Secretary William Simon in a dispute over Saudi Arabia's industrial-development program, he told me that the President would support Kissinger in anything he wished to do. Then came the shocker: I was asked to understand that Ford was barely aware that he'd moved from being House minority leader to occupying the vice-presidency, and I was warned that it would take the President at least another six months to get used to the Oval Office. With such a gap in leadership, and U.S. foreign policy being improvised by a secretary of state displaying every sign of megalomania, I saw little hope for progress toward peace in Lebanon or the Middle East as a whole. Both Ford and Kissinger had Congress to contend with: elections were coming up, and this inevitably brought in the domestic political considerations affecting any matters relating to the Middle East. Just to be certain that our legislators remembered this and that the American public would not forget Israel's "beleagueread peril," a stream of Israeli spokesmen (Dayan, Eban, Allon, and others) descended on Washington and appeared on national television.

During May 1975, the Israeli lobby mobilized three-quarters of the U.S. Senate to sign a letter to President Ford demanding that Israel be given "defensible" frontiers and massive quantities of military and economic aid. America's "only democratic ally in the Middle East" is what these perceptive (electioneering) senators called this small state upon which the United States supposedly should depend to "keep communism out of the area." I'd heard this often and I still wondered how an Israel desperate for "defensible" frontiers to protect against the dissension-torn and militarily inferior Arabs could be expected to combat the Soviet air force or navy. But President Ford, who was then considering appealing to the American people (as President Eisenhower had done in 1957) for domestic support of U.S. demands that Israel relinquish its captured territories, capitulated to this pressure from Capitol Hill. This symbolized the power of an unelected President who'd learned to like living in the White House.

In August 1975, Secretary Kissinger was sent back to shuttle between Cairo and Jerusalem (the Saudis, Jordanians, and Syrians had little to say to him, and he avoided Lebanon). A second Israeli-Egyptian disengagement was signed September 4, 1975. In it, America agreed to supply Israel with up to $5 billion in sophisticated superweapons (many still unavailable to our NATO allies or our own forces), and Israel was now certain of military superiority over the combined Arab states for at least a decade. Because Israel promised to give up the Egyptian oil fields, an energy-short America promised Israel a twelve-month petroleum reserve in storage and undertook to ensure that the country's oil requirements were met for the next five years—even if the U.S. should be restricted by an embargo or otherwise. (The oil fields were not returned until

1979, as a part of the Camp David agreements; then the United States guaranteed Israel's oil supplies for fifteen years—even as Americans were again forming lines to buy fuel that had escalated in price by 55 percent within three months.)

In a secret American-Israeli Memorandum of Agreement, Kissinger virtually granted Israel's right to veto U.S. policy relating to the Arab-Israeli conflict. Worse, he agreed that the U.S. would have no contact with the PLO—or recognize it officially—except on terms agreeable to Israel. If America had ever had any potential to mediate or resolve the Lebanese crisis, this abrogation of our right to have contact with one of the principal parties completely eliminated it. That took care of peace in Lebanon. Nearly five years later, the fighting continues.

With only the clothing I had on and a briefcase, I returned to America. Although the press carried vivid accounts of the war in Lebanon, the reactions I encountered were apathetic: "A bunch of Moslems are trying to kill off Lebanon's Christians" was the opinion I most often heard expressed. I still hoped that we'd learn, as the deaths mounted to the tens of thousands, but it was obvious that the U.S. wasn't moved to take direct action.

The CIA station in Greece supplied some support for the Christian-led militias; when this wasn't enough, the United States had Israel ship them large quantities of surplus and captured weapons. Then, concerned that a partitioned Lebanon might appear on its borders, Syria moved troops to rescue the militias from defeat by the PLO's fighters (who'd originally been equipped by Syria and supported by three battalions of Syrian-led PLO soldiers). Preferring instead a partitioned Lebanon, Israel drew an arbitrary line across southern Lebanon within which the PLO and Syrian troops might not operate without risking an Israeli invasion. The flaw in this (in addition to Lebanon's right to do as it wished within its own territory) was that the majority of the Christians Israel hoped might migrate to its borderline enclave lived north of Beirut and weren't budging from the safety of Mount Lebanon. Instead, Israel found a renegade Lebanese-Christian army major and sponsored his "breakaway regime" in southern Lebanon. This was hardly taken seriously, except by the Israelis, who were now eager to be portrayed as the saviors of Lebanese Christianity.

Although during times of past trouble in the Middle East U. S. citizens had been evacuated promptly from Lebanon, even if the fighting in the area didn't touch that country, over thirteen months went by before Washington decided that an American evacuation should be mounted. The incident that precipitated this was a tragic result of U.S. diplomatic blundering. An American ambassador-designate and the embassy's economic counselor (with their chauffeur) were kidnapped and murdered. This might never have occurred had the State Department not instructed its envoy to demonstrate America's displeasure with the situation in Lebanon. Instead of presenting his credentials to the chief of state—thus making his ambassadorship official—Francis Meloy was told to shun President Franjieh (whose term had four months remaining) and to call instead on the man who'd been elected to replace him. It was Washington's hope that this deliberate affront might induce Franjieh to resign prior to the end of his term. In the end, he did so, but America lost two foreign service officers attempting to accomplish what the U.S. Sixth Fleet had been landed to prevent in 1958—namely, a Lebanese president's having to leave office before the expiration of his constitutionally prescribed tenure.

The dilemma the United States faces in Lebanon epitomizes the failure of America in the Middle East. Instead of adopting policies based on recognition and consideration of the aspirations and rights of the overwhelming majority of the people of that area, we attempted to establish two small states—first Lebanon, then Israel—as models of the rewards for supporting American efforts to prevent the spread of communism and Arab nationalism. These efforts not only failed to stifle the ideologies we opposed but also placed in jeopardy the survival of the two states America selected as its allies.

In its relations with Lebanon, the United States violated its professed standards of morality in its international undertakings (that is, refraining from intervention in the internal affairs of other nations). By using Lebanon as a base for the CIA's covert operations, America undermined that country's stability and precipitated attempts by its Arab neighbors to bring down the Lebanese government. Although the might of U.S. military power saved Lebanon from possible fragmentation in 1958, the country never recovered completely and America was left with few friends in the Arab world.

When it turned to Israel as an ally, the United States strayed even further from its avowed principles by concluding secret agreements for joint clandestine operations with Israel against the Arabs. This collaboration weakened the CIA's capabilities to evaluate objectively intelligence relating to the Middle East and, in the end, led to America's tacit agreement that Israel might start the 1967 war. The fruits of this aggression and the failures of American intelligence ripened when Egypt and Syria launched the 1973 war against Israel. Once more, the might of America's military arsenal saved an ally from possible defeat, but Araby's oil and economic weapons were soon brandished, and the entire free world felt the effects of America's massive aid to Israel.

Finally, in Lebanon, the United States faced the consequences of its failure to apply impartially, in its dealings with the people of the Middle East, the principles of equal justice upon which the American republic was founded. The presence in Lebanon of the Palestinians made homeless by the creation of the state of Israel and its expansion in 1967 jeopardized the survival of another state, in which the descendants of the Phoenicians had lived for 4,000 years. The question of whether America's support of one ally (Israel) would lead to the destruction of another (Lebanon) can be resolved only by the United States. Until now, political rhetoric, lobbying in Washington, and fancied allegations that Biblical history supersedes international law have all been employed to obfuscate the issues and delay the resolution of a problem the United States has evaded for over thirty years. The basic question is a simple one, involving nothing more complicated than human rights:

Can there be any justice in denying to four million Palestinians, now living under Israeli occupation or abroad, the same rights of citizenship and statehood enjoyed by three million Israelis and guaranteed (by Israel's Law of Return and Covenant with the World Zionist Organization) to every Jew on the face of the earth?

CHAPTER THIRTY

LOOKING BACK AND TO THE FUTURE

Now, in late 1979, the various elements of the American presence in the Middle East since the end of the Second World War continue to haunt us and to threaten our hopes for peace and domestic economic stability. It appears, sadly, that we have learned little from our mistakes.

The Petroleum Industry

Thirty years of monopolistic practices by the oil companies provoked the formation of OPEC, but the petroleum industry soon devised means of profiting from the oil-exporting countries' cartel. Aided by the ill-advised regulatory measures of the Nixon, Ford, and Carter administrations, short-sighted opposition by conservationists and the Environmental Protection Agency, and Congress' failure to develop a workable national energy policy, the oil companies transformed a world crude-oil surplus in 1978 into the long service-station lines waiting to buy dollar-a-gallon gasoline that Americans endured in the spring of 1979.

▼ No longer the owners of the oil they produce abroad, the companies still control its transportation, refining, and marketing. Furthermore, they sell petroleum products in forms and at places that offer the highest profit margins.

▼ Lest the 1978 surplus of crude oil (forecast then at 3.5 million barrels a day through 1985) drive retail prices even lower, the oil companies slashed their imports of refined products and crude, while they drew down their own inventories to below levels of previous years. Making matters worse, the Department of Energy diverted the largest volume of crude oil ever to the Strategic Petroleum Reserve—the stockpile set aside for a national emergency (and from which must come the oil to meet the U.S. commitment to supply Israel's requirements). Thus, even before Iran (not a major U.S. source) reduced its exports, an artificially created energy shortage existed in America. By utilizing their ability to shift foreign oil to other markets, the oil companies sustained the shortage, used it as a justification for increasing retail prices, and reaped unprecedented profits.

▼ Only two "grass roots" (completely new) oil refineries have been built in America since the 1950s, making it necessary to employ inefficient and costly methods to meet long-anticipated requirements for unleaded, heating, and diesel fuel. Nor can crude oil shipped from Alaska and other non-OPEC sources be processed without costly shutdowns and conversions of existing refineries. Attributing far more blame than is justified to conservationists and restrictive government regulations, the petroleum industry has procrastinated in conducting new exploration, developing offshore fields, and building pipelines in the United States in order to preserve traditional marketing spheres of influence. Despite increasing demands by consumers, oil refiners operated for the past two years at 85 percent of capacity; crude used to make petrochemicals, fertilizers, and plastics produces higher revenues, but in justifying the huge earnings from their total operations the oil companies cite only their pennies-per-gallon profits from gasoline.

▼ Worse, by 1977 the oil companies owned over 80 percent of the U.S. reserves of uranium ore and controlled more than a quarter of our coal deposits. Thus the petroleum industry has the ability and financial strength to keep virtually all fuel supplies short and prices high.[107]

---

107 The oil companies also control 30 percent of America's copper resources; this is an essential element of solar heating systems.

▼ The American economy is just as dependent on the petroleum industry as it is on the power, water, and transportation companies whose activities and prices are governed by public-utility commissions. Also, the direct dealings of the oil companies with the governments of the oil-producing countries significantly affect American foreign policy and its impact on the domestic economy of the United States.

For all of these reasons, then, it is imperative that the petroleum industry be forced to comply with U.S. antitrust regulations. Nor should the fact that the oil companies profit internally from wholly owned, equity-controlled, or cartel operations at each stage between the wellhead and the gasoline pump be ignored; thus they escape the provisions of divestiture laws that affect other major industries. Power companies were forced to give up oil wells, bus lines, and coal mines; aircraft manufacturers were prevented from operating air carriers; financial institutions were made to choose between commercial and investment banking; and the railroads had to stop producing coal, timber, and other related commodities. Total-equity financing requirements for refining, marketing, and transportation divestiture are readily available on the domestic capital market: the giant oil companies' claim that forced sale of these operations would disrupt America's economy is just as flimsy as the contention by the U.S. government that antitrust legislation has failed. Neither remedy has been tried for over sixty-five years.[108]

OPEC and OAPEC[109]

America's failure to heed the warnings of the Arab oil-exporting states that they would use petroleum as a political weapon enabled the combined OPEC membership to establish

108 See Dr. John M. Blair, *The Control of Oil* (New York: Pantheon, 1977).
109 The Organization of Petroleum Exporting Countries (OPEC) consists of thirteen nations: Ecuador, Venezuela, Nigeria, Gabon, Indonesia, Iran, Iraq, Qatar, Algeria, Kuwait, Saudi Arabia, Libya, and the United Arab Emirates. Only the last seven listed are Arab countries: they also make up the Organization of Arab Petroleum Exporting Countries (OAPEC).

itself as a powerful determinant in the economic future of the free world. The American oil companies, whose credibility was rapidly fading, were unable in 1972 to convince the U.S. government that the Arabs meant business and that the other oil-exporting nations would support them. The petroleum industry's attempts to alert the American public to the need for a balanced policy in the Arab-Israeli conflict were drowned by a campaign charging that any change in America's support of Israel's policies would mean "trading Jewish blood for Arab oil." Trade restrictions and economic sanctions have long been employed by the U.S. government to support foreign-policy objectives and to punish regimes whose policies offend us, but America's politicians—led by presidential hopefuls Hubert Humphrey, Henry Jackson, and Frank Church—continued to brand the Arabs as "bloodthirsty blackmailers."

▼ Both before and since the 1973 oil embargo, the OAPEC members have made it clear that restrictions on oil exports would be directed solely at inducing Israel to comply with the U.N.'s dictates and to recognize the "rights" of the Palestinian Arabs.

▼ The communiqué issued by the combined OPEC-membership meeting in Geneva in June 1979 urged the industrialized nations to join in common measures for "restructuring the international economic order"; it announced an additional $800 million contribution to the OPEC fund to assist developing countries affected by increased oil prices; and the OAPEC members advised of their willingness to invest in a $500 billion European Common Market plan for developing alternative sources of energy for Europe.

▼ The same day, in Tokyo, President Carter condemned the new OPEC pricing formula by saying that "there is no one on earth who will fail to suffer from these extraordinary increases." From Washington, the President's principal domestic-affairs adviser, Stuart Eizenstat, urged Carter to attribute to the Arab oil-producing states all of America's economic problems, hoping, as Eizenstat wrote, to salvage the President's popularity ratings, which had hit a new low. Thus Jimmy Carter, who had spent more time salvaging poll ratings by trying to arrange peace between Egypt and Israel than he had addressing the domestic economic problems caused by the lack of a comprehensive Middle East settlement, convened another "summit" meeting at Camp David; at stake was public confidence in the administration's ability to solve the nation's economic crisis. Cabinet shakeups followed, but the President's vow that the United States would never increase oil imports by a "single drop" was the keynote of his address to the nation. None of the Camp David "summits" has, however, had any effect in making more and cheaper oil available.

▼ In fact, OPEC's price ceiling of $23.50 a barrel had little to do with what Americans paid for gasoline and fuel oil: independent tanker owners at sea conducted radio auctions for their "spot market" cargos, and prices of $40 a barrel were not unusual; also, the Aramco partners bought Saudi Arabian oil at a preferential rate of $18 without passing on a cent of their discount to consumers.

▼ Moreover, America's economic problems justify OPEC's price increases and its decisions to curtail oil production. The price of foreign oil is set in U.S. dollars; thus as the exchange rate of the dollar decreases, the true value of what the OPEC members receive for their exports drops. Similarly, America's inflation adversely affects the value of the investments we have persuaded the oil-producing countries to make in U.S. Treasury offerings for the purpose of supporting our economy. Decisions by OPEC to peg oil prices to the skyrocketing cost of gold or to withdraw the over $50 billion invested in America would precipitate a financial disaster in this country. Oil left in the ground will become more valuable than the price it presently fetches, and we can hardly criticize OPEC for emulating the American oil companies who decline to produce more domestic oil until it can be sold legally at OPEC's prices.

Still hoping that the United States will recognize that the availability of Arab oil is directly related to the U.S. position on the Arab-Israeli conflict, Saudi Arabia has temporarily increased its production by a million barrels a day in order to cater to America's apparently insatiable appetite for a finite commodity and to bolster our economy. It would be the height of foolishness, however, to expect the Arabs to wait out the five-year period set forth in the Camp David "Frameworks" to learn what, if any, degree of self-determination will be allowed the Palestinian Arabs, or how soon the U.S. government will come to grips with the basic problems that have for over thirty years obstructed a comprehensive Arab-Israeli peace settlement.

In the past, the prospect of war between the Arab armies and Israel posed the greatest threat of an American-Soviet military confrontation in the Middle East. An abortive Egyptian-Israeli peace treaty could lead to a renewal of hostilities, but the West's losses in Iran and Afghanistan make it even more vital for us to earn the goodwill of the OAPEC members.

The Arabs

In a military sense, the term "Arab-Israeli conflict" is a misnomer. The Arabs are no more united militarily today against Israel than they were in 1947 and 1948, when the armies of Egypt, Jordan, and Iraq were decisively defeated by Jewish forces and Zionist irregulars. Nor does the "Arab nation" exist as a cohesive entity in terms of significant political accomplishments. Domestic problems, intra-Arab quarrels, and petty jealousies have dogged every effort of the Arab states to federate: persistent attempts to unite Iraq and Syria both by coups and compacts continue to flounder even today. The Arab League has ostracized Egypt, the state that once held it together, and the league's records of its past failures are located in its new headquarters in remote Tunis. In the negative sense of opposing aggression and expansion by Israel, the Arabs have been united, however, and they continue to acquire supporters around the world.

▼ The 1956 Israeli invasion of Suez evoked international sympathy for Egypt and served to establish Nasser as a hero of the Arab masses from the Atlantic to the Indian Oceans.

▼ By 1966 Cairo had become a major capital of the Third World of nonaligned nations, and Egypt's geographical situation qualified it to be a leader of the Organization of African Unity. These developments strengthened support of the Arab cause in new areas: Israel's relations with the African and Asian nations and its position in the United Nations suffered as a result. By then, though, conflicts between radical and conservative factions had fragmented any semblance of united Arab political action.

▼ Israel's Six-Day War of 1967, by its conquest of additional Arab territory and the flight of more Palestinians from their homeland, brought the Arabs together again in opposition to both Israel and America, who were regarded as coconspirators. At this point the Arab-Israeli conflict assumed new dimensions: within a year the Palestinians organized to fight for the right to return to the home of their ancestors, and the sympathy of 200 million Arabs (if not all their governments) was behind them; simultaneously, Israel's "annexation" of Jerusalem and its environs in 1967 aroused the enmity of nearly 800 Moslems.[110]

▼ As we now appreciate daily, America's massive support of Israel during the 1973 war and thereafter has brought the Arabs support from the non-Moslem oil-producing nations of Africa and South America. The new Islamic republic of Iran has joined the Arabs in opposing Israeli policies, a swing toward solid support of the Arabs has become evident in Turkey and Pakistan, and most Western European nations now support self-determination for the Palestinian Arabs. In fact, only America, of the major powers, still consistently supports Israel in the United Nations.

▼ The Soviet bloc, in efforts to mend fences with the Arabs, wields a double-edged word under Russian leadership: it can either fuel the Middle East arms race—as it has done since it was Israel's chief supplier—by continuing to offer arms to the Arabs, or it can saddle Israel with enormous economic problems by releasing or expelling Jews living behind the iron curtain.

Thus, although the Arabs have only a small constituency and virtually no lobby in the United States to counter powerful Israeli

---

110   The King-Crane Commission's Report described the Jews as the least acceptable custodians of the Holy Land: "The places which are most sacred to the Christians—those having to do with Jesus—and which are also sacred to the Moslems, are not only not sacred to Jews, but abhorrent to them."

influence over American politicians and foreign policy, world support for the Arabs is growing stronger every day. Despite America's achievement in promoting the Egyptian-Israeli peace treaty, this pact alone cannot bring peace to the Middle East. Today it seems certain that the Arab states bordering Israel would agree to peace on the basis of slight modifications of the 1949 armistice agreements.

But the Arabs, who did little more for their Palestinian brothers than shower them with oratory and exploit their plight as a weapon of political negativism, must now share with Israel the obligation of ensuring that the Christians and Moslems who became homeless as a result of the creation of the state of Israel are able to exercise their right of self-determination—the same right once guaranteed by America and reaffirmed by the United Nations in 1974. Secure frontiers are no longer the only issue in an Arab-Israeli peace settlement: a homeland for the Palestinian Arabs has assumed equal importance. If a Palestinian state is to be created in the West Bank and Gaza areas, however, both Egypt and Jordan will have to be far more positive than they have been so far in affirming their willingness to live alongside a new independent Arab nation.

The Palestinian Question

The question of how the Palestinian Arabs became refugees has been obscured both by time and by propaganda. Fear of war, panic, and bewilderment unquestionably started their flight, both in 1947–48 and in 1967. But there is not one shred of evidence to substantiate the Israeli claims that the Palestinians were obeying Arab orders to flee. In fact, by remaining on their land the refugees would have frustrated the aspirations of the Zionists to possessing an exclusively Jewish nation. The partition plan approved by the United Nations (on which the Zionists based their claim for statehood) provided for a Jewish state whose population would consist of an almost equal number of Arabs and Jews, as well as an Arab state alongside it—a concept rejected by the members of the Arab League. Clearly, the Arab nations were at that time motivated more by the aim of preventing any partition of Palestine than by their concern over the creation thereby of a refugee problem.

Just before the expiration of Britain's mandate over Palestine in 1948, radical Zionists embarked on a campaign of terrorism directed at the destruction of the Palestinian Arab community.[111] Had the Arab armies not intervened and had the U.N. not imposed truces, the Zionist extremists who claim a "right" to all of Biblical Israel might have accomplished their initial objective of taking over all of Palestine in order to form the state of Israel.

▼ Tragically, while innocent people are being killed and the destruction of towns and villages creates yet more refugee problems in Lebanon, the questions of human rights and international justice inherent in the Palestinian problem are still being obscured by the obdurate, irreconcilable statements of positions advanced by both the PLO and the Israelis.

▼ To the distress of the Palestinians and the PLO (recognized as their spokesman by an overwhelming vote of the U.N.'s membership in November 1974), the Ford and Carter administrations have promised Israel that America will neither recognize nor negotiate with the PLO until that organization agrees to recognize Israel's right to exist under the provisions of a U.N. resolution whose requirements have not yet been fully met by any of the parties to the Arab-Israeli conflict. The Security Council's Resolution 242 of 1967 calls for every state in the area to terminate "all claims or states of belligerency" and to respect "the sovereignty, territorial integrity, and political independence of every state in the area." The word "Palestinian" does not appear in Resolution 242; instead there is the necessity "for achieving a just settlement of the refugee problem."

▼ Resolution 242 was passed to condemn Israel for, among other things, creating an even greater Palestinian-refugee problem

---

111   The results of this campaign have been described in the writings of former Israeli foreign minister Yigal Allon and Prime Minister Menachem Begin. As this is written, Israeli censors had prohibited the publication of former premier Yitzhak Rabin's first-person account of the explusion of 50,000 Arabs from their homes near Tel Aviv.

than that of 1948, and in emphasizing the inadmissibility of Israel's acquisition of territory by war it required the withdrawal of Israeli forces from the territories they had occupied (beyond the 1949 armistice lines). Israel has implied, and many Americans seem to believe, that 242 requires the Palestinians to recognize the second Israeli conquest of their homeland. This sleight of hand is unparalleled in international relations—and the United States has gone along with it.

▼ The question is that of just what "state of Israel" the PLO is being asked to recognize. Today Israel has no internationally recognized borders (it having renounced the 1949 armistice agreements in 1956), and the Israeli government continues to state unequivocally its refusal ever to return to its pre-1967 borders. Moreover, Prime Minister Begin has always been committed to reclaiming all of *Eretz Yisrael*, which by some Zionist definitions could include all the land between the Nile and the Euphrates. Never in history has a political entity been granted recognition on the premise that it would at some later date negotiate and define its borders.

▼ The PLO's deplorable acts of terrorism continue, provoking Israeli military retaliation, which threatens the survival of Lebanon. Unfortunately, many Americans regard the terms "PLO" and "Palestinian Arabs" as synonymous, and they tend to perceive the coalition that makes up the PLO as a monolithic body exercising direction and control over the guerrilla bands headed by leaders with divergent views and objectives. The PLO's role as a spokesman for the Palestinians is firmly established, however, and neither Anwar Sadat nor any other Arab chief of state is likely to be accepted by the Palestinians as either their spokesman or their negotiator. This brings us to Israel's present position that the PLO is nothing more than a gang of "terrorists and murderers" and that "recognizing the PLO would be tantamount to the recognition of genocide." Such accusations certainly justify a blunt and uncompromising examination of the role of terrorism in the history of Arab-Jewish relations.

▼ Terrorism is by its definition the cruel use of force or threats to demoralize, intimidate, and subjugate others in a wanton manner, and describing those who have resorted to it as "freedom fighters" cannot cloak their actions in respectability. Nor does the wearing of the uniform of a sovereign state make any less reprehensible the killing of innocent people by men wielding automatic weapons, firing artillery pieces, driving tanks, or flying aircraft. For those Israelis who once engaged in terrorism (and who continue it today behind the mask of preemptive military operations that kill hundreds of innocent people) now to condemn the Palestinians who have in desperation resorted to terrorist acts for an identical objective—the obtaining of a homeland in Palestine—is sheer hypocrisy.

▼ Nor does citing statistics to justify the invasion of another's sovereign territory excuse flagrant violations of international law by Israel. In March 1979, Aharon Yarif, director of the Israeli Institute of Strategic Studies (and former head of Israeli intelligence) reported that in the past fourteen years Israel had lost about 630 people to terrorism (adding, strangely, that "this is what we lose each year to traffic accidents," and that the PLO "have not disrupted normal life," "stopped immigration," or "stopped tourism"). In contrast to this, military action by Israel or its surrogates in Lebanon between April 1978 and September 1979 killed hundreds of innocent Lebanese men, women, and children; Israeli troops adopted a "scorched earth" policy, plundered archaeological treasures, and shot those who opposed them rather than taking prisoners. Over 200,000 people have been forced to flee from devastated southern Lebanon (where over 100 homes were destroyed in a twenty-four-hour period and, although the United States futilely protested, a State Department spokesman emphasized that the administration was not contemplating any reduction in the $2.7 billion in military aid already committed to Israel—a sovereign country in whose affairs we couldn't intervene. While this went on, new Israeli settlements proliferated in Israeli-occupied Jordan and Syria.

▼ Although there are increasing signs that Yasser Arafat would be willing to offer the PLO's recognition of Israel's right to exist in security in return for the recognition of the Palestinians' right to self-determination, the Israelis now reject the mutuality explicit in "recognition" by vowing never to negotiate with the PLO under any circumstances. Assuming that Israel will be unable indefinitely to resist world pressure in support of a Palestinian homeland, it is appropriate to examine the records of Israeli officials who would presumably influence Israel's position in exercising its right, under the Egyptian-Israeli peace treaty, to veto any form of Palestinian "autonomy" not acceptable to Israel.

▼ Menachem Begin, Moshe Dayan, Ariel Sharon, and Ezer Weizmann are hardly justified in shunning Yasser Arafat as a terrorist. Each of these men has ordered acts of terrorism that, in terms of brutality and the loss of innocent lives, exceed any act or operation for which credit has been claimed in the name of the PLO. Thus, Yasser Arafat and the Palestinians he speaks for can hardly be blamed for insisting that both Israel's final borders and the degree of self-determination that the Palestinian's will be allowed are defined in advance of agreement to recognize Israel[112]

Andrew Young ended his career as the U.S. representative to the U.N. by presiding over the Security Council's two-day debate on Israel's actions in southern Lebanon. As a part of his remarks to reporters after the session, Young compared the acts of Israel with those of the PLO and said that he was unable to differentiate between them. He then said, "I think that no group can consistently

---

112 Begin headed the *Irgun Zvai Leumi*, whose bombing of the King David Hotel on July 22, 1946, killed 90 people—Arabs, Jews, and Britons—and was instrumental in the British government's decision to withdraw from its mandate over Palestine. The operation Begin ordered against the unarmed village of Deir Yassin on April 9, 1948, resulted in the slaughter of 254 men, women, and children, and many bodies were stuffed into a well to conceal evidence (pregnant women were cut open and others raped). This atrocity surpasses all others in the entire history of the conflict between the Arabs and the Jews, and it led (according to Begin's own book) to the flight of the Arabs in terror from Palestine. In 1953 Dayan ordered the formation of the all-volunteer Unit 101, whose operations in raiding defenseless Arab villages and in revenge killings were covered up with false reports to the Israeli government. Sharon commanded Unit 101 in its first major operation on October 14, 1953, against Qibya, which left 53 innocent men, women, and children dead. Weizmann ordered Israeli forces into Lebanon in 1978, killing over 500 and employing the antipersonnel cluster and concussion bombs that the United States had furnished Israel after receiving assurances that they would never be used except against an invading army.

defy the universal consensus of the nations of the world and survive, whether it be a nation or a liberation movement."

Israel

"It's tragic to see people dooming themselves to a course of unbelievable peril." These were the words of Henry Kissinger to Prime Minister Yitzhak Rabin on March 22, 1975, in Jerusalem.[113] The American secretary of state had just abandoned his effort to persuade Israel to accept President Sadat's agreement to nonbelligerency as a further step in negotiating a Middle East peace settlement. On March 25, 1979, Egypt and Israel signed a treaty in Washington, and for the first time in thirty years the Israelis could feel secure against attack by the largest and most efficient Arab army. At last the peace process had been started, but over the four years since Kissinger's prophecy, more than 40,000 people had died in Lebanon—more than Israel has lost since its inception, and more than Egypt has lost in three wars with the Israeli armed forces.

Claiming that its survival is still threatened by the presence of Palestinian guerrillas in Lebanon, Israel continues to bomb, strafe, and invade Lebanese territory. It would be naive to believe that such a policy will make the Palestinians any more tractable. Nor should it be forgotten that the future of the Egyptian treaty with Israel hinges on the implementation of its provision for the establishment of a self-governing Palestinian Arab authority in the West Bank and Gaza no later than May 25, 1980. Surely the time has come for Israel to recognize that its only hope of true security lies in making peace with its Arab neighbors.

▼ That Israel has never experienced peace since the day it proclaimed statehood has undoubtedly affected the outlook of its peoples and governments. The possibility that Yasser Arafat's rhetoric may be as hollow as that of Nasser and the other Arab demagogues who've threatened to drive Israel into the sea provides little comfort to Israelis who live in fear of bombs planted in a marketplace or on a bus. Just as the rulers of the oil sheikhdoms fear uprisings sparked by the Palestinians on whom they are dependent for

---

113   See Edward R.F. Sheehan, *Foreign Policy* 22 (Spring 1976): 52.

labor, and just as the West fears PLO sabotage of ships to block the entrance and exit to the Persian Gulf oil ports, so the Israelis cannot be blamed for taking seriously the Palestinians' Covenant, which vows to eliminate Israel as extending sanctuary to all the world's Jewry.

▼ Most Israelis long for tranquility, and a significant segment of Israel's population sees peaceful coexistence with the Arabs as the only means of overcoming their country's isolation from the world community. Against them are arrayed the generals and politicians, who see the sword as the only key to security, and the pragmatists, who view peace as a threat to Israel's financial future.

▼ Meanwhile, devaluation of the Israeli pound continues, and triple digit inflation is forecast by 1980; only massive U.S.-aid grants and Jewish charity prevent Israel's bankruptcy. Even if peace came tomorrow, the future generations of Israelis would be plagued with the interest and repayment costs of their state's multibillion-dollar foreign debt. To this must be added the residual effect of vast military expenditures; even the operational, storage, and maintenance costs of armaments for which payment has been waived will be staggering. The number of Israelis leaving to live elsewhere rivals the number of Jews arriving as immigrants, and even though Russian Jews leave with Israeli visas, a majority of them settle in the U.S. or other countries—facts that Zionist fund raisers find increasingly difficult to explain.

▼ Sadly, Israel is expending another asset to which it shares joint title with the eleven million Jews who do not live in Israel: the friendship and admiration born of the Jews' great religious contribution to humanity and of their tragic sufferings and endurance. Because Israel has identified itself as a Jewish state, its actions redound to the credit or discredit of all Jewry.

Tsiyyon be-Mishpat tipadeh ("Zion shall be redeemed with justice") was the injunction of the Prophet Isaiah to the children of Israel. This admonishment also closed the open letter to Prime Minister Begin written by Rabbi Arthur Hertzberg, vice-president of the World Jewish Congress, in which he said that it would be a mistake to imagine that American Jews are united behind Israel's annexation policy on the West Bank.[114] More than any other people in the world, the Jews should know that even centuries of oppression and dispersion cannot destroy the determination of the Palestinians to acquire a homeland and a national identity.

President Truman, to whom Israel owes more gratitude for support of its statehood than it does to any other person, frequently expressed the fear that excessive political pressure from American Zionists would turn the country against their cause. Truman recorded in a letter to Eleanor Roosevelt the concern he often expressed to others: "I fear very much that Jews are like all underdogs. When they get on top they are just as intolerant and cruel as the people were to them when they were underneath."[115] Today, America's greatest contribution to the future of Israel and to peace in the Middle East would be to ensure that Harry Truman's apprehensions turn out to be unjustified. In the words of an Israeli friend of mine who writes to me from Tel Aviv: "America must save Israel from itself."

The Central Intelligence Agency

When President Truman created the CIA in 1947, he left no doubt that he strongly disapproved of clandestine operations and that he expected the new agency to limit its activities to the collation and evaluation of foreign intelligence gathered by conventional means (through our embassies, their military attachés, and openly accredited technical specialists). Allen Dulles was one of three men Truman charged with preparing recommendations for the CIA's organization; even then, Dulles was confident that he would one day head a peacetime spy agency, and the advice he gave helped lay its foundations. First, OSS veterans were assigned to our embassies and designated as political attachés; they were to advise our ambassadors on intelligence requirements and evaluate in the field information acquired through the embassies' usual sources. Dulles was named to head the CIA's clandestine services

---

114   See the *Christian Science Monitor*, Friday, June 28, 1979.
115   See Robert J. Donovan, *Conflict and Crisis* (New York: W. W. Norton & Company, 1977), p. 325.

in the wake of the agency's failure to forecast the Korean war. This provided the excuse he needed to convert the political attachés into covert operators and to supplement their staffs with deep-cover operatives.

When the shah and Premier Mossadeq nationalized Britain's oil concession in 1951, Allen Dulles was ready for a major operation. Behind President Truman's back, Dulles and Kermit Roosevelt planned Operation AJAX; Foster Dulles convinced President Eisenhower that Mossadeq could be replaced, and the green light was flashed. The operation was mounted despite the conclusions of the intelligence community that the shah could not rule without the support of Iran's religious leaders, the tribes, and the merchants of the bazaar who controlled the country's economy.[116] Ignoring all this, Roosevelt decided that the army would always support the shah, and the monarch was persuaded to defy

---

116 The highly respected Mossadeq was unanimously elected prime minister by the Iranian Majlis (parliament), in which the vested interests of the court, army, clergy, tribes, landlords, and businessmen were represented—the most powerful bloc was headed by the Shi'ite religious leader Mullah Kashani. The Department of State's intelligence analysts assessed this group's support of Mossadeq's program as being "one sure way of saving themselves and Iran without oil resources from an increased Communist threat."

In a move that appeared to defy prudence and logic, Kermit Roosevelt wrote a book entitled *Countercoup: The Struggle for Control of Iran*, released by McGraw-Hill Book Company, New York, on September 16, 1979, in which Roosevelt boasts of his role for the CIA in overthrowing Mossadeq and describes *inter alia* his access to a safe in the American embassy containing $1 million for support of the CIA coup. Serialized in the *Washington Post* on May 6, 1979 (even as the shah was seeking a home in exile), the book was suddenly withdrawn from circulation and some 7,000 copies of it "scrapped," just a few days after Iranian students had taken over the American embassy in Tehran and seized fifty hostages. Roosevelt's book fails to mention that over 300 Iranians were killed in the pro-shah riots the CIA had organized and supported with massive quantities of U.S. military equipment. Roosevelt's book does reveal that he had defied Secretary of State Dulles's orders to avoid any personal contact with the shah: a meeting between Roosevelt and the shah was reported to Prime Minister Mossadeq; the initially planned coup aborted, and this was the reason for the shah's having to flee from Iran until Roosevelt's (largely British SIS) agents could be supplied with arms and organize the riots that permitted the monarch to return to Tehran.

popular sentiment and turn the operation of Iran's oil fields over to an American-organized consortium of oil companies. For twenty-five years Operation AJAX was cited to justify the frequent, and often disastrous, substitution of clandestine and paramilitary operations for conventional diplomacy.

The extent to which the CIA's covert operators had misjudged the situation in Iran became evident in January 1979. Despite one of the agency's closest intelligence-liaison agreements, and although former CIA director Richard Helms served as our ambassador in Tehran while the opponents of the shah were mobilizing to overthrow him, the collapse of the monarchy caught President Carter and Director Stansfield Turner completely by surprise. The factions Dulles and Roosevelt ignored took over with a vengeance; when and how all this will end is still uncertain, but we must remember how the French Revolution spread over Europe and not dismiss this possibility in the Middle East.

Not only was the CIA left without any useful contacts through which the United States might initiate constructive relations with Iran's revolutionary government; the U.S. government disregarded normally routine measures by not evacuating American citizens or severing diplomatic relations with Iran after our embassy had been entered and the American ambassador briefly held captive. Influential factions, consisting of former U.S. government officials and prominent business figures, reportedly prevailed on President Carter to maintain a "business as usual" relationship with the constantly changing Iranian government officials. Worse, ignoring the advice of Secretary of State Vance and Under Secretary David Newsom (who had been present in Baghdad in 1952 when the British embassy was ravished and the USIS library destroyed), the President was persuaded to allow the shah to enter the United States for medical treatment, precipitating, thereby, the hostage crisis in Tehran.[117]

---

117   During an election year there is strong congressional opposition to proposals that a "Blue Ribbon" panel be convened to investigate business and personal relations among former U.S. government officials, prominent businessmen, and the shah of Iran. The influential role of Henry Kissinger, John

▼ What has happened in Iran was predicted by the CIA's career intelligence analysts; their estimates, based on data acquired from many sources, were simply ignored by the agency's hierarchy, however. The CIA brass *wanted* to believe that their covert sources in Iran were infallible, and for years they had been telling American presidents what the latter wanted to hear. Approximately 90 percent of the data the CIA collects come from open (as opposed to covert) sources or from technological means, such as satellites and communications intercepts; and it was this mass of information that the CIA brass chose not to read or to ignore.

▼ The events in Iran also illustrate that neither massive supplies of sophisticated weapons nor building up a secret-police organization can sustain indefinitely a chief of state's tenure. The armaments we furnish can be used against our interests, and repressive police are the first target of a successful opposition movement. (Resentment of the role played by Israel's Mossad in training the shah's dreaded SAVAK was an important factor in the new Iranian government's break in diplomatic relations with Israel and that country's loss of Iranian oil supplies.)

▼ CIA liaison agreements with foreign intelligence services have impaired America's ability to evaluate the intentions of its

---

J. McCloy, and David Rockefeller, of Chase Manhattan Bank, with Carter has received considerable publicity, but there has been no mention of Archibald Roosevelt's CIA-retirement position as Chase's vice-president for Middle East matters or of former state secretary William Rogers's role as legal counsel for the Pahlavi Foundation. Also, the oilwell-drilling firm formed by former deputy defense secretary William Clements (now governor of Texas), SEDCO, Inc., started its foreign operations in Iran, and the Pahlavi Foundation reportedly held 5 percent of SEDCO's stock during the period Clements was in Washington and the massive buildup of the Iranian armed forces was implemented. [See Robert Graham, *Iran: The Illusion of Power* (New York, St. Martin's Press, 1979).] Some observers claim that an investigation of the connections between the ex-shah and former U.S. government officials might make the Watergate revelations seem tame by comparison. In any case, if there are reasons to require CIA officials to refrain from revealing their former activities after retirement, there would seem to be equal justification for requiring that they abjure using their CIA-acquired connections for personal profit; Richard Helms, William Colby, and Kermit Roosevelt are examples of those who have acted as "consultants" for foreign governments or businesses.

covert partners and the real strength of their governments. In addition, the United States has been subjected to blackmail by threats of exposure of joint operations or the expulsion of CIA personnel. We have permitted friendly intelligence agents to operate freely in America in violation of our laws and the rights guaranteed to citizens and residents of this country, as well as in contravention of the inviolability extended to diplomatic missions and their personnel.

▼ Covert political-action operations by the agency have failed most often owing to ineptitude and exposure. Otherwise, they have merely postponed developments that were inevitable as a result of misguided U.S. policies, or they have temporarily supported regimes whose successors have acted contrary to America's interests.

▼ CIA director Turner found it necessary to fire or force the retirement of over 200 members of the clandestine services before he could even attempt to exercise effective control over the agency. Now Turner seeks legislation to "legalize" covert operations at the discretion of a president; to make disclosure (even from a public source) of the agency's activities a criminal offense; and to deny affected parties access to records through the Freedom of Information and Privacy Acts. The details of covert operations are denied to our ambassadors, and Director Turner's personal control of the intelligence community's $12 billion annual budget and its 200,000 employees has been tightened.

Acting entirely within its charter, the CIA has produced valuable intelligence estimates to guide foreign-policy decisions; outlawing covert activities will not impair this capability. Even if presidents ignore the CIA's warnings, the agency's responsibility to advise remains.

American Policy in the Middle East

More often than not, America's Middle East policy has been formulated in response to developments abroad instead of being planned on the basis of sound intelligence estimates and the recommendations of experienced professional foreign-service officers.

For example, the following are excerpts from secret CIA estimates prepared for the President of the United States:

▼ *"The future attitude of the Arab states, regarding both new concessions and the cancellation of existing oil agreements, will be determined by the policy of the U.S. and the U.N. on the Palestine issue. Responsible Arab leaders will be unable to curb the actions of the Arab fanatics, while the Jewish extremists may be expected to intensify their terrorist activity . . ."*

▼ *"It has recently seemed that the foundations for a comprehensive peace settlement in the Near East were being laid . . . [Troop movements] have, however, thrown the situation into its customary uncertainty. These will probably continue in view of the indisputably superior strength of Israel and the skill with which Israeli policy has fragmented the Arab position; but solutions reached by these means will contribute little to the stabilization of the Near East and nothing to the improvement of U.S. and U.K. security interests in the area."*

▼ *"The legality of conflicting claims in Palestine can be left to one side, for the essential fact of the moment is that the Arab judgment of U.S. intentions will become fixedly suspicious if no evidence is provided of a U.S. willingness to check the aggressive expansion of Israel."*

▼ *". . . although the [Middle East] situation is extremely fluid, the relative security positions of the U.S. and the U.S.S.R. have [not] significantly changed in the course of twelve months . . . There are signs that the Arab states are individually seeking to reestablish closer ties with the West to gain what protection they can from a successful Israel. . . . The decline of the Arab League as an important political force simplifies these individual approaches by permitting more realistic decisions. . . . However, the local power superiority and presumed ambitions of Israel prevent a final stabilization of the Near East."*

The fact that President Carter must today contend with every situation cited in these CIA estimates, even though they were prepared for President Truman more than thirty years ago, provides ample evidence of the failure of America's policies in the Middle East.[118] Each of these predictions by the CIA's intelligence analysts has materialized; only their estimate of the relative security positions of the United States and the Soviet Union has changed. The continuing lack of stability in the Middle East has adversely affected America's economy and defense capabilities; meanwhile, Russian influence in that area has increased as a result of our mistakes.

In October 1948, America's position as the world's strongest power was unchallenged, but Defense Secretary Forrestal complained that U.S. Palestinian policy had been made for "squalid political purposes" involving domestic political considerations instead of the U.S. national interest. In the same month, Under Secretary of State Lovett cabled Secretary Marshall to report that White House restrictions on U.S. action in the Palestine question could be expected to end when the "silly season terminates." As President Truman did in 1947–48, President Carter in 1979–80 must also face low popularity ratings and questionable reelection prospects; and Carter has emulated his predecessor in dealing with the Palestinian problem. Robert Strauss, the administration's Middle East peace "expert," has returned to full-time duties as Carter's reelection-campaign manager after admitting that Egypt and Israel had been unable to agree even on an agenda for discussing Palestinian "autonomy."

One must ask if we can afford to allow even a one-year preelection hiatus (Lovett's "silly season") to delay Middle East peacemaking. Moreover, we should ask whether the injection of domestic considerations into foreign policy will really benefit Israel's long-term interests or enhance Anwar Sadat's ability to survive as America's one-man Arab link to the peace process. In 1976 Jimmy Carter and Gerald Ford vied for votes by promising aid that Israel had yet to request; now, a year before the elections, Carter's challengers speak of basing America's entire Middle East policy on Israel. John Connally incurred accusations of anti-Semitism when he dared propose that America's security interests be isolated from

---

118 *Papers of Harry S. Truman*, Series CIA 1948–1949 (3–48, 3–49, and 4–49), National Archives, Washington, D.C.

domestic politics—the same challenge Carter issued to members of Congress who sought to make political capital of the belated discovery of Soviet troops in Cuba by threatening to block ratification of the Strategic Arms Limitation Treaty with Russia.

Seven American Presidents have held office during the period of Israel's statehood. Only one ever put to a test the perception that opposition to Israel's policies could lose an election: it was Dwight D. Eisenhower, and he won by a landslide after condemning Israel's invasion of Egypt. Some American President can go down in history as the man who saved Israel and also brought peace to the Middle East—even if he lost an election by doing it.

Iran was defined as a "U.S. security interest," and in 1948 we considered "untenable" that country's trend toward a policy of balance between the United States (7,000 miles distant) and the Soviet Union (with whom Iran shares over 1,000 miles of frontier). The CIA warned President Truman that Iranian nationalists and leftists opposed U.S. missions and arms credit, but the agency concluded that unless U.S. aid was forthcoming our influence in Iran would diminish. While an American aid program was being developed, the shah and his government yielded to popular demands that Britain's oil concession be nationalized, and its citizens were expelled from Iran. Then, despite Britain's inability to sustain Iraq's monarchy as the keystone of Western influence in the Middle East, America initiated a massive program to build up the shah for personally assuming a similar role for the United States.

The collapse of the Iranian monarchy in 1979 sounded the death knell of CENTO (the Baghdad Pact's successor), on which we relied to bar Russia from the Middle East. The governments of Turkey and Pakistan, to whom U.S. commitments to defend their borders with Russia were made, have been turned out of office; their replacements have been denied American aid under our selective applications of eligibility criteria. The Turks' use of U.S. arms to protect the Turkish minority on Cyprus and the Pakistanis' efforts to match India's nuclear capability were punished; Israel's use of American arms against the Arabs and its development of nuclear weapons evoked either futile protests or silence while U.S. aid to Israel was increased by huge amounts.

No one knows the extent to which America's losses in the Middle East might have been reduced had we concentrated on achieving peace between Israel and its Arab neighbors instead of building defense alliances against Russia. It is certain, however, that there never will be stability in that strategic area until secure borders for Israel have been settled in viable peace treaties with the countries on its borders.

There is no need to develop new policies to settle the question of peace between the Arabs and the Israelis and the future status of the Palestinians; no presidential mediation or "shuttle diplomacy" by the secretary of state or special envoys will be required—save between Washington and United Nations headquarters. The key to peace for both the Arabs and the Israelis is contained in existing resolutions, and the United States is committed to ensuring compliance with the Security Council's rulings, seeking their enforcement, if need be, by the same economic sanctions President Carter had demanded to punish Russia for invading Afghanistan and Iran for holding Americans hostage.

The threat of such sanctions by President Eisenhower in 1957 produced Israeli compliance with the Security Council's resolutions and its withdrawal from Arab territory captured by an invading army. To the people of Egypt, Jordan, Syria, and Lebanon the invasion of their territory by (largely American-supplied) Israeli forces was just as illegal and repugnant as we now find the Soviet invasion of Afghanistan. The President and the American people poured out sympathy for the families of the hostages held in our Tehran embassy, and the invasion of its grounds and buildings was condemned as an act of war. Were the families of the thirty-four Americans killed aboard the defenseless U.S.S. *Liberty* any less entitled to expressions of sympathy, indignation, and outrage; and was not Israel's determined effort to sink an American naval vessel tantamount to an act of war?

As the leader of the free world the United States must not be seen reverting to the U.N. and demanding immediate compliance with international law only when it suits our purposes. Yet that is precisely what we've done since 1967 when Israel was concerned. Should we now be surprised that we are unable to manipulate the world organization, when our Western European and Japanese allies view their own interests as incompatible with our belated efforts to recover from our own policy failures? In 1947 America's U.N. delegates and our ambassadors abroad exerted extreme pressure on Latin American and Asian countries that were dependent upon us for aid in order to arrange passage of the Palestinian Partition resolution. Next we blocked an Arab attempt to appeal to the International Court of Justice to adjudicate the right of the General Assembly to partition a country contrary to the wishes of its inhabitants; we then induced the Arabs to accept partition and negotiate the U.N. armistice agreements that Israel repudiated seven years later. Since 1967 we have tolerated—even tacitly approved—Israel's defiance of the Security Council's resolutions and international legal rulings that the annexation of Jerusalem is illegal. Should we now be surprised to find that some nations refuse to support our demands for U.N. sanctions after we have opposed by threat of veto those who advocate punishing Israel for having established a record of having been condemned more than any other member state?

By cutting off shipments of foodstuffs, medicines, and other materials to Egypt we merely drove Nasser into closer relations with Russia. An embargo against Iran will do little more than increase our inability to communicate with that country; the Iranians survived, albeit frugally, for forty months under Mossadeq without exporting petroleum (other than to China and Israel). Naval blockades of the Iranian Persian Gulf ports ignore the fact that Iran shares the Caspian Sea with Russia; there is no surer way to force Iran to depend on the Soviets for support.

The specters John Foster Dulles feared in the 1950s have now emerged in reality: Iran has opted for neutrality in the East-West conflict and the "northern tier" has been breached in Afghanistan. Meanwhile, the Arab states have been divided by our attempts at peacemaking, our covert intervention, and our selective applications of morality. And, as Dulles feared, Israel has adopted and implemented Zionist expansionist policies—the ones he warned the Israelis that the Arabs feared more than communism.

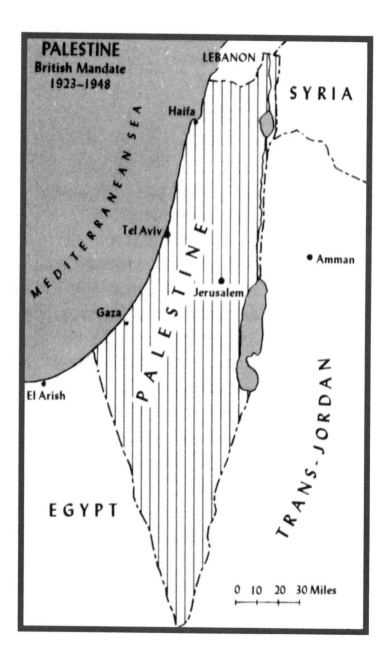

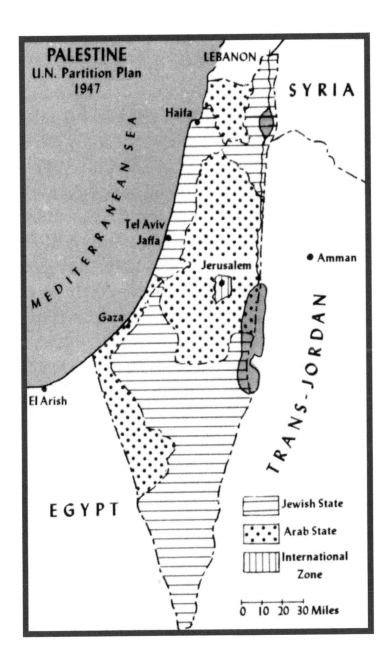

PALESTINE
U.N. Partition Plan
1947

LEBANON

SYRIA

MEDITERRANEAN SEA

Haifa

Tel Aviv
Jaffa

Jerusalem

Amman

Gaza

El Arish

TRANS-JORDAN

EGYPT

Jewish State

Arab State

International
Zone

0 10 20 30 Miles

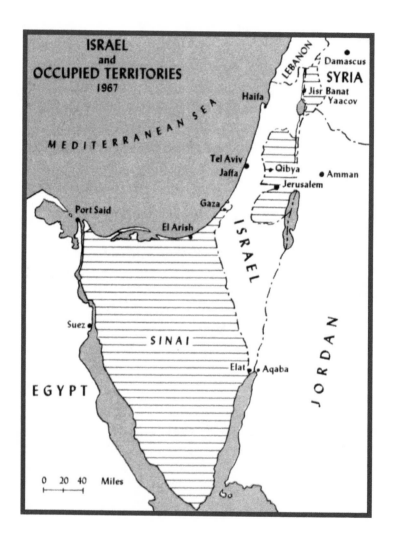

We seem to have forgotten that Nasser condemned foreign military bases just as much as he did Israel's creation; we now seek to renew alliances with nations we'd formerly penalized by cutting off arms aid. Even before Pakistan asked for help, President Carter offered military equipment to counter the Russians in Afghanistan; not surprisingly, our offer to lift our arms embargo evoked Pakistani inquiries of what we'd been giving and what we'd expect in return. Having lost Iran, we have sudden afterthoughts about Turkey, whose listening posts are essential for monitoring Russian movements: to renew an expiring agreement, we proffered a $2.5 billion arms grant over a five-year period—less than Israel has asked for in 1980 alone. After the Egyptian-Israeli peace-treaty framework had been negotiated, the Carter administration sent high-level representatives to seek Saudi Arabian and Jordanian agreement to participate with Israel and Egypt in a new "Maginot line" to protect the Middle East oilfields; predictably, this proposal was refused by the Arabian monarchs who'd seen the fate of the shah in his role as the American "policeman" for the area. History has shown that defense alliances cannot solve our problems in the present vortex of world power politics; nor is there any possibility whatever of Israel's playing a useful part in the direct military or strategic sense.[119]

During the past thirty years America has envisaged a grand Soviet design to take over the Middle Eastern arc of instability; this ignores the fact that Russia fears the wrath of the Islamic world just as much as the West should in formulating its policies. This great force has been compared to a drum: if you tap on any part the whole instrument vibrates. The first sounds were generated when the Arab Moslems were expelled from Palestine, when the third-holiest place in Islam—Jerusalem—was taken over and declared to be Israel's capital, the timpani pitch increased and it emerged with an anti-American roar in Iran. The crises in Iran and Afghanistan have eclipsed the problem of Palestine for the moment, but they have not replaced it in order of importance. They have been added

---

119 See "The Coming Crisis in Israeli-American Relation," by former under secretary of state George W. Ball, *Foreign Affairs,* Winter 1979–80.

to the older problem, and none can be solved in isolation from the others.

The events of the past thirty years have forced Americans to pay attention to the Middle East and its problems. Today we see live television coverage of the results of our failures, and radio stations broadcast half-hourly "Iranian-crisis updates." Most people have learned about the difference between a Sunni and a Shi'ite Moslem; they understand that an ayatullah is superior in rank to an imam. Mainly, they recognize that events in the Middle East may determine whether they must endure the hardship of selling their third and fourth cars and drydocking their yachts. This, then, is a time for sober stock taking, not one in which to line up to enlist in a war to be launched to rescue fifty hostages—our 1958 landing of troops in Lebanon was the last we'll ever make in the Middle East without risking thermonuclear war with Russia.

If we use reasoned judgment (suppress the usual inanities of our "silly season") and take lessons from the history of our past failures, our adversities can be turned to an advantage. The American government has an unprecedented opportunity to obtain the support of an aware and aroused electorate; nothing foreign to our principles or prejudicial to our national security need be asked. The United States must demonstrate to the Third World nations that we are concerned foremost with the people of the Middle East and that we do not regard that area as merely a source of oil or a platform for military bases. This will require blunt and frank dealings with the heads of the Middle Eastern governments that we consider to be our allies. As our former ambassador to Saudi Arabia, James E. Akins, has pointed our, "We are no more capable of protecting the Saudis [or the rulers of the Persian Gulf sheikhdoms] against internal subversion than we were the shah or Iran." Such views were not received well in Washington: Akins and his career foreign-service successor, William J. Porter, were replaced by a southern politician who seems now to be reporting the things President Carter wants to hear. But as Akins warns us, the reasons for popular discontent are not land reform, women's rights, rights of minorities, and the things stressed in the American media. Corruption is one major issue—that deriving from huge military expenditures and grandiose industrial-development projects—and the other involves popular demands to participate in the governments that are dominated by family regimes. We must also insist that the Egyptian-Israeli peace treaty move forward to the comprehensive settlement envisaged in the Camp David Accords, including the right of self-determination for the Palestinians.

Finally, resolution of the Arab-Israeli conflict would strengthen America's position in dealing with the energy shortage, the Iranian crisis, Soviet gains in the Middle East and Africa, and increasing hostility in the Moslem world. Our commitment to Israel's survival has been immutable for thirty years, and making peace with its Arab neighbors could be Israel's greatest contribution as an American ally. The people concerned are all Semites, and the solution to enabling them to live in peace remains in America's hands. One thing is certain: we don't have another thirty years to find the answer. The world's stake in the Middle East is nothing less than peace itself.

ACKNOWLEDGMENTS

Publication of this book in itself will express my gratitude to those who have over the years encouraged me to write it. I name only a few, to illustrate the diversity of their viewpoints: Rabbi Elmer Berger; Israel's retired ambassador, General Chaim Herzog; Lebanon's ambassador to the United Nations, Ghassan Tueni; Lebanese rebel leader Kamal Jumblatt; "professional CIA alumnus" Miles Copeland; Russian spy Kim Philby; and an Israeli intelligence officer who shall remain nameless.

For helping me define the scope of the book, I am indebted to John Marks. He also introduced me to Thomas Farber, without whose literary talents and constructive criticism my first draft might still be wallowing in a quagmire of purple prose. Joe Matthews spent many hours reading the manuscript for errors and cumbersome language. No editor could have been more tolerant of a first-time author than Starling Lawrence of W. W. Norton & Company; his "fussing" was both welcome and enlightening. Judith Sonntag's helpful suggestions concerning the manuscript turned my apprehensions about a copy editor's pencil to admiration and appreciation. Because references to history are essential in order to bring this book into perspective, I thank Dr. Harry N. Howard (retired dean of the Department of State's Middle East historians) for his critical review of these chapters. My sister Marjorie

Newnan's encouragement and experience as a librarian were assets on which I could always count.

There could have been no book had it not been for the generous cooperation and proofreading of Daisy Gellatly (and the understanding of her daughters: Jill, Allison, and Kim).

Few things could please me more than being able to thank in peaceful surroundings two valued friends who facilitated my departure from embattled Lebanon: Abu Said Abu Rish and Roger Tamraz. Also aiding my return to California was Congressman Paul N. McCloskey, Jr.; his membership on the House Committee on Government Operations helped expedite the initial responses of the Department of State and the CIA to my Freedom of Information and Privacy Act requests.

Finally, I want to acknowledge my debt to two wonderful women, each of whom at one time shared the problems of my life in the Middle East: Marge and Mimi. And, in gratitude for their counsel and companionship, I mention four friends who will never read this book: Sam Pope Brewer, Sam Kopper, Joe Alex Morris, Jr., and Walt Kelly—whose "Pogo" diagnosed the problem of which I write: "We have met the enemy and he is us!"

INDEX

ABOUT THE AUTHOR

Wilbur Crane Eveland (1918–1990) was a World War II veteran, CIA station chief, and critic of US foreign policy in the Middle East. His memoir, *Ropes of Sand* (1980), details the many failures of the CIA vis-á-vis the Middle East during the Cold War.

FORBIDDEN BOOKSHELF

FROM OPEN ROAD MEDIA

James Stewart Martin
With an Introduction by Christopher Simpson and a Foreword by Hank Albarelli

All Honorable Men

The Story of the Men on Both Sides of the Atlantic Who Successfully Thwarted Plans to Dismantle the Nazi Cartel System

FORBIDDEN BOOKSHELF

Robert Fitch
With a New Introduction by Peter Kwong

The Assassination of New York

FORBIDDEN BOOKSHELF
SERIES EDITED BY MARK CRISPIN MILLER

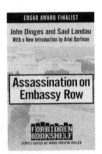

EDGAR AWARD FINALIST

John Dinges and Saul Landau
With a New Introduction by Ariel Dorfman

Assassination on Embassy Row

FORBIDDEN BOOKSHELF
SERIES EDITED BY MARK CRISPIN MILLER

Christopher Simpson

Blowback

America's Recruitment of Nazis and Its Destructive Impact on Our Domestic and Foreign Policy

FORBIDDEN BOOKSHELF

Lewis Mumford
With an Introduction by Thomas Fisher

The Culture of Cities

FORBIDDEN BOOKSHELF
SERIES EDITED BY MARK CRISPIN MILLER

Peter Dale Scott

Dallas '63

The First Deep State Revolt Against the White House

FORBIDDEN BOOKSHELF
SERIES EDITED BY MARK CRISPIN MILLER

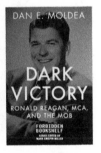

DAN E. MOLDEA

DARK VICTORY

RONALD REAGAN, MCA, AND THE MOB

FORBIDDEN BOOKSHELF
SERIES EDITED BY MARK CRISPIN MILLER

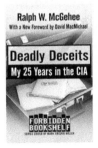

Ralph W. McGehee
With a New Foreword by David MacMichael

Deadly Deceits

My 25 Years in the CIA

FORBIDDEN BOOKSHELF
SERIES EDITED BY MARK CRISPIN MILLER

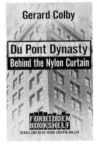

Gerard Colby

Du Pont Dynasty
Behind the Nylon Curtain

FORBIDDEN BOOKSHELF
SERIES EDITED BY MARK CRISPIN MILLER

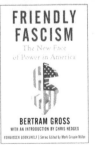

FRIENDLY FASCISM

The New Face of Power in America

BERTRAM GROSS
WITH AN INTRODUCTION BY CHRIS HEDGES

FORBIDDEN BOOKSHELF | Series Edited by Mark Crispin Miller

OPEN ROAD
INTEGRATED MEDIA

OPEN ROAD

INTEGRATED MEDIA

Find a full list of our authors and titles at www.openroadmedia.com

FOLLOW US

@OpenRoadMedia

CPSIA information can be obtained
at www.ICGtesting.com
Printed in the USA
BVHW08s1136250618
519964BV00001B/17/P